PARTIES, PATRIOTS AND UNDERTAKERS

Parties, Patriots and Undertakers

*Parliamentary Politics
in Early Hanoverian Ireland*

Patrick McNally

FOUR COURTS PRESS

This book was typeset for
FOUR COURTS PRESS LTD
55 Prussia Street, Dublin 7, Ireland
e-mail: fcp@ indigo.ie
and in North America for
FOUR COURTS PRESS
c/o ISBS, 5804 N.E. Hassalo Street, Portland, OR 97213.

A catalogue record for this title
is available from the British Library.

ISBN 1-85182-255-0

Printed in Great Britain
by Hartnolls Ltd, Bodmin, Cornwall

For Paddy

Contents

List of Abbreviations

The stylistic conventions of *Irish Historical Studies* have normally been followed. With the exception of quotations from printed sources (which are reproduced as in the original), spelling has been modernised in all quotations. The original punctuation has normally been preserved, being altered only where it was felt necessary for the purposes of clarity.

In referring to the respective religious communities in Ireland 'Catholic' has been used to refer to the Roman Catholic community; 'Protestant' or 'Anglican' has been employed to describe adherents to the Church of Ireland; 'protestant' refers to members of all protestant churches; 'protestant dissenters' to all protestants bar members of the Church of Ireland.

References to secondary texts are given in full in the first citation, in an abbreviated form thereafter. Full references are given in the bibliography. The following abbreviations are employed throughout:

Add MS	Additional Manuscripts
IHS	*Irish Historical Studies*
BL	British Library
PRO	Public Record Office, London
PRONI	Public Record Office of Northern Ireland
NLI	National Library of Ireland
SP	State Papers
Lords Journals	*Journals of the House of Lords [Ireland]* (8 vols, Dublin, 1779-1800)
Commons Journals	*Journals of the House of Commons of the Kingdom of Ireland* (3rd ed., 23 vols, Dublin, 1796-1800)
DNB	*Dictionary of National Biography*
SRO	Surrey Record Office
TCD	Trinity College, Dublin
Bod Lib	Bodleian Library, Oxford
New History of Ireland	T.W. Moody *et al.* (eds.), *A New History of Ireland* (5 vols, Oxford, 1976-)

Preface

Many people have helped in the production of this book and in facilitating the research upon which it is based. Financial support from the School of Humanities and Social Sciences of Worcester College of Higher Education over a number of years significantly facilitated the completion of this book.

The help and cooperation of the staff of the libraries and record offices outlined below was invaluable. For permission to consult and quote from manuscripts I would like to thank the following: the Deputy Keeper of Records of the Public Record Office of Northern Ireland; the Director, National Archives of Ireland; the Bodleian Library, Oxford; the library of Christ Church College, Oxford; the Public Record Office, London; the British Library; the Rt Hon the earl of Shannon; Cambridge University Library; the library of Worcester College of Higher Education; the National Library of Ireland; the Linen Hall Library, Belfast; the library of Queen's University, Belfast; and the library of Trinity College, Dublin.

Versions of chapters four and seven have previously appeared in print elsewhere. I am grateful to the editors and publishers of *Irish Historical Studies* and *Parliamentary History* for permission to reproduce this material here.

I have been fortunate in working with colleagues at Worcester who recognise the importance of research output. The general support and encouragement of my colleagues over the past five years was warmly appreciated. In particular, the enthusiasm and determination of Dilwyn Porter and Ronald Kowalski in pursuing academic research over many years in an environment which has not always been conducive to such activity was an admirable example of what can be achieved. The former was also kind enough to read and comment upon sections of this work in draft.

Readers will quickly realise the extent of my debt to the work of a number of historians of late seventeenth- and eighteenth-century Ireland. The repeated references to a large body of work speak for themselves. However, I would like to single out a small number of people without whose work this book could not have appeared in its present form. I was first attracted to the history of early eighteenth-century Ireland by the pioneering work of Dr David Hayton. All of us who have followed in his footsteps are only too aware of the debt we owe to his work over the past two decades. In addition, the advice and encouragement

11

which I (and many others) have received from David over many years is a testimony to his personal and professional generosity. As a result of the publication of Sean Connolly's *Religion, Law and Power. The making of Protestant Ireland 1660-1760* (Oxford, 1992) the historiography of early eighteenth-century Ireland will never be the same again. The repeated references to Professor Connolly's work throughout this book indicates the impact which it has had on my own research. Finally, I would like to thank Toby Barnard for patiently listening to my often incoherent ramblings on a number of occasions. The influence of Toby's work on my views of the nature of early eighteenth-century Irish society is manifest in chapter two.

The following friends and colleagues have also materially assisted me in a variety of ways: John Regan, Darren Oldridge, Joep Leerssen, Ted Townley and Gerry Douds. I am also grateful to all of those with whom I have worked for a number of years at the Open University A318 summer school at York University. In addition to forming many valued friendships, the opportunity to converse with and learn from historians of a wide variety of experiences, backgrounds and interests has been a privilege.

For granting me the opportunity to air some of the ideas expressed in this book I am grateful to the organisers and participants of the following conferences and seminar series – the annual conference of the *Eighteenth-Century Ireland Society*, University of Limerick, May 1996; *Irish Encounters*, Bath College of HE, July 1996; the *Long Eighteenth Century Seminar*, Institute of Historical Research, January 1997. The comments and suggestions offered on these occasions have been invaluable.

I am grateful to Michael Adams, Martin Fanning and the rest of the staff at Four Courts Press for agreeing to publish this book in the first place and for all their help during its production.

I would like to express my heartfelt gratitude to my wife, Lois, for her patience and encouragement during the writing of this book. Having been a 'PhD widow' for almost five years, the prospect of yet more years of angst cannot have been a welcome one. However, Lois and my son, Philip, have tolerated my repeated absences and (worse) moody presence with patience and good humour. Lois is also responsible for proof-reading and type-setting this book, a job made no easier by my frequent errors.

More than anyone, my mother and late father made my educational career possible. At every stage, their support and encouragement was of critical importance and I am forever grateful for their support of a not always enthusiastic subject. It is to the memory of my father that this work is dedicated.

1

Introduction

I

It would be misleading to claim that the study of early eighteenth-century Irish history has been characterised by controversy. Contrasting emphases and varying nuances have led, at most, to polite disagreement. Certainly, the historical debate relating to eighteenth-century Ireland has (mercifully) lacked the rancour and bitterness sometimes associated with the study of the sixteenth and seventeenth centuries. There may be a number of reasons for this uncharacteristic gentility among academic historians but the most important, undoubtedly, is the subject matter in question. The eighteenth century has traditionally been regarded as a period of respite in the depressingly turbulent history of Ireland. From the Williamite war until the violent decade of the 1790s, the centuries-old struggle between England and Ireland, Protestant and Catholic, appeared to be, temporarily at least, in abeyance. There is, in other words, little to stir the hearts and excite the imagination of a proponent of either of the rival schools of Irish nationalism which, despite the attempts of the so-called 'revisionists', continue to dominate the writing of Irish history.

The history of early eighteenth-century Ireland, in particular, appears uncontroversial, unproblematic, even boring. At least the latter half of the century saw the rise of the 'Patriots' (the 'good Protestants' of nineteenth- and twentieth-century nationalist mythology) and the exciting decade of the 1790s. The first half of the century, on the other hand could not muster a decent rebellion, something managed twice even by British Jacobites. It appears that many of today's historians would differ little from the judgement of those two great nineteenth-century adversaries, W.E.H. Lecky and J.A. Froude. Writing of the first half of the eighteenth century, Lecky concluded that, with the exception of the Wood's halfpence dispute, 'there was little, during the period I am noticing, of political interest in Ireland'.[1] Froude, characteristically, went further: 'For the half century between the Duke of Grafton's government and the revolt of the American colonies, Ireland was without a history.'[2]

As a result of this widespread perception, historians have tended to steer clear of the first half of the eighteenth century. The judgements of Lecky and Froude would appear to be confirmed by many general accounts of Irish history. Professor Beckett's standard history of modern Ireland from 1603 to 1922, for example, devoted only 5.8 per cent of the book to the political history of the period from 1692 to 1767 (23.4 per cent of the period covered in the book) – and Beckett was an historian of the eighteenth century! What is clear is that the period from 1690 to 1770 is one of the most neglected periods of Irish history and one about which we know startlingly little.

The foundations for the modern study of early eighteenth-century Irish history were laid in the 1940s and 1950s by J.L. McCracken and J.C. Beckett. McCracken's research and publications on the structure of Irish politics under the first two Georges established an orthodoxy which was to remain unchallenged until the 1970s. He argued that after the Wood's halfpence dispute the British government decided to appoint Englishmen to the highest offices of state and church in Ireland and to introduce a system of managing the Irish parliament through 'undertakers', that is, local political magnates who would guarantee the government a majority in parliament in return for office, a share in the distribution of patronage, and a limited influence in government policy.[3]

Beckett's contribution to the history of early eighteenth-century Ireland lies primarily in his articles on the Church of Ireland in this period and in his books *Protestant Dissent in Ireland, 1687-1780* (London, 1948) and *The Making of Modern Ireland, 1603-1923* (London, 1966). This work by McCracken and Beckett was followed by that of J.G. Simms who concentrated on the period from the restoration to the reign of Queen Anne. Simms' work on Jacobite Ireland, the Williamite settlement in Ireland, and the origins of the penal laws remains the most authoritative work to have been published on this important period.[4]

More recently, a new generation of historians has begun to build on the pioneering efforts of McCracken, Simms, and Beckett. In particular, a small number of overtly political historians have broken new ground in the realm of national politics. Whilst the majority continue to concentrate on the history of the last three decades of the eighteenth century, people such as David Hayton, James McGuire, F.G. James and Sean Connolly have tackled an earlier and more mysterious era. James' *Ireland in the Empire, 1688-1770* was innovative both in emphasising the importance of early eighteenth-century politics and in attempting to locate Ireland in an imperial context. James' book remains the best narrative account of Irish politics in this period. It was, however, the publication in 1979 of articles by Hayton and McGuire in the excellent *Penal Era and Golden Age. Essays in eighteenth-century Irish history* which marked an important milestone in the study of early eighteenth-century Ireland. McGuire provided a new insight into the parliamentary politics of the period immediately following the 'glorious revolution', demonstrating that undertakers were much in evidence well before the reign of George I. Hayton's important research into the reigns of Queen Anne and George I illustrated the intensity of the Whig-Tory party conflict of the former reign and has confirmed McGuire's view that 'undertakers' existed before 1725.[5] Taken together, this research convincingly challenged McCracken's contention that the Wood's halfpence episode marked an important turning point in the political history of early Hanoverian Ireland. Much of this work has been incorporated into some of the general histories of Ireland published in recent years and has assumed the status of a new orthodoxy. More importantly, this work by McGuire and, especially, Hayton has encouraged new interest in this period. One indication of this changing attitude is that the most up-to-date general history of Ireland between the restoration and the union devotes one-third of the space allocated to the political narrative to the 1692-1760 period.[6]

With the publication of Sean Connolly's *Religion, Law and Power. The making of Protestant Ireland, 1660-1760* (Oxford, 1992), the 'revisionist' debate finally reached the hitherto becalmed waters of early eighteenth-century Irish historiography. This book is the most important to have been published on this period since the early 1970s and Connolly has added a new dimension to the debate surrounding the nature of Irish politics and society in the first half of the eighteenth century. In a thoughtful and thought-provoking study Connolly consciously attacks what he regards as 'reductionist' interpretations of the politics of this period which concentrate on the influence of patronage in influencing political behaviour. A more controversial argument (and one which has received more attention) is his assertion that Ireland in the first half of the eighteenth century was a society which was more akin to contemporary *ancien régime* states in Europe than a 'colony'. This is an argument which directly challenges the traditional nationalist interpretation of eighteenth-century Ireland and, as such, has laid itself open to the charge of being 'revisionist'. Nationalist historians have tended to regard the hundred years or so after the Battle of the Boyne as an era of unbridled oppression of the Irish people by an alien and bigoted ruling class, transplanted to Ireland in order to serve their 'colonial masters' in London. Connolly seriously challenges such a view by questioning whether the vast majority of the 'Irish people' cared very much whether their landlord was Irish or English, Catholic or Protestant. He also points out that the notorious 'Penal Code', even when enforced, directly affected very few Irish Catholics for the simple reason that the laws were aimed at the propertied classes. These are important issues which merit serious consideration.

Whilst the political historians are revising the work of the 1940s and 1950s, economic historians have been at least as busy. The detailed studies of the nature of landownership in eighteenth-century Ireland produced by Louis Cullen and those inspired by his example, have forced a re-examination, in particular, of the impact of the penal laws on Irish society. This work, carried out by Cullen, Kevin Whelan and Thomas Power, has implications far beyond purely economic history, encouraging a re-evaluation of the way in which historians view the nature of Irish society and politics in the eighteenth century. This work is certainly among the most exciting to have been undertaken on eighteenth-century Ireland in recent years demonstrating, as it does, that Irish society in the eighteenth century was much more complex than was previously thought. The simple dichotomy between 'Penal Era and Golden Age' no longer appears sufficient.

Despite the important advances made in our knowledge of early eighteenth-century Irish history in recent years, the historiography of this period is still, relatively speaking, in its infancy. Our historical understanding of this period continues to be dependent upon a small number of (thankfully excellent) historians. Increasingly, however, there are signs that the status of early eighteenth-century Ireland as something of an historical blind spot may be changing. The appearance of a number of important doctoral theses, combined with the publication since 1986 of the journal *Eighteenth-Century Ireland* suggests that for historians of this hitherto neglected period the future will be more promising than the past.

II

This book attempts to make a contribution to the study of the nature of Irish politics and society in the early eighteenth century. An overt and unashamed work of political history (and a history of national politics at that), this book has no pretensions to being a comprehensive history of early Hanoverian Ireland. Those seeking detailed discussion of the economy, the nature of society, law and order, popular culture, and the role of women or children will be disappointed. These are all important and worthy fields of research which certainly need to be investigated for this period, but they are beyond the scope of this study.

What this work will do is examine the nature of parliamentary politics during the reign of George I and the early years of his son. The book will develop and expand upon the work which I carried out for my doctoral thesis 'Patronage and Politics in Ireland, 1714 to 1727'.[7] Whereas that thesis specifically concentrated upon the role of patronage in the political culture of Ireland in the reign of George I, this book has, I hope, a much wider scope. In addition, the period under discussion has been extended to the early 1730s in order to take in the rise of Henry Boyle to a position of prominence in Irish national politics. The book aims to make sense of the often confused and confusing national politics of this period. A number of important themes run through this work – the Whig-Tory party conflict, the court-country dichotomy, the politics of 'patriotism', the role of patronage, the rise of the undertakers. All of these themes will be addressed throughout. In addition, the nature of the Irish political system will be examined and structural factors affecting political stability identified.

Chapter two attempts to place the subsequent analysis of the early Hanoverian political system in some kind of broader context by addressing some of the wider questions relevant to the nature of early eighteenth-century Irish society. Inevitably superficial, the chapter at least provides an indication of my own views on some of these important questions. Chapter three is designed to provide sufficient background information to enable the non-specialist reader to understand the context in which the politics of the post-1714 period operated. In particular, the fundamental importance of the 'revolution' of 1688 in establishing permanent parliamentary government in both England and Ireland and the consequences of this development is emphasised. Chapter four analyses the impact on Irish politics of the accession of George I to the throne in 1714. Detailed attention is given to the rapid decline of the Tory party and the consequences of the establishment of a Whig ascendancy in both Britain and Ireland. Chapter five attempts to examine the role of patronage in the political system of early eighteenth-century Ireland. It has been commonly asserted that the pursuit of patronage was the most important influence on the behaviour of Irish politicians in the first half of the eighteenth century. How patronage was actually employed for the purposes of parliamentary management, especially in the early part of the century, has been less often examined. This chapter attempts, to some extent, to remedy this neglect. Chapter six analyses the key relationships which dominated early eighteenth-century Irish parliamentary politics, that is, those between the government and viceroy, the viceroy and his parliamentary managers ('undertakers'), and the undertakers and parliament. Chapter seven examines one of the most notable political conflicts which affected early Hanoverian Irish politics, that between the Irish and English 'interests'. Chapter eight attempts to make a contribution to the on-going debate concerning the nature of the 'patriotism' of the Anglican élite in the first half of the eighteenth century. It is argued that this patriotism was primarily concerned with the defence of the rights of the Irish parliament and the well-being of the Irish economy and that it lacked any meaningful proto-nationalistic agenda.

It is impossible for an Irish historian to treat any period of his/her country's past with objectivity. A work of history concentrating on the Anglican élite of the eighteenth century offers itself (for those inclined to take them) more than enough opportunities to pillory, condemn, even ridicule the historical record and legacy of the Protestant ruling class. Readers will no doubt quickly identify only too clearly where this book strays from the straight path of impartiality. Issues such as the penal laws and the nature of Protestant patriotism are sufficiently complex to allow for vigorous, but legitimate, debate and for the drawing of widely differing conclusions. The nature of those conclusions no doubt reflects our respective preconceptions. It is hoped that the conclusions which are drawn in the following pages are based at least as much upon documentary evidence, objectively selected and reasonably interpreted, as personal bias or anachronistic indictment.

2

Early Eighteenth-Century Irish Society

This book will concentrate on the parliamentary politics of early Hanoverian Ireland. Inevitably, by focusing on the parliamentary arena an incomplete and, perhaps, misleading picture of Ireland at this time will emerge. It is self-evident that the political activity which will dominate this work did not operate in a vacuum. What happened at Dublin Castle and College Green was fundamentally affected by (and impacted upon) Irish society as a whole, in Dublin and in the provinces. In order to place the parliamentary politics of this period in a wider context, therefore, some discussion of the nature of early Hanoverian Irish society as a whole is necessary. Hopefully the following discussion will qualify to a certain extent the inevitably incomplete impression which will emerge in the following chapters.

I

What sort of society was Ireland in the early eighteenth century? Was it, as some would have it, a colonial society or was it more akin to those of *ancien régime* Europe?[1] It would be very surprising indeed if we were unable to trace similarities between early Hanoverian Ireland and, say, contemporary Britain. In fact it is not hard to do so. The histories of Ireland and Britain had been inextricably bound together for centuries. The political élites of both societies shared a common culture, educational experience, and were closely linked by marriage and personal connection. The political structures and systems of law and order in both societies were almost identical. Irishmen served in the British army, a third of which was based in Ireland at this time. Economically too, Ireland, although relatively underdeveloped, had many features in common with early eighteenth-century Britain. Like everywhere else in Europe, the economy in Ireland was still dominated by agriculture and Britain had not yet embarked on the process of industrialisation which would by the early nineteenth century set that country apart from the rest of the world. It is sensible and reasonable, therefore, to highlight the extent to which Irish society in the early Hanoverian era, like all other societies in pre-industrial Europe, was one which was characterised by an hierarchical social structure, the different ranks or 'orders' being bound together by vertical ties of patronage, dependence, and deference.

Patronage and dependence were central to the functioning of Irish society, economy, and politics at this time. On the face of it, there is little reason to believe that the relationship between landlord and tenant, master and servant, husband and wife, parent and child, patron and dependant, employer and employee was any different in Ireland than in any other society. Indeed there is ample evidence to suggest that such relationships operated in Ireland exactly as they did elsewhere. On the other hand, we need to be clear what exactly we mean when we speak of 'deference' or 'dependence'. E.P. Thompson has written of the limits of deference in the context of eighteenth-century England, going so far as to say that 'the eighteenth century sees the old paternalism at a point of crisis'.[2] Aspects of Thompson's thesis may well be inappropriate to the Irish context, but what is striking is just how much of Thompson's analysis of the relationship between rulers and ruled in England can be applied to eighteenth-century Ireland. Anyone who has explored the manuscript collections of this period can only concur with Thompson's important observation that, 'the sources give a historiographical bias to overemphasize the deferential element in eighteenth century society – a man put, perforce, into the stance of soliciting favours will not reveal his true mind'.[3] When analysing the relationship between the different orders of eighteenth-century Irish society historians should bear this bias of the sources in mind. Of course, manuscript sources and contemporary printed matter give little insight into the feelings of the poor towards their employers and governors. What they do contain is evidence of the attitudes of the propertied classes towards the 'lower orders' and there are abundant examples of the kind of complaints against the 'insubordination' of the poor which Thompson has claimed was the 'most characteristic complaint throughout the greater part of the [eighteenth] century' in England. We can even find examples in Ireland of those increasingly independent employees whom, Thompson argues, 'felt their client relationship to the gentry very little or not at all'.[4] In 1721, for example, *Whalley's Newsletter* reported that, 'Yesterday the Owner of a Hackney-Coach was Committed by the Rt. Hon. the Lord mayor till he pay 40 shilling, or produce the Driver of his Coach to be Whipt for abuseing a Gentleman he carried in his Coach, a Custom too Common among that sort of Fellow.'[5]

Such parallels with the changing nature of English society would appear to support the view that we should locate eighteenth-century Ireland firmly in the context of *ancien régime* Europe. However, we must not be too hasty in our conclusions. Class or economic and social status is obviously a crucial factor in determining the relationship between individuals in any society at any time. Early eighteenth-century Ireland was no exception in this respect. Considerations of patronage and deference played an important part in relations between members of the Anglican community, the community about which, of course, we know most. But how important were these same considerations in determining relations between Anglicans and Catholics, or Anglicans and protestant dissenters? While it may have been the case that a Catholic tenant cared little whether his landlord was a Protestant or Catholic, it is also conceivable that on certain occasions the religion of a landlord could have mattered a great deal. It is impossible to generalise about this issue. Different conditions existed in different parts of the country, for example. The work of Louis Cullen has shown just how complicated was the structure of landholding in eighteenth-century Ireland and how extensive the Catholic interest in land may have been.[6] However, there are occasional insights into how religion might have affected relations between governors and governed at this time.

Returning from England in 1723 after the arrest of the bishop of Rochester for treason, the Anglican bishop of Derry stopped off at Larne in County Antrim. His account of the treatment that he and his party received there at the hands of the Presbyterian population suggests that deference to authority had its limits:

> There, I and my children went ashore, and dined in the neighbouring village. My character could not be concealed; and I hope[d] the money we scattered amongst them, would have secured us against any insults of the populace. But, at our return to the ship, several bawled out, 'the bishop of Rochester, the bishop of Rochester', etc.[7]

These Presbyterians at least, appear to have regarded themselves as distinct from the Anglican élite in terms of religion as well as class. Catholics too were on occasion prepared to antagonize the Anglican clergy. Henry Maule, the dean of Cloyne, described one such incident to the archbishop of Canterbury in 1724:

> Your Grace will be surprised to hear that a body of my Popish parishioners had lately the assurance to come to my vestry met together [*sic*] for the repairing of our parish church, and there by a majority of voices claimed their right of voting as parishioners against the annual usual rate for repairs etc. of the parish church.[8]

To regain control, Maule had to adjourn the meeting and impose the oaths of abjuration and allegiance against this 'lawless crew'. It could be argued, of course, that such incidents are unrepresentative. They were also directed at the clergy, a highly visible and, perhaps, more bitterly resented group than the Anglican laity. However, landlord-tenant relations could also be complicated by religious divisions. In 1715 John Percival sent his land agent in Ireland a list of instructions one of which ordered him 'To be diligent in getting in the tenants' rents and arrears, especially of the Papist tenants.' It is unclear why Percival issued such an order but it is evident that, for whatever reason, his Catholic tenants were being singled out for special treatment.[9] These and similar incidents suggest that tension between the Anglican and non-Anglican communities was a factor tending to undermine deference in Ireland at this time. Authority in early eighteenth-century Ireland was, of course, Anglican authority. It would be astonishing if Catholics and protestant dissenters did not on occasion take delight in undermining or ridiculing the representatives of the Anglican élite. One or two further examples might illustrate this process at work.

In 1738 Lord Castledurrow wrote to Sir John St Leger, a judge, complaining at the treatment he had received at the hands of the previous court of assize. He and one Captain Lyon had fined William Fitzpatrick of Harristown, Queen's County, £20 for having harboured 'a popish priest'. Fitzpatrick appealed to the assize judges who condemned the action taken by Castledurrow and Lyon and ordered that Fitzpatrick's fine be repaid to him. Clearly furious at such treatment which he would have regarded as tending to undermine his authority, Castledurrow complained of 'the boasts Fitzpatrick has since made, his rejoicings, and the very great indulgence a popish cause met with, from the judges'.[10] The enforcement of the law always had the potential to lead to sectarian conflict for those responsible for upholding law and order were Anglicans. It was inevitable under these circumstances that the law might on occasion be regarded as less than impartial. Owen Gallagher, land agent to Oliver St George, asked the latter in 1730 to intervene on behalf of his friend, one Mills, who had been arrested in Galway for killing a Catholic. Arguing that the jury there would be packed with Catholics, Gallagher asked St George to see that the case be brought to the attention of Judge Ward and Councellor Upton who would be serving on the circuit there. Six months later Mills was acquitted.[11] Of course, the accused may well have been innocent of the crime but this case does raise questions about the impartiality of the law whenever Catholic and Protestant interests conflicted. What is clear is that Protestants could ask members of parliament to intervene with Protestant judges in favour of their friends.

The complaints of Irish gentlemen about the 'insolence' of the poor had an edge which was absent from comparable grumblings in England, for in Ireland the 'poor' were normally (although not exclusively) Catholic. Indeed the complaints of Anglican gentlemen were normally directed, not towards the poor as such, but towards the 'papists'. References to popish insolence (and of Presbyterian cheek) were very common and this was often given as the justification for further anti-Catholic legislation or for denying relief to protestant dissenters. Forwarding a bill for disarming Catholics in 1731, Chief Secretary Cary commented, 'You know the state of the Kingdom so well, that it is needless to inform you how zealous people are here to keep the papists in awe, whose licentiousness and growing insolence has given great offence.'[12] The continued longevity of intense politico-religious rivalries in Ireland can be seen from complaints on the part of Anglicans about the 'uppishness' of Catholics at times of acute political tension or, more commonly, when there was a prospect of war with or invasion by Britain's foreign enemies. In 1734, for example, Primate Boulter complained that the Catholics were 'more than ordinarily insolent' following the French victories in the War of the Polish Succession in the summer of that year.[13] Clearly some Catholics at least continued to take delight in taunting the Protestant élite with the bogey of Jacobitism. It would appear, furthermore, that there was at least one politically-motivated murder in this period, that of Colonel Henry Luttrell in 1718.[14] There is sufficient evidence, therefore, to indicate that in Ireland religious divisions could at times cut across the ties of deference and patronage which would normally dominate relations between the social classes in *ancien régime* Europe. The persistence of such tensions between the leaders of Irish society and the Catholic community means that Irish society was not a carbon-copy of that of Britain or of any other in *ancien régime* Europe.

II

It is incumbent on an historian to attempt to avoid anachronistic judgements and not to read history backwards. An historical period must be viewed on its own terms. There are clear dangers in selecting material from the past in order to explain why certain eventualities came about. Events and issues which may have been of great concern to contemporaries can easily be ignored or downplayed because we know that, in the event, they proved to be of limited importance. The Jacobite movement in Britain is a good example of a phenomenon which was considered by contemporaries to have been a major threat but which, until recently, has been virtually ignored by historians who, unlike those who lived at the time, know that it failed. The historian must, therefore, recognise what was of concern to the people who lived in his or her chosen period. However, there are also dangers in attempting to analyse an historical epoch in isolation. While historians must endeavour to explain and evaluate the behaviour of individuals by the standards of their own time, it is also important to recognise that such behaviour had an influence upon later generations. It is futile to confine strictly one's analysis and comment to a period defined by two dates, often chosen for the practical convenience of the historian.[15] Some will argue that historical figures did not know what the future held in store and that we should not, therefore, analyse their behaviour with subsequent events in mind. This is, of course, correct. However, the avoidance of anachronistic judgements does not preclude analysis of the future impact of events. For example, it is perfectly correct for an historian to comment upon the impact of the penal laws on later generations of Irish people, so long as he or she recognises that these laws may not have been passed in order to achieve such an effect.

Less contentious, perhaps, is the observation that the events which preceded one's chosen period should not be overlooked. While early eighteenth-century Irishmen and women did not know what the future held in store, they were perfectly conscious of what had happened in the past. Those people who lived in Ireland in the decades following the 1688 revolution were only too aware of the history of their country and of its relevance to their own lives. The civil war, Cromwellian conquest and, more recently, the conflict of 1688-91 would have been recalled by many with the sort of immediacy which a seventy- or eighty-year-old in the 1970s regarded the world wars of the twentieth century. The seventeenth century had been a period of conflict in Ireland unprecedented in its scale, brutality and in its consequences. The turbulent and violent events of 1641-52 and 1688-91 must have made a deep and lasting impression on those who had lived through those traumatic years or who heard the first-hand accounts from others who had done. The memory of the Gaelic rising of 1641 or the Cromwellian military conquest of Ireland, for example, were strongly embedded in the folk memory of Irish people, as they still are today. Among Protestants, references to the 1641 rising and the events of the reign of James II were very common. Moreover such episodes were not merely regarded as unfortunate occurrences which deserved to be remembered for the sake of the victims; they were also held up as warnings as to what the future might have in store.[16] At times of tension references to past conflicts came readily to mind. Reacting to rumours of an impending Catholic insurrection in 1719, Bishop Evans of Meath was quick to refer to the Irish rebellion of 1641:

> my Lord Lieutenant had last Thursday <u>certain notice</u> that the Papists have a design of a general insurrection by surprise to cut all Protestants' throats as they did in 1641 – this is fully expressed in the proclamation published this noon, how our poor countrymen will escape in the country time must show, but I trust God will assist us in this city to be in a posture of readiness against those blood thirsty villains.[17]

The remembrance of past conflicts between Catholic and Protestant directly impinged upon relationships between the respective communities in Ireland. The eighteenth-century calendar was replete with politically and emotionally charged anniversaries. Nicholas Rogers has described the 'politicisation of the calendar' in seventeenth- and eighteenth-century Britain and the same phenomenon is apparent in the Irish context.[18] The most important dates in the calendar were 30 January (the martyrdom of Charles I), 10 June (the Pretender's birthday), 1 July (Battle of the Boyne), 23 October (1641 uprising), 4 November (the birthday of William III), and 5 November (Gunpowder Plot and William III's landing at Torbay). As in Britain, some of these commemorations could play an overt role in the political conflict between the Whig and Tory parties. Celebrations of the exploits of William III were always likely to be enjoyed with particular enthusiasm by Irish Whigs and to be regarded with more ambiguity by Tories. The commemoration of the 'martyrdom' of Charles I, on the other hand, provided an opportunity for Tories (particularly the Anglican clergy) to express regret at the excesses of the parliamentary régime which could easily be interpreted as an implicit criticism of the Whig party with whom the republican administration was associated. All Anglicans, however, could comfortably combine to commemorate the 'treachery' of the Catholic Irish in 1641 and undoubtedly the most significant date in the Irish Protestant political calendar was 23 October.

Rogers has argued that public ceremonies and celebrations in Britain served a number of functions, the most important of which were to remind the 'nation' of its common heritage and to promote a sense of unity within the community through demonstrations of ruling-class liberality and display. Such occasions could, therefore, serve to reinforce feelings of deference and loyalty on the part of the masses towards their social superiors. The officially organised annual commemorations of the 1641 uprising; Lord Santry's provision of 'a splendid entertainment' for 'all estates of men, women, and children' in Londonderry to celebrate the reconciliation between George I and the Prince of Wales in 1720; the corporation of Londonderry's staging of a feast to celebrate the king's birthday; and the erection of bonfires outside the house of William Conolly upon the surrender of Wood's patent in 1725 are examples of such occasions.[19] Such treating of the lower orders 'sanctified the political order and at the same time elevated the status of its principal guardians'.[20] However, the parallels with the political culture of Britain should not be stretched too far. It has been pointed out by a number of historians that deference and loyalty in Britain was largely based upon common religious identity, protestantism in general, Anglicanism in particular.[21] Naturally those in Ireland participating in such public ceremonials were also united by religious affiliation. As a result such public occasions served as reminders to non-Anglicans that they were not members of the political nation. Whilst serving to unite the bonds between all sections of the Anglican community, these occasions were also, in Toby Barnard's words, 'rites of exclusion'.[22] How this could operate in practice can be seen from the intervention of the lord mayor of Dublin in an apparently unpolitical civic ceremony in 1734. On St Crispin's Day[23] 'the Society of Journeymen Shoe Makers walked in Procession through this City ... Our Lord Mayor stopped them as they passed by the Tholsel, disarmed St Crispin's Guards, took their Kettle Drums and trumpets from them, and made some of them take the Oaths of Allegiance'.[24]

If 23 October and 4-5 November were the classic occasions for demonstrations of Anglican solidarity, 10 June quickly became the equivalent occasion for those of Jacobite sympathies.[25] It is perhaps surprising to find examples of overt displays of Jacobite sentiment in Dublin but these did occur. In 1717, for example, bonfires were lit in Dublin and several women wore white roses in St

Stephen's Green to celebrate the Pretender's birthday.[26] The Pretender's birthday also provided an excuse for 'almost ritualized clashes' between Protestant and Catholic mobs in Dublin.[27] Primate Boulter described a particularly serious incident of this sort which took place in 1726. Boulter described how 'a very numerous rabble' of Catholics had assembled on St Stephen's Green. This was clearly no minor affray since the crowd attacked the lord mayor, sheriffs, aldermen and constables 'with stones, bricks, and dirt'. In the end the mob was only dispersed when forty foot and 'the like number of horse' arrived on the scene and fired on the crowd. Boulter thought that more Catholics than usual took part in the affray that year due to rumours of war which resulted in them being 'better in heart'.[28]

Public celebrations in Ireland, therefore, served to reinforce the bonds between the different sections of the Anglican community, as they did in Britain. However, celebrations of a common Protestant (or Catholic) historical experience inevitably reinforced divisions between the minority Anglican community and the majority non-Anglican population. This constant commemoration of events relating to political and religious conflict in the relatively recent past must have served to reopen at regular intervals the fissures afflicting Irish society and to reinforce the political loyalties of the respective communities.

The most important long-term structural feature affecting Irish society from the sixteenth century until the present day has been sectarian distrust and conflict between the Catholic and Protestant communities. The eighteenth century did not escape the consequences of this conflict. Although, during the first half of the eighteenth century the leaders of the Catholic community adopted a policy of 'discretion' in their relations with the Anglican élite (when they did not ignore them altogether by negotiating directly with the British political establishment), it would be a mistake to assume that old sectarian enmities were forgotten. The re-emergence of the 'Catholic question' from 1760 onwards, the vigorous opposition of many Protestants to any concessions to Catholics, and the outbreak of sectarian violence in the Ulster countryside in the 1780s clearly demonstrated that sixty or seventy years of relative tranquillity had done little to diminish the suspicion and hostility which characterised the relationship between the respective communities.[29]

Eighteenth-century Ireland, therefore, was not merely a mirror-image of its larger sister kingdom across the Irish Sea. Above all, of course, Ireland differed from Britain and all other *ancien régime* kingdoms in one important respect, making the country a special case. In terms of denominational composition, something approaching eighty per cent of the Irish population was Catholic. Uniquely in Europe at this time, this large majority was totally excluded from any direct participation in politics or public employment, explicitly on the grounds of religious affiliation. Of course, as is often pointed out, many other religious groups throughout Europe suffered similar or worse disabilities –

French Protestants, English Catholics, and Jews everywhere, to name only a few. However, the fact that these groups were in every other case minorities and that the Irish Catholics comprised the overwhelming majority of the population of their country is a circumstance which cannot be simply glossed over or normalised. Moreover, that Catholics had until the mid-1600s owned a majority of land in Ireland further differentiates them from the case of religious minorities elsewhere. Within a few decades a ruling élite which shared the religion of the majority of the population had been forcibly displaced by one which did not. The exclusion of the majority population of Ireland from political participation and public employment is far and away the most important factor in the history of Ireland in the eighteenth century. The course of events in Ireland in the nineteenth and twentieth centuries was and is, after all, dominated by endeavours to overcome the poisonous legacy of the eighteenth-century penal era.

It is certainly justifiable to question the importance and impact of the 'penal laws', the series of anti-Catholic acts passed by the Irish parliament between 1695 and 1728. It is now universally accepted among academic historians that many of these laws (those relating to religious worship, for example) were rarely, unevenly or only half-heartedly enforced. Even the impact of those penal laws which appear to have been consistently and rigorously enforced (especially those affecting land ownership and political activity) has been questioned. Louis Cullen has argued that 'the material, as opposed to the more psychological effects of the penal laws have been exaggerated'.[30] On balance, Sean Connolly surely has a point in questioning whether the structure of early eighteenth-century Irish society would have been radically different if the penal laws had never existed. His conclusion that it would have looked more or less the same is indisputable:

> It was of course the case that Ireland in the late seventeenth and early eighteenth centuries was an unequal and exploitative society, in which power and wealth were monopolized by a small group. But the same was true of contemporary England, and indeed of the whole of western Europe, regardless of the religious composition of the population. Ireland's penal laws operated mainly to exclude one segment of the country's natural ruling élite – by this time a small minority – from the advantages that would normally have gone with their economic and social position. They did not determine the relationship between that élite and the remainder of the population. If the penal laws had been removed or if the whole population had been transformed overnight into Protestants, then a few new faces would have made their appearance in the ranks of the ruling class. [31]

On the other hand, early eighteenth-century Ireland must be placed in its proper context. The reason why society would have looked so similar if the laws had been repealed or had never been passed is that the job of restructuring Irish society had been more or less done by 1692. The old Catholic élites who would have suffered badly under the penal laws had been largely displaced by the actions of a combination of successive Tudor and Stuart monarchs and Oliver Cromwell. We should not be surprised if we find that the penal laws apparently achieved little – there was little left for them to do.

Just as it is enlightening to question whether early eighteenth-century Irish society would have looked very different had the penal laws never been passed, it is equally profitable (indeed essential) to ask if late eighteenth-century Ireland would have been a different society if this body of legislation had never existed. It is, of course, impossible to answer this question with precision for we are in the realms of hypothesis, dangerous ground for the historian. However, it is likely that in the absence of the penal laws the Ireland of the 1780s and 1790s would have been a significantly different society to the one which in fact existed. In all probability Catholic landownership would have increased throughout the century rather than decrease as it did; a small but increasing number of Catholic peers and MPs would have sat in parliament; Catholic lawyers would have played an important role within the Irish legal profession without having to trouble themselves with converting to Anglicanism; Catholic merchants would have operated under the same conditions as their Protestant countrymen; Catholic freeholders would have voted at parliamentary elections; propertied Catholics would have served as magistrates and justices of the peace; and Catholics would have been able to sit on town corporations. Perhaps most importantly, the politics of Great Britain and Ireland would not have been dominated from the late 1770s until 1829 by the 'Catholic question', for without the penal laws there would not have been a 'Catholic question'.

It is not enough to look simply at the material impact of the penal laws on early eighteenth-century Irish society in order to assess their real significance. The long-term effects of these laws which denied opportunities to successive generations of Irish Catholics must also be taken into account. Catholics in eighteenth-century Ireland must have regarded the penal legislation as designed not simply to attack current Catholic landowners and holders of public office but also to prevent Catholics from owning land or being employed by the state in the future. Whereas the legislation might directly affect relatively few people, it was an obstacle to the aspirations of all. Certainly the social structure of early eighteenth-century Ireland would not have been materially different had the penal laws never existed, but the nature of society (in its broadest sense) depends upon much more than the economic relationships between classes. To argue that the penal laws made little difference to the nature of Irish society in the eighteenth century would be to suggest that religion played little or no part in the politics and life of eighteenth-century Irish people, a proposition difficult to uphold.

It is difficult to accept the argument that the penal laws did not impact upon the relationship between the Irish ruling élite and the remainder of the population. As has been seen, relations between the Protestant community and the Catholic Irish were determined at least as much by their common historical experience as by calculations of the current balance of power. The penal laws legally recognised and confirmed in statute the mistrust and suspicion which divided the three main religious communities in Ireland. Although they were not responsible for creating the divisions which afflicted Irish society, they did nothing to overcome and much to reinforce them.[32] The implications of the Anglican supremacy established by the Williamite victory were thereafter enshrined in law. The penal laws were not an isolated phenomenon imposed on the non-Anglican communities simply for the sake of it. They were not merely the legislative 'icing', so to speak, on the 'cake' of the Williamite military victory. Irish Protestants went to a great deal of trouble over a period spanning several decades in order to have this legislation passed. It has been convincingly argued that the penal laws did not amount to a 'systematic "code" reflecting a consensus among the Protestant élite as to how its security could best be preserved'.[33] It is true that when one follows the progress of individual pieces of legislation and discovers the manner in which bills were altered at each stage of the tortuous Irish legislative process, penal legislation does appear in a new light. In order to gain the assent of both houses of the Irish parliament and the privy councils of both Britain and Ireland all important Irish legislation of the eighteenth century was, by definition, an act of compromise. In this sense, it is correct to describe the penal laws as 'a rag-bag of measures'.[34] There was certainly no clear consensus of opinion among Irish Protestants about the precise way in which Irish Catholics should be treated by the state. Furthermore, Irish Protestants (especially the clergy) argued over the final purpose of the legislation. Were the laws designed to convert the Catholics or merely oppress them? Whereas some clergymen were keen to promote schemes to convert Catholics, few laymen displayed a similar enthusiasm.

> The true reason the natives have not been converted, is because no true methods nor pains have been taken with them, all the care has been to get their lands and make them hewers of wood and drawers of water, but to provide them teachers or apply to them in a tongue they understood was never in earnest attempted, nor will it yet be suffered.[35]

This said, it is possible to over-emphasise the divisions within the Protestant community over the Catholic question. Disagreement there certainly was, but there was also a considerable degree of consensus. How many Irish Protestants of the early eighteenth century advocated that Catholics should be allowed to sit in parliament, vote in parliamentary elections, serve in the army, hold public office, practise law, bear arms, or buy and inherit land from Protestants? How many argued that Catholic priests should be allowed to travel with impunity to and from the continent? One will search long and hard to find such proposals.[36]

Clearly the penal laws had a variety of purposes for disparate interests at different times. In particular, some Protestants hoped that they would lead to conversions to Anglicanism amongst the Catholic community, although the majority clearly displayed little interest in this objective. The official papers and private correspondence of this period bear witness to the disagreement within the Protestant establishment about the detail of penal legislation. However, the silence of the records on the major questions of the rights and status of Irish Catholics speaks volumes. For despite their differences, Irish Protestants were able to agree on the fundamental objective of the penal laws – to protect and preserve a victory which had been won at great cost. This clear and precise purpose – so obvious that it did not require explicit assertion – was (to borrow James Joll's concept) an 'unspoken assumption' of the Protestant establishment in eighteenth-century Ireland.[37] For the penal laws were not, in the main, designed to change Irish society in a dramatic way, rather to maintain that society as it was in the period immediately after the Williamite victory. They were, furthermore, very successful.

III

The persistence of intense politico-religious rivalries between the different religious communities in Ireland, combined with the existence of a body of discriminatory legislation, passed by a tiny minority of the population and directed at the overwhelming majority, provides powerful ammunition for those who argue in favour of regarding eighteenth-century Irish society as 'colonial' in nature.[38] However, 'colonial' is an unhelpful and misleading adjective in this context. Two characteristics are normally found in a colonial situation. The constitutional relationship between the colony and the metropolitan power is one of explicit dependence of the former upon the latter with the metropolitan power retaining ultimate sovereignty. In addition, a racially-defined élite originating from the metropolis normally dominates the government and administration of the colony. Although elements of these characteristics can certainly be discerned in the relationship between Britain and Ireland in the eighteenth century, neither can be said wholly to apply.

In terms of its constitutional relationship with Britain, Ireland was not a colony but a kingdom. It is true that the Irish government was appointed from Westminster, that the freedom of action of the Irish parliament was hampered

by the provisions of Poynings' Law, that the terms under which Ireland con-
ducted its foreign trade (and, of course, foreign policy) were determined by the
Westminster parliament, and that with the passage of the Declaratory Act of
1720 the Westminster parliament explicitly claimed the right to legislate for
Ireland. If the British parliament had exercised the powers it claimed under the
Declaratory Act, Ireland would indeed have been nothing more than a colony.
It is all the more important, therefore, to emphasise that the Westminster legislature did not exercise these theoretical powers. The British parliament very
rarely passed legislation which affected Ireland. Neither the British parliament
nor government ever displayed any serious inclination to attempt to legislate
directly for Ireland. Although some Irishmen feared that they would be taxed
from London should relations between the rival parliaments sufficiently dete-
riorate, there is no evidence that the government ever seriously considered taxing
Ireland without the consent of the Irish parliament.[39] In the aftermath of the
constitutional dispute over the Sherlock–Annesley case when the government
did seek a way to avoid calling the Dublin parliament, the only option suggested was to cut government expenditure to enable it to be met from the
hereditary revenues. It did not seem to occur to anyone in London that Ireland
could be taxed from Westminster, theoretically possible under the terms of the
Declaratory Act. Charles Delafaye assured Isaac Manley that taxing Ireland
from Westminster 'has not been once thought of'.[40] This assumption on the
part of the British political establishment was of huge constitutional significance and it is important to stress that this perception was not shaken by the
passage of the Declaratory Act.

As is well known, the provisions of Poynings' Law, originally intended to
restrict the independence of the lord deputy in Ireland, had come to assume
over the centuries the purpose of restricting the legislative independence of the
Irish parliament.[41] Poynings' Law denied the Irish parliament the right to initiate any legislation, all bills having to take their rise in either the British or Irish
privy councils. Theoretically, therefore, the role of the Dublin parliament was
confined merely to the acceptance or rejection of legislation which had been
initiated by either of the privy councils and approved by both, for the Irish
parliament could not amend bills. The provisions of Poynings' Law, if they had
been strictly enforced, would have severely restricted the operation of parliamentary government in Ireland. Indeed the English government was so impressed
by the value of Poynings' Law that an attempt was made to introduce similar
legislation to define the powers of the Jamaican and Virginian representative
assemblies. This explicit equation of Ireland with the American colonies on the
part of the English government once more raises the question of Ireland's colonial status. Moreover, the fact that Westminster's attempt to enforce legislation
similar to Poynings' Law on Jamaica and Virginia ended in failure might even
suggest that in the 1690s the 'kingdom of Ireland' was even more constitution-

ally dependent upon England than were the American colonies.[42] Such a conclusion, however, would overlook the fact that since 1692 the restrictions imposed on the Irish parliament by Poynings' Law were being systematically circumvented. Most importantly, the Irish parliament developed a procedure by which both houses were enabled to initiate legislation.

In a colonial situation the ruling élite is normally defined by racial origin. This was the case, for example, in the eighteenth-century British colonies in North America. This was not the situation in Ireland. Any attempt to define the Anglican ruling class in terms of racial origin is doomed to failure.[43] As in Britain and elsewhere in *ancien régime* Europe the Irish ruling élite was defined by religious affiliation and wealth. In order to become a member of this élite, a person had only to go through the motions of conversion to the established church. Many Irish Catholics, for sensible and pragmatic reasons, did exactly this. The tendency for Irish Catholics in the nineteenth and twentieth centuries to regard eighteenth-century converts as 'traitors' to their religion and country overlooks the strong temptation for Catholics at the time to protect their property and the privileges associated with their social status by conforming to the established church. In a true colonial situation the transformation from being a 'native' to a member of the ruling class is not so straightforward as it was in eighteenth-century Ireland. The factor which defined the conflicting communities in Ireland in the eighteenth century was the same factor which continues to define those communities today – perceived religious affiliation. The fate of the Old English had demonstrated that the possession of English racial origins cut no ice with a Protestant establishment. The problematic nature of the colonial label is further highlighted by the example of William Conolly, who from 1714 to 1729 served as speaker of the Irish House of Commons, was a lord justice and chief revenue commissioner and was the most wealthy and powerful politician in Ireland. Can Conolly, a man of Gaelic Catholic origins, be termed a 'colonist' and the term retain any real meaning?

If, as has been argued, it is misleading to describe early eighteenth-century Ireland as a colonial society, how then should it be described? Eighteenth-century Ireland was certainly a 'confessional state' like all others in Europe and, strictly speaking, this is perhaps the most appropriate label to accurately describe the reality of Ireland at this time. However, it must always be borne in mind that, unlike other states in contemporary Europe, the confession of the Irish ruling élite was shared by perhaps as little as ten per cent of the population.

3

The Glorious Revolution and Ireland

I

The 'glorious revolution' (so-called) of 1688 fundamentally altered the course of Irish history. Generations of Irish people up until the present day have unquestioningly regarded William III's victory over James II at the Battle of the Boyne as a decisive turning point in the history of their country. William's triumph on 1 July 1690 resulted in the establishment of a 'Protestant Ascendancy' in Ireland and confirmed the position of the Anglican landowning class as the ruling élite of Ireland for the subsequent century and a half.[1] The war had been brought about, of course, by what proved to be the final attempt by an English monarch to establish an Ireland firmly connected to England but governed by the leaders of the majority Catholic community.

The accession to the throne of James II in 1685 had raised the question of how the minority Protestant community in Ireland would fare under a Catholic monarch. As a result of the civil war and the Cromwellian régime Irish Protestants (or 'New English') had replaced the 'Old English' as the dominant political and economic force in Ireland. Whereas before the civil war Catholics had owned around sixty per cent of land in Ireland, following the restoration land settlement only around twenty-two per cent of land remained in Catholic ownership. The rest was now in Protestant hands. The implications of such a change in the ownership of land became manifest when only one Catholic was elected to the Irish House of Commons in 1661.[2] In restoration Ireland, therefore, central and local administration was firmly under Protestant control. The accession to the throne of a Catholic, however, threatened to undermine this state of affairs.

Shortly after the accession of James II, an Old English Catholic, Richard Talbot, was created earl of Tyrconnell and placed in charge of the army in Ireland.[3] Thereafter he implemented a determined and successful policy of 'Catholicising' the Irish army and administration. This policy was accelerated after Tyrconnell was appointed as lord deputy in January 1687 and received James' backing at his meeting with Tyrconnell at Chester in the summer of that year. Tyrconnell's ultimate aim was to reverse the transfers in land ownership which had taken place since the civil war and thus to restore the Old English Catholic community to a position of political pre-eminence in Ireland. By November 1688 Tyrconnell had made significant progress towards realising his objec-

32

tives. The Irish army had been systematically purged of Protestants and was overwhelmingly Catholic in composition; a majority of Irish judges was Catholic; and central and local government had been put into Catholic hands. On the other hand, so long as Protestants continued to own the bulk of Irish land such changes would be easily reversed after James' death and the accession of either of his Protestant daughters to the throne. For Catholics to retain control of the Irish administration after James' death the restoration land settlement would have to be substantially altered. Tyrconnell may have had some success in convincing the king of the necessity of such an alteration but after the birth of James' son in August 1688, bringing with it the prospect of a succession of Catholic monarchs, the political initiative swiftly passed to the Prince of Orange and the Anglican élites of England. The English ruling classes had tolerated James out of fear of provoking another civil war and because they could take comfort in the knowledge that he would be succeeded by his Protestant daughters and their heirs. The birth to James of a male heir completely changed the situation. Three weeks after this unwelcome development, seven leading politicians informed William of Orange that he could expect considerable support if he chose to invade England in order to protect the right of his wife to succeed her father and preserve the Protestant succession.[4] When William of Orange landed at Torbay with 20,000 Dutch troops in November 1688, James quickly lost his nerve and, after a little difficulty, eventually managed to flee to France. The 'revolution' in England, therefore, passed off without undue fuss.

While the English political establishment struggled to rationalise what had happened and to restore a semblance of constitutional normality, James II's supporters in Ireland were faced with a dilemma. William had managed to seize the crowns of England and Scotland but that of Ireland remained unsecured. The Irish government, controlled by James' Catholic allies, was confronted with the problem of choosing which king to support – the 'legitimate' James in France or the 'usurpers' (but *de facto* monarchs) in London.

The flight of his king to France left Tyrconnell in a difficult situation to say the least. Tyrconnell may have considered attempting to come to an agreement with William but, in truth, there was little to recommend such a compromise to either party. It has been suggested by John Miller that Tyrconnell had been for some time considering the possibility of placing Ireland under French protection in the event of James' death and succession by either of his Protestant daughters.[5] Certainly, the much-improved status of Irish Catholics so laboriously built up by Tyrconnell was unlikely to survive the accession of a Protestant monarch. Whatever his original plans may have been, once it became clear that Louis XIV was prepared to devote the resources of France to an attempt to reinstall James on his throne, Tyrconnell did not hesitate. Deciding that James' success was vital if he were to protect the achievements of his period in office, Tyrconnell placed the full resources of the Irish government at James' disposal and prepared for war. Accordingly, James arrived in Ireland in March 1689, entering Dublin in triumph on 24 March. Meanwhile, in the north a Williamite army under the duke of Schomberg landed just outside Belfast in August 1689, a fortnight after the raising of the siege of Londonderry. With the exception of some posturing around Dundalk, however, no serious fighting took place until William himself arrived in Ireland in June 1690 to take personal command of military operations.[6]

The presence in Ireland of rival monarchs personally leading two large professional armies into battle provided an appropriately dramatic climax to the struggle for power between the Catholic and Protestant élites which had been in progress in Ireland since the English Reformation. James was supported by the vast majority of the population whereas William was backed by those Ulster protestants who had held the Jacobite army at bay outside Derry and had harassed James' forces around Enniskillen.[7] This internal Irish conflict was, of course, only one aspect of the wider European conflagration which had been in progress since November 1688 between Louis xiv's France and the League of Augsburg headed by William of Orange. When major hostilities finally broke out in Ireland at the Battle of the Boyne on 1 July 1690, therefore, many issues were at stake. James ii hoped to defeat William in battle and secure Ireland as a launching-pad for an invasion of mainland Britain. Tyrconnell and the Old English Catholics hoped that a victory for James would lead to a reversal of the Cromwellian and restoration land settlements and establish a 'Catholic Ascendancy' in Ireland. William's Irish Protestant allies sought to use his armies to restore and strengthen the position of dominance which they had enjoyed in Ireland since the end of the civil war and which had been seriously undermined by Tyrconnell's régime. William's priority was to pacify Ireland as quickly as possible in order to free those of his troops who were tied down there for campaigns on the continent. The Prince of Orange's main reason for invading England and deposing his father-in-law had been to secure English involvement in the continental war. Having secured the English and Scottish thrones, there was little point in having badly-needed troops bogged down in Ireland for any longer than was absolutely necessary. In the background, Louis xiv calculated that by supporting James' campaign in Ireland he would tie down the Williamite armies there in a protracted and costly struggle.

Although, it is clear, the Williamite war was by no means a purely Irish affair, there is no doubt that the consequences of the conflict were greatest in Ireland. Hostilities lasted for a total of three years, at a cost of over 20,000 battle fatalities and many more deaths from disease. The war, furthermore, wrought devastation in large areas of the Irish countryside. The common assumption in British historiography that the revolution of 1688 was 'bloodless' is curious indeed when viewed from the Irish perspective.[8]

The crushing Jacobite military defeats at the Boyne (1 July 1690) and, even more so, at Aughrim (12 July 1691) did not only serve to ensure William's status as the popular icon for future generations of Irish protestants; more importantly, William of Orange's triumph gave the Anglican community in Ireland a virtual monopoly of political power for the next one hundred years. The confiscation of the land of those of James II's Irish supporters who had capitulated before the surrender at Limerick (October 1691) further reduced the proportion of Irish land owned by Catholics from the approximate twenty two per cent in 1688 to around fourteen per cent by 1703.[9] The amount of Catholic-owned land was to fall further as a result of the conversions which followed the passage of the 'Act to prevent the further growth of popery' of 1704 which placed a number of severe restrictions on the ability of Catholics to inherit, buy, or rent land. The Jacobite military defeat, combined with the impact of the penal laws, confirmed and completed the transformation of the economic and political élite in Ireland which had been proceeding throughout the seventeenth century. After the restoration of Charles II the Irish Catholic élites had had some success in recovering their former position through the purchase of land.[10] It soon became clear that no such possibility would exist after the defeat of James II. After 1691, the complete dominance by Anglicans of the Irish political establishment was no longer open to question.[11]

II

The penal laws, passed between 1695 and 1728 by an increasingly assertive and powerful Irish parliament, formally excluded Catholics from a direct participation in all areas of political life. However, as Sean Connolly has forcefully argued, it was primarily the impact of the wars of the 1640s and 1690s (especially the former) in transferring the bulk of landed property from Catholic to Protestant hands which ensured Anglican political hegemony. Even after the repeal of the penal laws the 'Protestant Ascendancy' in Ireland was to display what some might regard as a stubborn longevity. With the benefit of hindsight, it can be seen that the Jacobite surrender at Limerick in October 1691 witnessed the final defeat of the attempts of the Old English in Ireland to combine their Catholicism with loyal service to the English government. After Limerick, attempts to differentiate between Old English Catholics and their Irish co-religionists (a division still prominent in the Jacobite Parliament of 1689) became increasingly meaningless. The Williamite victory, therefore, soon resulted in the formation of a single Catholic political community in Ireland. In contrast, the coalition of Anglican and Presbyterian forces during the war had been an uneasy one which did not long survive the defeat of the Jacobite armies. The emergence of a politically-united Irish protestant community followed only after the Act of Union of 1800, and even then the transformation was a slow one.

The Williamite war not only decided the struggle for power between the rival Catholic and Protestant communities in Ireland in the latter's favour, it also led to a dramatic alteration in the relationship between the political establishments of England and Ireland. One result of the wars in Ireland and in Europe, was that the way in which Ireland was governed changed fundamentally. William Speck has written that 'In 1689 [the English] parliament was finally transformed from an event into an institution.'[12] The Williamite revolution had a similar impact on the status of its sister parliament in Dublin for, after 1692, the Irish parliament for the first time became a regular and influential partner in the government of Ireland.[13] Prior to 1692, the Irish parliament had sat very rarely. Before 1688, only five parliaments had assembled in Dublin during the whole of the seventeenth century – 1613-15; 1634-5; 1640-1; 1661-6 and 1689. These assemblies had been summoned only when the crown had urgent need of Irish parliamentary assent, normally for taxation or legislation relating to land ownership. When these needs had been met, no further thought was given to holding regular meetings of parliament in Ireland. Prior to 1692, therefore, parliaments in Ireland (as in England) were regarded as 'events', the exception rather than the norm. However, after 1692, until its final demise in 1800, the Irish parliament usually met for six months every other year. This dramatic change in the role of the Dublin parliament in the government of Ireland (which closely mirrored changes in crown-parliament relations in England) occurred mainly because the government badly needed Irish money. As in England, government indebtedness rather than deliberate constitutional innovation resulted in the establishment of permanent parliamentary government.

The hereditary revenues granted to Charles II by the Irish parliament in 1666 had proved sufficient to meet the Irish government's expenditure until the outbreak of the revolution in 1688. In fact, these revenues had often produced a surplus for the crown.[14] As a result, the government could dispense with the necessity of calling a parliament in Ireland. With the outbreak of war between the Jacobite and Williamite forces in Ireland this situation changed, with long-term implications for the role of the Dublin parliament. Upon his arrival in Ireland, James II immediately faced pressure to call a parliament. The king found it impossible to resist such pressure for he desperately required funds to enable him to raise forces against William. Accordingly a parliament dominated by Old English Catholic interests was elected and met in May 1689.[15] This 'Patriot' or 'Jacobite' parliament as it has come to be known by historians, proved surprisingly uncooperative and meddlesome as far as James was concerned. Instead of concentrating on the task at hand, that is, defeating the Williamite forces in Ireland, Catholic peers and MPs insisted that, before granting him supplies, the king should address a number of their long-standing grievances. Their most pressing concerns were, of course, the land question and the status of the Catholic church in Ireland. Parliament demanded that the Cromwellian and restoration land settlements be amended in order to return land to those who had owned it in 1641. The lands which had changed hands as a result of earlier confiscations were not, it will be noted, to be restored. Those most affected by these earlier transfers had been, of course, the Gaelic Irish. The 1689 Parliament eventually announced the confiscation of the lands of around 2,000 Protestant landowners who had fled the country after the revolution. If such a programme of confiscation had been put into effect it would have dramatically altered the balance of landownership (and hence political power) between the Protestant and Catholic communities in Ireland.

Viewed in the light of the constitutional conflicts which were to occur between the Protestant Irish parliament and the English government and parliament after 1692, the proceedings of the 'Patriot Parliament' are highly suggestive. The Catholic-dominated assembly of 1689 passed a Declaratory Act denying the right of the Westminster parliament to legislate for Ireland and made an unsuccessful attempt to repeal Poynings' Law. Although the Jacobite defeat rendered all of the efforts of the 1689 Parliament redundant, these constitutional issues would raise their heads repeatedly during the period from 1692 to 1800. It is evident, therefore, that constitutional conflict between the Irish and English parliaments was virtually inevitable in a situation in which both legislatures were meeting regularly. These disputes, in short, were structural rather than 'ideological' in nature. Whether the parliament in Dublin was dominated by 'Irish' Catholics or 'colonist' Protestants was, apparently, irrelevant.

Consequently James II was not the only king of England who had to face an unexpectedly troublesome Irish parliament in these years. After the Williamite military victory the king felt obliged to call an Irish parliament in order to have it ratify the terms of the Treaty of Limerick. More pressingly, William also needed the Dublin parliament to vote additional revenues to meet Irish government expenditure. The economic disruption brought about by the war in Ireland had naturally reduced the government's revenue severely. The civil and military establishments, on the other hand, had both increased. The hereditary revenues were no longer proving sufficient to meet the costs of the Irish military establishment; new taxes were needed and these required the consent of the Irish parliament.

The Dublin administration was to find the by now exclusively Protestant parliament of 1692 puzzlingly obstructive. It might reasonably have been expected that within a year of the Jacobite surrender at Limerick Irish Protestants would have been in a grateful and cooperative frame of mind. The Williamite armies had, after all, recently delivered the Protestant community in Ireland from disaster, defeated their enemies and restored them to their estates. The parliamentary session of 1692, however, graphically demonstrated that the political situation in Ireland was very different to that which had prevailed when the last Protestant Irish parliament had met in the 1660s.[16] The lord lieutenant, Henry, Viscount Sydney, and the lords justices, Sir Charles Porter and Thomas, 1st Baron Coningsby, were deeply unpopular among the Anglican community. Irish Protestants particularly resented what they regarded as the unnecessarily lenient elements of the Treaty of Limerick which, they feared, kept open the possibility of a Catholic resurgence. Furthermore, there was strong resentment among Irish Protestants of alleged corruption among senior figures in Dublin Castle. When viewed in this context of widespread distrust of the government by the Anglican community, rather than in the context of the recent Jacobite-Williamite conflict, the failure of the 1692 Parliament comes as less of a surprise.

It is clear that Irish Protestants were determined to use the forthcoming session of parliament in order to gain concessions from the administration at Dublin Castle over the 'Catholic question' and the post-revolutionary land settlement. Like any representative assembly at this time, the Irish parliament's only real instrument for influencing government policy was in its power to approve or reject government supply bills. Irish members of parliament in 1692 sought to extend their influence over government finances by demanding the 'sole right' of the House of Commons to frame money bills, that is, to decide how much should be voted to the government in additional taxation and the 'ways and means' in which such money should be raised. Such a right was in direct conflict with the provisions of Poynings' Law which denied the Irish parliament the power to initiate any legislation whatsoever. When the government presented two money bills to parliament, the Commons responded by rejecting the main bill and asserting their sole right to initiate money bills. The lower house then passed the other money bill to help the government meet its immediate financial needs. It had now become clear that Lord Lieutenant Sydney had seriously misjudged the mood of the Anglican gentry. When the Dublin parliament refused to play the role of ratifying body (and also to prevent a Commons debate about alleged corruption within the Castle administration) Sydney had no choice but to prorogue it only four weeks after it had first met. At its prorogation on 3 November, Sydney revealingly accused the House of Commons of not answering 'the ends for which they were called together'.[17]

The collapse of the 1692 session of parliament resulted in a transformation of the relationship between the English government and the Protestant community in Ireland. It had been made abundantly clear that Irish Protestants were demanding a price from the government in return for supplying taxation. The price demanded was an enhanced role for the Irish parliament in the government of the country. The long period when parliament had failed to meet after 1666, followed by the dramatic developments in Ireland during the reign of James II and the Williamite wars (when the Irish Protestant community had faced virtual extinction) had convinced Irish Protestants that neither the executive in Dublin nor the ministry in London could be relied upon to guarantee the

Protestant interest in Ireland. The (in their view) excessively lenient Treaty of Limerick was further proof, if proof were needed, that an English government could not be trusted to protect the interests of Irish Protestants.[18] The representatives of the Protestant community, therefore, determined that their parliament should have a permanent and meaningful role to play in the future government of their country. From now on, Irish Protestants resolved to rely upon no one but themselves in order to guarantee their liberties, property and privileges. It was recognised that securing control of government finances was the key to the achievement of such an objective.

In adopting such a policy, Irish members of parliament were closely following the example of their counterparts at Westminster. English parliamentarians had shown a similar disinclination to entrust their future to the new Williamite government by deliberately voting the king insufficient funds to meet normal (that is, peacetime) expenditure. The spiralling costs of William's prolonged war against the French ensured that the king's ministers would regularly have to seek additional supplies from the English House of Commons. The increased taxation and national debt which resulted from the war of 1689-97 brought about a 'financial revolution' in England which had hugely significant and permanent constitutional consequences. Previous Tudor and Stuart monarchs had been able to govern without the necessity of calling parliament so long as they avoided drawn-out and costly wars. The reigns of Charles II and James II had demonstrated only too clearly that the civil war had done nothing to guarantee that parliament would meet on a regular basis. The creation of a permanent national debt after the 'glorious revolution', however, ensured that no future English monarch would ever be in a position to dispense with parliament.[19]

After the disastrous session of 1692, a reappraisal of the mechanisms for governing Ireland was clearly necessary. The collapse of the parliamentary session had indicated the extent of the gulf which existed between the Castle and College Green. The solution and the establishment of an effective system of government came only with the appointment of a new lord deputy, Henry, 1st Baron Capel, in May 1695 and the election of a new parliament in the same year. James McGuire has described Capel's policy for the government of Ireland as follows:

> From the time he became a lord justice [June 1693] he consistently struck an optimistic note when reporting to London on the possibilities of an Irish Parliament. All that was needed, he implied, was a change in government policy, adroit and politic handling of the local political leaders, and a willingness to concede to Parliament a de facto initiative in legislation without reneging in principle.[20]

If this was 'all that was needed' then it amounted to a very great deal. Capel's policy amounted to a fundamental shift in the manner in which Ireland would be governed in the future. The lord deputy was recommending that the government should compromise with the Irish Protestants over the question of 'sole right'. However, it quickly became clear that such a compromise was exceedingly favourable towards the Irish House of Commons. When parliament met in August 1695, the lord deputy presented a minor excise bill in order to confirm the government's right to initiate money bills but left it to the Commons to frame the main supply bill. As a result Capel obtained the government's supply with relatively little trouble. At the same time, however, the government was implicitly accepting the claim of the Irish House of Commons to have the dominant say in initiating and framing finance legislation. As a result of this compromise, the Irish parliament effectively regained the ability to initiate legislation and removed at a stroke possibly the most important restriction imposed by Poynings' Law.

Capel had recognized that the situation had changed in Ireland. Parliament was now an important factor in the government of the country. Irish peers and MPs could no longer be dictated to and then sent home. So long as the government needed additional revenues to meet the increased costs of the Irish civil and military establishments, parliament would have to be managed and the only way in which this could be done was by giving local politicians posts of responsibility. Accordingly, the second aspect of Capel's recommendation was implemented. Two of the main opponents of the government in the 1692 session (both of whom, significantly, were lawyers) were brought into the Castle administration – Robert Rochfort as attorney general and Alan Brodrick as solicitor general. This can be regarded as the first step in the establishment of what later came to be known by historians as the 'undertaker system', whereby local politicians agreed to manage the government's business in parliament in return for office, some influence in the formation of policy, and a share in the distribution of government patronage.[21]

The Irish parliamentary session of 1695 was arguably the most important session to take place between 1692 and 1800. It witnessed three crucial developments for the future government of Ireland. Firstly, leading Irish parliamentarians were brought into the government; secondly, parliament's right to initiate legislation through the 'heads of bills' procedure was recognised; and thirdly, the predominant role of the House of Commons in deciding the amount of money to be granted to the government as a supply, and the ways and means in which it was to be raised, was implicitly accepted. The session of 1695, in other words, established the pattern by which Ireland would be governed for the next one hundred years.

The permanence of such an arrangement was not, of course, apparent to contemporaries. Indeed if the government had been able to reduce its expenditure at the conclusion of the European war in 1697 it may not have been necessary to call the Irish parliament on a regular basis thereafter. In this respect the king's difficulties with the English parliament had a crucial effect on the future government of Ireland, demonstrating once again the extent to which the Irish and English political scenes were closely connected. At the conclusion of the Nine Years War in 1697, the English parliamentary opposition demanded that William III reduce the size of his standing army in England to a mere 7,000 men. Permanent standing armies had long been a sensitive political issue in England, the painful experience of military dictatorship under Cromwell never being far from the minds of parliamentarians. Charles II's stationing of troops in Oxford when his last parliament had met there in 1681 and the expansion of the standing army under James II had, no doubt, further deepened this distrust of the military. William III, on the other hand, was convinced (rightly as it turned out) that the peace between England and France was little more than a temporary truce and was extremely reluctant to disband an army which he believed would be needed once again in the near future. Parliament, however, was adamant that the troops should be disbanded and the king was eventually forced to give in. As a consolation, the English parliament passed an act allowing the government to maintain a permanent standing army of 12,000 men in Ireland, these troops to be paid for out of Irish taxation. Quite apart from the constitutional implications of the English parliament deciding that Irish taxes should support an English army in Ireland, this decision was to ensure that the Irish parliament, like its counterpart at Westminster, was transformed from being an occasional event into a permanent institution.

No doubt with a close eye on developments in London, the Irish House of Commons in both 1692 and 1695 had attempted to ensure a continued role for their parliament in the affairs of Ireland by voting the additional revenues needed by the government for only two years or less at a time. On no occasion after 1692 did the Irish Commons vote taxes for more than two years duration; on a number of occasions, indeed, taxes were voted for less than two years.[22] The government's decision to station 12,000 troops on Irish soil, combined with the Irish parliament's refusal to vote permanent taxes, inevitably meant that so long as the Westminster government wanted these troops to remain in Ireland it would have to allow the Irish parliament to meet every two years or so. After 1695, until its demise in 1800, with one exception, the Irish parliament met at least once every two years.[23] The fact that the Dublin parliament was now a permanent partner in the government of Ireland raised a completely new set of problems for the English ministry. Since the beginning of the seventeenth century the English government had been in a position in which it could normally carry out its policy towards Ireland (if it had one) with relatively little interference from the Irish (Catholic and Protestant) themselves. The presence of a parliament, sitting regularly in Dublin, changed Anglo-Irish relations in a dramatic way.

III

The single most important factor leading to instability in Anglo-Irish relations in the eighteenth century was the complex relationship between the government in London, the executive in Dublin Castle, and the Irish parliament. Under the provisions of Poynings' Law, the Irish parliament had no right to initiate legislation, merely to pass or reject bills which had taken their rise in either the English or Irish privy councils and had been approved by both.[24] The parliament of 1661-65 had witnessed the first steps in the process whereby the Irish parliament would regain the legislative initiative. During this parliament, the practice of drawing up 'heads' of bills (as opposed to bills) by either house of the Irish parliament was developed. Theoretically heads of bills had the status only of requests for legislation but in practice they were treated by both houses of the Irish parliament as if they were bills proper. The heads of a bill were read three times in the house in which they had arisen. If approved by that house in the normal way it was presented to the Irish privy council to be drawn up into a proper bill. It will be noted that, unlike a bill at Westminster, heads of bills were not presented to both houses of parliament. Such a development was occasionally suggested in Ireland but this was always opposed by the government. Ministers no doubt feared that heads of bills which had been approved by both houses of parliament would carry greater authority than those which had been assented to only by one. The rejection of such legislation at council would clearly be a more problematic process.[25]

Once the heads of a bill had been presented to the Irish privy council it could be amended, accepted or rejected. If approved (even in amended form) the bill then passed to the privy council in London where it could be similarly accepted, rejected or amended. If the bill had survived thus far it was then returned to Ireland where it had to pass both houses of the Irish parliament to become law. The bill could not be amended by parliament, merely accepted or rejected. In this way, the provision of Poynings' Law that only the Irish or English privy councils could initiate bills was theoretically adhered to whilst the Irish parliament in fact regained the legislative initiative. This became the established practice after 1692 and during the eighteenth century the vast majority of Irish legislation began its life in the form of heads of a bill.[26] Thus, the Irish parliament in the eighteenth century had, in practice if not in theory, the power to initiate legislation.

The major factor which tended to strain the relationship between the government and the Irish parliament was the fact that the executive in Dublin Castle was in no way responsible to the Dublin parliament. This would not have mattered very much if the government had had a stable and significant 'interest' or following in parliament. However, it had not. Although the government could normally control the House of Lords with the votes of a combination of bishops and dependent peers, it had very little direct interest in the House of Commons. A situation arose, therefore, where the government had little control over the House of Commons, which in turn had no control over the government. Clearly, if Ireland was to have any kind of effective government, a *modus operandi* would have to be devised between the executive and legislature. The next one hundred years or so were to see various attempts by the British government to come to terms with this new situation, their final solution being, of course, the legislative union of the two kingdoms.

It has been seen how during the session of 1695 parliamentary managers or undertakers were used by Lord Deputy Capel to manage parliament on the government's behalf. This use of local expertise to ensure the relatively smooth passage of government business was inevitable given the lack of a government party in the House of Commons. During the reign of William III, activity in the Irish House of Commons was complicated and confused, at times appearing to be organized along court and country lines, on other occasions resembling a conflict between the personal followers of Lord Capel and Sir Charles Porter respectively. David Hayton, however, has argued that an 'incipient two-party system' existed at this time which later matured into the Whig-Tory political divide which characterised the reign of Queen Anne.[27] In support of this argument, Hayton demonstrated the large degree of continuity in the personnel of those who were involved in the court-country and Whig-Tory conflicts.[28] Certainly, the followers of the two most important political figures in the 1690s, Lord Chancellor Porter and Lord Deputy Capel, eventually metamorphosed into the Tory and Whig parties respectively. It is also the case that important ideological questions contributed to the court-country division of the 1690s which was not simply a battle for office between 'ins' and 'outs'. In particular, the parliamentary conflicts about the legal status of Irish Catholics after the Treaty of Limerick bore obvious relevance to the party conflict about the state's religious policy during Anne's reign. However, the 1690s proved to be a confused and unstable period in Irish politics. Whilst the executive was trying to create a stable system of government which would ensure the passage of money bills, peers and MPs were debating the merits of anti-popery bills, arguing over the final form of the Treaty of Limerick, and attempting to protect the interests of those Irish Protestants who had bought land from those who had been granted forfeited estates by William III after 1691, grants which were later challenged by the English parliament.[29]

At the same time, Irish Protestants were beginning to question the nature of the constitutional link with England. The dispute between the Irish and English Houses of Lords over who should be the final court of appeal in Irish legal cases caused by the case of the *Bishop of Derry versus the Irish Society* commenced a constitutional wrangle which was only settled with the passage of the Declaratory Act in 1720. The publication of William Molyneux's *Case of Ire-*

land being bound by Acts of Parliament in England stated followed by the passage of the Woollen Act of 1699, brought to the fore the question of the powers of the increasingly assertive English parliament as regards Ireland. The legislatures in Dublin and Westminster had both been relatively impotent under Charles II and James II. Under William III, however, both parliaments significantly increased in power and influence raising the question of what would happen if and when they came into conflict. Clearly the Westminster parliament would be the winner in any such dispute but this would inevitably arouse resentment among Irish Protestants (or 'the English in Ireland' as they commonly styled themselves) on the grounds that they were being bound by legislation passed by a legislature in which they had no direct representation. The emergence of such fundamental constitutional issues provoked discussion about how the interests of Irish Protestants could be best protected. One solution to this constitutional muddle was a legislative union with England such as the one in which Scotland was soon to engage and it appears clear that at this stage such a union was the preferred option in Ireland.[30] In this way, Irish representatives could sit in the parliament at Westminster and represent Irish Protestant interests at the centre of government. When, however, it became clear that a union would not be acceptable to the English political establishment, Irish Protestants were left with no option but to attempt to protect their interests by defending the powers of their own parliament in Dublin against the attempted encroachments by that at Westminster.

The consistent efforts on the part of Irish Protestants to defend what they regarded as the rights of the Irish parliament should not necessarily be interpreted as evidence of an embryonic 'colonial nationalism'. Only by exploiting to the full the potential influence of their own parliament could Irish Protestants hope to defend their interests (particularly their economic interests) against interference from an increasingly assertive Westminster parliament. Given the lack of Irish representation at Westminster, the preservation of the privileges and status of the Irish parliament was a practical necessity for the Protestant community.

IV

Despite having a common monarch with Great Britain, Ireland in the eighteenth century was theoretically a separate kingdom. Ireland had its own government, privy council, parliament, judiciary, and established church, leading some Irish Protestants to claim that Ireland was a kingdom of equal status to Britain. Not surprisingly, this view was rejected in England. Indeed some British politicians claimed that Ireland was not a kingdom, but a colony, and therefore subject to the laws of the mother country.[31] Historians have continued this debate about the status of Ireland in relation to Britain. Like many of the questions relating to the nature of eighteenth-century Irish politics and society, there is no simple answer. Whatever constitutional claims Ireland may have had to being treated as an equal by Britain, in practice Ireland's status lay somewhere between equality and subjection – a kingdom certainly, but a dependent one, despite Swift's rejection of the validity of such a concept.[32] The government based in Dublin Castle and headed by the lord lieutenant was appointed by the ministry in London and was expected to carry out the policy of the British government towards Ireland. So long as the Irish executive was controlled from London, Ireland would remain in practice under British rule. On the other hand, the British government recognized the sensibilities of the Anglican community by rarely attempting to legislate for Ireland and there was never any serious suggestion of the Irish people being taxed from Westminster.[33]

Although the British government was directly responsible for the government of the country, Ireland and Irish affairs had a very low priority in London. The archbishop of Dublin described the attitude towards Ireland of those British politicians whom he had met in 1726: 'I have been in London and discoursed several statesmen there, but I do not remember that any of them ever asked me a question about Ireland, nor did I find that they knew anything of it, or were fond of hearing anything about it'.[34] The chief advantage of Ireland for the British ministry in the early eighteenth century was in its role as a base for 12,000 troops of the British army at a time when the Westminster parliament would allow a standing army in Britain of only 7,000 men. Throughout the first half of the eighteenth century, in particular, the forces stationed in Ireland were used as a strategic reserve to be called upon whenever necessary and they played a crucial role in the defence of the British Isles and the colonies. The fact that these forces – which comprised about one-third of George I's army – were paid for by the Irish Exchequer was an additional bonus for the ministry in London and the top priority of all lords lieutenant of Ireland was to obtain sufficient funds from the Irish House of Commons to support the military establishment.

Other matters relating to Ireland rarely received serious attention in Britain. Two exceptions, however, should be mentioned. The first regarded the state's religious policy. After 1704, successive Whig administrations in Britain made repeated attempts to repeal the sacramental test as it affected protestant dissenters in Ireland, possibly as the first step to its removal in England. The Irish parliament, however, steadfastly refused to comply with this policy and this issue strained Anglo-Irish relations throughout this period. In deference to the sensibilities of its Catholic allies in Europe, the British government tended also to tone down or to veto bills sent from Ireland 'to prevent the further growth of popery'. Such differing stances on the question of religion were not likely to produce an harmonious relationship between executive and legislature.

Economic disputes also soured relations between the government in London and the Irish parliament at this time. Ever since the passage of the Woollen Act of 1699 Irish Protestants had felt, rightly or wrongly, that England would always impede any Irish industry or trade which threatened her own. The wool issue continued to occupy the minds of the British ministry who, spurred on by the complaints of English merchants, repeatedly accused the Irish revenue service of not doing enough to prevent the illegal export of wool to France.[35] For their part, Irish merchants resented the controls placed upon their trade with the colonies. The House of Commons, in addition, repeatedly saw bills to encourage tillage in Ireland vetoed in England through fear of Irish competition, even when these bills had the strong support of the lord lieutenant.[36] It is perhaps significant that the most serious crisis in Anglo-Irish relations in this period, the Wood's halfpence dispute, was over an economic issue.

For most of the eighteenth century the Irish political nation was comprised of a social, economic, and religious élite. The series of penal laws passed between 1695 and 1728 resulted in political power at all levels in Ireland being concentrated in the hands of Irish Protestants.[37] From 1728 until 1793 Irish Catholics were totally excluded from a direct participation in political life. Protestant dissenters, too, were stripped of much of their political influence due to the imposition of the sacramental test which had to be taken by all office-holders. The test effectively debarred dissenters from sitting on town corporations, although they were still allowed to sit in both houses of parliament. Catholics, on the other hand, were denied any direct access to the political system being prevented from sitting in parliament and effectively disenfranchised by the Act of 1704 to prevent the further growth of popery. The effective removal of the Catholics' right to vote was made explicit in 1728.[38]

The Irish executive comprised the lord lieutenant (viceroy), the lords justices, and the privy council. With the single exception of the duke of Ormonde (1703-7 and 1711-13), the lord lieutenant was always an English nobleman. The viceroy was a member of the government at Westminster and, until the arrival of George, 4th Viscount Townshend in 1767, he normally resided in Ireland only during the parliamentary session, that is, for about six to eight months every two years.[39] During the early Hanoverian period, the calibre of those viceroys who came to Ireland, with the notable exception of John, 2nd Baron Carteret, was not high.[40] A top-ranking British minister would have regarded being appointed as lord lieutenant of Ireland as a demotion. Although the Irish viceroyalty was not regarded by senior politicians in England as a prestigious post, it was nevertheless a lucrative one. The basic salary of the viceroy was £11,000 per annum plus £3,000 for equipage which he received upon his appointment. Out of this salary the lord lieutenant had to pay his entertainment expenses while in Dublin and the salaries of his deputies, the lords justices, but even allowing for these expenses the viceroy's salary remained a considerable one.[41]

Probably of more importance than the viceroy's salary was the patronage attached to the post. With the exception of a very few senior posts, the lord lieutenant controlled the disposal of all Irish civil offices in the gift of the crown, amounting to about one hundred and fifty posts.[42] The viceroy was head of the army in Ireland, until 1727 personally deciding the disposal of ensigncies and cornetcies and having a major influence in the disposal of more senior commissions. He also played an important role in the disposal of ecclesiastical patronage, having control of all benefices in the gift of the crown except for bishoprics and, after 1727, Irish deaneries. Only the revenue service was beyond his immediate control, but even here a determined viceroy such as Sunderland or Carteret could exert considerable influence in the disposal of patronage.[43] Given this enormous source of patronage, an Irish viceroy was able to provide for many of his friends and relatives and, perhaps more importantly, to oblige his political allies by granting them favours in respect of jobs for themselves and their dependants.

The role of the viceroy in the early eighteenth century was not as passive as it has sometimes been portrayed. In addition to his parliamentary managers, the lord lieutenant himself occasionally played an active role in drumming up support for his administration. On 25 and 31 June 1719, for example, the duke of Bolton summoned sixteen leading parliamentarians to Dublin Castle to find out how far they would go to relieve the protestant dissenters. One month later, Bolton wrote to Secretary of State Craggs that, 'I had between 50 and 60 members with me last night, and they have promised to go into the supply today.'[44] The extent of such activity by a viceroy largely depended upon the personality involved. Carteret was undoubtedly the lord lieutenant who was most actively involved in the day to day management of the Irish parliament during the reign of George I. Charles Fitzroy, 2nd duke of Grafton, however, seems to have been happy to let his managers, chiefly the speaker of the House of Commons, William Conolly, take responsibility for the management of parliament. Even Grafton, however, was said to have personally intervened to persuade Charles Stewart, MP for County Tyrone and a naval officer, to stay in Ireland at the height of the Wood's halfpence crisis.[45] The lord lieutenant, therefore, was not an entirely remote figure, rather he tended to intervene as a *deus ex machina* at crucial moments.

The lords justices, usually three in number, were leading Irish politicians who were appointed to head the government in the viceroy's absence. In addition, during the 1715-16 parliamentary session, the duke of Grafton and Henri de Massue, 1st earl of Galway, were sent from Britain to act as lords justices due to Sunderland's refusal to travel to Ireland. This was an exceptional situation, however, and was not to reoccur. The commission of the lords justices was normally drawn from the lord chancellor, the speaker of the House of Commons, the primate of the Church of Ireland, and the commander-in-chief of the army. In spite of the not inconsiderable salary of £100 per month, to serve as a lord justice appears to have been something of a burden.[46] William King, archbishop of Dublin from 1703 to 1729, served as a lord justice on four occasions (1714-15, 1717, 1718, 1722-3) and clearly did not enjoy the experience. King's first experience of serving as a lord justice had made him anxious to avoid being chosen to do so again.[47] In February 1717, Martin Bladen wrote to Charles Delafaye that 'I must tell you the Archbishop [of Dublin] is very averse to being in the commission [of lords justices], yet I am of opinion when his name is once put in, he will not absolutely decline acting.'[48] Dr King was, in the event, chosen to act as a lord justice, despite his being in London at the time. His reaction to the appointment confirms Bladen's impression that he was unwilling to serve:

> I do not remember anything has happened more uneasy to me than being in the present circumstances in the government of Ireland. You must be sensible that it is not out of any kindness to me and may be very inconvenient to me. I (God willing) will keep out of harm's way as long as I can, and hope the job will be very short.[49]

In 1722 King was again chosen to act as a lord justice, allegedly after he had been 'followed by the duke of Grafton and begged as for an alms' to accept the commission. The archbishop apparently insisted in return for agreeing to act as a lord justice that he would not be forced to consecrate Josiah Hort as the new bishop of Ferns and Leighlin and that John Parnell would be appointed as a judge.[50] It would appear that these terms were agreed to by the government for King did not consecrate Hort and Parnell was shortly afterwards appointed as a judge of the King's Bench. The archbishop, however, still insisted to a friend that he had 'been forced into the government'.[51] Henry Downes, the bishop of Killala, was understandably sceptical of the archbishop's protestations, writing that 'His Grace seems not pleased with the trust reposed in him and told me that he was sure it would kill him. But I do not believe him; perhaps he would have been as uneasy had he been left out of the government.'[52] However, King's genuine distaste for this post was further demonstrated by the pointed (but characteristic) instruction which he directed to one of his correspondents to address him according to his ecclesiastical title of 'your Grace' rather than 'your Excellency', his title as a lord justice.[53]

In spite of the burdensome nature of the office, the advantage in being chosen to act as a lord justice lay in the fact that it was a public signal that a person was in favour with the present ministry. Anyone who hoped to have influence in either house of parliament had to demonstrate that he had influence and credit with the Westminster government. When the lords justices were being chosen at the end of 1717, the speaker of the Commons, William Conolly, was fearful that he would not be included in the commission. In October, Conolly wrote to Charles Delafaye that he did not know who were to be the new lords justices:

> But as usual I can understand I shall not have the honour to be one of the number, if the greatest Minister of State here [Lord Brodrick, the Lord Chancellor] can prevent it. You know me too well to imagine it will give me any concern (whatever it may be to our friends) but if it be effected it will be apparent that his Grace [the Duke of Bolton] can place no greater indignity upon me, having found me in that station, than to leave me out [having gone] into every step and measure for his Majesty's service and the ease of his Grace's administration.[54]

In November 1719, when Archbishop King was left out of the commission of lords justices due to his opposition to the government in the House of Lords, the bishop of Killala doubted whether King's professions of relief at the decision were genuine. Highlighting the real significance of being appointed as a lord justice, Henry Downes wrote that King 'seemed as pleased with his release from trouble, as others can possibly be with the addition to theirs; but his heart you can guess at as well … because it looked as if he had far less credit and power on the other side of the water than he has on this'.[55]

Although the post of lord justice was clearly an important and prestigious one, the powers attached to the post were strictly limited. William Conolly wrote in January 1718 that 'The lords justices are tied down by instructions from the lord lieutenant (as usual) which makes my colleagues uneasy. The truth is there is little in our power.'[56] Lord Drogheda had refused a request to serve as a lord justice in 1709 'as thinking his Commission too restrained'.[57] The constraints imposed upon the lords justices led to complaints that they were being expected to shoulder the responsibility of government without being given the necessary authority to carry out the task.[58] The lords justices had very little say in the disposal of government patronage, for example. They could recommend people for vacant posts but there was no guarantee that their recommendations would be heeded. Archbishop King complained in March 1718 that the duke of Bolton was ignoring the views of the lords justices about the disposal of patronage:

> my lord lieutenant disposes of all things in England without consulting anybody here, or giving any regard to our recommendation,… I suspected this would be so, and therefore desired to be excused from being one of the justices, and now I find it so, I am heartily tired of it and hope soon to be released …[59]

There is some evidence to suggest that the lords justices were reluctant even to recommend people to certain posts lest it give offence to the ministry in London.[60] Responding to a suggestion that he might be asked to serve as a lord justice in 1733, Marmaduke Coghill observed that 'a man in that station without the power to oblige and satisfy applications in matters of no great importance, will be a man rather despised than respected'.[61]

It would appear that the influence of the lords justices increased somewhat after the Wood's halfpence dispute. The death of Primate Thomas Lindsay in 1724 and the resignation of Lord Chancellor Midleton in April 1725 allowed the government to fill these key posts with Englishmen who were considered to be more reliable, Hugh Boulter and Richard West, respectively. From now on the lords justices were normally the primate, the lord chancellor, and the speaker of the Commons, with the latter being the only Irishman. From a situation where all of the lords justices (except lords justices Grafton and Galway) from September 1714 to October 1724 had been Irishmen, two of the lords justices after 1725 were always English-born. Because two out of the three lords justices from 1725 onwards were regarded to be primarily in the English interest, the views of the lords justices and their recommendations concerning government patronage were more likely to receive a sympathetic hearing from the British ministry.[62]

The role of the Irish privy council was to assist the lord lieutenant and lords justices in the exercise of executive power. The council was theoretically a large body, the one appointed in September 1714 having fifty-six members. The council also increased in size during the reign of George I. By 1725 there were sixty-six members of the council and the government became very reluctant to appoint additional members, even when they were recommended by the lord lieutenant.[63] Despite this increase in membership, attendances at council meetings were usually small. During parliamentary sessions attendances normally varied between twelve and twenty. When parliament was not in session attendances were even lower, so that it was sometimes impossible to gather enough members together in order to form a board. The situation became most difficult in this respect when twice a year the judges went on their circuits of the country and were unable to attend.[64]

The council was called to issue proclamations, usually relating to law and order or to the economy; to approve the election of local government officials; and to discuss parliamentary legislation with the lord lieutenant. The council also had the power to initiate, alter, or veto legislation in the Irish parliament. It was this legislative role which was perhaps the most important function of the privy council, a role which sometimes brought it into conflict with parliament. It would appear that the House of Commons increasingly resented the privy council's legislative powers and that bills which had taken their rise in the privy council were often attacked, and occasionally defeated, in the Commons for this reason. When two bills were rejected by the Commons in July 1707, Sir Richard Cox explained that 'several dislike that the Privy Council should model bills for them', adding 'You may judge what this will come to in time'.[65] When a bill for preventing riots in the city of Dublin was thrown out by the Commons in 1730, Primate Boulter commented that 'It is very common in debates in the Commons to abuse the privy council, but this is the first time since my coming hither, that a bill has been in plain defiance of our constitution, thrown out for rising in the privy council.'[66] The fact that this bill had been framed by Boulter and Lord Chancellor Wyndham seems to have made some MPs particularly keen to see it defeated in the Commons.[67] Bills which had been amended by the privy council were also occasionally dropped by the Commons and any amendment to a money bill was particularly resented. As a result, privy councillors could find themselves in a difficult position since many heads of bills sent to the council were extremely loosely drawn and required considerable amendment in order to render them fit to be forwarded to London.[68] Councillors could, therefore, attract opprobrium for altering bills when, in fact, they were acting in good faith. Due to the sensitivities of the Irish parliament over 'interference' by the privy council, Irish councillors quite naturally sometimes preferred to let bills pass over to England with the recommendation that they be altered by the council there.[69]

Membership of the council does not seem to have required a member to support the government line in parliament or even in the privy council itself. The council was often divided on important questions of policy. In 1716 and 1719, for example, the council was split evenly over the question of relief for protestant dissenters even though the bills in question had strong government support.[70] Because all of the active members of the privy council also sat in the Irish parliament they sometimes found themselves facing a conflict of loyalties. In January 1722, the House of Commons threw out three bills because they had been altered by the privy council. The bishop of Derry, William Nicolson, commented that:

> In the course of these debates a great many heavy reflections were darted at some particular members of the council; and not a few at the whole board in general. It was observed [that] the[re were] eleven commoners then in the house, who were privy councillors, and not one of them opened his mouth in defence of himself or his brethren.[71]

Lord Chancellor Midleton was also angered by the behaviour of these privy councillors. He named seven men who, he claimed, 'were mute', one of whom, amazingly, was the chief secretary to the duke of Grafton, Edward Hopkins.[72] In 1726, Lord Chancellor West and Archbishop Boulter both wrote to the duke of Newcastle pointing out that privy councillors were opposing the government in parliament. Boulter unsuccessfully urged the ministry to dismiss the leaders of the opposition from the council *pour encourager les autres*.[73]

The privy council was overwhelmingly Irish in composition, a fact which made it unreliable as far as the government was concerned. During the Wood's halfpence dispute, the privy council simply refused to comply with the orders of the ministry in London to advise the government about what should be done to resolve the situation. With the appointment of Hugh Boulter as primate in 1724, the conflict for political power in the Church of Ireland and House of Lords between the so-called 'Irish and English interests' which had been in progress since 1715 intensified. Boulter was determined to extend this struggle to the privy council and to build up the representation of the English interest there.[74] Boulter's efforts were undermined, however, by Carteret's insistence on promoting Irishmen to the council in order to consolidate his support in the House of Commons. In the summer of 1726, for example, Carteret had appointed to the privy council Viscount Charlemont, the earl of Clanrickard, the earl of Kerry, Lord Newtownbutler, Lord Southwell, and Sir Thomas Taylor. None of these men could have been considered to have been in the English interest and Archbishop Boulter was furious. Writing to the duke of Newcastle, Boulter complained that the new list of privy councillors had offended the king's friends in Ireland and that it would lessen their influence. Explaining that, except for one, the appointments had been made upon the recommendation of the lord lieutenant, Newcastle rather unhelpfully replied that 'since the thing is over and not to be recalled, I doubt not but that your Grace will endeavour to make the matter as easy as possible'.[75] Boulter continued to be largely unsuccessful in establishing the English interest in the privy council. There simply were not enough English-born politicians of sufficient calibre resident in Ireland to counterbalance the weight of the Irish privy councillors. In March 1730, Boulter responded to rumours that the privy council was to be further enlarged by complaining that 'the weight and power of the privy council is not sufficiently understood in England'.[76]

The representatives of the Anglican political nation sat in parliament at Chichester House at College Green in Dublin. The Irish House of Lords closely resembled its counterpart at Westminster, though it had far fewer members.[77] The power of the Lords rested upon two factors: firstly, all of its members (except for the judges) were members for life; and secondly, many peers controlled the return of members of the House of Commons. Throughout the eighteenth century, however, the government was normally able to control the Lords with relative ease. Many lay peers were dependent upon government patronage of one form or another and were effectively 'bought' by the ministry. It was the government, too, which appointed the bishops and the judges and only those men who had proved their loyalty and worth to the government could expect to be appointed. In addition, in Ireland the judges held their places during pleasure and if they failed to follow the government line in the Lords they could be dismissed. It is true that the bishops once appointed were members for life and could behave as they wished. However, if a bishop sought promotion he had to be a faithful servant of the government in parliament. In the last resort, the government had the power to create new peers to strengthen its position in the upper house.

For most of the eighteenth century, therefore, an Irish government could afford to pay relatively little attention to the House of Lords. The first priority of the government was to get funds additional to the hereditary revenues voted by parliament to support the civil and military establishments. The amount of money granted to the government in the form of additional duties was decided by the House of Commons alone, the Lords having no say in this matter. Not surprisingly, therefore, a viceroy tended to concentrate his attention upon building up his support in the Commons and paid relatively little attention to the normally subservient upper house. Edward Southwell, the chief secretary to the duke of Ormonde, went so far as to say that 'I never trouble you with what the House of Lords do, because in truth they have hardly any business before them.'[78] However, due to a combination of exceptional circumstances, the House of Lords during the reign of George I proved to be unusually difficult for the government to control. Indeed the Lords were so troublesome that for most of the 1715-27 period the ministry found it easier to manage the House of Commons than it did to keep the Lords under control. In 1719, for example, as the conflict over the Sherlock–Annesley case reached its climax, the duke of Bolton's chief secretary, Edward Webster, wrote that, 'everything goes as easy as can be desired in the House of Commons though matters are carried so extravagantly in the other house'.[79] The troublesome nature of the Lords' proceedings from 1715 to 1727 is a useful reminder of the dangers of falling into teleological traps and underestimating the significance of allegedly 'declining' institutions.

The most important group in the Irish House of Lords was the bishops, reflected by the high proportion of the business of the Lords which was devoted to ecclesiastical affairs.[80] Although three Whigs had been appointed to vacant Irish bishoprics between the death of Queen Anne and the meeting of the Irish parliament in November 1715, most of the Irish bishops had been appointed before 1714 and tended to be Tories. The government's problem was that these men could not be removed. The situation for the government was made even worse by the fact that the bishops were among the best attenders of the Lords to the extent, indeed, that they could sometimes form a majority. In addition to Tory sympathies among many bishops, a feeling of anti-Englishness became evident among the Irish-born bishops as the reign of George I progressed. This antipathy towards England was largely due to the practice of the British ministry of appointing English candidates to Irish bishoprics, particularly to the more lucrative ones. The division between the Irish and English interests within the episcopal bench first became evident during the controversy over the judicial rights of the Irish House of Lords between 1717 and 1720, when the English-born bishops sided with the government against those who sought to defend what they regarded as the constitutional rights of the Irish upper house. This dispute led to the formation of a kind of 'Irish party' in the Lords led by the archbishops of Dublin and of Tuam and Robert, 1st Viscount Molesworth.[81] During the reign of George I, the 'Irish party' in the Lords was among the British ministry's most implacable opponents in Ireland. The English-born bishops and judges, on the other hand, increasingly became the ministry's most loyal supporters. The battle between the English and Irish interests for control of the Lords continued throughout this period, though by the late 1720s the English interest was clearly coming out on top.

The Irish House of Commons was made up of 300 MPs. Thirty-two counties, 117 boroughs, and Trinity College each returned two members. Catholics were excluded from sitting in the Commons but protestant dissenters were not and there were always a few of the latter in the lower house. In 1715, twelve Presbyterians were elected to the Commons, only one of whom came from outside Ulster.[82] The House of Commons was a fairly incestuous institution, most MPs being related to at the very least one other member.[83] To take a fairly crude measure of this, of all the MPs who sat in the Commons from 1715 to 1727, over half had at least one fellow member with the same surname. One surname (Hamilton) occurs nine times; another (Moore), eight times. Four surnames occur five times; seven surnames occur four times; nineteen surnames occur three times; and fifty-one surnames occur twice. Although not all members with the same surname were necessarily related to each other, it can be safely assumed that the vast majority of Irish MPs who shared the same surname were indeed close relatives. Furthermore, of course, many MPs who did not share surnames were also closely related. The three Brodricks, four Barrys, and two Hills who sat in the House of Commons between 1715 and 1727, for example, were all connected by Alan Brodrick's marriage first to Catherine Barry and then to Anne Trevor, the widow of Michael Hill.[84] To take another example, Stephen Ludlow was father-in-law to two MPs, John Rogerson and Francis Bernard, and a further member from each of the Ludlow and Bernard families also served as MPs in this period. William Conolly was closely related to only one MP, the husband of his sister Jane, Thomas Pearson. However, he was indirectly related by his marriage to Katherine Conyngham to the Gores, the Hamiltons of Derry and Donegal, the Montgomerys, and the Knoxes who together returned twelve MPs during the reign of George I.[85]

It cannot be assumed that MPs who were close relatives necessarily voted on the same side in the house; Ludlow and Bernard, for example, were Tories whilst Rogerson was a Whig. However, what is abundantly clear is that the members of the Irish House of Commons were drawn from an extremely narrow section of Irish society. Indeed, the number of people in Ireland who would have been realistic candidates for a seat in parliament must have been relatively small. The Anglican community itself made up at most one-sixth of a population of around two millions.[86] The landowning element of the Anglican community amounted to an estimated 5,000 families. Within this community only the sons of peers, the greater gentry, army officers, and wealthy lawyers and merchants could have aspired to a seat in parliament.

The exclusive nature of the Irish political nation was due to two main factors: the transfer in landownership from Catholic to Protestant hands during the seventeenth century, and the Irish electoral system. In Ireland, even more so than in Britain, political power depended upon the ownership of land, both as a generator of wealth and as a means of dominating elections. By 1703, after the land confiscations of the previous century, only fourteen per cent of land in Ireland was held by Catholics and this figure was to fall to five per cent by mid-century. Even if the legislation debarring Catholics from voting and sitting in parliament had not existed, the virtual monopoly which Anglicans possessed in terms of landownership would have guaranteed their political ascendancy.

The electoral system reinforced the political power of the Anglican community. The franchise in the counties was based on the forty shilling freehold property qualification. Until 1793, when Catholics were again given the franchise, all but one of the Irish counties had electorates of less than 4,000, five having less than 1,000 voters.[87] The county elections were dominated by the more important landlords who vied with each other for the control of these prestigious constituencies. The vast majority of borough constituencies had relatively small electorates and were controlled by one or more patrons although it was possible for the control of a borough to change hands. Contests for parliamentary seats in early eighteenth-century Ireland could take the form of a public election or a struggle between rival factions to gain the dominant interest in a county or borough, making a formal election unnecessary. The important point to note, however, is that when elections were contested, formally or informally, they were contested between members of the Protestant élite.[88]

Over two-thirds of the 300 men elected to the Irish House of Commons in 1715 had sat in parliament before, so the Commons in 1715 was a very experienced body. Fifty-nine of these MPs were holders of patentee offices from the crown.[89] These offices varied from outright sinecures to important posts such as those of attorney and solicitor general and the revenue commissioners. The army was the single greatest employer of the Anglican gentry. A military career was one of the very few professions which were available to the son of a peer without a loss of social status. Of those MPs who sat in the Commons between 1715 and 1727, at least thirty-four held army commissions during the same

period and this is probably an underestimate.[90] More, of course, would have
served in the army before 1714 and others may have been on the half pay list.
There was also a senior naval officer among those elected in 1715.[91] Along
with the army officers, lawyers were very strongly represented in the House of
Commons. Many MPs had had a legal education and fourteen of the MPs elected
in 1715 held legal posts from the government.[92] Apart from the army, the revenue service was the biggest public employer in Ireland though few revenue
posts were sufficiently lucrative to attract an MP. Nevertheless, in 1720 nine
MPs held important posts in the revenue.[93]

Some members of parliament were regarded as being members of the government by virtue of their office or by their relationship with the chief governor.
The chief secretary to the viceroy, the under-secretary at Dublin Castle, the
chancellor of the exchequer, and the attorney and solicitor generals are some of
the officials who can be regarded as 'servants' of the administration. The speaker
and other influential MPs might also be considered as 'government men' if
they happened to be on good terms with the viceroy. However, this was a very
informal arrangement and the position of these men could change virtually
overnight. About eleven MPs in 1715 could be regarded as 'government men'.[94]
Of course many other members would normally have been expected to support
the government in the Commons. The army and revenue officers, for example,
would have been expected under most circumstances to follow the administration's line. In 1719, William Conolly drew up a list of members 'in employment'
for the benefit of the lord lieutenant, the duke of Bolton. Of the seventy-two
people named on his list (one of whom was not an MP), thirty-one were in the
army, ten were in the revenue service, twelve were law officers, one was in the
navy, and eight were in government posts.[95] However, the votes of these men
could not have been taken for granted and it was the dozen or so MPs referred
to above who formed the core of the Castle party in the Commons and who
were expected to manage the lower house on the government's behalf.

In contrast to the turbulent sessions of the latter years of Queen Anne's reign,
the House of Commons gave the government relatively little trouble in the
following two decades. The Commons always granted the government additional supplies, for example. A notable exception in this period of calm was, of
course, the Wood's halfpence dispute. Even during this dispute, however, the
government's money bills were passed. The relationship between the Commons and the government was not, however, one-sided. Although the
government's supplies were always granted, they rarely amounted to the sum
requested by the Castle administration. The significant increase in the Irish
national debt after 1715 is a testimony to the government's difficulty in persuading the Commons to grant sufficient funds to support the establishments.[96]
In general, the government adopted towards the House of Commons a policy of
'letting sleeping dogs lie', a phrase which has also been employed to describe

the policy pursued by Sir Robert Walpole in early Hanoverian Britain.[97] The Westminster government never attempted to introduce a land tax in Ireland, nor did ministers push the issue of relief for protestant dissenters to extremes. On both of these issues, the Irish parliament would not budge.

V

The political history of Ireland in the hundred years after the 'glorious revolution' was dominated by the attempts of the British government to develop an harmonious working relationship with the representatives of the Protestant community in Ireland. This meant, above all, that a *modus operandi* between the Dublin administration and the Irish parliament had to be found. In short, the Irish government needed to find a way to get its business consistently and safely through the Dublin legislature. As has been pointed out, as early as 1695 it had become clear that local politicians, whether they be called managers, undertakers, or simply 'friends', would have to be employed by Dublin Castle to manage the parliament on the government's behalf. The party conflict of Queen Anne's reign introduced an element of instability and invective into Irish politics and possibly retarded the further development and refinement of the undertaker system. The removal of ideological controversy from Irish politics following the decline in party conflict after 1714 did, however, leave a vacuum. Men who had united with like-minded individuals under a party banner now found themselves operating in an environment in which their hitherto foes, the Tories, were largely absent. The following chapters will examine how Irish politicians reacted to this transformation of the political landscape.

4

The Hanoverian Accession

'the people here are possessed with such implacable spirits and
such a humour for parties, that a poor fiddler can hardly put up a
bill for a benefit, but immediately a party is formed for or against
him, and no regard ever had to his deserving or not, that I am
quite sick of them and Dublin'.[1]

George I's accession to the thrones of Great Britain and Ireland in August 1714
resulted in a rapid transformation of the Irish political landscape. As demoralised Tories retreated to the country or distanced themselves from their former
associates, the intense party rivalry of the previous reign seemed to disappear
like an apparition. This development does, of course, raise serious questions
about the nature of the Whig-Tory conflict in Ireland. Was it a genuine ideological dispute between committed parties or a mere struggle for power between
rival factions employing party nomenclature as labels of convenience? The first
part of this chapter will attempt to address this question by analysing the nature
of the party conflict and examining the fate of the Tories after August 1714.
The remainder of the chapter will analyse the transformation in parliamentary
politics brought about by the accession of George I. After the Hanoverian accession parliamentary politics in Ireland was dominated by the split which
affected the Irish Whig party during the first session of George I's parliament.
The session of parliament which sat between November 1715 and June 1716
established the pattern which was followed by Irish parliamentary politics for
the remainder of the reign of George I and this session will be given detailed
attention below. Between 1715 and 1727 the House of Commons consisted of
four main blocs or factions – the Conolly Whigs, the Brodrick Whigs, the remnants of the Tory party, and the 'country gentlemen'. In the Lords the situation
was rather different. The proceedings of the upper house quickly became dominated by an intense conflict between what became known as the Irish and English
interests with the Anglican episcopate playing the leading part. This conflict
will be examined in detail in chapter seven. From 1727 to 1729 the situation
was transformed by the deaths of most of the leading political figures who had
dominated Irish politics since 1714. The new configuration of Irish politics
after 1729 will be examined in chapter six.

I

Research carried out in the 1970s by David Hayton demonstrated that Irish parliamentary politics during the reign of Queen Anne was dominated by a party struggle between Whigs and Tories.[2] The labels attached to this party conflict had been imported from contemporary English politics and the increasing intensity of the party conflict in England during the reign of Queen Anne was mirrored in Ireland. From about 1706 to 1714, it seems, it was virtually impossible for Irish MPs to avoid being connected with one party or the other no matter how hard some tried to remain outside the fray. The strength of this party conflict was best illustrated by the failed attempts of lords lieutenant Pembroke and Shrewsbury to form mixed administrations in 1707 and 1713 respectively. An important consequence of the dominance of the political scene by party conflict was that a lord lieutenant had little choice but to rule through the Irish equivalent of the party with which he was identified at Westminster. Therefore, the duke of Ormonde could only govern through Tory support and the earl of Wharton had to rely on the Whigs. This close connection between the English and Irish parties was taken for granted by contemporaries, as successive lords lieutenant discovered. Government in Ireland during the reign of Queen Anne was, therefore, fairly straightforward. The choice was between a Tory or a Whig government, supported by their respective allies in Ireland and in Britain, the complexion of the administration depending upon which party was in the ascendancy in London. So long as the party struggle continued, therefore, incoming lords lieutenant had little room for manoeuvre in choosing who would be their parliamentary managers.

It does at first appear peculiar that Irish Protestants engaged in a bitter and long-lasting party conflict at a time when they were at war with France and had real fears about a Jacobite invasion and Catholic rebellion. The correspondence of contemporaries, however, leaves no doubt that this party conflict was a serious one which increasingly came to dominate Irish parliamentary politics during the reign of Queen Anne. Despite the strength of the Whig-Tory conflict in Ireland it has to be admitted that the party battle was riddled with ideological contradictions. Few Irish Tories, for example, could have seriously considered supporting the claim of James III (the so-called 'Pretender') to the throne. Whatever emotional attachment Irish Tories may have had for the Stuart dynasty, to have supported a Catholic king would have called into question the restoration and Williamite land settlements upon which depended most Tory gentlemen's estates. In 1715 the archbishop of Dublin neatly summed up the dilemma of the Irish Tories as follows: 'I can't say that many of our Tories here are in their hearts for the Pretender, our case is different from yours, not only our religion and liberty but estates depend on the Revolution. Every man [knows] the old proprietors that claim his land, and most gentlemen are attainted by name in the late King James's Parliament here, which would return with the Chevalier.'[3] Hayton claims that there was probably only one Jacobite member of the Irish parliament throughout the reign of Queen Anne. In 1707 Sir Richard Cox, the Tory lord chancellor, wrote that there were not five Protestants in Ireland worth £300 per annum in favour of the Jacobite cause. Two weeks after the death of Queen Anne, Cox claimed that he did not know a Protestant in Ireland who was not zealous for the Hanoverian succession.[4] The refusal of the Pretender to convert to Protestantism necessarily meant that there could be very few Jacobites among the Anglican community – they had simply too much to lose.

Irish Whigs also failed to live up to the ideological expectations of their English counterparts. The greatest failing of Irish Whigs in this respect was in their refusal to support the repeated attempts by the British government to repeal the sacramental test as it affected protestant dissenters in Ireland. This refusal on the part of Irish Whigs to back relief for the dissenters even led to some of them being accused of being Tories in England, a misunderstanding of the Irish political situation which has been perpetuated by at least one modern historian.[5] It was alleged in March 1716, for example, that George I had complained that the Brodrick family had been represented to him as being Whigs but that their ambiguous behaviour regarding a bill to relieve protestant dissenters in Ireland led him to believe otherwise. Informed of this charge, Lord Chancellor Brodrick wrote to his brother in exasperation, 'If I am not a Whig, what am I?'[6]

It should not be surprising that Whigs and Tories in Ireland did not adopt in full the ideological precepts of their English counterparts. Circumstances in Ireland were, after all, very different from those prevailing in Britain. Surrounded by a large dispossessed Catholic population, Irish Protestants simply could not afford the luxury open to some English Tories of calling into question the revolution of 1688. In addition, the large influx of Scottish Presbyterians into Ulster during the 1690s led many Irish Anglicans, and especially the clergy, to regard protestant dissenters to be at least as much of a threat to the political and religious establishment as was the Catholic population. Finally, the war against Louis XIV (and its domestic ramifications) was not a serious political issue in Ireland despite being one of the most bitterly contested issues between the parties in Britain. However, if the parties in Ireland were not divided over ideology to the same degree as the Whig and Tory parties in Britain, they were nonetheless divided.

The names which the Irish parties adopted might reveal more about how they perceived themselves. It is indicative of the hostile attitudes of contemporaries to party conflict that Irish politicians were loath to use the terms Whig or Tory of themselves. These party labels were normally reserved for their opponents and certainly carried negative connotations. The Tories called themselves the 'Church party' while the Whigs liked to think of themselves as the 'honest gentlemen'. Both parties, particularly when in opposition, claimed the honour of being the 'country party', the one party label regarded by all in a positive light.[7] Self-appointed defenders of the established church, the Tories were characterized by a strong defence of the rights and privileges of the Church of Ireland, an intense dislike of protestant dissent, and a strong regard for the monarchy in the person of Queen Anne, a Stuart and friend of the church. The Whigs, on the other hand, were the descendants of a wing of the 'sole right' or 'country party' of the reign of William III, specifically those who had followed Lord Capel. The main priority of the Whigs was to preserve the rights of the Irish parliament in relation to the crown and, increasingly as time went on, against the attempted encroachments by the parliament at Westminster. The Whigs were staunch supporters of the Williamite revolution and the ensuing political and land settlement in Ireland and were, in addition, strong advocates of further anti-Catholic legislation. They portrayed the Tories as being 'soft' on the Catholic question, a charge to which the latter were indeed vulnerable given the support shown by Catholics for Tory candidates at parliamentary elections and the obvious reluctance of the Tories to support anti-Catholic legislation. The fact that as many as twelve converts from Catholicism may have been returned as Tory MPs in the 1713 general election lent further credence to Whig charges that the Tories could not be trusted to maintain the Protestant establishment.[8] That this Catholic connection could be a serious embarrassment for Tories is clear from the comment made by Sir John Percival in 1713: 'The Papists here are insolent, some have said, if the Whigs and we fall out, the Papists will be on our side; a great comfort that.'[9] The Whigs, of course, made full use of the Tories' Catholic and Jacobite connections. The Tories for their part responded by raising the cry of 'the church in danger' and by accusing the Whigs of being schismatics and republicans.[10] It was religion, however, which was probably the major cause of conflict between the Irish parties. The Tories were generally more tolerant of Catholicism than the Whigs who tended to look upon the protestant dissenters with more favour. Although the bulk of the Anglican clergy strongly supported the Tories, both parties were united in their determination to uphold Anglican supremacy. As Sean Connolly has rightly argued: 'The difference between Whig and Tory was not a matter of positive favour towards either of the two non-Anglican denominations. Instead, the debate was over which of the two presented the greater threat to the position of the Church of Ireland.'[11]

The Whig-Tory dichotomy cannot always be regarded in black and white terms. Just as there were Hanoverian Tories ('whimsicals') in Britain, there was a group of 'Church Whigs' in Ireland. The latter, whilst recognising the Whig party as the safest guarantor of the Protestant succession, were determined to defend the privileges of the Church of Ireland against the possible threat from protestant dissent. Such people (William King, for example, or Jonathan Swift before his switch to the Tories) were in their general politics Whigs but adopted 'Tory' principles in regard to the religious establishment.

Having stressed the genuine ideological differences which existed between Whigs and Tories in Ireland it is nevertheless true that the Whig-Tory battle in Ireland was not a party conflict in the modern sense. The number of people who were in a position from which to exercise political power or influence in Ireland was in relative terms very small. Peers, bishops, and MPs were well acquainted with each other, many of them being related to one another or being on friendly (or unfriendly) terms. It is inconceivable under these circumstances that personal and family considerations would not on occasion have conflicted with a person's party loyalties. During the general election of November 1713, that is, at the very climax of the party rivalry in Ireland, the Tory earl of Abercorn supported the Tory interest in County Tyrone but backed two Whigs, Sir Ralph Gore and Frederick Hamilton, in County Donegal. These men were Abercorn's kinsmen and he justified supporting them because they were 'gentlemen of so good sense and principles in the main, in relation to the established church and monarchy, that I have thought fit to use my endeavours to prevent their being exposed to the mortification of a disappointment'.[12]

During electioneering in County Cork in the early months of 1714 when an election was anticipated following the collapse of the 1713 Parliament, Henry Boyle and Alan Brodrick set up as Whig candidates against Sir John Percival and Francis Bernard who stood in the Tory interest. When Boyle sought the votes of his relations for himself and Brodrick they apparently agreed to give him one of their votes but refused to support Brodrick. In other words, their personal distaste for the Brodrick family overcame any loyalty to the Whig cause. At the same time, other Cork Whigs who thought well of Sir John Percival and were happy to drink his health, refused to vote for him because he 'being a Tory and joining interest with one, and being opposed by two Whigs, they thought they ought to support the interest they were of themselves, since the dispute was between Whig and Tory'.[13] Clearly party loyalties and personal friendships could easily come into conflict eliciting a variety of responses.

A final example of family ties conflicting with party loyalties came about during the investigations carried out by the House of Commons into the behaviour of the Irish judiciary during the latter years of Queen Anne's reign. In June 1716 a Commons' committee, chaired by the solicitor general, John Rogerson, reported on its findings. Lord Chancellor Brodrick, whilst admitting that Rogerson was an honest Whig, reported that the latter

> and the late Solicitor Mr. Bernard are married to two sisters, the daughters of Stephen Ludlow; and the wife is a furious Tory if not a degree beyond it, and this inclined people to mutter that he delayed making the

report in favour of his brother Bernard and other Tories to the end things might cool and be forgotten toward the end of the session.[14]

Such instances of Whigs protecting Tories (or vice versa) who were friends or relations were not uncommon. Similarly it is very likely that the party battle was taken up by some in order to pursue local rivalries, factional disputes, and personal grievances. However, families were divided by party loyalties. It is surely just as significant that Rogerson, with a Tory wife and father-in-law, supported the Whigs as that he tried to protect his brother-in-law. Whilst accepting that personal loyalties and grievances continued to be of importance it would be a mistake to underestimate the ideological basis of the Whig-Tory party conflict in Ireland.[15]

As in Britain, the party conflict in Ireland intensified as Anne's reign progressed. The appointment of Thomas, earl of Wharton to the viceroyalty in 1708 certainly exacerbated party tensions in Ireland. Wharton was regarded by Tories as possibly the most obnoxious of the Whig 'Junto' and his viceroyalty undoubtedly added venom to parliamentary politics in Ireland. Wharton was personally despised by many in Ireland for his blatant use of patronage to reward favourites and, allegedly, to enrich himself. His personal morality was also very much open to censure. Swift's vicious attack on Wharton in *A Short Character of His Excellency, Thomas Earl of Wharton, Lord Lieutenant of Ireland* is a devastating example of political character assassination and reflects, no doubt, the views of many Irish Tories at the time. Accusing Wharton of being 'a Presbyterian in politics, and an atheist in religion', Swift added 'but he chooses at present to whore with a Papist'.[16] However, it was more than personal unpleasantness on the part of the viceroy which led to the embitterment of party conflict in Ireland. Specifically, Wharton launched a significant purge of the Irish administration replacing Tories with Whigs.[17] The connection between office and political allegiance was thereafter explicit with increasingly thorough purges following each change in government. Wharton also raised the political temperature by tackling the divisive and controversial question of religion. His attempt to repeal the sacramental test imposed in 1704 guaranteed a strong Tory reaction and placed Irish Whigs in a very uncomfortable position. The passage of additional anti-Catholic legislation on the other hand served to unite the Whig party behind the viceroy and highlighted the Tories' uncertainties over the Catholic question.[18] The restoration of the duke of Ormonde to the viceroyalty in 1710 was of less significance than the appointment of Sir Constantine Phipps to the lord chancellorship in the same year. For the next four years Phipps did more than anyone to heighten the tension between Whigs and Tories by his provocative and, in Whig eyes, possibly traitorous activities.[19]

During these years the party battle in Ireland reached its climax over two major issues – the Dublin mayoralty dispute (when the Tory-dominated Irish privy council refused to approve the election of a Whig lord mayor of Dublin), and the campaign by the Whigs to have Phipps removed from office. By the end of 1713, political deadlock had been reached in Ireland between the Tory government and the House of Commons in which the Whigs had a narrow working majority, despite the Tories' victory in the 1713 general election. On the first day of the new session, the leader of the Irish Whigs, Alan Brodrick, was elected as speaker of the Commons in opposition to Shrewsbury's candidate, Sir Richard Levinge. After John Forster, another leading Whig, was elected chairman of the crucial committee of elections by 127 votes to 121, Sir Richard Cox complained that 'they (who are not above 120) attend to a man, and also in case of particular persons gain 9 or 10 of the Tories, whereas our friends are negligent and do not attend'.[20] The ability of the Irish Whig party to prevent the Tory government in Dublin implementing its policy in parliament is an impressive demonstration both of its national party organisation and of its electoral support among the Protestant community in Ireland. Whereas it seems clear that the Tory party had most popular support in England at this time, the situation appears to have been the reverse across the Irish Sea.

Unable to command a majority in the Commons, Shrewsbury's administration had no choice but to seek the support of leading Whigs to ensure the passage of the government's money bills. The price demanded by the leaders of the Whig party in return for a promise to grant the usual two years' additional revenues was the dismissal of Lord Chancellor Phipps and the settlement of the mayoralty dispute. The lord lieutenant was not prepared to pay such a price. Consequently the Commons refused to vote a supply beyond the end of 1713 and the government had no choice but to prorogue parliament which had sat for only one month.[21] The account given by the earl of Abercorn of the attempt by Shrewsbury to persuade the leaders of the Whig party to support the government graphically indicates the gulf which had developed between the Whig party and Shrewsbury's administration by early 1714.[22]

Following the collapse of the parliamentary session the Irish political scene was dominated by preparations for the expected death of the Queen. The Irish executive was strongly suspected of harbouring Jacobite sympathies and a series of apparently partial judicial decisions in favour of Catholics combined with the alleged disbandment of the militia appeared to confirm Whig suspicions about the Irish government's commitment to the Hanoverian cause. Rumours of Catholic mobilisation and enlistment for the forces of the Pretender were also widespread. This atmosphere of mutual suspicion served to foster a sense of paranoia on both sides. The Anglican primate, Thomas Lindsay, for example, appeared to view more positively those who had been arrested for enlisting for the Pretender than his Anglican opponents in the Whig party. Having expressed the hope that 'her Majesty's mercy' would prevent the 'great carnage' of the execution of the condemned men, he added 'At the same time the Whigs have armed and are arming themselves in all parts, and some of them have bought up such quantities of arms as would make one suspect thay had other designs than barely opposing the Pretender.'[23]

A letter from Daniel Dering, written five weeks before the death of the Queen, is probably representative of the fears and concerns of many Irish Protestants in the first half of 1714:

> People here, (I mean those that fear there is a design to bring in the P[retender]) are in the greatest uneasiness. Every pacquet brings in something that adds to their alarms; but besides what they hear from your part of the world, they are daily put in frights from the insolence of the Papists, in marking peoples houses in the night, as if they intended mischief, in posting up written papers, some of w[hi]ch I saw myself, threatens destruction to the Protestants if the Pretender men suffer, and the like. For my part I can't think the Papists dare yet make any open attempt upon us, or if they had a design that they w[oul]d give us such public notice to be upon our guard. But in the meantime 'tis melancholy to see them so uppish, and our friends in such real uneasiness. I am assured that the common people sit up most of the night; and a great many of the better sort keep watches in their houses for fear of being surprised and having their throats cut; to complete all, never were Protestants more divided than now, party animosities increase daily, and thence hatreds to one another, and malicious backbitings; so that I have sometimes thought that even common danger w[oul]d hardly unite them to defend one another.[24]

In the event, such fears proved to have been unjustified. Following the death of the queen on 1 August 1714, George I's accession to the throne was proclaimed in Ireland without significant controversy. Writing the day after the proclamation of the new king in Dublin, Dering, so apprehensive six weeks previously, remarked that 'today people look as calm and unconcerned as if nothing had happened'.[25]

Whilst Irish Whigs were to see their worst nightmares vanish from the horizon, the proclamation of a Hanoverian monarch clearly presented the Tories with an uncomfortable prospect. Although it would take some months before the political situation in Britain and Ireland stabilised, it was evident to all that the Tory party could only lose from the accession of the new king. Ultimately the impregnable hold which was soon taken on government at Westminster after 1714 by the British Whig party was to have a devastating impact on the Tory party in Ireland. George I had a long-standing distrust and resentment of the Tories due to the uncertain nature of their commitment to his family's right to succeed to the throne and because a Tory ministry had, in his view, abandoned its continental allies (including Hanover) in 1713 by signing the Treaty of Utrecht. The king also felt that the Tory party could not be trusted with office so long as the Jacobite threat remained a real one, which it clearly did in 1714-15. In the knowledge 'that the Whigs would venture all to support the Protestant succession in your Majesty's family; on the other hand, that many Tories would rejoice to see [the] Pretender restored', it was understandable that the new monarch preferred to take no chances and he placed his trust in the Whigs.[26]

After a number of indications in the immediate aftermath of his accession that George I might include some Tories in his government, it soon became clear that the British Tories had no realistic prospect of office under the new king. Those Tories such as William Bromley and Sir Thomas Hanmer who were offered places had little choice but to refuse them in order to preserve the unity of their party. During the general election in Britain at the beginning of 1715 the Tories deeply offended the king by their implicit attacks upon him and his court. As a result of the election, the Tory majority of 239 gained in the electoral landslide of 1713 was transformed into a Whig superiority of around sixty-five.[27] By losing the election, and alienating the king in the process, the Tories condemned themselves to opposition for the foreseeable future. The flights of Bolingbroke and Ormonde to James III's court at St Germain, the arrest of the earl of Oxford and the outbreak of the Jacobite rebellion in September 1715, only served to make the situation even more hopeless for the Tories since the party was now firmly identified with treason and conspiracy, an image industriously reinforced by the Whigs over the succeeding years. In short, after 1715 the Tory party in Britain was finished as a credible party of government.

The revelations regarding the potentially treasonable activity of some Tory ministers left Irish Tories in a very uncomfortable situation. Archbishop King reported in October 1715 that, 'the discoveries made lately' had 'stunned and surprised those that call themselves Tories'. King, however, was sceptical about these protestations of ignorance, finding their claims that they had been unaware of the moves of the late government to bring in the Pretender as 'so strange a stupidity to me, that it then seemed incredible'.[28] The collapse of Tory power and influence in Britain ended any lingering hopes Irish Tories may have had that their allies across the water would come to their rescue. The complexion of the Irish government was always decided in London, not in Dublin, and by the summer of 1715 it was apparent that the Whigs would, in all probability, remain in power for a very long time. It soon became clear that the 'Whig ascendancy' at Westminster would be replicated in Dublin as the new administration sought to reward those in Ireland who had been its allies for the preceding ten years.

II

The precedent had been established in the second half of Queen Anne's reign that whenever the government of Ireland passed from the hands of one party to the other, a purge of office-holders was carried out. This occurred on a major scale for the first time when the Whig earl of Wharton was appointed as lord lieutenant in 1708 and dismissed many Tories from their jobs. In turn, when Wharton was replaced by the duke of Ormonde in 1711, many Whigs were turned out of office and replaced by Tories.[29] After the Queen's death in August 1714 it was assumed that a purge of Tory office-holders would take place to the benefit of the Irish Whigs who were understandably anxious to take their revenge for those previous purges carried out by their rivals. At the end of September 1714, Robert Molesworth wrote to Archbishop King that, following the appointment of the new lord lieutenant, 'we shall have a thorough reformation'. This was to involve a new lord chancellor, a new privy council and judiciary, and 'a great change in all subordinate civil employments'.[30]

The Whig purge of Tory office-holders which followed affected to varying degrees almost every level of every branch of the Irish administration. There was strong pressure put on the new administration by place-hungry Whigs to implement a thorough purge of Tory office-holders. Archbishop King noted that 'many ... have great expectations both in Church and State, and nothing will serve some but making a clear board'.[31] Sir Richard Cox described how 'a vast number' of Whigs had gone to England to seek jobs and found it 'wonderful to see what assurance ordinary fellows had, of their being able to place and displace whom their faction pleased'.[32]

Any office-holder who had been in any way associated with the late Tory administration was in a vulnerable position. Although it is difficult to state precisely which criteria were used to decide if someone should be dismissed, the position which a person took during the Dublin mayoralty dispute and a man's voting record in parliament, particularly in the 1713 Parliament, were obvious indicators as to his political affiliation. With regard to the judges, privy councillors, peers, and MPs their record on these issues was used to justify their removal. Promising to send a list of all patentee officers to the new viceroy, the earl of Sunderland, Archbishop King recommended that those who had 'misbehaved themselves in the late government ... will not deserve any favour' but that 'honest, quiet men' should be continued in office.[33]

It would appear that it was often enough for a man to be simply accused of being a Tory sympathiser or to have been associated with the Tories for him to lose his post. This was particularly true if the accusation was made by someone in London and the accused was in Ireland with little opportunity of defending himself. Archbishop King noted with disapproval this tactic employed by those in London to vilify people in Ireland writing 'I believe our friends there follow the old path of blackening and supplanting one another for those here generally lose and those that are there gain all.'[34] The collector of excise at Cork, Warham Jemmett, found himself accused of being a Tory towards the end of 1714. He sought the protection of, among others, the archbishop of Dublin who told him that 'I have no reason to believe you have enemies, but your having an employment that is reckoned pretty profitable'.[35] Having received a representation from Archbishop King in Jemmett's favour and a certificate from the corporation of Cork stating that Jemmett had not involved himself in politics, Sunderland admitted that Jemmett did not deserve the ill-character which he had received of him. However, Jemmett still eventually lost his post.[36] William Whitshed had to write to Sunderland to deny rumours that his brother-in-law, John Parnell, had Tory sympathies. Parnell had been recommended by the Irish lords justices for the post of counsel to the revenue commissioners and a rival for this post may have hoped to discredit Parnell by employing smear tactics. Whitshed suspected another motivation for the rumours commenting that 'I wish his having a better interest in a borough he stood for than a very valuable man, that stood against him may not have given rise to what has been said to his prejudice.'[37] On this occasion the smear campaign was unsuccessful and Parnell obtained the post for which he had been recommended. However, Parnell was very fortunate in that he had several powerful patrons and this episode raises the question of how many men in Ireland without influential friends suffered due to malicious rumours being spread in London. Sunderland attempted to verify the information which he was receiving about the character of alleged Tories since, as Joseph Addison explained to Archbishop King, 'some have not appeared so unprejudiced and impartial, as might have bin wisht, in the accounts they have given on such occasions'.[38]

On the other hand, it was not simply the case that all office-holders identified as having been Tories were dismissed for, although the purge of 1714-15 was extensive, not a few Tories kept their places. The most common way a Tory office-holder kept his post was through the protection of a powerful patron. There is evidence that in the revenue service, in particular, many Tories survived due to the protection of one or more of the commissioners in Dublin. There were limits to this protection, however, and if it could be proved that a man had been an active supporter of the Tories prior to 1714, there was little that even the most powerful patron could do to protect him. Charles Melvin, a Tory MP under Queen Anne, was removed as collector of excise in Dublin in 1715 but the commissioners immediately reappointed him as a surveyor general arguing that 'he seems to be very quiet and calm as to his politics and though he was under the character of a Tory, yet he never concerned himself as we can hear, in the late disorders of this City'.[39] In August 1717, however, William Maynard sent a memorial to the Treasury asking that Melvin be dismissed claiming that he had been 'removed from being collector of excise at

Dublin upon account of his disaffection to His Majesty and the present government'. Maynard wanted Melvin to be replaced as surveyor general by the collector of Cork with Maynard himself obtaining this latter post. When the Lords of the Treasury recommended this proposal, the Irish commissioners claimed that Maynard was mistaken, that Melvin was removed from his post in 1715, not upon account of his disaffection to the present government, but to make room for a nominee of Sunderland.[40] Maynard responded by visiting the commissioners in Dublin and producing a record of Melvin's voting behaviour in the 1713 session of parliament. In the face of such evidence, the commissioners had no choice but to dismiss Melvin.[41] This episode demonstrates that even powerful patrons such as the revenue commissioners (who included William Conolly) could not protect a man if positive proof of activity in the Tory interest could be provided.

Occasionally a man's personal political interest might be sufficient to save him from dismissal, although such cases were rare. Sir Richard Levinge had been dismissed as attorney general in November 1714 but was immediately offered a place as a judge of the King's Bench. The government apparently feared that Levinge would cause trouble in the new House of Commons and thought that it would be best to appoint him as a judge in order to prevent him sitting as an MP. Levinge, however, refused the post, suspecting that the government would remove him once the parliamentary session was over.[42]

The first step in remodelling the Irish government came on 4 September 1714 with the appointment of Archbishop King and the earl of Kildare as lords justices in the place of Primate Thomas Lindsay and Lord Chancellor Phipps. Archbishop John Vesey of Tuam remained from the former commission of lords justices, probably because the government did not want to appoint any leader of the various Whig parliamentary factions for fear of offending the rest and Vesey was, in any case, old and in poor health and took little part in the government's business.[43] The appointment of the new lords justices was followed on 21 September by the appointment of Charles Spencer, 3rd earl of Sunderland, as lord lieutenant of Ireland. This appointment was something of a surprise, to Sunderland more than anyone else and he was far from pleased. Archbishop King had expected the duke of Shrewsbury to continue as lord lieutenant and speculated that Shrewsbury had been removed in order to spare him the embarrassment of dismissing from office many of his former colleagues in Ireland.[44]

The next step in purging the Irish government was the replacement of the privy council. There had at first been some doubt as to whether the Irish privy council was automatically dissolved on the death of the queen. However, on 14 August 1714 lords justices Phipps and Lindsay wrote to Bolingbroke that the council was 'not determined by the demise of the late Queen' and that it would continue to act.[45] This seems to have been accepted in Britain for at the beginning of September Robert Molesworth wrote to Archbishop King warning him that the Tory-dominated privy council could prove to be troublesome to the new administration. The ministry in London then ordered the new lords justices to have the city of Dublin elect a lord mayor and to instruct the privy council to approve the election. The council, however, 'being spirited by the Primate and the Chancellor, and animated by the Judges present' still refused to accept the candidate of the Dublin aldermen.[46] The government responded by issuing orders to the Irish lords justices on 30 September to dissolve the entire privy council and to appoint a new one of around fifty-six members. The appointment of a new Whig-dominated privy council meant that the long-running Dublin mayoralty dispute could be finally settled. On 9 October 1714, seven members of the new privy council took their oaths and proceeded to approve the election of the lord mayor of Dublin.[47]

The appointment of a new lord lieutenant necessarily meant the employment of a new chief secretary (Joseph Addison) and private secretary (Charles Delafaye) for both of these posts were in the gift of the viceroy. The undersecretary at Dublin Castle was also changed. This post was in the gift of the chief secretary but the holder of this office normally remained even when the administration was changed. The man who held this post on the death of Queen Anne, Joshua Dawson, had held the position for thirteen years under both Whig and Tory administrations. Addison, however, dismissed Dawson and appointed a relation, Eustace Budgell, to be his deputy.[48] Addison told Archbishop King that, if he had been given the choice, he would not have turned Dawson out, but the appointment of Addison's relation as successor undermines somewhat the credibility of this claim. It would appear that Dawson did not take his dismissal gracefully and contrived to make life as difficult as possible for his successor.[49]

As for the minor officers in the Castle administration it is difficult to know who performed which job and when, for most of them were deputies and are not to be found in lists of office-holders.[50] Many Castle employees held patentee offices or were the deputies of those who did and thirty patentee offices changed hands in the two years after September 1714, the majority probably for party reasons.[51] This would seem to indicate that some form of clearout of staff took place at Dublin Castle. This suggestion is supported by Archbishop King's numerous complaints about the chaotic state of the offices at Dublin Castle. In November 1714, King complained that 'our officers are changed so fast on us, that before our orders are half executed we are obliged to begin anew, and with new men that know nothing of the matter that was ordered.'[52] King complained that those officers who were turned out were inclined to 'delay and intricate everything as much as they can, and leave their successors in the dark'. That patentee officers who held their posts *durante bene placito* were seriously affected is suggested by King's hope that people would be less likely to buy such offices in the future. Among the Castle employees most affected by the change in government were the military staff of whom four leading office-holders lost their jobs.[53]

The behaviour of the Irish judiciary during the Dublin mayoralty dispute and in the late parliament had left a great deal to be desired as far as the Irish Whigs were concerned. All of the Irish judges in their capacity as members of the privy council had taken the side of the council against the Dublin aldermen. Consequently, almost the whole of the Irish judiciary was suspect in Whig eyes.[54] The unwillingness of the Irish judges to compromise with their new masters in London, even after the Queen's death, was graphically demonstrated by their stubborn refusal to approve the election of a Whig lord mayor of Dublin. Unlike their British counterparts, Irish judges held office only 'during pleasure' and could be removed at any time. Within four months of the accession of George I, all but two of Anne's ten judges, the three serjeants at law, and the attorney and solicitor generals had been removed from office. The one judge to eventually survive this clearout was Sir Gilbert Dolben who had spent most of his time in office in England serving as a member of parliament.[55]

The first judges to be dismissed, in September 1714, were the lord chancellor, the chief justice of the King's Bench, the chief justice of the Common Pleas, the chief baron of the Exchequer, and a justice of the King's Bench. It seems that initially it was intended to dismiss only six of the ten Irish judges. This was the impression given to the new lord chancellor, Alan Brodrick, before he left London in early October 1714.[56] However, in November, Brodrick wrote in alarm to his brother when he heard that Sir John St Leger and Jeffrey Gilbert were also to be appointed as barons of the Exchequer: 'Be sure it is time to think of stopping, unless it is resolved to remove all the judges, which I suppose is not intended; nor do I think it politic or advisable; and if that be intended to make room for men who are perfectly strangers to the constitution and people of the country, it will create unhappiness.'[57] Brodrick clearly thought that the purge of Anne's judges had gone far enough and added that he thought that the current barons of the Exchequer should be continued in office. His suspicion appears to have been that men were being removed, not because of their politics but, merely to vacate lucrative offices which could be filled by the nominees of the British government. It is also clear that Brodrick was already concerned about the number of Englishmen being appointed to the major judicial offices in Ireland. It seems that it had been decided in London, apparently without Brodrick's knowledge, that virtually all of the Irish judges were to be removed. Robert Molesworth had written to Archbishop King as early as 28 September 1714 that the judges were to be purged and that they would be 'almost entirely new'.[58]

In addition to the replacement of the two barons of the Exchequer, November saw the dismissal of a justice of the Common Pleas, the attorney general, and the solicitor general. The virtual clean sweep of the Irish judiciary was completed in December with the dismissal of the three serjeants at law. By the end of 1714 only two of Anne's judges remained in office and justice of the King's Bench, Thomas Coote, was dismissed in May 1715 on account of his Tory background. Only Sir Gilbert Dolben, a Westminster MP, remained in office until his resignation in 1720.[59] Upon hearing confirmation that the two barons of the Exchequer were to be dismissed, Brodrick wrote to his brother bemoaning his lack of interest with the government in these matters. The fact that Sir Gilbert Dolben would be the only judge to remain in office clearly only served to add insult to the lord chancellor's injury. As Brodrick complained to Addison, 'unless Sir Gilbert Dolben's service in parliament in England was such as atoned for making his cushion almost a sinecure for a dozen years past, he had better luck than the barons to sit safe when they were removed'.[60]

The Irish revenue service was also subjected to a purge of some of its Tory elements. At the end of November 1714 Stephen Ludlow, Francis Roberts, Samuel Ogle and Thomas Keightley were removed as revenue commissioners and replaced by Sir Thomas Southwell, William Strickland, William Conolly and Philips Gibbon. Conolly, Strickland, and Southwell were former commissioners who themselves had previously been dismissed by the Tories.[61] Only three commissioners survived the accession of George I – Horatio Walpole, Sir Thomas Medlicott, and Sir Henry Bunbury, all three of whom were English Tories. Walpole was the uncle of Robert Walpole a connection which perhaps explains his continuation in office until his resignation in May 1716. Bunbury was discovered in May 1715 to have been involved in treasonable correspondence with Tories in Britain and Ireland and was forced from office. Medlicott, a Hanoverian Tory with powerful friends in Britain, remained in office until his removal upon the accession of George II.[62]

In addition to the four commissioners who lost their posts, at least five collectors were dismissed along with a surveyor general, and the secretary, the solicitor and the counsel to the commissioners.[63] It is more difficult to quantify exactly how many lesser officers in the revenue service were dismissed for their political affiliation as the records of the meetings of the Irish revenue commissioners for this period are missing, but it is likely that their numbers were considerable. In May 1715, Archbishop King believed that between forty and fifty revenue officers had been dismissed. In July 1715, Sir John Percival found 'many ... murmuring at the numerous changes of inferior officers in the Revenue'. Writing in November 1715, Archbishop King claimed that there had been a greater transfer of offices in the revenue service than in any other branch of the administration. He was told by the commissioners that 'about a hundred have been changed' but that only twenty-six of them were removed 'about party business and the rest for notorious misdemeanours in their employments'.[64]

Although there was undoubtedly a major transfer of offices in the 1714-16 period, it was not simply a matter of replacing all Tories with Whigs. Thomas Medlicott, the commissioner, is just one example of a Tory who stayed in office and it has been seen how the commissioners attempted to protect Charles Melvin. Medlicott and Melvin, moreover, were not isolated examples. At the beginning of 1715 Archbishop King commented on the slowness of the purge of the revenue service telling Addison that 'I find the commissioners of the revenue are afraid to change their collectors suddenly, the state of the revenue being somewhat dubious'.[65] This fear of harming the efficiency of the service crops up regularly as a reason, or as an excuse, for retaining existing officers. In response to complaints that some Tories were being protected, the commissioners had explained to Sunderland that:

> Mr. Thompson, Clerk of the Quit Rents, Mr. Roberts, Comptroller of the Stores, and some few others are old officers, and have the character of Tories, but being very modest in their behaviour, do yet continue in their several employments being so necessary in their respective stations, that we apprehended some hazard to the revenue by their removal ...[66]

In the end Sunderland was forced to write formally to the commissioners instructing them to dismiss those who had been active in the Tory interest. Sunderland complained to William Conolly that he had received reports 'from several hands, of honest men being turned out and ill ones kept in, through an interest made to Sir Thomas Southwell and Mr. Medlicott by such means as are very unjustifiable'.[67] However, Sunderland discovered that it was no easy matter to direct the actions of the commissioners in Dublin. Upon receiving the lord lieutenant's orders to purge the service of Tories, the commissioners had dismissed Brettridge Badham (collector of Youghal) and John Lloyd (a surveyor general) because they were 'as obnoxious as any in the revenue of all Ireland by their late behaviour to the public'. Both Badham and Lloyd had previously been specifically recommended by Sunderland to be continued in their posts.[68] Clearly it was the commissioners who decided whether people's previous political behaviour warranted their dismissal or whether they were 'so necessary in their respective stations' that it was inadvisable to remove them.

Given the threat posed to the Hanoverian régime by potential rebellion and invasion in 1714-15, it was essential that the loyalty of the army should be beyond doubt. In Ireland, eight commanders suspected of Jacobite sympathies were ordered to dispose of their regiments. The commander-in-chief, General William Stewart, was dismissed and replaced by Charles O'Hara, Lord Tyrawley. Along with the commander-in-chief and the seven other regimental commanders, the advocate general, the physician general, and the master general and lieutenant general of the ordnance were all dismissed. Seven men, including General Stewart and at least five other army officers, were also deprived of their pensions on the military establishment.[69] In general, dismissals on political grounds were confined to the upper ranks

of the officer corps and army administration. The possibility of a Jacobite rebellion or invasion and the actual outbreak of rebellion in September 1715
would have made the government think twice about implementing large scale
dismissals in the army, even if such a thing had ever been intended. Moreover
in response to the rebellion in Great Britain, thirteen new regiments were raised
in Ireland making large scale dismissals in the army both impracticable and
unnecessary, since many Whigs could now be given commissions in the new
levies without removing existing officers.[70]

At least one officer apart from the regimental commanders did lose his post,
however. Archbishop King and Lord Chancellor Brodrick both wrote on behalf
of Brinsley Butler who had been removed from his post as captain of the
Battleaxe Guards because of his Tory connections. Butler was an MP and the
brother of Theophilus Butler, a leading Irish Whig and privy councillor. Brodrick
argued that although Captain Butler had hitherto taken the Tory side he should
be allowed to keep his place as a favour to Theophilus Butler who had given
assurances of his brother's good behaviour in the future. Dr King claimed that
Brinsley Butler had been obliged by the late government to vote on the Tory
side in parliament in order to keep his job which, being a younger son and a
father of nine children, he could ill afford to lose. Butler's dismissal, however,
would seem to have been an exceptional case. William Whitshed, in fact, told
Sunderland in November 1714 that Butler 'is the only man in a military way
that has been removed here'. Even Butler was later compensated for the loss of
his post with a pension.[71]

After the initial purge of the army, no officers on the Irish establishment
appear to have lost their commissions for political reasons. However, it is impossible to be certain of this. An officer may have been forced to sell out, for
example, and it would be difficult to distinguish this transaction from the numerous 'normal' ones. Furthermore it is also likely that men with Tory
backgrounds, even if they were allowed to retain their commissions, found the
path to promotion blocked after 1714. On the other hand, it was alleged in 1715
that the army surgeon general, Thomas Proby, refused to appoint any army
surgeons who were not 'of a Tory kind like himself'.[72] It is impossible to sub-
stantiate this allegation but the fact that Proby's son was later forced to leave
the army after priest's garments were found in his quarters and then travelled to
London to become an abbot provides some food for thought.[73]

The Church of Ireland was certainly the institution which was most Tory
both in sentiment and in composition. Unlike the other branches of the establishment, however, the church could not be purged since the clergy could not
be dismissed from their posts. This problem would become acute for the government whenever the Irish parliament eventually met for the bishops played
an extremely influential role in the business of the House of Lords. In 1714 the
new Whig administration found itself confronted by an Irish episcopal bench

which was dominated by Tory prelates. Of the nineteen bishops in Ireland in September 1714 the majority, perhaps as many as thirteen, were Tories.[74] Unable to dismiss the Tory bishops, the government could only follow a policy of filling each vacant see with a Whig. Only the passage of time and the death of Queen Anne's bishops would remove the threat posed by the Tory episcopate. To start with, the three vacant bishoprics of Raphoe, Killaloe, and Kilmore were filled with Whigs: respectively, Edward Synge and Nicholas Forster from Ireland and Timothy Godwin, an Englishman who had been chaplain to the duke of Shrewsbury. This policy of appointing only Whigs to bishoprics, while successful in reducing the number of Tories on the episcopal bench, created its own difficulties. As soon as the Tory threat was removed, the Whig prelates in the Irish House of Lords quickly began to quarrel among themselves, primarily about the distribution of ecclesiastical patronage. These resentments over patronage soon led to the emergence of opposing Irish and English interests within the episcopate.[75]

On the death of the queen the Irish House of Lords had a clear Tory majority. This was in part due to the very active and leading role played by the Anglican bishops in the activities of the upper house. Robert Molesworth recognised the problems which a Tory-controlled House of Lords could pose to the new régime. Writing to Archbishop King in September 1714 he explained that 'All our difficulty in Ireland will be to have a good House of Lords. You know what an odd set of men commonly attends there, and I can think of no speedy way of mending it.'[76] There were, in fact, three ways in which the government could attempt to 'mend' this difficulty by weakening the Tories' hold on the Lords – by the appointment of Whigs to vacant bishoprics; by the creation of new peers who would support the government; and by winning over existing peers to the government's side.

Although a purge of the Irish episcopal bench was impossible to implement since the bishops held their posts for life, the government had made a start by appointing Whigs to the three vacant bishoprics. The judicial bench had also been purged of the Tory judges but this did not increase the government's voting strength in the Lords, the judges sitting in the upper house only as 'assistants'. The quickest way to strengthen the Whig presence in the upper house was to ennoble Whig politicians. On the other hand, this was not the simple matter which at first sight it might appear to have been. The main difficulty for the government was in finding a sufficient number of politically reliable men who also had the financial resources to support a title. In January 1715 William Whitshed complained to Sunderland that 'Our Kingdom is so poor as not to have very many commoners of great estates'.[77] The danger for the government was that if men of moderate incomes were granted peerages in order to serve the new administration in the House of Lords, they would feel entitled to seek some form of compensation in order to live in a style commensurate with their enhanced social status. In August 1717, for example, John Moore, who had been elevated to the Lords as Lord Tullamore in 1715, sought the post of chancellor of the Exchequer, arguing that he would never have agreed to accept his peerage 'but that I was told His Majesty's service at that time required a balance to the then wicked majority'.[78]

Having decided which gentlemen to elevate to the peerage, the government was faced with the problem of deciding which title to confer on them. If some men were given a more senior rank than the rest the latter might well be offended and more harm than good would have been done to the government's cause. The simplest solution was to confer the same rank on everyone and this is what the government did. All of the new peers were granted the title of baron despite pressure from at least two of them, Gustavus Hamilton and Alan Brodrick, to be created a viscount. Asking Archbishop King to persuade Hamilton to accept the title of baron, Sunderland explained that 'doing otherwise would displease more persons than it would oblige'.[79]

In all, eleven men were elevated to the peerage in 1715, ten of whom attended the Irish House of Lords in the 1715-16 session. Five of these newly-created peers each attended more than half of the sittings of the upper house during this session.[80] This mass-creation appears to have had the desired effect as far as the government's control of the House of Lords was concerned. In January 1716, Lord Chancellor Brodrick wrote confidently to his brother that 'Our Tories in a certain house are so humbled, that as I told you formerly no danger need be apprehended from that quarter'.[81]

Also subjected to a politically-motivated purge were the pensions on the Irish civil establishment. For a year after the death of Queen Anne there was widespread confusion in Ireland about which pensions would be continued and which would be removed from the establishment. This uncertainty over the future of the civil list put the new administration in a strong bargaining position from which it could extract promises of political support in return for the continuation of existing pensions. In November 1714 Alan Brodrick wrote to his brother regarding the pensions of the earl of Granard and his sister, the countess of Donegall, both of whom were well-known Tories. Brodrick commented that although Granard's 'sentiments have been hitherto otherwise than I could wish, yet I shall be troubled to have his Majesty's bounty to him struck off'. As for Lady Donegall, Brodrick argued that her pension should be continued on account of her husband's having been killed in action at Barcelona. Brodrick then explained how the government might benefit from this situation:

> But may it not be reasonably expected that the interest of his lordship in the boroughs of Mullingar and St Johnstown, and of Lady Donegall at Belfast and Carrickfergus will not be made use of to send up members whose business it will be to distress the government and obstruct the

King's affairs in parliament. I do not say, that either of the interests will be so used, but if those pensions instead of being put actually on the establishment were left a little to be considered till my Lord Lieutenant landed, I cannot see but it would have a good effect.[82]

It is clear that pressure was being put on the government by its allies in Ireland to reduce the pension list. Those who were going to be responsible for managing the House of Commons probably felt that it would ease their task if they could obtain the removal of a number of unpopular pensions. In January 1715 Brodrick told Sunderland that he believed that the Irish parliament would be pleased to see certain pensions struck off. The following month Sunderland told Conolly that he would do his best to have some pensions withdrawn but that it would be no easy matter 'such persons as have them, though undeserving, seldom wanting advocates to intercede for them'.[83] At this time Brodrick, Conolly and the chief justices examined the pensions on the civil establishment, presumably to decide whom they considered should have their pensions removed. In early July, when the new establishment was agreed, Addison informed Archbishop King that the lord lieutenant had struck off 'about a dozen' pensions and had 'made a separate list of some to be continued until further order, by which means it is hoped they will deserve them by their future behaviour'. In all, by the time that the Irish parliament met in November 1715, seventeen pensions had been removed from the establishment and another had been reduced to half of its former value.[84] A list of the Irish civil pensions in the Blenheim Papers gives the reasons for striking them off the establishment. Eight people lost their pensions because they were Tories or suspected Jacobites; four because there appeared to be no foundation for the pension; three because the holders were considered to be wealthy enough not to need a pension; and one because the holder was a Catholic.[85]

The pensions of the earl of Granard and the countess of Donegall which, as has been mentioned, Brodrick tried to preserve were among those struck off. The countess of Donegall was described as a 'violent' Jacobite who had 'two or three boroughs at her disposition which return members of parliament to which she will only allow to be chosen people of her own sentiments'. Granard, on the other hand, although described as 'zealous for the Jacobite party', was considered to be 'a man of honour'. It was proposed that, if he promised to give the government his vote in the House of Lords, his pension could be continued although not put on the establishment immediately.[86] Granard may well have agreed to some such undertaking for in April and again in June 1716 Archbishop King is found writing to Sunderland and Addison respectively asking for Granard's pension to be confirmed. To Sunderland, King argued that 'My Lord Granard has behaved himself very well on the revolution on the Queen's death and since, and so far as I can learn, has come into all measures for his

Majesty's service, that could be expected, the parliament men in several boroughs under his influence have concurred in every vote'.[87] King wrote again to Addison in March 1717, asking him to remind Sunderland about Granard's pension. The archbishop concluded, 'I write this to you, because of the part both you and I had in giving my Lord Granard these hopes, and therefore think myself concerned in honour to push it as far as I can.'[88] Clearly King felt that some kind of promise had been made to Granard in return for his vote in the Lords and for helping to return MPs who would serve the government in the Commons. The fact that Eustace Budgell, the under-secretary at Dublin Castle, was returned as member for Mullingar, a borough in which Brodrick claimed Granard had an interest, lends credence to the theory that some kind of deal had been struck between Granard and the administration in Dublin Castle.[89] Nevertheless, Granard's pension was never replaced on the civil establishment.

Granard was not the only pensioner who may have promised to support the new administration. The pensions of Lord Athenry, the earl of Roscommon, and the earl of Cavan were all recommended to be continued because all three men were poor and dependent upon their pensions. Consequently, they were expected to support the government in the Irish House of Lords, although Athenry for one was known to be a Tory.[90]

By the time that the general election was held in Ireland in October 1715 the highest levels of the Irish administration had been thoroughly purged of Tories. The purge had also affected many lesser office-holders, especially within the revenue service, and had even extended to justices of the peace of whom an estimated seventy-two had been dismissed.[91] The message from the government during the year prior to the meeting of parliament in November 1715 was clear – Tories could expect little favour from the new régime.

III

Since the death of the queen, Irish Tories had become increasingly demoralised. In October 1714 Sir Constantine Phipps had left for England and in the same month Primate Thomas Lindsay wrote despondently about the future prospects of the church party in Ireland. Referring to the coming elections in Britain, Lindsay rightly asserted that 'Upon the goodness of them our future happiness and prosperity seem very much to depend and when I consider the great weight there will be against us, I must own I cannot be without my fears. The Church Interest hath been so much shattered and broken in this Kingdom of late, that … all our hopes and support must come from your side.'[92] The following month Archbishop King claimed that 'Sir Constantine's party give up all their hopes as to a majority' in the next House of Commons. Although King wrote the same day that the Tories were raising the cry of 'the church in danger' in order to try to win a majority and force the government to return them to office, he believed this to be impossible.[93] If the future looked bleak for the Tories in the immediate aftermath of the queen's death, the situation soon went from bad to worse. The flight of the duke of Ormonde to the Continent, the Whig victory in the British general election, and the outbreak of the Jacobite rebellion in Great Britain deprived the Tory party of its leadership and completely undermined its political credibility. The morale of the Tories progressively disintegrated throughout 1715. When the general election did take place in October 1715, King and the joint chief secretary to the lords justices, Charles Delafaye, both commented on the lack of enthusiasm shown by the Tories. Delafaye wrote that the Tories were 'in most places giving up very tamely' and King noted that 'several Tories that might undoubtedly have been elected have declined standing'.[94] It has to be remembered that by the time of the election in Ireland the Whigs had been firmly in power for over a year and had thoroughly purged the civil and military administrations of Tories. Under these circumstances, it is perhaps not surprising that many Tories were reluctant to raise their heads above the parapet by standing for election in opposition to Whig candidates.

The 1715 election resulted in a comfortable, although not overwhelming, victory for the Whigs. In contrast to the bitterly-contested election of 1713, that of 1715 passed without notable controversy with many seats being uncontested. As William King put it, 'Most of the elections for our Parliament are over, and they have passed with the greatest quiet imaginable, insomuch that I verily believe that no Parliament was ever chosen with so little expense or trouble to the candidates'.[95] However, although clearly defeated, the Tories had not been annihilated. At least 209 of the MPs elected in 1715 had sat in the Irish Commons before. Of these 209, eighty-two can be identified with a degree of certainty as having been Tories before 1714.[96] The situation after the election, therefore, was that although the Whigs had a comfortable majority of around one hundred or more, the Tory party had not been wiped out. A potential strength of around eighty MPs combined with a strong representation in the Lords meant that the Tories were, theoretically at least, in a position to cause the new government serious difficulties. However, this potential for making trouble was never fully realized, certainly as far as the House of Commons was concerned.

Once parliament met in November 1715 the Whigs ruthlessly attacked former Tory office-holders, launching enquiries into their behaviour while in office. Tories who had signed county addresses in support of Lord Chancellor Phipps were forced to apologize to the House of Commons and Anne's judges were summoned before a Commons committee to account for their behaviour whilst in office. The Tories' control of the corporations of Kilkenny and Galway was later broken by acts of parliament.[97] The reaction of most Tories to the purge of office-holders and the political harassment by the Whig authorities was to give up politics altogether or to try to switch sides.[98] The earl of Anglesey, leader of the Irish Tories since the flight of Ormonde and dismissal of Phipps, left Ireland in January 1716 depriving the party of yet another of its leaders. A week after his departure a Commons motion accused Anglesey of being 'an enemy to the King and Kingdom'. When the House of Commons censured the behaviour of the Irish judges during Anne's reign, only Richard Stewart (who had assumed leadership of the Tories in the lower house) came to their defence whereas 'several reputed Tories voted against them'.[99] The Irish Tory party had always been less disciplined than the Whigs and this lack of organization may have hastened its demise. In early November 1714, Archbishop King sardonically commented on the tendency of Tory office-holders to distance themselves from their former colleagues: 'All *bene placito* officers are trembling, apprehending a rout, if not a rot amongst them, and there's not one of them that ever were violent, or concerned themselves about elections, in so much that it is a miracle who made all the bustle we pretended to observe.'[100]

By May 1716 the active Tory party in the House of Commons had been reduced to about thirty members and never again would the Tory party be a considerable independent political force in Irish parliamentary politics.[101] However, when 'patriotic' or 'country' issues or matters relating to the Church of Ireland arose the spirit of the Tories could revive. The repeated attempts by the government to raise the question of relief for protestant dissenters may have been an indication that they were dismissive of the Tories' potential to cause trouble. However, it was foolish to completely ignore the threat from the Tories for they represented a body of support which could ally itself with any other group or faction which, for whatever reason, decided to oppose the government over a particular issue. As late as 1728, the bishop of Elphin, Theophilus Bolton, confided to Lord Carteret 'that there is no one thing so necessary to make a Lord Lieutenant easy here, as to prevent a union of' the Tories and the country party.[102] The point should be emphasised, however, that by itself the rump Tory party was powerless.

After the purge of Tories from high office, the weakening of Tory influence in the upper house, and the electoral defeat of October 1715, the Tory party was exiled to the political wilderness. Although normally a weak and ineffective parliamentary force, the party nevertheless retained its separate identity until 1727 at least. A group of thirty MPs could not be entirely ignored and on a few occasions the Tories were able to exert some influence in the House of Commons. They generally threw in their lot with whoever was in opposition to the court, this normally being the group of Whigs led by the Brodrick family. In 1716, for example, St John Brodrick, the son of the lord chancellor, joined with the Tories in opposing a bill to abolish the test clause relating to militia commissions and to remove it for ten years for army commissions.[103] As well as opposing such 'Whiggish' religious legislation, the Tories also took advantage of 'patriotic' issues to embarrass the court. As at Westminster, the Tories united with 'discontented Whigs' in pursuing popular causes such as a reduction in the size of the establishment. The number and size of civil pensions, especially those of absentees, was by far the most useful grievance in this respect.[104]

The splits which affected the Whig party in both Britain and Ireland gave the Tories in London and Dublin some room to manoeuvre. In both parliaments Tories and discontented Whigs were a useful body of support with which either of the major Whig factions could ally in order to attack the other. The Irish Whig party had split into two main factions by the end of 1715, one led by William Conolly, the other by Alan, Lord Brodrick (created Viscount Midleton in 1717). In Britain, the split became overt with the resignation of Robert Walpole and Viscount Townshend in 1717. Walpole certainly showed no hesitation in allying with Tories at Westminster after he left the government in 1717. The earl of Sunderland was similarly willing to seek the support of the Tories even when in government.[105] The situation in Ireland was possibly less clear-cut for, until 1725, both Midleton and Conolly were leading members of the adminis- tration and could not, therefore, openly side with the opposition as Walpole was able to do after 1717. On the other hand, whereas Midleton himself could not be seen to cooperate with the opposition, his son, St John ('Sinny') Brodrick, very often associated with the Tories in the House of Commons. Charles Delafaye described the long debate in the Commons in 1716 over a clause removing the sacramental test from militia and army commissions 'for which we were beholding to young Broderick whose zeal for the church gave encour- agement to the Tories to battle it out'.[106] It is true that the Irish Tories' options were limited since Midleton seems to have had closer connections with them than did Conolly. In 1724, the Tories supported a motion in the House of Com- mons defending the lord chancellor in response to a motion of censure of Midleton which had been passed by the Lords. The Tories in the Lords had also voted on Midleton's side. It was alleged that the Tories in the Commons turned against Conolly because they were angry at having lost a disputed election. The bishop of Ferns and Leighlin, Josiah Hort, claimed that the Tories had hoped to break up the parliamentary session before the money bill was passed by setting the Lords and Commons against each other. Hort tried to use the Tories' support for Midleton to undermine the latter's credit with the govern- ment and consequently strengthen that of Conolly: 'You will never find the Tories and Jacobites join with the Speaker, and this is a true touchstone.' On the other hand, Bishop Godwin believed that prior to their anger over the disputed election, the Tories had 'stuck to Mr Conolly'.[107]

Until 1724 at least, it seems to have been assumed that the Tories were a party of permanent opposition. However, upon his arrival in Ireland as viceroy, Lord Carteret, himself a former Tory, appears to have made a concerted attempt to win the support of the Tory party for the parliamentary session of 1725. One government supporter was clearly surprised by the Tories support of the opposition in that session writing 'we all thought by the favour and countenance they have had from my Lord Lieutenant they would have done everything they could to make my Lord Lieutenant easy in his administration'.[108] However, that Carteret had felt it worthwhile to try to win the Tories' support, combined with the fact that their opposition to his administration may have been due to a relatively unimportant dispute between Carteret and Lord Forbes, seems to suggest that the hitherto automatic opposition of the Tory party to the court was by this time wavering. Despite the failure of Carteret's attempt to work with the Tory parliamentary party, the possibility was not, it seems, ruled out for the future. As has been seen, Theophilus Bolton wrote to Carteret in 1728 stressing the importance of preventing the union of the Tory and country parties, he added, however, that 'so unaccountably narrow are the notions of some people here that they almost look upon a man as a deserter that shows common civility to those they call Tories'.[109] This comment may indicate that whilst the government (at least under Carteret) was prepared to work with the Tories, many Irish Whigs continued to harbour serious doubts about the propriety of such a relationship.

The perception that some Tories were 'coming in from the cold' is supported by the appointment of a few Tories to office after 1720. Since the accession of George I it had been taken for granted that Tories would continue to be proscribed from office and denied a share in government patronage. In 1719, Bishop Godwin of Kilmore, informed the archbishop of Canterbury about the anger of 'all the Whig clergy who look on themselves to be in the way of preferment' about the appointment of William Nicolson to the bishopric of Derry. Godwin added that, 'The Tories are well enough pleased, because they were not [in] competition.'[110] However, the exclusion of Tories from government patronage began to be eased by the early 1720s.

The appointment of the duke of Grafton as lord lieutenant in 1720 seems to have produced a change in the previously hostile relationship between Dublin Castle and the Irish Tories. The previous year the earl of Anglesey had supported the government position in the dispute over the Sherlock–Annesley case and Grafton's viceroyalty saw the beginning of the end of the policy of proscribing former Tories from office.[111] Shortly after Grafton's appointment Sir Richard Levinge, removed as attorney general in 1714, was appointed as a judge of the Common Pleas and throughout his period in office Grafton appointed clergymen who were allegedly Tories. Bishop Godwin claimed that Grafton had appointed 'Atterburian Tories' to the deaneries of Down, Limerick, and Cork, for example.[112] During a debate in the House of Lords over Wood's patent, the earl of Anglesey, according to the bishop of Kilmore, 'behaved in that debate like a Minister more than like a discarded man'. Godwin also praised the behaviour of the bishop of Limerick, Thomas Mills, both over the Sherlock–Annesley controversy (when 'He constantly left the House') –

and in the debate on Wood's patent.[113]

This limited rehabilitation of Irish Tories was accelerated under Carteret. In 1725 Francis Bernard, removed as solicitor general during the purge of 1714-15, was appointed by Carteret as prime serjeant and was made a judge of the Common Pleas the following year. Henry Singleton was another Tory who moved over towards the court at this time. Hitherto a leading opponent of the Castle in the House of Commons, Singleton was described by Speaker Conolly in February 1726 as 'now very hearty with our friends'.[114] Singleton was soon rewarded with the post of prime serjeant upon Bernard's promotion in May 1726. The Tory bishop of Kildare, Welbore Ellis, who pursued a campaign of political rehabilitation from 1717 at least, was eventually rewarded for his services to the English interest in Ireland after 1715 with an appointment to the prestigious bishopric of Meath in 1732.[115]

There is some evidence, therefore, that by the time of Grafton's viceroyalty the proscription of former Tories from office in Ireland was coming to an end and that this rehabilitation of former Tories was accelerated under his successor. It seems likely that by the mid-1720s the issues which had lain behind the Whig-Tory conflict were coming to be regarded, in Ireland anyway, as increasingly irrelevant. Carteret's Tory background, furthermore, meant that he was on good personal terms with some Irish Tories, most notably Jonathan Swift. William Percival, a strong Tory before 1714, certainly seized the opportunity of Carteret's viceroyalty to seek preferment in the church. Percival had known Carteret at Oxford and in the changed circumstances of the mid-1720s was prepared to declare himself 'as well affected to the present Royal Family, as any person whatsoever'.[116] Although it would be foolish to push this line of argument too far, what does seem to be clear is that a few ambitious former Tories such as Ellis, Singleton, Bernard and others were now prepared to support the court in return for preferment and that under Carteret they were met with encouragement.

That the party battle in Ireland during the reign of Queen Anne was a real one seems to be beyond doubt. The widespread purge of Tory office-holders after August 1714 is surely the best proof of the seriousness of that conflict. As a result of this purge the Tory party was effectively rendered powerless in Ireland. Harassed by the government, deprived of the opportunity to obtain a share of government patronage, and tainted with the charge of Jacobitism, the party quickly declined towards relative insignificance after 1714. After 1720, the prospect of rehabilitation for ambitious former Tories probably encouraged a further weakening of party distinctions until by the early 1730s the Irish Tory party had virtually disappeared.[117]

IV

The recent historiography of eighteenth-century British politics has established that the British Tories continued to be a significant political force long after 1714. 'Debate there may be over the extent to which Tories were, or were not, Jacobites; the party's existence as a coherent political grouping until at least the 1750s is agreed.'[118] The decline and eventual disappearance of the Irish Tory party by the early 1730s is, therefore, in stark contrast to the fate of its British counterpart. How can these conflicting fortunes be explained?

One important difference between the Irish and British Tory parties is that the latter had a much stronger electoral base. It has been seen how, even at the height of their power in 1713, Irish Tories were unable to obtain a stable parliamentary majority. Given the electoral strength of the Irish Whigs even in the 'worst of times', it should not be surprising to find them firmly establishing themselves in government when they controlled the levers of power.

Historians are divided about the extent and role of Jacobitism within the British Tory party. Was the restoration of a Stuart monarchy a serious objective or a romantic fantasy to which gentlemen merely paid lip service? The current state of research does not allow this question to be answered with certainty and, given the problematic nature of the evidence, firm conclusions are likely to remain elusive. However, it is surely reasonable to assume that Jacobitism (even of a romantic variety) gave the British Tory party a sense of unity and coherence which helped it to survive the long Whig ascendancy. J.C.D. Clark has posed the question 'If the Tory party was not Jacobite, then, what held it together?'[119] In the Irish context the answer would appear to be attachment to the established church, anti-dissenter prejudices (feelings also common, by the way, among Irish Whigs), distaste for the Hanoverian dynasty, and the presence of a small convert or 'crypto-Catholic' interest. These factors enabled the party to survive for a decade and a half after 1714, but apparently for no longer. The lack of significant Jacobite sympathies among Irish Tories deprived the party of that unifying factor which, it has been argued, enabled the English Tory party to survive until the last years of the reign of George II.

Eveline Cruickshanks and Bruce Lenman have claimed that because British Tories were apparently denied the prospect of political rehabilitation there was little incentive for them to abandon their party allegiances and even a positive reason to resort to Jacobitism.[120] From the early 1720s in Ireland, on the other hand, leading former Tories were brought back into the centre of political life and Tories obtained posts in the church and judiciary. If the nature of the relationship between Walpole's government and the Tory party in England in the early to mid-1720s is considered, the contrast with the Irish administrations of Grafton and, especially, Carteret becomes quickly apparent.

After 1714 the Tory parties in Britain and in Ireland engaged in tactical parliamentary alliances with disaffected Whig elements in order to oppose the government. It has been pointed out that such cooperation in Britain centred upon non-partisan issues which can be broadly termed as 'patriotic' or 'country'. Again, the nature of these alliances at Westminster has been a subject of controversy.[121] It seems, however, that in spite of this cooperation against the court the opposition Whigs and Tories retained their separate party identities.

> A Country party manifested itself from time to time; the Country party did not have a continuous existence. Whigs and Tories co-operated – in Parliament on Country measures, at elections sometimes, on a Country platform – but they did not lose their identity. They still remained Whigs and Tories first and foremost.[122]

Or as Eveline Cruickshanks has put it, 'There was indeed a "country platform" …, but there was no country party.'[123] However, in Ireland parliamentary cooperation between Tories and discontented Whigs had at least two ingredients which were missing at Westminster. As with their British counterparts, Irish Tories and discontented Whigs attacked the administration on country issues – the size of the national debt, levels of taxation, and the number and size of civil pensions. However, Irish Whigs and Tories also united to oppose repeated governmental schemes to repeal or weaken the operation of the sacramental test as it applied to protestant dissenters. Such cooperation indeed occurred in the first session of the Irish parliament after the Hanoverian accession.[124] Perhaps of even more significance is that the patriotism of the parliamentary opposition in Ireland was not simply anti-court in nature – it was also anti-English, often violently so. It is likely that cooperation between Irish Whigs and Tories was made much easier by attacking an English court, increasingly regarded as 'foreign' and 'oppressive'. Joining in common cause to oppose a 'foreign' court may well have led to a more rapid lessening of partisan differences in Ireland. In a similar way, the emergence of a 'national' conflict in the House of Lords after 1715 certainly facilitated cooperation between the Whig and Tory wings of an English interest increasingly under attack from Irish Protestants. On the other hand, it would be dangerous to assume the existence of a 'country party' in Ireland before 1730. Contemporaries certainly used this term to describe the opposition but, as in Britain, it would seem that, with the possible exception of some English-born bishops in the Lords, party identities remained paramount. Even when Whig and Tory members of the House of Lords united to defend their judicial rights during the controversy caused by the Sherlock–Annesley case, the legacy of past conflicts remained. One Whig reported that 'The Tory Lords were with us, but I am afraid some of them had rather views to embroil us, than assist us, but we kept a watchful eye over 'em.'[125]

V

The virtual elimination of the Tory party as an independent force in the Irish House of Commons which could realistically hope to regain office had important implications for the future government of Ireland. During the reign of Queen Anne, the choice of an Irish government had been relatively simple. Whichever party was in the ascendancy in London appointed its Irish allies to office. From September 1714, however, the Whigs were permanently in office at Westminster and an Irish lord lieutenant had to form his administration, not between Whigs and Tories, but from the Whigs alone. On the face of it, this should have led to a more stable and unproblematic situation for a viceroy who no longer had to contend with a united and well-organised opposition. The 'Whig Ascendancy', however, brought its own difficulties.

An inevitable consequence of the establishment of permanent Whig government was the emergence of division within the governing party. In the aftermath of the purge of Tory officials some Whigs were either left out of office or dissatisfied with the positions they had achieved. Such people felt resentful that they had not, in their opinion, been sufficiently rewarded for their services to the party in the past. These men would be strongly tempted to cause trouble in parliament in an attempt to force the government to buy them off with office. As early as 26 August 1714, the archbishop of Dublin feared that this would happen. Speaking of the great expectations of Irish Whigs who would be seeking favours from the new administration, he warned that 'many will be discontented'. By November 1714, Alan Brodrick had come to a similar conclusion. Barely three months after the death of Queen Anne, Brodrick wrote to his brother pointing out the political consequences which would follow from men feeling that they had been let down, saying, 'by the petulancy of some men, whose unreasonable expectations are not gratified, and [by] the perverseness of others, I foresee my Lord Lieutenant will meet [with] difficulties in his Government'.[126]

As soon as parliament met in November 1715, an opposition of Tories and discontented Whigs quickly emerged in the House of Commons uniting under a 'country' or 'patriot' platform. This opposition concentrated upon attacking the establishment which had increased by over £70,000 since 1713. They focused their attention in particular upon the pensions on the civil establishment demanding that some old ones be struck off and also questioning some of those added since the accession of the king.[127] The injudicious attempt by the government to repeal the sacramental test served as another useful issue upon which 'patriotic' Whigs and Tories could unite. In April 1716, Charles Delafaye offered an analysis of the nature of the opposition in the Commons. Advising the ministry against another rather insensitive proposal, namely to increase the value of the pensions paid to Huguenot ex-soldiers, he argued that it:

would give a very plausible handle to those who from Tory principles, from disappointments of preferments they pretended to, or from a natural peevish disposition, do not like the present administration, to clamour against the court, against the ministry and more particularly against my Lord Gallway, for loading them with new pensions and creating a necessity of new taxes to be lavished away upon foreigners ... And believe me there are not wanting those who profess themselves Whigs who would fall in with the cry: ... Every man who was honest in the worst of times, gave a vote against Sir Constantine Phipps or but drank his confusion, has created thereby such a merit in his own opinion that all the employments the King has to bestow were not a sufficient recompense.[128]

When a month later the Commons voted on a motion to decrease the establishment, Delafaye estimated that of the sixty who voted against the government thirty were Tories and the rest discontented Whigs.[129]

The structure of party politics in the Irish parliament after 1714 closely resembled the situation at Westminster. In both countries the governing Whig party quickly split in two, largely due to personality clashes and a fairly blatant struggle for power. These schisms within the Whig parties in Britain and Ireland were not unconnected. Midleton identified strongly with the Sunderland–Stanhope faction at Westminster (where he sat as MP for Midhurst from 1717 to 1728) whereas William Conolly was on better terms with the Walpole–Townshend interest.[130] These alliances were, however, neither straightforward nor permanent. Midleton fell out of favour with Sunderland after refusing to support the latter's Peerage Bill in the British House of Commons in 1719. In contrast, Conolly managed to remain on reasonable terms with Sunderland even when, apparently, siding with Walpole and Townshend. This conflict between Conolly and Midleton for the position of chief undertaker was to dominate Irish parliamentary politics until the latter's death in 1728. Chapter five will examine the relationship between these men and successive viceroys in detail. First, however, it is necessary to examine the most important factor which affected the behaviour of early eighteenth-century Irish politicians – the pursuit of patronage.

Patronage and Politics

I

The political culture of eighteenth-century Ireland was dominated by patronage. The management of the most obscure borough corporation, the drumming up of votes for a fiercely contested county election, the winning of majorities in the Irish houses of parliament, all depended upon the pursuit and distribution of patronage. Of course, in this respect the Irish political system was no different from that in Britain or indeed any other European society of the time. In the eighteenth century as in the twentieth, politics and patronage were inseparable.

Historians of eighteenth-century Ireland have long accepted that patronage played, to a greater or lesser degree, a key function in the Irish political system at both national and local levels. However, agreement about the precise way in which patronage affected politics has been more elusive. W.E.H. Lecky, for example, emphasised what he regarded as the important role played by Irish patronage in the operation of British politics: 'The Irish establishments were out of all proportion to the wealth and to the needs of the people, and they formed a great field of lucrative patronage, paid for from the Irish revenues, at the full disposal of the English ministers, and almost wholly beyond the cognizance of the British Parliament.'[1]

Lecky was clearly suggesting that some Irish patronage had been created by the crown and government at Westminster, was controlled by the British government, and was used by British ministers in order to buy votes in the Westminster parliament. An examination of the list of Irish civil pensions in the early eighteenth century would certainly appear to provide strong evidence to support Lecky's contention. Many large pensions, paid for by the Irish taxpayer, were granted to leading English politicians and courtiers. It is also easy to find examples of posts in the Irish church, army, judiciary and revenue service being given to English candidates. Moreover, titles in the Irish peerage were given (almost as consolation prizes) to English men and women who were deemed unworthy of a British title. There is, therefore, considerable truth in Lecky's perception of the value of Irish patronage as a means by which British ministers could buy political support at Westminster.

More recent historians, however, have taken a different view of the true significance of Irish patronage. Edith Mary Johnston has argued that Irish patronage was primarily used by the Dublin government in order to buy support in the

Irish House of Commons. She has claimed that 'the administration had to build up its majority by a judicious distribution of patronage among the greater and lesser borough proprietors'.[2] J.C. Beckett has supported Johnston's view regarding the use to which Irish patronage was put. While warning that the importance of patronage should not be exaggerated, he felt compelled to admit that 'Members were more commonly concerned about appointments or pensions for themselves or their dependants than about constitutional rights; and, as in England, the government regularly used its patronage to purchase support in the house.'[3] David Hayton has gone further than either Johnston or Beckett regarding the motivation of the leading members of the Irish parliament in the early eighteenth century, describing them as 'hard-headed jobbers' who were, he argues, 'principally concerned to advance their own careers and get the better of their rivals'.[4] David Dickson lends support to Hayton's view by emphasizing the change which he believes occurred in the Irish political scene after the Hanoverian accession to the throne. Dickson claims that the reign of George I witnessed:

> ... in the Irish house of commons the replacement of ideologically committed party blocks by a number of 'factions' or informal associations of MPs, which were held together by family connection or personal loyalty to the leading member, the common objective being to maximize the group's access to government patronage.[5]

While all of these historians agree that patronage had an important part to play in the political process, they disagree about the precise nature of its role. Lecky is alone in giving precedence to the use made of Irish patronage by the British government in order to buy votes at Westminster and it is impossible to support the view that this was the primary purpose to which Irish patronage was put. Johnston and Beckett are on much firmer ground in arguing that the administration in Dublin Castle used patronage to buy votes in the House of Commons and this view is supported by both Hayton and Dickson. However, whilst agreeing with the view that patronage was used to build a Commons majority, Hayton and Dickson appear to place more emphasis upon the role of the Irish politicians in this process. Put crudely, they see leading Irish politicians demanding and receiving patronage from the government rather than gratefully accepting whatever was dispensed from on high.

This emphasis on the importance of patronage in the early eighteenth century political process has recently been subjected to challenge from Sean Connolly who questions what he describes as 'reductionist' approaches which regard early eighteenth-century Irish politics as being dominated by 'the pursuit of private gain'.[6] Building upon A.P.W. Malcomson's analysis of the role of patronage in late eighteenth-century Irish politics, Connolly has argued that 'the role of patronage as a political cement has been exaggerated'. He contends that an 'interpretation of early and mid-eighteenth century Irish politics as amounting to no more than the self-interested pursuit of office and profit ... repeatedly fails to do justice to the manner in which individuals actually behaved'.[7] Considerations of personal honour, 'patriotism', 'personal contacts', and parliamentary rhetoric, claims Connolly, were also important factors in deciding an individual's behaviour.[8] Connolly's book is the first to go beyond a fairly superficial approach to the role of patronage in the early eighteenth-century Irish political system and his objections to an excessive emphasis upon the importance of patronage in deciding political behaviour merit careful consideration.

It is clear that all recent historians of early eighteenth-century Ireland, Connolly included, generally agree that the building of a relatively stable majority in the House of Commons was the prime objective of the Castle administration and that patronage was used by the government, to a greater or lesser extent, in order to achieve that goal. So much is clear. The way in which patronage was used to achieve that objective and the extent to which its use was successful is much less evident.

A number of questions quickly present themselves when the function of political patronage is considered. Most obviously, who controlled the distribution of patronage? The crown, ministry, viceroy, peers, MPs, generals, bishops, secretaries – who controlled what? Could they dispense this patronage as they pleased, to whom they pleased, or did they act under certain constraints? Who received patronage? What did they have to do in order to be one of its beneficiaries? Were political behaviour and the receipt of patronage explicitly connected? Was all patronage employed for political purposes? Was the receipt of patronage a reward for past services or an inducement to future good behaviour? Did people feel grateful for obtaining patronage or did they consider it their right? Did the award of favours necessarily guarantee the loyalty of the recipient in the future? These are only some of the questions which will be addressed in this chapter. Only by a detailed analysis of how patronage was distributed and an examination of the political consequences can firm conclusions be drawn. It will quickly become apparent that the links between politics and patronage were not so simple and straightforward as is often assumed to have been the case.

II

The following areas provided the main sources of patronage in early eighteenth-century Ireland – the army, the church, the judiciary, the revenue service, government posts, pensions, and titles. All of these areas were governed by their own specific rules and conventions for the distribution of favours. It is difficult to generalise, therefore, about the operation of the patronage system because it was so diverse and fragmented. Different people controlled the distribution of different forms of patronage and they operated under different rules.

The army was by far the biggest employer of state officials in Ireland. There were approximately between 650 and 700 regimental officers normally on the Irish military establishment, not including the half pay officers. In addition, there were about sixty-seven non-regimental posts in 1716 and around one hundred personnel in the Irish artillery train.[9] The financial affairs of the army were dealt with by the muster office which was staffed by civilians. The army also had its own ordnance office and the barracks were looked after by the barrack masters, civilians who had bought their office.[10] Next to the army, the revenue service was the largest public employer in Ireland. Revenue patronage consisted of two types – fifty-two patentee offices, originally created to collect the medieval duties of tunnage and poundage, and around 1,100 posts under the control of the revenue commissioners.[11] Most of the patentee offices had become virtual or actual sinecures by the early eighteenth century. They were often regarded as private property and were freely bought and sold. Of more importance than the patentee offices were the approximately 1,100 people employed by the revenue service. These consisted of around fifty two senior posts – seven revenue commissioners, their secretary, solicitor, English solicitor, and counsellor,[12] three surveyors general, and thirty-eight collectors of customs and excise. The remainder of the officers were gaugers and, at the ports, surveyors, tidewaiters, coast officers and boatmen.[13]

In addition to the four archbishops and eighteen bishops, the Church of Ireland employed approximately 600 beneficed clergymen and 200 curates.[14] Most of the occupants of these livings were very poorly paid. It was estimated in 1716 that there were perhaps only two hundred livings in Ireland worth £100 per annum or more. The Irish legal establishment in the eighteenth century consisted of four main courts: Chancery, King's Bench, Common Pleas, and Exchequer. The court of Chancery employed the lord chancellor, the master of the rolls, and four masters in Chancery. Although the court of Exchequer was officially headed by the lord treasurer and his deputy, the vice-treasurer, the actual business of the court of Exchequer was overseen by the chief baron and the second and third barons. The courts of Common Pleas and King's Bench each had a chief justice supported by two puisne justices.[15] Apart from the above posts, the state employed an attorney general, a solicitor general, a prime serjeant, a second and third serjeant, and several King's counsel. In addition to these major posts, there were about fifty other legal patentee offices in Ireland with salaries ranging from £1.5s. to £280 per annum.[16]

One form of patronage which has received more attention than most others is, of course, pensions. There were three main types of pension which were granted on the Irish establishments. Although the most important was pensions on the civil establishment, pensions were also granted on the military establishment and there was a separate list of French pensions (small pensions granted to Huguenot soldiers and their families) on the civil establishment.[17] Military pensions were of two kinds – half pay pensions paid to officers of reduced regiments and a separate list of pensions on the military establishment which were granted to army officers and their widows for a variety of reasons. After 1714, pensions on the civil establishment became increasingly more important than the French, half pay, or the military pensions, their cost more than doubling between 1715 and 1727.[18]

In the early eighteenth century there were around 120 Irish peers. The reign of George I saw the creation of thirty-eight new Irish peerages and fourteen promotions of existing peers to a higher rank.[19] After an initial mass creation of peers in 1715 to strengthen the Whig vote in the House of Lords, more new peerages were granted to Englishmen than to Irish residents, the figures being fourteen and ten respectively.[20] This use of Irish titles to reward Englishmen once again demonstrates that Lecky's contention that Irish patronage could be utilised for the purposes of managing the Westminster parliament cannot be entirely dismissed.

On the face of it, the government had an impressive fount of patronage at its disposal with which to influence the political loyalties and behaviour of Irish parliamentarians. With such a collection of jobs and favours to dispose of it might appear that the control of an assembly of 300 MPs and around forty active peers and bishops should have been a relatively straightforward task. However, it is clear from the political history of early Hanoverian Ireland that the control of parliament proved to be an extremely arduous task for the administration. Unless a high degree of incompetence on the part of the Dublin government can be demonstrated, it is necessary to conclude that the distribution of patronage was not the all-powerful tool of parliamentary management which, on the surface, it might appear to have been.

The first point to make about the disposal of patronage is that it was not all under the control of the government. Many patentee offices, for example, were regarded as the personal property of the holder. Some of these posts were held for life or a term of lives and reversions to these offices were also commonly granted. Primate Boulter brought to the attention of the ministry the consequence of these practices, arguing that 'the granting places for more than one life, or the reversion of places now full … tends to loosen that small hold the crown still retains in this nation'.[21] Although many of these offices were held 'during pleasure' and the holders were consequently liable to dismissal, in practice this was rare. Only following the death of the monarch did holders of such offices during pleasure have real cause for concern. Under normal circumstances the government's influence over the disposal of many of these posts was minimal. Many posts in the army were also, to some extent, outside government control. Where commissions had been bought, for example, they were regarded as the property of the holder. Despite determined efforts on the part of George I and his son, the purchase system proved impossible to eliminate from the army. On the other hand, increased efforts were made to limit and regulate the sale of commissions and each transaction required the permission of the king.

Although, in theory, the disposal of the patronage of the Irish revenue service was under the control of the British Treasury, in practice only the revenue commissioners and a few other major office-holders were normally appointed by London. The rest of the patronage attached to the revenue service tended to be controlled by the commissioners themselves. Two factors tended to discourage interference from the Treasury in the distribution of all but the top posts in the Irish revenue service. Firstly, the majority of posts in the Irish revenue service were not very lucrative. Secondly, when the Lords of the Treasury did try to make recommendations for posts in the Irish revenue service, the commissioners in Ireland often found some reason for not complying. Archbishop King commented of the revenue commissioners that it was 'no easy matter to obtain anything of them, when they can make any excuse for their not complying'.[22] In general, the Treasury did not interfere too much with the running of the Irish revenue service. The majority of revenue patronage in Ireland was simply not lucrative enough to arouse the interest of most of those in the Treasury in London. It should be emphasised, however, that when the Treasury did issue a positive order to the commissioners in Ireland, they had to obey it. There was never any doubt as to who was ultimately in control.

Much ecclesiastical patronage was outside of the government's control. Bishops, for example, controlled much of the patronage within their own dioceses, and lay patrons also nominated to church livings. However, it is clear that the government did control most of the more lucrative posts within the Church of Ireland. The bishoprics and deaneries were all under the crown's control and these were the most sought-after and, therefore, most politically important positions. The most important legal posts in Ireland were, of course, under the control of the crown. The judges and other senior legal officers were all appointed by the government. Furthermore, they held these posts during pleasure and could be removed at any time. Some minor patentee offices could be bought and sold but these were of relatively little importance. It was expressly forbidden to buy or sell active judicial posts.

Even where the government did control the distribution of patronage, there was a limit to the resource and only a finite number of jobs or favours to go around. The number of army commissions might increase dramatically in time of war but the service was then expected to contract in peacetime with officers dropping onto the half pay list. In theory, the government could award as many pensions and titles as it wished but there were a number of practical limitations. The Irish House of Commons proved itself quick to show displeasure if it felt that pensions were being awarded to 'unworthy' people or if their cost was becoming excessive. The size of the civil list was one of the most powerful weapons in the hand of the government's 'patriot' opponents in parliament and the administration had to be wary of adding pensions to the Irish establishment. In order to appease a truculent parliamentary opposition and ensure the passage of its money bill in 1716, the administration had to agree to stop payment of certain pensions previously objected to by a Commons' committee and refrain from adding new ones.[23] Neither could the government award titles on a lavish scale. Put simply, if too many were awarded they would quickly lose their prestige and, hence, their value. Furthermore, candidates for the peerage had to be deemed 'worthy', both in terms of their social status and their wealth.

Another limitation on the government's ability to employ patronage to obtain political support was that not all patronage could be used solely for this purpose. Many positions required formal qualifications and/or experience. Officially, for example, all candidates for the revenue service had to undergo formal 'instruction', either in the customs, in the excise, as a coast-officer, in 'the business of the tide', or in the hearthmoney. This kind of mandatory instruction was unique in the early eighteenth-century Irish civil administration. Although ability or experience played very little part in the choice of personnel for the minor posts in the revenue, in order to obtain a senior post previous experience in the service was normally necessary. William Conolly outlined the board's general rule in 1726 as 'no person can be appointed an officer in any of the upper stations, who has not first served in some inferior post of the same branch'.[24] This insistence upon previous experience appears to have been enforced with increasing vigour from around 1720 following a scandal over the mismanagement of the collectorship of Dublin and the revenue commissioners showed themselves perfectly willing to block recommendations, even from the Treasury, on such grounds.[25] It should not be surprising to find that some experience and professional ability was required from the more senior revenue officials; after all, it was they who were ultimately responsible for the collection of the overwhelming majority of the government's revenues. In addition, if a collector was not doing his job properly, or if there was a suspicion of peculation, relatively swift action was usually taken by the revenue board to rectify the problem.

Aspiring clergymen not only had to have formal educational qualifications, at least a degree, they then had to be ordained by a bishop, not always a straightforward matter when positions were in short supply. Candidates for the highest positions in the Church of Ireland were normally required to have a doctorate, although exceptions were made. Similarly judges and other legal officers had to have the normal legal training. Although army officers did not require formal qualifications, they did normally need experience. In getting an initial commission, financial resources and political interest were the key factors and it was not unknown for children to have commissions.[26] Although wealth and political interest could take a man so far in the army, experience and some degree of ability were necessary if he aspired to high command. The number of senior commissions was limited so the officer corps could afford to be fairly exclusive. Hayes has calculated that of 290 men who were appointed to colonelcies in the period between 1714 and 1763, over half had served twenty-five years or more in the army before their appointment and that most of the rest had served at least fifteen years.[27] The personal interest which was taken in military affairs by the first two Georges certainly seems to have had a positive impact on the way in which appointments and promotions were made within the army. Although it is not difficult to discover exceptions, senior officials in the judiciary, revenue service, and army generally had to display an acceptable level of competence. The consequences of appointing unqualified people to such positions of trust could prove to be extremely serious. Consequently, although the exigencies of parliamentary management might well be very important, this could not be the sole criterion when filling senior posts.

In spite of the limitations outlined above, political considerations did play a major part in the distribution of government patronage. The necessity to employ Irish parliamentary managers meant that these undertakers had to be offered something in return for their labours. Traditionally it has been said that, in return for managing parliament, undertakers were offered office, some influence over policy, and a share of government patronage. Only the ability to reward dependants with the spoils of office enabled an undertaker to maintain a stable parliamentary following which could be employed in the service of the ministry. As has been seen, the government did not control all state patronage, nor could it employ all of the patronage which it did control for the purposes of securing political support. Given such constraints, the administration had to be careful to employ to the maximum effect such patronage which could be utilised for political purposes.

Although patronage was the most powerful weapon in the hands of the government, it is clear that it was a double-edged sword. The distribution of patronage certainly brought the ministry political support, but it is also the case that under certain circumstances more support could be lost than was obtained. Put simply, whenever a particular post was vacant there would be many people seeking to obtain it, only one of whom could be successful. Furthermore, given the limitations in the supply of patronage outlined above, the government could never hope to fulfil everyone's expectations. As the future Viscount Bolingbroke put it in 1711, 'the number of discontented must always exceed that of the contented, as the number of pretenders does that of employments'.[28] Of course, it was not essential for the administration to please everyone, just enough to enable it to govern effectively. It is also true that the government was ultimately the fount of all significant places and honours. However, disgruntled politicians might react to disappointments not only by trying harder to win the favour of those currently in power but by plotting their downfall or by paying court to opposition politicians who might come to power in the future. Marmaduke Coghill alleged in 1733 that 'ever since he was refused an employment', Agmondisham Vesey 'has always appeared against the Court'.[29] The business of filling vacancies was, therefore, a delicate and sensitive task. The need to distribute patronage in a manner which would satisfy the expectations of the most influential politicians, whilst avoiding creating widespread and long-lasting resentment among those who had been overlooked, was the single most difficult task which faced the Dublin administration.

It might be thought that the filling of vacancies during the parliamentary session was the perfect opportunity for the government to buy support when it was most needed. However, the reverse appears to have been the case. The filling of posts while parliament was in session was an especially dangerous activity for the government for, although the recipient would be inclined to be cooperative, the much larger number of disappointed candidates and their patrons had an immediate opportunity to express their displeasure. For this reason, appointments were routinely delayed until the parliamentary session was over. This tactic brought two main benefits. Firstly, it encouraged those who were seeking appointment to be especially supportive of the government. The earl of Sunderland refused to confirm several pensions in 1715 in order to encourage the people concerned to behave themselves during the 1715-16 session. During this same session, it was claimed that the secretaries to the lords justices were delaying making any recommendations for the vacant archbishopric of Tuam 'till they see how the bishops behave as to this bill they are fond of'.[30] When baron of the Exchequer Pocklington died in October 1731, the duke of Dorset recommended that the place be filled with a candidate from England, 'but as the parliament is now sitting, this place while vacant will have some influence, and therefore the keeping of it open till the session is over, will certainly be for His Majesty's service'.[31] Arguing that Thomas Carter should receive some favour in return for agreeing to hold the office of master of the rolls during pleasure, Dorset added 'But I choose to defer any application on that account for the present, being desirous to have some experience of the session here, in which I am informed by the King's servants, that Mr. Carter's abilities may be of use in carrying on His Majesty's service.'[32]

The second, and more important, reason for delaying appointments was that it minimised the damage caused by disappointed expectations. When parliament rose the disappointed had no real opportunity to express their discontent and they would have eighteen months in which to cool their passions. This was a particularly important consideration when the administration intended to appoint an English candidate to a post, an eventuality likely to arouse widespread resentment among the Irish political community. When in August 1727 Primate Boulter recommended that an Englishman succeed Lord Chief Justice Whitshed he suggested that the announcement should be made only when 'the approaching sessions of parliament is pretty well over'.[33] Following the death of Archbishop King in May 1729, Boulter advised that his successor be appointed before parliament met in order to allow time for the resentment over the appointment of an Englishman to die down. Finally, during the session of 1729-30, Boulter suggested that the appointment of an English candidate to the bishopric of Clonfert should wait until 'the season of grumbling is over'.[34] The filling of vacancies outside parliamentary sessions became so common that it can be regarded as virtually a systematic policy on the part of the government. When George Berkeley hoped to be appointed as dean of Dromore in 1722, he explained that he would have to wait 'till the time when things can be declared, which cannot be far off, if the parliament rises in a fortnight'.[35]

Another limitation on the ability of the government to employ patronage for political purposes was the delegation of the power of disposal by the crown or ministry to subordinates. As a result, credit and gratitude for the appointment could go to the subordinate rather than directly to the government. Perhaps the best example of this process in action can be seen in the revenue service. With the exception of the most senior posts in the service, the patronage of the customs and excise was in practice controlled by those commissioners who were resident in Dublin. William Conolly, the leading undertaker of this period, was also the only commissioner to permanently reside in Ireland and thus established an unrivalled control over revenue patronage which could be employed to strengthen his personal position in the Irish parliament. In 1724, for example, Robert Wilson asked Oliver St George to intervene with William Conolly in order to obtain a revenue post. Since two commissioners were at that time about to leave for England, only Conolly and one other commissioner would remain and it would, therefore, be easier 'to do for' Wilson.[36] Clearly it was Conolly who was regarded as the ultimate controller of this type of patronage. Neither the government nor Treasury appear to have come into the picture. In order to obtain such a post, the consent of the commissioners was all that was needed and the fewer commissioners in Dublin the easier it was to obtain such approval. In a case such as this, St George would receive the gratitude of Wilson and both men would be in the debt of Conolly. No one would feel particularly obliged to the administration. Where recipients of patronage considered that they had received favours due to the intercession of an intermediary, rather than directly from the government, a sense of gratitude and loyalty to the administration might prove to be very short-lived, or even absent altogether, with obligation to the intermediary lasting much longer.

Such devolution of credit for appointments was not confined to minor posts.

Referring to the vacant bishopric of Clogher in 1717, Lord Brodrick hoped that it 'may be well disposed of; bishops should owe their preferment to the king, not to one another'.[37] Obviously, when deciding upon the filling of any vacancy, the ministry was influenced by recommendations from a variety of interests. Since each case was treated individually, it is impossible to generalise about the political ramifications of appointments. Whereas one recipient of favour might consider himself to be in the debt of the government, another might consider it the result of a patron's influence, and another as just reward for his own merit. In short, it cannot be assumed that in all cases the distribution of patronage (even when done explicitly by the government) brought direct political support for the administration.

As has been seen, control over the Irish government's patronage was divided between several – often competing – institutions and individuals. The majority of Irish patronage was controlled by one of four individuals or organisations – the crown, the viceroy, the Treasury, and the 'Irish', the latter referring to a variety of people, normally resident in Ireland, who had some influence over the disposal of patronage. The revenue commissioners, lord chancellor, bishops, lords justices, and army administration would all come under the latter general heading. The obvious point to be drawn from this dispersal of control over patronage distribution is that government patronage as a whole could not be employed in a pre-determined and systematic manner to achieve precise political objectives. Such a use of patronage was simply impossible given the fact that those individuals and institutions who controlled it often had different, even conflicting, political goals. This is most clearly seen in the divisions which existed between the 'Irish' and the 'English interest'. In the broadest sense, the 'Irish' represented the Irish-born Anglican gentry and professional classes, with the English interest comprising the viceroy, his secretariat, and certain British-born officials (especially bishops and judges) resident in Ireland.[38] Disputes between these groups over ecclesiastical and judicial patronage, in particular, graphically highlighted their conflicting objectives. To emphasise this 'English-Irish' division alone, however, would be a gross simplification. It is abundantly clear that divisions existed within both the English and Irish camps and that elements from both sometimes cooperated with each other in order to frustrate the objectives of a rival institution or individual.

Conflicts within the English interest over patronage were common. The main source of such conflicts lay in a structural feature of the Irish political system, that is, the necessity on the part of the viceroy to reward his Irish parliamentary supporters with appointments for their friends. The tendency of successive viceroys to appoint Irishmen to positions in the church, judiciary, and privy council caused considerable resentment among many of the English in Ireland who regarded this as a weakening of the English interest. This resentment became serious during the viceroyalty of the duke of Grafton (1720-24). Bishop Godwin repeatedly alleged that the lord lieutenant was neglecting the English interest in Ireland, claiming that Grafton had ignored 'us English' because he knew that he could rely on their support in parliament.[39] This split within the English interest was exacerbated by Carteret's viceroyalty (1724-30) when the lord lieutenant's patronage of Irish candidates brought him into repeated conflict with Primate Hugh Boulter. In 1727, for example, Carteret supported the candidature of Theophilus Bolton, the Irish-born bishop of Elphin, for the vacant archbishopric of Cashel despite the vigorous opposition of Boulter. Although the primate blocked Bolton's appointment on this occasion when Cashel again became vacant two years later Boulter was reluctantly forced to agree to Bolton's appointment in order to win parliamentary support, or as the primate put it, in order 'to keep things quiet in this country'. The relationship between Carteret and Boulter was further complicated by factional rivalries at Westminster.[40]

The major source of conflict among 'the Irish' was caused by competition for patronage between rival parliamentary factions. In particular, the rivalry between Speaker Conolly and Lord Chancellor Midleton, leaders of the two most powerful political factions in Ireland at this time, for the position of chief undertaker caused the deepest schism among Irish politicians. In addition to bringing the victor political influence with the Castle administration, the position of chief undertaker brought with it the potential to gain a significant influence over the disposal of government patronage. On occasion this rivalry could lead to Conolly or Midleton supporting the claims of English candidates against those of Irishmen. In 1716, for example, Thomas Brodrick supported an English candidate, Josiah Hort, to succeed as chaplain to the Irish House of Commons because his rival for the post, William Gore, would have been regarded as Conolly's candidate. After Conolly and Archbishop William King had engineered a vote of censure against Midleton in the House of Lords in 1723, Bishop Godwin remarked that 'these people quarrel with one another as heartily as all of them do with us English strangers'.[41]

III

Having looked at some of the general features associated with the disposal of government patronage which detracted from its effectiveness as a tool of parliamentary management, it is now necessary to look at the other side of the coin. It would be a mistake to conclude from the above discussion that patronage was of little or no use to the administration in securing political support. Although the government could not use the patronage at its disposal to promote a pre-determined and systematic policy, it did employ patronage to sustain its following and to defuse political opposition in the Irish parliament.

Given the small number of regular attenders, it is easier to see this process in action in the upper house. The administration had a number of distinct advantages in managing the House of Lords. First of all, in stark contrast to the position in the Commons, the crown had a major influence over its composition. The crown appointed all bishops and judges and could, if necessary, ennoble sufficient men to ensure a majority. Before parliament met in November 1715, George I created eleven new Irish peers in order to guarantee a strong Whig presence in the Lords. These peerages were explicitly political in motivation. Informing Sir George St George that he would be offered a peerage, Archbishop King made it clear that this was being done to strengthen the government's position in the House of Lords. When William Whitshed recommended Theophilus Butler for a peerage he told Sunderland that Butler would have Charles Delafaye elected for the borough of Belturbet 'in case your Excellency shall think it proper to have him made lord'.[42] Accordingly, Butler was raised to the peerage and Delafaye elected for Belturbet. Similarly, it was agreed that the duke of Dorset's son should succeed William Flower as MP for Portarlington upon the latter's elevation to the peerage in 1733.[43] That the newly created peers in 1715 were expected to serve the court in parliament is clear from the reaction of the earl of Sunderland and his wife to the proposal that Lord Percival should return to England before the session. Percival had suggested that because Sunderland would not be going to Ireland, and that he himself had only gone to Ireland to serve the lord lieutenant, he might return to England. Sunderland and his wife responded 'with some warmth', commenting that, 'sure My Lord Percival would never have received favours from his Majesty without intending to serve him in return'.[44] Of the eleven men given baronetcies in 1715, ten attended the House of Lords in the 1715-16 session, five of whom each attended more than half of the Lords' sittings.[45] The link between patronage and political behaviour was, in this context, explicit.

In addition to creating eleven new peers, between 1715 and 1717 the government also granted military pensions to Viscount Longford, Lord Stackallen and Lord Blayney. Longford was a French refugee who lived in England but both Stackallen and Blayney were regular attenders of the House of Lords during the 1715-16 session.[46] Following the purge of civil pensions, the earl of Granard was given the impression that his pension might be replaced on the civil establishment if he supported the new administration. Seeking the confirmation of Granard's pension in June 1716, Archbishop King argued that 'My Lord Granard has behaved himself very well on the revolution on the Queen's death and since, and so far as I can learn, has come into all measures for his Majesty's service, that could be expected, the parliament men in several boroughs under his influence have concurred in every vote'.[47] The qualified nature of King's testimonial may explain the failure of Granard to have his pension restored. On the other hand, the pensions of Lord Athenry, the earl of Roscommon, and the earl of Cavan were all recommended to be continued because all three men were poor and dependent upon their pensions. Consequently, they were expected to support the government in the Irish House of Lords, although Athenry for one was known to be a Tory.[48] Thereafter, pensions continued to be employed as one of the most important means by which the government secured support in the Lords. In 1720, for example, the duke of Bolton requested that Lord Blayney's military pension of £182.10 be augmented by £300 per annum to enable him to continue serving the government in the House of Lords where he had been useful in the past.[49] During the first two years of Carteret's viceroyalty (a period which saw an unprecedented increase in the number of civil pensions), Lords Altham and Athenry each received £200 per annum, while the earls of Roscommon and of Cavan had their existing pensions increased by the same sum.[50]

The government's control over appointments to the Lords, combined with the distribution of pensions and jobs to many peers, gave the administration considerable influence in the upper house. During the 1715-16 parliamentary session, for instance, twenty-two lay peers attended over half of the sittings of the House of Lords, of whom only five can be positively identified as Tories. Of the seventeen 'non-Tory' peers, ten were occupants of civil or military posts or were in receipt of pensions on either the civil or military establishments. Another peer, the earl of Kildare, had served as a lord justice between September 1714 and October 1715. Two more had been raised to the peerage since the accession of George I and can, therefore, be assumed to have been generally supportive of the administration.[51] The three remaining 'non-Tory' peers were all named by Charles Delafaye in February 1716 as likely supporters of the projected bill to remove the sacramental test as it affected protestant dissenters, a measure which only the staunchest of Irish Whigs would have supported. Furthermore, two of these three peers were in the future to support the government line over the Sherlock–Annesley case, something which only two other lay peers were prepared to do.[52]

Therefore, of the twenty-two lay peers who attended over half of the sittings of the Irish Lords between November 1715 and June 1716, seventeen can be taken to be supporters of the government and only five to be consistent opponents. It must be stressed, however, that not all of these seventeen were likely to have supported the administration with equal fervour. In drawing up a list of those whom he believed were likely to oppose the removal of the sacramental test, Charles Delafaye included Lord Gowran who had only recently been given a peerage by the King. Another recent creation, Lord Carbery, was also thought likely to oppose this sensitive measure.[53]

The ability to appoint peers and bishops, combined with the fact that most lay peers who regularly attended the Lords were in some respect financially dependent upon the crown, might suggest that control of the House of Lords was a fairly straightforward matter in the early Hanoverian period. However, at least until 1727, the upper house proved to be remarkably troublesome to the administration. This was mainly due to the unreliability of the bishops (who were, of course, appointed for life) and the continued attendance on a regular basis of a group of Tory peers usually amounting to between five and nine individuals.[54] Under these circumstances, even a slight weakening of the government's support could quickly lead to defeat. Over the Sherlock–Annesley case, Wood's patent, and religious legislation, Irish peers (even those dependent upon the administration) showed themselves perfectly willing to defy Dublin Castle. The point must be made once more, therefore, that although under normal circumstances patronage could secure support in parliament, that support was not, and could not be, taken for granted.

In contrast to the House of Lords, the government had little direct influence over the composition of the lower house. Unlike the situation in Britain, the government had virtually no influence over the election of Irish MPs. Moreover, the active membership of the House of Commons was much larger than that of the Lords. This presented the administration with two problems. Firstly, the court's strength could not be directly enhanced as it could in the upper house. Secondly, a great deal more patronage was needed to control an assembly with an active membership of over 200 than one in which a maximum of forty people regularly attended. In short, a policy of winning over individual members by the distribution of patronage, feasible in the Lords, was impracticable in the Commons. Only by delegating the task of management to undertakers could the government ensure the relatively smooth passage of its business.

Instances of state patronage being employed to secure political support in the Commons are not difficult to find. Despite the consideration given to experience and merit, membership of parliament was a distinct advantage in seeking, for example, a military commission. Early in 1715, Charles Irvine wrote to Archbishop King that he had heard that the earl of Sunderland had advised those who were seeking army commissions 'to get themselves elected members to the next parliament and promised to do for them'.[55] In November 1715 the Irish lords justices recommended the MP for the borough of Fore, Patrick Fox, for a vacant major's post. They claimed that Fox was the eldest major on the Irish half pay and that he was 'a man of a general good character, well affected to the King's interest and a Member of Parliament here'.[56] Six months later Grafton and Galway recommended Fox for a lieutenant-colonelcy arguing that his 'long services and his steadiness in the King's interest, especially in Parliament, do justly entitle him to His Majesty's favour'.[57] In 1716, George I recommended Captain Smith for a troop of dragoons in return for his 'merit and services ... both during the sitting of the late Parliament of Ireland and also since his Majesty's accession to the Throne, for which as yet he has had no recompense'.[58] The duke of Bolton justified his appointment of Major-General Owen Wynne to the command of a regiment in 1719 on the grounds that he was 'one that has on all occasions taken care both to do his duty, and to show his regard to the King's service both in his command and likewise in supporting His Majesty's commands in everything that he thinks for his service, and particularly in parliament'.[59]

The raising of thirteen new regiments in Ireland after the outbreak of the Jacobite rebellion in 1715 demonstrated the very close connection between political considerations and the disposal of army patronage. It was decided, presumably in the interests both of economy and fairness, that the policy decided upon earlier in the year 'that no commissions should be granted but to half pay officers' should also apply to the new levies.[60] In filling the vacancies, the lords justices generally followed the policy of recruiting from the half pay list but also granted commissions to 'some few officers who deserve extremely well and are all in his Majesty's service though not within the general rule'.[61] In early March, the lords justices sent a list of those lieutenant-colonels and majors who were on the Irish half pay requesting that the king choose whom he pleased for the new commissions. However, in spite of the king's explicit instructions that only half pay officers were to be employed, they also sent the names of seven men whom they recommended for commissions who were neither on the English nor the Irish half pay lists. The reasons which they give for recommending these men are interesting. In recommending Samuel Whitshed, MP for Wicklow borough, to be a lieutenant-colonel of Dragoons, they described him as 'a gentleman of merit and brother to the Lord Chief Justice Whitshed who has been very serviceable to his Majesty here'. In recommending Dudley Cosby, MP for Queen's County, for a major's commission, they argue that his 'long and good services both in the army and in Parliament, entitle him to his Majesty's favour, he has a brevet of Major, and is particularly recommended by an address of the house of commons'. John Etchingham Chichester, MP for Belfast, was recommended to be a major 'in regard to his quality, being uncle to the earl of Donnegal, and a great sufferer on account of his honest principles'. Recommending John Tichburne for a major's commission, they argued that he was 'of a family of consideration and good interest in this country, and very zealous for his Majesty's service'.[62] On 27 March, Stanhope sent the lords justices the names of fifteen men from whom they were to choose thirteen majors. Three of the seven men recommended by Grafton and Galway who were not half pay officers were included in this list of fifteen, all three being members of the Irish House of Commons. Each of the three men were given a major's commission.[63]

Tension between the king's concern for the welfare of the army and the half pay officers and the lords justices' need to buy support in Ireland did not go away. In November 1716, Galway attempted to justify himself in response to an order from the king 'not to recommend for vacant commissions, even of cornets and ensigns, any but half pay officers'. Galway sent a list of the Irish half pay officers pointing out that many were unfit for service. Some of them, he said, were Irish protestants who had been put on half pay as a reward for taking up arms against James II and it would be unfair to ask these men to serve in the army. He continued:

> The rest were not put into the new levies, either because they were minors, or absent, or that their affection to his Majesty's Government were suspected ... I shall not fail punctually to observe his Royal Highness's commands, and where half pay officers are wanting for those posts, I shall recommend young gentlemen who serve as cadets in the army, or who by the interest or abilities of their friends and relations to do his Majesty's service, or from some other good reason may not be undeserving of that favour.[64]

The implication of this letter is that ensigncies and cornetcies in the new regiments had been given to men who were not on half pay, notwithstanding the lords justices' claim in February 1716 that all captains and subalterns had been taken from the Irish or English half pay. Clearly, as far as the lords justices were concerned, 'the interest or abilities of ... friends and relations to do his Majesty's service' was a crucial element to be taken into consideration when army commissions were being distributed. In the end about twenty-three members of the Irish House of Commons were given commissions in the new regiments along with one member of the Lords. However, many more of those officers commissioned in the new levies were relations of MPs and peers. The raising of thirteen new regiments made available over 350 officers' commissions, presenting the Irish lords justices with a heaven-sent opportunity to buy support in the Irish parliament.[65]

What is interesting about this dispute is that no matter how often and how explicitly the king ordered that commissions were to be distributed only to those on half pay, the lords justices continued, sometimes successfully, to recommend people for overtly political reasons. Such conflicts between the king and his governors in Ireland over the disposal of military patronage did not disappear. In 1722, Archbishop King commented on Grafton's neglect of the half pay officers. Responding to a recommendation from the earl of Pembroke to obtain a commission for one Wood, King informed him that 'He is an half pay officer and it is hard to get any of them preferred, for the Lord Lieutenant reasons thus, this man has some provision, I have a friend who has nothing, and if I gratify this half pay man he can have nothing, I will therefore post my friend on this occasion and let the other stand as he is.'[66]

Political considerations played at least as great a role in the disposal of jobs in the army administration as they did in the allocation of officers' commissions. When in 1715 it became known that eight new horse barracks were to be built, the government was swamped with applications. Samuel Molyneux wrote to Lord Justice King in February 1715 asking that he be allowed to build one of the barracks at Castledillon. Pointing out that the government had already received some very advantageous proposals and that barracks were supposed to be built in market towns because 'men can't send three or four miles for a joint of mutton', King nevertheless added that he was certain that 'your interest will easily break through all these objections'. King said that nothing would be decided about the barracks until the arrival of Sunderland in Ireland but was sure that 'gratifying eight Parliament men will be sufficient motive to secure their votes'.[67] In March 1715, a list of reasons in favour of building a barracks at Cloghnakilty in County Cork was presented to the government. It is surely significant that the first reason given was that Cloghnakilty 'sends members to parliament'.[68] With over two hundred applications and only eight barracks to be built, it was inevitable that many more people would be disappointed than would be gratified. Sunderland was, therefore, in agreement with a suggestion of William Conolly's that the barracks should not be built until after the parliamentary session was over. It should come as no surprise to discover that two of the barracks were awarded to Irish peers and six to members of the House of Commons.[69]

Other forms of military patronage could be used to obtain political support and to reward dependants. Posts such as muster master general, commissary of musters, master general and lieutenant of the ordnance, and advocate general were all commonly held by members of the Irish parliament. Governorships of towns and forts and posts in the barracks office were also regularly given to peers and MPs. In 1717, for example, Henry Hawley (MP for Kinsale), the earl of Inchiquin, and Lords Ferrard, St George, and Barry were all governors of towns or forts, whilst Luke Gardiner (MP for Tralee) was registrar of barracks and Samuel Bindon (member for Ennis) was a barrack master. In 1715, furthermore, military pensions of the value of £1,247. 10s. were held by three Irish peers and two members of the Irish House of Commons.[70] The military contingency fund was also apparently used to make cash payments to favourites. Viscount Midleton argued in 1727 that all payments on this fund should have to be justified. He claimed that 'if a favourite is to have a sum given him or her the method hath (sometimes or somehow) been to pay £100 to A.B. without saying for what and to place the sum on the account of money to be issued for military contingencies'.[71] This fund (commonly known as the viceroy's 'privy purse') was apparently a favourite target for the patriot opposition who demanded that the particulars of each payment should be revealed to the committee of accounts. In 1733, the Commons voted that such details should be made available in future.[72]

In terms of providing jobs, pensions and cash payments for members of parliament, therefore, it would appear that the army provided the Dublin administration with its most important source of patronage. The revenue service, on the other hand, represented the single greatest source of patronage under the control of Irish-based politicians. The important political function of the Irish revenue service in the later eighteenth century has been well-documented and it would appear that the reign of George I saw the transformation of the Irish revenue service into an institution which had a crucial function within the Irish political system.[73] The responsibility for this change in the role of the revenue service can be largely attributed to William Conolly, 'first' commissioner of the revenue, speaker of the House of Commons, and a lord justice on nine occasions. Conolly's occupation of these posts enabled him to build up the most powerful political following in Ireland, making him chief manager or undertaker of the government's business in parliament. Conolly had been appointed as a revenue commissioner in 1709, allegedly paying the then lord lieutenant, the duke of Wharton, £3,000 for the post. From his removal by the Tory government in 1710 Conolly's chief ambition seems to have been to regain his commissionership. When asked to stand as the government's candidate for speaker of the Commons in 1714, Conolly's main concern appears to have been that this might affect his chances of regaining his commissionership. For Conolly at least, a seat on the revenue board was a more attractive proposition than the speaker's chair.[74]

Over the succeeding fourteen years Conolly's judgement regarding the potential value of a revenue commissionership was proved to have been correct. Since most of the commissioners in this period were Englishmen who were reluctant to spend too much time in Ireland, revenue patronage tended to become concentrated in the hands of those commissioners who resided most regularly in Ireland. Whoever gained control of this patronage would have the opportunity to become one of the dominant figures in Irish politics. For most of the reign of George I three men tended to dominate revenue patronage – William Conolly, Sir Thomas (later Lord) Southwell, and Thomas Medlicott. However, because Conolly was the only commissioner in this period never to have left Ireland, his control over revenue patronage became unrivalled. As the reign of George I progressed Conolly's ascendancy at the Customs House became widely recognized. Very simply, Conolly was more prepared than anyone else to spend a great deal of his time attending to revenue business. In June 1729, Katherine Conolly told Charles Delafaye that Conolly had been able to visit his country house at Castletown only three times during the preceding nine months. She complained that 'he is every day at least six hours at the Custom House ... I wish some of the commissioners were ordered to their business – for I think it is hard he should always have the labouring over him'.[75] Despite Mrs Conolly's understandable objections, by devoting more time to revenue business than anyone else, Conolly's influence over revenue affairs, and by implication over revenue patronage, became greater than that of any of the other commissioners. To enable him to establish and consolidate his position as chief manager of the government's parliamentary affairs Conolly required a reliable and substantial source of patronage with which to reward his political allies and dependants. The control of revenue patronage enabled him to keep his own followers content and gave him a distinct advantage over his political rivals. Conolly's eventual successor as chief undertaker, Henry Boyle, also realised the political significance of the revenue board and sought to emulate Conolly by demanding the post of 'first' commissioner when he joined the board after becoming speaker of the Commons in 1733.[76]

The government itself was not slow to realise the political potential of revenue patronage. At the beginning of 1715 the earl of Sunderland sent Conolly a list of men whom he wished to be provided for or continued in the service. All of these men had been recommended to Sunderland by a variety of people including the earl of Rochester, the earl of Orrery, Lord Chancellor Somers, and the king himself. Two months previously John Forster had advised Sunderland to recommend to the revenue commissioners that they should favour men who would be MPs in the new Irish parliament when disposing of revenue posts. Forster himself recommended that Henry Bellingham be given a collectorship on the grounds that he, his father and several relations would in all probability be members of the new House of Commons. In March 1715 Oliver St George asked that John King be given a collectorship adding that King and his father had been in the Commons for fourteen years and that neither of them 'ever gave a wrong vote'.[77]

Whereas conflicts within the English interest over patronage were normally related to the management of the House of Lords, disputes amongst Irish-born politicians mainly revolved around a struggle for influence in the House of Commons. Disputes over patronage certainly played a fundamental part in the battle for power between Midleton and Conolly. In order to operate effectively as the manager of government business in parliament, an undertaker had to be able to demonstrate his ability to obtain preferments for his followers. There was, after all, little reason for a member of parliament to follow the lead of a particular politician other than his ability to obtain favours from the government. This need to reward followers became even more important after the decline of party rivalry. When in 1717 it became clear that the chancellorship of the Exchequer would soon become vacant, Conolly and Midleton pressed the claims of rival candidates. Whereas Conolly recommended Sir Ralph Gore, Midleton attempted to have Michael Ward appointed, describing Gore as 'a creature of' Conolly who 'hath a spirit low enough not to disdain being thought a dependant' of the speaker.[78] A good example of how divisions amongst the Irish could open the door for an English candidate can be seen from the circumstances surrounding the appointment of a new chief justice of the Common Pleas in 1724. When Sir Richard Levinge died in July 1724, Conolly and Midleton were both acting as lords justices and a recommendation with the approval of both men may have carried considerable weight with the ministry. However, not surprisingly these two great rivals proved unable to agree on a single candidate and instead engaged in a struggle to nominate Levinge's successor, Midleton recommending Justice Macartney and Conolly supporting Justice Gore. As a result of this failure to agree on a single Irish candidate, neither Macartney nor Gore was appointed and an Englishman, Thomas Wyndham, was appointed to the place instead.[79]

Even relatively minor posts could take on a disproportionate significance as was seen when the deanery of Cork, worth around £100 per annum, became vacant in 1720. Being out of favour with the lord lieutenant at the time, Midleton asked his brother Thomas to recommend to the duke of Bolton the son of the previous incumbent, Richard Davies who also happened to be a relation of the Brodricks. When informed that Bolton had promised Davies the post, Midleton expressed his relief to his brother:

> ... it would have been [a] matter of great triumph if that deanery in that part of the country should have fallen into other hands, on the recommendation of Mr. C[onoll]y who I know was applied to and hath wrote on behalf of Dr. Maule; it would really have been looked on as a designed and avowed honour done to one and indignity placed on those to whom Mr. Davies is related, and especially when it is in a country where our estate and friends are, and where the other hath no pretences.[80]

At the height of the Wood's halfpence dispute in March 1724, Conolly managed to have Arthur Price appointed to the bishopric of Clonfert. Midleton was furious at Conolly's victory which was all the more impressive given the highly strained relationship which then existed between the ministry and its supporters in Ireland. Bishop Downes of Elphin claimed that when the lord chancellor heard the news of Price's appointment it had 'made him swear' and Midleton refused to congratulate Price when he met him at the Castle. Secretary of State Townshend had informed Grafton that Carteret, Midleton's ally at that time, had suppressed the news of Price's appointment 'perhaps on account of Mr. Conolly's desiring it'.[81]

Conolly and Midleton both needed to be successful in obtaining patronage for their followers for two reasons. Firstly they needed to keep their followers content. Secondly, and more importantly, they were desperate to demonstrate that they had influence with the ministry. Conolly's successful recommendation of Price in 1724 is an excellent example of the importance of obtaining favours from the court. Despite the anger of the king and ministry over Conolly's ambiguous behaviour over the Wood's halfpence affair he still managed to obtain a bishopric for his client. This was a clear message to everyone in Ireland that, despite current difficulties, Conolly was still on good terms with the government. It is little wonder that Midleton reacted so angrily to the news of Price's appointment. When in 1720 the government went back on a promise to appoint St John Brodrick as solicitor general Midleton commented, 'This I took to be intended as a public declaration to the world in what credit his father stands with the great ones, and that it is so understood by everybody.'[82] The outcomes of disputes over patronage amounted to public demonstrations as to the extent of the rival patrons' interest with the present ministry. A victory brought enhanced status and increased political support as people discovered who was in a position to obtain favours from those in power. For an aspiring undertaker, the ability to obtain patronage from the government was a fundamental prerequisite to his ambition to build up and maintain a significant parliamentary following.

Patronage was important, therefore, not simply as an end in itself but as a means to an end. The adoption of a 'patriotic' pose in opposition to the administration could persuade significant numbers of MPs to support a parliamentarian over a particular issue, especially if the leaders of the opposition were gifted in the art of parliamentary oratory.[83] However, because such coalitions were normally based on single issues, they were inevitably impermanent and short-lived and support could ebb even more quickly than it had arrived. Given the absence of significant ideological conflict and strong party discipline after 1714, a parliamentary manager could only create and preserve a large and steadfast personal following in parliament by making clear the extent of his interest with the government. The best and most public way in which to demonstrate this interest was to obtain favours from the court. Therefore, the attempts by patrons such as Conolly and Midleton to obtain patronage for their followers should not be judged in moralistic terms. They were not simply 'on the make'. Such men, if they hoped to have influence in the Irish parliament, had no choice but to engage in such activity. Patronage, in other words, amounted to more than an army commission for a brother, a revenue post for a nephew, or a pension for a destitute widow. Above all, the ability to obtain patronage from the government was the yardstick by which political interest was measured. Interest in parliament gave a man influence over patronage which in turn resulted in increased political interest. In this self-perpetuating circle the ability to influence the disposal of patronage was the key to political power.

IV

Although the most important function of patronage was to reward the dependants of the government's chief parliamentary managers and thereby maintain a stable following for the administration, it could also be used to buy off individual members of the parliamentary opposition. This had been done successfully by Lord Capel in the 1690s and thereafter troublesome opponents of the administration continued to be offered patronage in return for cooperation. However, like other aspects of patronage distribution, the link between the granting of favours and the receipt of a political dividend was not always straightforward. After Pembroke replaced Ormonde as viceroy in 1707, the lord chancellor, Sir Richard Cox, warned against attempting to win over the Whig party to the court. Cox argued that 'changes in favour of that party' would disoblige more people than it would win over. He also claimed that 'the very men who whilst they personate patriots delude many and seem to have great interest, the minute they turn Courtiers (as they call it) lose all their popularity and signify little. In short their talent is in doing mischief and not in doing good.'[84] As a leading Tory, Cox's evaluation of the Whigs cannot be taken at face value. However, he was not alone in warning about the dangers and limited benefits of buying off troublemakers. During the turbulent session of parliament following the revocation of Wood's patent, Primate Boulter (experiencing an Irish parliament for the first time) warned the ministry against attempting to appease the opposition with favours. Adopting a martyred posture, Boulter declared that he was prepared to suffer the trials and tribulations of facing the parliamentary opposition so long as:

> no new encouragement is given to such doings, by buying off any discontented persons here; for if any body is bought off, there will always arise a succession of people to make a disturbance every session; and there wants no accident here to furnish a bottom of popularity, every one having it always in his power to grow popular, by setting up for the Irish, in opposition to the English interest.[85]

Discussing who would succeed Sir Ralph Gore as speaker of the Commons in 1733, Marmaduke Coghill was sceptical about the amount of support which either Thomas Carter or Henry Boyle could bring to the administration, believing that 'they will hardly be able to bring off any or at least but very few of the country party with them'.[86] The point which both Cox and Coghill were making was that, whereas it was relatively simple to buy off individual troublemakers, it was unlikely that the support of those members of parliament who had supported such 'patriots' would follow. Indeed those in opposition to the court may even be encouraged to continue such behaviour. When it became apparent that the court would probably support Boyle's candidacy for the speaker's chair in 1733, Coghill was vociferous in his disapproval of the court's strategy. He lamented 'I shall not trouble myself much in these matters, let them do as they think fit, I am not in their confidence, and I find those persons are in greatest esteem, who have always been violent in opposition to the court, it is a piece of politics I don't understand, and it is a certain method to create further opposition.'[87] Whilst Coghill was clearly piqued at being excluded from the court's confidence, his analysis also contained a valid observation – that buying off opponents of the administration merely served to encourage such opposition in the future.

One man who was apparently prepared to link explicitly his voting behaviour in parliament to the government's willingness to prefer him was Theophilus Bolton. A protégé of Archbishop King who obtained the patronage of Conolly, Bolton was an extremely able clergyman who displayed ruthless ambition. Primate Boulter consistently attempted to block Bolton's advancement and the two men were described in 1733 as being 'as great enemies as Christianity will permit'.[88] Boulter's quite justified fear was that Bolton would succeed Archbishop King as leader of the Irish interest within the church. However, unlike King, Bolton was above all a pragmatist, primarily concerned about his own career. Appointed as bishop of Clonfert in 1722 and subsequently translated to Elphin in 1724, Bolton (with the support of Conolly and Carteret) sought the archbishopric of Cashel in 1727 only to have his candidature blocked by Boulter. Explaining why he would not trust him with his proxy vote in the Lords, Bishop Carr of Killaloe pointed to Bolton's behaviour after Boulter blocked his translation to Cashel:

> I could no more trust my proxy to [Bolton] than my daughter with a bawd or my purse with a pickpocket. How could I answer a refinement he is capable of making, had he given my proxy in favour of the bill, and I could expect nothing less from a man that could speak so long and used such arguments (as he can never answer) against the Quakers Bill, and yet turned on his heel at the two last lines and was most astonishingly for it. But I need not tell you the reason of his present alteration, he missed Cashel.[89]

During the same session, Boulter described how the bishop of Elphin led an opposition of lay lords against a privilege bill which was sponsored by the bishops, concluding that 'His view no doubt was to make himself considerable enough by being at the head of this strength to be bought off.'[90] If this was Bolton's intention then it certainly worked since he was appointed archbishop of Cashel the following year. Boulter is undoubtedly a hostile witness regarding Bolton. In 1733, on the other hand, Marmaduke Coghill recalled that Conolly had 'found this prelate greatly serviceable to him' and that Carteret had 'found this man absolutely necessary for his service'. However even Coghill added that 'I must say this much for Cashel, he can be a great friend in assisting a chief governor, but if he opposes, can be as great an enemy'.[91]

Although the government could win the support of individual parliamentarians through the distribution of favours, that was not the end of the story. Even men who were firmly within the government's interest required careful handling by the court if their support was to remain constant. Towards the end of 1732, for instance, Boulter suggested to the duke of Dorset that the earl of Cavan be appointed governor of the Royal Hospital at Kilmainham. The primate argued that Cavan served the government in the Lords where he was the only lay peer who could be considered 'a man of business'. Boulter added that if Cavan were given this post he would 'always be at hand to assist in the Privy Council'. Dorset, however, chose instead to give the position to his own half-brother. When in March 1735 Boulter's recommendation that Cavan be made governor of Londonderry was disregarded, he warned that 'I fear we may have some occasion for his help in the House of Lords, except he is made some way easy.' The following year when Boulter sought the post of governor of Derry or governor of the Royal Hospital for Cavan he made it clear that otherwise 'we may find the want of him in the session of Parliament'.[92]

In addition to buying off opponents and keeping others content, patronage was employed by the court to reward those who had served the government well in parliament. This was seen most explicitly following the Hanoverian accession when the Whig ministry launched a widespread purge of office-holders and rewarded its Irish allies. It has also been seen how parliamentary supporters of the court benefited from the raising of new regiments in 1715. Such rewarding of past services continued to occur. In May 1719 the duke of Bolton recommended that Brinsley Butler be granted a pension which he received later that year. Butler had been removed in 1714 as captain of the Battle Axe Guards due to his support of the Tory administration but, according to the viceroy, Butler had served the government well in the Irish Commons since 1715. Lord Carteret gave Bartholomew Purdon a small revenue post for supporting his administration in parliament. Being an MP for a constituency in County Cork, he had apparently suffered much from 'the Munster gentlemen' led by the Brodricks.[93] Such compensation for overtly political services inevitably led on occasion to the appointment of unsuitable candidates. The appointment of Charles Carr as bishop of Killaloe certainly scandalised one of his political opponents:

> ... there could hardly in the whole kingdom be picked out another clergyman so distinguished for weakness of understanding, and want of literature, and this to so great a degree, that when any of those who are called Tories had a mind to say a reflecting thing on the designs of the other party, they would charge them in a sneering way, that they de-

signed to make Charles Carr a bishop which was always resented as an injury and slander. ... His only plausible title is being chaplain to the House of Commons which was nothing but the effect of party, his competitor being what they call a Tory.[94]

Despite lacking any previous experience in the revenue service, Sir John Eccles was appointed in 1715 as collector of the port of Dublin on the recommendation of the earl of Sunderland. His appointment was defended because Eccles had 'been bred a merchant' and could be expected to have some expertise in the methods of the customs. The revenue commissioners also thought that he could not get into much difficulty in Dublin 'where the whole Board is so near to his Assistance'.[95] Contrary to the rules of the revenue, Eccles employed a relation as his clerk and left the management of the port to him. When he was finally dismissed in November 1720 Eccles allegedly owed the government over £5,000. William Conolly remarked that, although Eccles' clerk had 'used him ill, ... Sir John was in no ways capable of so great a post'.[96]

V

How useful was patronage, therefore, as a tool of parliamentary management? Is it crudely 'reductionist' to suggest that Irish politicians in the early eighteenth century were strongly motivated by ambition or greed and that the Irish parliament served as a market place where men's allegiances (and votes) were bought and sold? The first point which must be stressed is that it would be unreasonable for historians to expect to find evidence of explicit 'deals' between the court and members of parliament in which the latter promised to support the government in return for favours. The parliamentary code of honour would not allow gentlemen openly to admit to such a degree of dependence. There was certainly no reason to commit any such bargain to paper and many good reasons to refrain from so doing. Absence of documentation, therefore, cannot be taken at face value. Fortunately sufficient evidence survives to make it clear that promises of political support in return for preferment did take place. In 1732, for example, Boulter recommended the son-in-law of Agmondisham Vesey for the deanery of Ardfert. Vesey had promised Boulter that he would support the government in the next session in all measures 'which a man of honour could possibly join in'. Dorset apparently 'had been mentioning Mr. Vesey, as one proper to be gained'.[97] While Vesey promised to be cooperative in parliament, it is important to realise the significance of the qualification which he placed on that engagement. Vesey was indicating that he was not prepared to jeopardise his reputation and his own sense of honour by voting for controversial government-sponsored legislation. Boulter had apparently accepted these terms assuring Vesey that he 'was very sure the government would never desire any thing a man of honour could not comply with'.[98] It is perhaps surprising that the government was prepared to accept such qualified support in return for favours. However, it is evident that the administration recognised the limited nature of the demands which it could realistically make on its supporters. It was accepted, for example, that members of parliament could not be dictated to on sensitive questions such as religious legislation, particularly repeal of the sacramental test. Similarly, there were no thoughts of 'disciplining' peers and MPs who had opposed the government over the Sherlock–Annesley case or Wood's patent. The government clearly realised that men could not support measures in parliament which were violently opposed by the Anglican community as a whole.

While it is easy enough to present examples of parliamentarians who were employees or otherwise dependent upon the state, this does not mean that all state employees were necessarily consistent supporters of the court. Army officers could generally, although not invariably, be relied upon to support the government in parliament. In July 1715 Archbishop King claimed that all of the military officers were Sunderland's 'creatures' and would have been 'at his service' had he chosen to come to Ireland as viceroy.[99] In 1723 Lord Chancellor Midleton listed twelve MPs who had military posts or were on half pay who had voted according to the wishes of the court in the case of a disputed election. Midleton also noted, however, that Brigadier-General David Creichton had absented himself from the vote despite having been solicited by Speaker Conolly.[100] However, the advantages to the government of important members of the Anglo-Irish community holding military commissions can be seen from Grafton's request that the King should express his appreciation to Lieutenant-General Viscount Shannon when the latter returned to London. Grafton explained that 'he has been of great use and service, he having a great many relations and friends which have stood by us, that perhaps had not if he had not been here'.[101]

There is evidence, however, to suggest that army officers did on occasion vote against the government in parliament. In January 1726, the government carried a vote in the Commons by 108 votes to ten. Lord Chancellor West noted that among the government's ten opponents there were three captains.[102] Praising Major-General Wynne in 1719 for his service to the government in parliament, the duke of Bolton added that he wished that he could do likewise for those with more senior commands, commenting that there 'are too many here that rather do disservice than otherwise that have the best employments'.[103]

In 1720 thirteen members of the Irish House of Commons held senior positions within the revenue service. Discussing the prospects of a bill in the Irish parliament to establish an Irish national bank in December 1721, Lord Chancellor Midleton described a group of MPs as being 'dependants on the Custom house'. In October 1723 Midleton listed a group of ten MPs (excluding Conolly himself) whom he described as 'collectors and concerned in the revenue'. All of these men had voted for the court's, and Conolly's, candidate in a case of a disputed election.[104] What is unclear, however, is what exactly was meant by the term 'dependants on the Custom house'. Were these men under the control of the British Treasury, of Dublin Castle, or were they personal dependants of William Conolly? One of those named, Thomas Medlicott, could not be described as a dependant of Conolly's since he was himself a revenue commissioner and, after 1722, a British MP. On the other hand, another of the men named, Thomas Pearson, was a relation of Conolly's and would fall into the category of a dependant of the speaker.[105] It is unlikely that all of these men were either dependant upon the Treasury, upon the Castle, or upon Conolly. However, in a sense, this did not matter for Conolly and the Castle were almost invariably on the same side throughout this period. What does seem to be clear is that the 'dependants of the Custom house' represented a bloc of MPs who, led or 'managed' by Conolly, could normally be relied upon by the Castle administration to support its line in the House of Commons.

Although, in general, those dependent upon the government normally supported the administration, complaints that office-holders, pensioners or privy councillors were opposing the government were not uncommon. Primate Boulter was particularly resentful of this apparent lack of loyalty and pressed the ministry to take action against the guilty men. In the midst of the troublesome parliamentary session of 1725-26 Boulter advised that:

> if those who have places here, and yet have joined in the late measures, are remembered after the sessions; and if nobody finds his account in having headed the opposition made now to his Majesty's service, I do not doubt but the face of affairs will here gradually alter, and we may hope that the next sessions will be more easy and successful.[106]

The primate complained that the leaders of the opposition had persuaded 'many well-meaning members' to support them by 'telling them that by their opposition they were making court on the other side of the water'. Such an interpretation of the political situation would have been widely credited given the strained relationship which existed between Carteret and the ministry at that time. Boulter argued that the country gentlemen would only be persuaded that this was not the case by dismissing the leaders of the opposition from the privy council.[107] Boulter bore a particular resentment against Thomas Carter whom he recommended 'should be made an example of'. Boulter promised soon 'to point out such a way of dealing with him, as will make his opposition in future sessions of little weight'.[108] It is significant that Boulter's repeated requests for the dismissal of disloyal employees went unheeded, once more emphasising the limited control which patronage gave the government over the political behaviour of its followers. The administration obviously felt that the possible advantages of making 'examples' of such men would be outweighed by the negative consequences of making martyrs of those who portrayed themselves as 'patriots'. Robert Walpole made this point quite explicitly when the Irish lords justices refused to obey the government during the Wood's halfpence dispute. Walpole believed that 'to remove them avowedly and expressly for this behaviour would possibly make them so popular all over the Kingdom that with the interest and influence they have already they might be able to render the King's Government absolutely impracticable'.[109] Walpole was absolutely right. Quite simply, the government could not dismiss men every time they voted against the court. Such a policy would have made impracticable the creation of a stable parliamentary following and would have merely swelled the ranks of an even more disaffected opposition.

The limits of the court's ability to influence state employees can be seen from the failure of the attempt to repeal the sacramental test in 1733. After the House of Commons passed a motion refusing to receive such a bill after Friday 14 December a meeting of government advisers and representatives of the dissenters was held at Dublin Castle to make a final decision about whether to attempt repeal. After all of the government's advisers declared their opinion that repeal stood no chance of success, the dissenters urged the lord lieutenant to 'use his influence'. Dorset replied that 'he had done all that was proper for him to do, unless he should tell those in employments, that they should be turned out unless they complied, which he thought not proper, having no directions to do so'.[110] Marmaduke Coghill, a revenue commissioner, had previously told Dorset that he hoped that he would not be offended if he voted against repeal of the test even if it had the support of the court. Dorset replied that 'he should never expect anything of me in any matter of importance, which was contrary to my opinion and judgement, and he should have the better opinion of me, for acting accordingly'.[111]

While certainly being the strongest weapon in the government's arsenal, therefore, there were clear limits to the utility of patronage as a 'lubrication' for the political machinery of early eighteenth century. Opponents could be bought off, supporters rewarded, waverers persuaded, and enemies punished. However, followers continued to demand favours and could be easily offended, the votes of even state employees could not be taken for granted, and some opponents could not be won over by the distribution of patronage alone. Finally, when 'patriotic' issues raised their head in parliament, considerations of patronage were often quickly swept aside. Parliamentary management, therefore, involved much more than the mere distribution of patronage. However, an appreciation that the distribution of patronage was complex and that its ramifications were uncertain does not detract from its pivotal political function. Irish parliamentary politics in the two decades following 1714 simply would not

have been practicable without the widespread disposal of patronage to the Anglican political élite. Despite the limitations outlined above, the most convincing
interpretation of early Hanoverian parliamentary politics remains one which
accepts that the single most important factor influencing the behaviour of Irish
politicians was the pursuit of patronage.

VI

To conclude this analysis of the operation of the patronage system, an illustration of the atmosphere surrounding the competition for posts might be
enlightening. An account from Philip Percival of the rivalry between the Irish
clergy for vacant benefices in 1722 depicts a scene which would not be out of
place in *The Warden*.

> I believe it may be wondered at in England that his Grace continues so
> long here, but the great number of livings and deanerys which have lately
> become vacant by death or promotions, have occasioned such variety of
> schemes that I believe his Grace has not been a little perplexed how to
> dispose of them, the legion of candidates being many and very importu-
> nate, they certainly are good sollicitors, and were you sometimes at the
> Castle, it would make you laugh to see the whole Piazza crowded to that
> degree that Dr. Berkeley was ashamed to be seen among them and used
> to retire to the Garden. It was really comical to see long Northcote stalk-
> ing, and little Shadwell waddling about whilst fat Dean Daniel was
> storming at Berkeley's having the Deanery of Derry, a man who he said
> had never declared himself, so that he could not tell what principles he
> held, where himself had declared himself in the worst of times vehe-
> mently; which (to do him justice) he certainly did constantly twice or
> thrice every day in Lucas's Coffee house, Sundays even not excepted.
> He was inveighing bitterly one day in this manner to the Bishop of Fernes,
> who let him run on for about half an hour, and then whispered him in the
> ear Berkeley will have it for all that, which made him rage ten times
> more.[112]

6

Viceroys, Undertakers, and Parliamentary Management

'these people are not easily governed'.[1]

The previous chapter examined in some detail the role of patronage in the operation of the Irish parliamentary system. Although clearly possessing a pivotal function, the distribution of patronage was only one aspect of the management of parliament. Essential to the effective management of the Irish parliament was a stable and trusted relationship between the court and its parliamentary advisers. It is evident, however, that the establishment and maintenance of such a relationship was an extremely difficult affair. This chapter will attempt to analyse the often shadowy relationship between a viceroy and his parliamentary managers or undertakers. Having examined the function of the viceroy and his managers, some of the problems associated with running a session of parliament will be analysed.

I

The work of Hayton and McGuire has demonstrated that undertakers or parliamentary managers came into existence in Ireland after the collapse of the 1692 Parliament.[2] Sydney's failure to take into account the concerns of the Protestant community, particularly regarding the terms of the Treaty of Limerick, left him with a disaffected House of Commons lacking any direction from the court. Consequently, to the government's discomfiture, the leaders of the Protestant community were enabled to seize the political initiative and to direct the business of parliament as they chose. Sydney's failure to appreciate the realities of the new situation in Ireland and the determination of the Irish Protestant community to be consulted in the affairs of their own country only served to bring the viceroy personal humiliation. However, the failure of the 1692 Parliament did lead his eventual successor to realise that local political magnates had to be taken into the government's confidence. Managers had to be given posts of responsibility both as public demonstrations of the government's recognition of their status and as a vote of confidence in their ability. Moreover the advice of these confidants about what would be acceptable to the wider Protestant community (and what would not) had to be taken seriously if major and perhaps unnecessary disputes were to be avoided. In short the job of these undertakers was to act as a direct line of communication between the court and parliament. As shall be seen, however, Sydney was by no means the last viceroy to underestimate the necessity for a close relationship with the leading Irish parliamentarians.

There were two main reasons why such managers were essential to ensure the smooth running of the parliamentary session. Arriving in Ireland to all intents and purposes as a colonial governor, the viceroy normally had little or no personal knowledge of the political culture of the country and of the issues which were of particular concern to the Anglican community. He also lacked detailed information about the interests, ambitions and idiosyncrasies of individual members of parliament and of the connections and rivalries between them. Normally arriving in Ireland only a few weeks before the opening of the parliamentary session, neither the viceroy nor his chief secretary (who always sat as an Irish MP) had any realistic opportunity to build up a stable following for the court in parliament. In addition, the government had no 'interest' (or following) worthy of the name in the Irish House of Commons. The government had virtually no electoral influence in Ireland and showed little inclination to acquire one.[3] In contrast to the situation in the Westminster House of Commons, therefore, the government had no bloc of votes in the Irish lower house upon which it could consistently rely. Under the circumstances, an incoming viceroy had no choice but to come to terms with the self-appointed leaders of the Irish parliament and to govern through middlemen or undertakers. This task was not made any easier by the absence of any great borough owners in the early eighteenth century. The diffusion of electoral interest among a large number of people meant that it was difficult for anyone to establish a large and stable parliamentary following, the leaders of each parliamentary faction being liable to desert the court over contentious legislation or due to a perceived personal slight.

The necessity for a viceroy to employ the leading Irish parliamentary power-brokers might lead to the conclusion that he was effectively their prisoner. To some extent this is true but the situation was never so clear-cut. Certainly the party conflict of the reign of Queen Anne, by adding a further complicating factor to the practicalities of parliamentary management, did have the effect of limiting a viceroy's room for manoeuvre. In one respect the Whig-Tory conflict made the political situation clearer in that a viceroy was normally so strongly identified with one of the parties that the Irish leaders of the opposite party simply refused to cooperate with him. This was especially true of the viceroyalties of Ormonde and Wharton, less so of Pembroke and Shrewsbury. However, even the latter two lords lieutenant found it impossible to form mixed administrations. The party political dichotomy, therefore, had the effect of removing the viceroy's decision as to which faction to employ as his servants. In one respect this made the viceroy's job easier since he did not have to make the difficult decision about whom to favour and, consequently, whom to offend. On the other hand, by effectively removing the viceroy's ability to choose his own managers, there was a strong temptation for his followers to try to dictate terms, or at least to exert an influence unimaginable under 'normal' circumstances. In other words, the parliamentary tail might begin to wag the viceregal dog, especially over emotive party issues.

The accession to the throne of George I in 1714 effectively ended the party conflict in Ireland by leading to the rapid weakening of the Tory party. Although initially the Whig administration had no option but to appoint to office those men who had led the Whig party in Ireland, in time the demise of the Tories would restore to some extent the initiative to the viceroy as to whom he should choose as his parliamentary advisers. Indeed during the first weeks of the parliamentary session of 1715-16 splits began to appear among the leaders of the Irish Whig party. While viceroy, the earl of Sunderland had consulted apparently without overt favouritism with all of the most important of the Irish Whigs. As the acknowledged leader of the Whigs during 'the worst of times', Alan Brodrick was accorded a natural prominence but the advice of men such as William Conolly, John Forster, William Whitshed, Oliver St George and Lord Tyrawley was also regularly sought and given. Indeed these men appeared to act as an informal cabinet in Ireland preparing the ground for the forthcoming session of parliament. Brodrick and Conolly, for example, seem to have worked closely together with the former spending considerable time at the future speaker's residence at Castletown.[4] Although Sunderland's decision to resign the viceroyalty threatened to undermine this cooperative approach by introducing an atmosphere of uncertainty as to his successor, it was not until the arrival of Lords Justices Grafton and Galway and their joint chief secretaries, Charles Delafaye and Martin Bladen, that a serious deterioration in relations occurred. It quickly became clear that the new administration favoured Conolly in opposition to Brodrick and the latter's relationship with the Castle administration rapidly deteriorated. A clash between Bladen and St John Brodrick may have been the catalyst for this breakdown in trust but deeper rivalries within the Irish Whig party must have been at the root of the problem. In any case, Brodrick was quickly excluded from the Dublin administration's discussions in relation to the lower house at least. Writing to his brother on 18 December, Brodrick claimed that 'I have not for this fortnight been spoken to about anything in the House of Commons.'[5] According to Brodrick, a 'junto' was managing the Commons and that in order to be taken into the court's confidence men had to pay Bladen 'the most entire submission I ever heard of'. Brodrick claimed that the chief justice (probably John Forster), the speaker and the secretary 'are entirely and solely confided in'.[6] It is unclear whether St John Brodrick's opposition to the court in the Commons was the cause or effect of the lord chancellor's exclusion from the confidence of the Castle administration. However, the former certainly exacerbated the extent of the latter rendering a reconciliation much more difficult to effect. In retaliation for the perceived lack of consultation with and trust in the lord chancellor, St John Brodrick began to attack Martin Bladen and oppose Conolly in the House of Commons which, of course, only served to increase the court's distrust of the Brodricks.[7]

The ramifications of the personal rivalry between Conolly and Brodrick were to be one of the main causes of political instability in Ireland for the next dozen years or so. However, this schism within the Whig party did to some extent restore to the viceroy the power of choosing his own managers. Whereas Conolly was certainly in the ascendant in 1716, Brodrick had replaced him as chief undertaker by the following year after the appointment of the duke of Bolton as viceroy. Bolton showed no hesitation, however, in turning to Conolly as his chief adviser after Sunderland's quarrel with Midleton over the British Peerage Bill. Carteret, moreover, having worked closely with the Brodricks for several years, quickly abandoned the lord chancellor when circumstances changed, like Bolton eventually coming to an accommodation with Conolly. The government, therefore, did not become the prisoner of individual undertakers. Perhaps unconsciously, a policy of 'divide and rule' was very successfully employed during the early Hanoverian period. The possibility of the government employing a rival undertaker was usually enough to keep in check the ambitions of the current favourite. Certainly the letters of Conolly and Midleton very often display a strong sense of insecurity. However, whilst the split within the Whig ranks allowed the viceroy a choice as to whom should be his chief manager or undertaker, it also created the potential for a powerful opposition party led by whichever man felt that he had been discarded or badly-treated. Such a disaffected Whig faction, in alliance with the remnants of the Tory party and periodically supported by the country gentlemen, would be well placed to lead a formidable 'patriotic' opposition to the court. Such a powerful coalition indeed manifested itself immediately after Midleton finally resigned the lord chancellorship in 1725 and engaged in open opposition to the government. Until Midleton's resignation successive viceroys were faced with the delicate problem of keeping both lord chancellor and speaker relatively content in order to prevent one of these powerful figures opting for open and determined opposition. Midleton's resignation in 1725 finally resolved the question as to who should dominate and thereafter the government was able to lend full support to Conolly and his eventual successors Sir Ralph Gore and Marmaduke Coghill. As shall be seen, however, the relationship between the court and their successor, Henry Boyle, appears to have been rather different.

II

The precise nature of the relationship between undertaker and government is, of course, shrouded in secrecy. There were very good reasons for maintaining the essentially private nature of the relationship. It is clear that the term 'undertaker' (like 'party') was a pejorative one to contemporaries. Politicians were extremely careful to avoid giving the impression that they had dared 'undertake' for a parliament's future behaviour. Such an impression would have been deeply insulting to members of parliament who prided themselves upon their independence, however fictitious this may have been in practice. When in January 1714 the duke of Shrewsbury asked the leaders of the Irish Whig party if they thought parliament would 'proceed with temper' should he recall it, he was careful to concede that 'he knew very well that in such assemblies no wise man would undertake for more than himself'. Despite Shrewsbury's admission, several of the Whigs 'could not forbear wresting some of his expressions to have the opportunity of carping at the unreasonableness of putting them upon being undertakers'.[8] The following year, these same gentlemen, now in the service of a Whig government, were equally anxious to avoid the impression that they had undertaken for parliament's future behaviour. Although in regular contact with the viceroy and his chief secretary from the autumn of 1714 to the following summer, offering advice as to what policies should be pursued in Ireland, Alan Brodrick emphasised to Sunderland how important it was to keep such negotiations secret:

> Nothing will be of worse consequence than to have it known that opinions have been asked and given of what a parliament will probably do when they meet, the persons advised with are branded with the name of undertakers ... and I am persuaded your Excellency will not subject us to that character by taking notice, or letting a secretary know you have done us the honour to ask our opinions.[9]

It seems clear that rumours were circulating in Ireland about the existence of undertakers and what they were promising to obtain for the government. A few weeks previously Brodrick had described how some were claiming 'that there are undertakers for a land tax, an augmentation of forces, and indeed for everything: you know how an odious a term that is, and that nothing is so likely to disappoint a reasonable thing as possessing men with an opinion that it is stipulated for'.[10] Men continued to be careful to avoid the impression that they were prepared to undertake for parliament's future behaviour. When Midleton was asked after his resignation as lord chancellor what he thought would be necessary to produce a quiet session in 1725 he stressed that he could only speak for himself for fear of being thought an undertaker. When a few months later Henry

Boyle was asked what would satisfy those country gentlemen who were at that time opposing the court in parliament, he refused to answer at all.[11]

To be accused of agreeing to act as an undertaker could do great harm to a politician's reputation. The Brodricks consistently accused William Conolly of undertaking for particular measures in an attempt to blacken his reputation. Such accusations began as early as 1715 when Lord Brodrick alleged that Conolly had undertaken to achieve more additional taxation than had already been agreed to and to obtain relief for protestant dissenters. In 1719, Midleton claimed that Conolly had lost support in the Commons because it was believed that he had undertaken to have passed a bill granting relief to protestant dissenters.[12] In the Commons, St John Brodrick apparently openly accused Conolly of undertaking for a repeal of the test, a charge vehemently refuted by the speaker.

> Young Mr. Br[odric]k said very warmly he heard there were undertakers to England for this affair, so destructive to the constitution; and plainly pointed at the Sp[eake]r who so much thought himself concerned herein that he rose up and insisted that gentlemen would name who they were for he said they deserved the severest censure; as for his part he was clear of being an undertaker or over with a word about it.[13]

Following the withdrawal of the court's toleration bill and the acceptance of one drawn up by the Commons it was reported that 'there seems to be a general joy and triumph at pinning down this matter as it is, and as if the Court and their undertakers were defeated'.[14] During the Wood's halfpence crisis, Midleton claimed that Conolly had undertaken the defence of the patent. Alleging that the speaker and others had given the ministry the impression that it would be accepted in Ireland, Midleton added that 'they must now see they misjudged the thing and must confess that they have not the power to do every thing which they undertake'.[15] Following the withdrawal of the patent, Midleton again accused Conolly of undertaking for parliament's gratitude and future cooperation. According to Midleton, after Carteret informed the privy council of the patent's withdrawal the speaker promised to draw up an address of thanks to the king 'and I think ventured to undertake for one if not both houses of parliament that the thing would be done'.[16] Midleton is obviously an extremely hostile witness as regards Conolly's actions but, on this occasion at least, his accusation receives some support from a letter to Charles Delafaye from the speaker. After thanking the king, Walpole, Grafton and 'all the ministry' for the withdrawal of the patent, Conolly suggested that this 'extraordinary instance of favour and indulgence from the Crown will I hope put the parliament in such temper that they will demonstrate that they are truly sensible of His Majesty's goodness to them'.[17]

Conolly himself was not above indulging in public mud-slinging in an attempt to damage the reputation of his opponents. After the appointment of the duke of Bolton as viceroy in 1717 it was taken for granted that Brodrick would thereafter act as chief undertaker and rumours began circulating in Ireland that either a land tax or poll tax would be introduced to pay off the national debt. Reporting that the majority of MPs were opposed to the former, Charles Dering informed Lord Percival that 'Mr. Conolly and all those he has an interest over, which is a very considerable number will certainly with all their power oppose it, and he openly declares it's one of his constant toasts at table is to the not having a land tax.'[18] Clearly it was important for aspiring parliamentary managers to maintain the appearance of independence and not to insult their followers or other members by promising or taking for granted their acquiescence in particular measures. Moreover, the insinuation that one's rivals were making such promises could prove to be extremely useful. A number of historians have emphasised the importance of the sense of personal honour among the Anglican élite in the early Hanoverian era.[19] Any suggestion that the votes of members of parliament could be 'delivered on a plate', so to speak, would have aroused widespread righteous indignation among the followers and dependants of the main parliamentary power brokers. The independence of MPs may often have been in practice a fiction, but it was a fiction which had to be maintained in public at least. Dependence, it is clear, was a very private affair.

The portrayal of Conolly as a 'sycophant' who was prepared to follow whatever orders were issued by the government is a recurrent theme in the correspondence of Midleton. The latter consistently portrayed himself as a loyal servant of the crown but one who was not prepared to jeopardise the well being of his country by blindly following the orders of the ministry. His opposition to the peerage bill, the establishment of a national bank, a variety of religious legislation, and Wood's patent tend to lend credence to Midleton's overtly self-serving protestations. Once again forced to accept Conolly's preeminence during the viceroyalty of Grafton, Midleton argued that 'it is plain whom the Castle supports, and always will; viz. those who will go into all their measures without reserve'.[20] Three months later, the lord chancellor rationalised his political eclipse as follows:

> If there must be either a bank or a patent for halfpence or some such contrivance carried on every session I am fated to be always opposite to the government here and shall be content to be out of the strife. But I hope the Kingdom hath shown it will not easily allow such things [to] be imposed upon them; and that we are not so far under the direction of any Lord Lieutenant, assisted with his Conollys and other sycophants to persuade us to swallow our own destruction.[21]

Midleton repeatedly adopts this stance of moral superiority in explaining his difficulties with those in power and many of his comments, particularly those about Conolly, need to be treated with extreme caution. Although Midleton's description of Conolly as a 'flattering sycophant' may well contain an element of truth, it does not do the speaker justice.[22] Conolly triumphed over Midleton because he realised that to be successful as an undertaker a man needed the support of the government as much as it needed his and that to try to hold the court to ransom was a futile exercise. In contrast, the lord chancellor repeatedly made life difficult for the government. Midleton's personality may have been responsible for his failure to remain on good terms with the government. In September 1714, Sir Richard Cox noted the extent to which Brodrick was in favour with the government at that time but prophetically added that he was 'sure it can't hold'.[23] Midleton himself admitted that 'I am one of those people whose fate it will never be to stand favourable in the opinion of those who surround and besiege great men and always have their ear.'[24] A few days before his resignation in 1725 Midleton claimed that he had been forced from office because 'I have not been able to bring myself to a slavish subserviency to the sentiments of some ministers (the rock I have split upon)'.[25]

In contrast to Midleton, Conolly appeared able to remain on reasonable terms with whoever was in power. Whilst having close connections with the Townshend–Walpole faction, Conolly managed to maintain a good relationship with the earl of Sunderland. This interest with Sunderland protected Conolly's position during the viceroyalty of the duke of Bolton when Midleton tried to have the speaker excluded from the commission of lords justices. When Conolly was appointed as a lord justice in Bolton's absence Midleton complained that he was 'a happy man who by wishing well to and acting for one set of men renders or keeps himself gracious with the other'.[26] Conolly realised, given the power of the court, that it was futile to oppose the government and he was careful during Bolton's first session not to give the ministry any excuse to dismiss him. Expecting to be excluded by the duke of Bolton from the commission of lords justices Conolly declared:

> I am easy when I have this Parliament discharged my duty and that I defy my enemies to tax me in any one instance that I have not gone in (with all my friends) for his Majesty's service and the ease of his administration, though perhaps I had not that treatment that might be expected.[27]

Conolly's reward for refraining from opposition came when Bolton was instructed by London to continue the same lords justices who had served before his arrival.[28] It is important to stress, however, that Conolly's appointment as a lord justice was primarily a result of his good behaviour and not because the ministry feared his power to create opposition in parliament. Midleton's rift with Sunderland over the Peerage Bill gave Conolly the opportunity to resume once more his position as chief undertaker, a position confirmed when his ally, the duke of Grafton, was appointed as viceroy in 1720. Grafton and the speaker had worked closely during the session of 1715-16 and this close relationship was quickly re-established. Indeed, Grafton's viceroyalty perhaps saw Conolly's influence at its height. Grafton was a second-rate politician who was apparently content to leave the bulk of government business to Conolly's direction. The viceroy made public his close relationship to Conolly by spending considerable time at Conolly's residence at Castletown. At the same time, Grafton's viceroyalty saw Midleton's fortunes plunge to a new low and the lord chancellor appears to have expected dismissal at any time. Indeed the ramifications of a failed attempt to have Midleton dismissed provides perhaps the clearest written evidence of a deal between the government and an undertaker in the early Hanoverian era.

After Midleton's refusal to vote for Sunderland's Peerage Bill the Irish lord chancellor found himself with few friends and many enemies in London and following his appointment to the viceroyalty, Grafton attempted to secure Midleton's removal. However, Grafton's candidate for the lord chancellorship, Jeffrey Gilbert, refused to take the post and no alternative candidate could be found before the Irish parliament was due to meet. Under these circumstances even Conolly argued that it would be foolish to remove Midleton. In fact, Conolly had all along advised against the appointment of Gilbert, realising how unpopular such an appointment would be in Ireland because of Gilbert's role in the recent Sherlock–Annesley affair.[29] Grafton, therefore, asked Thomas Brodrick to find out if Midleton would serve as chancellor in the coming session. Midleton responded that he would only agree to remain as lord chancellor if he received 'some mark of his Majesty's Royal favour to wash me from the little imputations of being in his displeasure, disaffected to the government or having acted in opposition to his interest'.[30] He further stipulated that he would only serve as lord chancellor if he was assured that he would be allowed to resign with honour after the parliamentary session and, in addition, be granted a pension. Midleton continued 'But after all this I would not be understood to undertake to do anything but barely not to withdraw; I am to be at liberty to act as I always have for the good of my country as well as the King's service, and to oppose whatever I may think not for both.'[31] Midleton then made it clear that he would agree to remain in office only if 'I shall meet such countenance as a chancellor ought to expect, and not see little people advised with and confided in about matters out of their spheres, and properly within his'.[32] Grafton apparently agreed to these terms and authorised Thomas Brodrick to inform Midleton that he could expect better treatment than he had received of late. Midleton immediately began preparations for the new session, asking Grafton to get the Irish peers in England to either come over to Ireland or send their proxies.[33]

This was a rather unusual bargain between viceroy and undertaker, for each side was convinced of the ill-intentions of the other. Midleton knew that he had been on the point of dismissal, only remained in office because the government could not find a replacement, and that he could expect removal from office at the end of the parliamentary session. However, he agreed to refrain from open opposition in order to continue to enjoy the material benefits of office and the influence which accompanied the post of lord chancellor. Grafton, for his part, was merely making the best of a difficult situation. Unable to remove Midleton, he could only hope to limit the damage which could be done by him.

This episode could be interpreted as an illustration of the power of the undertakers in that, Midleton had openly disobeyed the court, Grafton had decided to remove him but, having failed, then had little choice but to treat with him. On the other hand it must be acknowledged that in this instance Grafton acted with a characteristic lack of foresight and himself created an unnecessarily difficult situation. Given a suitable replacement, Midleton's removal could have been achieved with relatively little trouble so long as Grafton publicly threw his full support behind Conolly. After this inauspicious beginning Grafton's viceroyalty eventually come to its disastrous conclusion during the Wood's halfpence dispute. The progress and aftermath of this episode is worth examining in some detail for it highlights the most important structural features of the relationship between government, viceroy, undertakers and parliament.

III

As is well known, the Wood's halfpence dispute was the result of Irish resentment over the issuing of a patent to William Wood to coin copper halfpence for Ireland.[34] When news of the patent became known in Ireland in 1722 Lord Justice King and the Irish revenue commissioners separately wrote to the ministry warning that the patent would arouse strong opposition in Ireland due to fears that the issuing of such large quantities of copper coins would destroy the Irish economy. The revenue commissioners (who included William Conolly) explicitly warned that government revenues might suffer and that the affair 'may be very prejudicial to His Majesty's affairs in Parliament'.[35] Grafton, however, simply ignored these warnings and consequently faced a united parliamentary opposition when parliament met in September 1723. By this time resentment against the copper halfpence was so strong in Ireland that no one could be persuaded to defend the patent in public and the undertaker system simply ceased to function. The Brodricks (supported by Lord Carteret) exploited the episode to rally opposition to Conolly, Grafton and Walpole, but the opposition of Midleton and his son was not the major problem for the court. Much more serious was Conolly's refusal to undertake the defence of the copper coinage. As Grafton himself put it, even the government's closest friends 'dare not undertake the defence of this patent'.[36] To do so would have exposed them to such a degree of obloquy as to render them politically useless. This highlights the first limitation of the policy of governing by undertaker. In the admittedly exceptional circumstances produced by the Wood's halfpence dispute, parliamentary and public opinion was so strong and so united that to oppose the popular tide in order to defend the government would have amounted to political suicide. As a result Grafton could not find an undertaker for Wood's patent. Despite his long-standing and excellent relationship with Conolly, and despite continuing to support the speaker's recommendations for patronage, when it came to the crunch Conolly refused to jeopardise his political future by defending the copper halfpence.[37] What this demonstrates is the inability of the British government to enforce a policy which aroused virtually unanimous opposition in Ireland. This conclusion, however, was not immediately apparent to the government in London. Walpole and Townshend alternatively put the blame for the crisis on the Brodricks, Carteret, Grafton, and Conolly – anyone, in fact, except themselves. It was to take almost two years for the ministry to accept that the problem lay neither with the viceroy nor his undertakers, but with the policy.

The government's immediate reaction to the crisis was to buy time by agreeing to set up an inquiry into the patent. When the inquiry's recommendation to reduce the quantity of halfpence to be issued proved insufficient to allay the opposition in Ireland, Grafton (described by Walpole as a 'fair weather pilot') was recalled and replaced by Carteret.[38] The absence of a viceroy after Grafton's recall, however, led to a further deterioration in the situation as far as the government was concerned and highlighted another structural weakness in the British government's ability to enforce its policy in Ireland. When the ministry demanded the advice of the Irish privy council about how to end the crisis, the councillors (overwhelmingly Irish-born) simply refused to comply. It was clearly not appreciated in London that to suggest solutions to the problem of the halfpence would be, in effect, to undertake for the behaviour of parliament in the future, something no one dared contemplate in the circumstances of 1724. To make matters worse, the Irish lords justices (Archbishop King, Conolly, Midleton and Lord Shannon), also all Irish, refused to obey an instruction to direct the Irish revenue commissioners to revoke any order they may have given to their officers to refuse to accept Wood's coinage. In other words, the Irish government was refusing to obey the positive instructions of the king's ministers.[39]

Clearly a flock of chickens had come home to roost by the summer of 1724. The disinterested and sometimes cavalier attitude of successive British administrations towards Ireland since 1714 at least, had resulted in an over-reliance upon the goodwill and cooperation of key figures within the Anglican élite in Ireland to ensure the smooth-running of the Irish political system. When the advice of these figures was ignored over Wood's patent, their goodwill was forfeited, their ability and inclination to implement government policy disappeared, and the political system consequently ceased to function. In response to the refusal of the Irish lords justices and privy council to obey instructions, it was decided to take the unprecedented step of sending Carteret to Ireland almost a year before parliament was due to meet. If the ministry hoped that the presence of the viceroy would restore governmental authority in Ireland they were to be sadly mistaken. Carteret's presence led to the removal of the lords justices but nothing else changed. The privy council continued to oppose the patent and public opinion was as inflamed as ever, further stoked by the publication of the fourth and most powerful of Swift's *Drapier's Letters* on the day of the new viceroy's arrival. The prospects for a satisfactory session of parliament whilst the patent continued in existence were very bleak.[40]

Unlike Grafton, Carteret at least recognised that the crisis over Wood's halfpence made government by undertaker impracticable. From his appointment the new viceroy apparently decided to govern himself without depending upon any single faction in Ireland.[41] There seemed little point in relying on Conolly who had repaid Grafton's support with a refusal to undertake the defence of Wood's halfpence. Moreover, since the speaker was a long-standing confidant of the Walpole–Townshend faction, Carteret could not have placed much faith in Conolly's loyalty. The new viceroy also made it clear to the Brodricks that he would not place himself in their hands which, given their recent cooperation, might have been expected. Midleton's widespread unpopularity at Westminster made him a man with whom it was impolitic to be closely associated.

Carteret's unwillingness to closely identify with any single faction was immediately apparent to contemporaries. The change in Conolly's situation, in particular, was widely noted. Whereas in the past Grafton had spent Christmas in the country with Conolly, Carteret spent his Christmas in Dublin. Indeed, it was reported in May 1725 that Carteret had yet to visit Castletown and that Conolly was 'not so much at the Castle as in former days'.[42] One observer noted at the start of 1725 that 'Mr. Conolly is not as great a favourite at the Castle as in the Duke of Grafton's time. It's observed that Lord Carteret is not particularly great with any, for very few or none are admitted to his Closet as formerly, but wait till he comes to them in the drawing room.'[43]

Carteret, in fact, found himself in an extremely difficult situation in Ireland. Indeed it is hard to imagine a more challenging combination of circumstances with which any viceroy could have been confronted. Presented with the task of defending a patent which aroused unanimous opposition in Ireland, serving a ministry in London which was busily undermining his credit with the king and his authority in Ireland, Carteret had been thrust into a situation in which he could not possibly hope to succeed. His only option was to buy time and hope to avoid sole responsibility for the inevitable surrender to Irish public opinion.

In the meantime, the lord lieutenant attempted to strengthen his own position in Ireland by winning over certain key individuals through the distribution of patronage, by reforming the Irish administration, and by wooing the Tory party. Carteret seems to have hoped that, by these means, he could build up a court party in the Irish parliament thus removing the viceroy's dependence upon undertakers. When parliament reassembled in September 1725 he was to be rapidly and rudely disabused of such a notion.[44]

By the spring of 1725 even the British ministry realised that a surrender of Wood's patent was necessary to restore some semblance of political normality in Ireland. When Primate Boulter and Lord Chancellor West, both recent appointees of the ministry, readily concurred with Carteret's eventual recommendation to this effect, the government had no option but to permit the lord lieutenant to announce the patent's withdrawal at the opening of the new session of parliament.[45] The ministry's surrender should have resulted in a relatively unproblematic parliamentary session but trouble immediately began to brew, initially in the House of Lords, then in the Commons. Following an acrimonious dispute over the wording of the Lords' address of thanks to the king for the revocation of the patent, Carteret was able to restore the government's control in the upper house by a personal intervention with a number of dependent peers.[46] When the opposition gained control of the House of Commons, however, the limitations of Dublin Castle's parliamentary influence became only too obvious.

A disastrous combination of circumstances in the autumn and winter of 1725 threatened to wreck Carteret's viceroyalty. Moreover, the responsibility for the situation largely rested with the lord lieutenant himself. The resignation of Midleton in April 1725 made the opposition of the powerful Brodrick faction inevitable. Carteret's efforts to win the support of the Tory party through the distribution of patronage eventually failed due to a disagreement with Lord Forbes.[47] More crucially, Carteret apparently continued to keep Conolly at arm's length prior to the meeting of parliament. Whilst the speaker continued in office with the official support of the Castle, the personal relationship between the viceroy and Conolly cannot have been an easy one.[48] Conolly's long-standing alliance with Walpole, combined with consistent rumours of Carteret's imminent dismissal, made it virtually impossible for the two men to form a working relationship based upon mutual trust. Carteret felt that he could not rely on the speaker and Conolly was understandably reluctant to gamble his political future on a 'lame duck' administration. To make matters worse, the ministry undermined the viceroy's authority in Ireland by refusing to support his recommendations for the distribution of government patronage.[49]

Having started badly, the parliamentary session threatened to end in disaster when the Commons disputed the government's estimate of the national debt and refused to vote the additional taxation requested by the Castle. Carteret's efforts to reform the Irish administration had unearthed serious irregularities in the Treasury which eventually led to the arrest of the deputy vice-treasurer, John Pratt. The opposition in the Commons (calling themselves the 'Country party') exploited to the full rumours of government corruption and confusion over the size of the debt to persuade the country gentlemen to rally behind the slogan of 'No New Taxes'. It was a relatively easy matter to persuade backbench MPs that the court was trying to trick them into passing additional taxation to replace funds embezzled by government officials and to pay for pensions for foreigners. Consequently, the Commons voted that the national debt was around £80,000 less than the figure claimed by the Castle and that the usual additional duties would be sufficient to service it.[50]

What had gone so wrong for Carteret? Contemporaries suggested a number of reasons for his failure. Although lack of support from London was noted by a number of commentators, Carteret himself came in for criticism even from government supporters. Marmaduke Coghill had no doubt that the viceroy was himself responsible for the failure of the session.[51] Philip Percival believed that much trouble could have been avoided 'had my Lord Lieutenant followed the steps of some former politic governors in taking care before the sessions to have cultivated a good correspondence with the gentlemen of the country, and he was long enough here to have done it'. Percival continued:

> You know a little eating and drinking well timed goes a great way with our country gentlemen, and this has contrary to custom been sparing, and according to the general opinion it proceeded from too great frugality which is no way conducing to popularity, for one bellyfull of good meat and drink is more acceptable to the generality than twenty courteous smiles which people imagine to be put on as occasion serves, and perhaps the next day no more notice is taken of you than if you were never seen before. This I have often heard remarked and some gentlemen of fortune and in the House have told me they had almost resolved to go no more to court since they were so soon forgot.[52]

Percival also mentioned what was perhaps the fundamental cause of Carteret's troubles, namely that he was 'above consulting and seeming to despise the services of others as one capable of doing all himself'. Carteret's refusal to accept advice was also noted by Marmaduke Coghill, the duke of Newcastle and Sir Edward Southwell.[53] Coghill alleged that Carteret 'was often told the ill consequences' of presenting the government's accounts to the Commons as they then stood. As a result, when the viceroy insisted that they be so presented, none of the government's Treasury officials 'took upon them to justify the accounts' when the opposition questioned their accuracy.[54] Primate Boulter also suggested that 'his Majesty's friends have not been so diligent in undeceiving the country gentlemen as might have been expected from them'.[55] Edward Southwell correctly concluded that Carteret's insistence on governing himself meant that none of the government's traditional supporters 'thought themselves particularly bound or engaged to fight the battle against the popular current'.[56]

Carteret's refusal to confide in the government's traditional advisers, there-fore, had two consequences. Firstly, the viceroy continued to pursue a policy which he had been warned would bring disaster. Secondly, when the predicted trouble materialised, the government supporters felt no strong obligation to support him. The ambiguous behaviour of the government's supporters even led to speculation that they had been given secret instructions from London to engineer Carteret's humiliation.[57] It is impossible to verify such rumours but what does seem clear is that Carteret was more than capable of creating diffi-culties for himself. Having let the situation get out of control, the lord lieutenant seems to have turned to Conolly to try to salvage something from the fiasco. Boulter informed Newcastle on 12 October that the management of the Com-mons had been put into the speaker's hands and that he was confident that things would now go smoothly.[58] However, it soon became clear that Carteret had delayed too long for the situation in the Commons continued to deterio-rate. Only during the Christmas recess did Carteret and Conolly begin to re-establish the court's control. Even so, only the prospect of war with Spain led the Commons to vote additional taxes to augment the army.[59]

The Wood's halfpence dispute, therefore, did not lead to the implementation of a policy of government by undertaker. Instead the episode represented a crisis in the viceroy–undertaker partnership and led, for a time at least, to a complete breakdown in that relationship due to an absence of mutual trust. The dispute and its immediate aftermath demonstrated, however, that there was sim-ply no alternative to the 'undertaker system' if the Irish parliament was to function in relative harmony with the Dublin administration. Carteret's efforts to govern alone by creating a court party in the Commons to match that in the Lords, understandable in the circumstances, led only to disaster. Only in the 1760s when a viceroy took the, perhaps unpalatable but essential, decision to reside permanently in Ireland, would the strategy of creating a government party in parliament become feasible and the role of the undertakers be seri-ously diminished.

IV

The Wood's halfpence dispute highlighted the undertakers' role as mediators between government and parliament rather than their traditionally perceived role as power-brokers and parliamentary manipulators. This function of the undertakers as a channel of communication between executive and legislature can also be seen in operation under more 'normal' circumstances than those which prevailed from 1723 to 1725. Prior to Bolton's first session of parliament in 1717, for example, Lord Brodrick advised that the establishment should be decreased and that 'care ought to be taken lest his Grace and the King's servants and friends here be laid under insuperable difficulties by means of the dissenters panting after what cannot I think be obtained here'.[60] When Bolton arrived in Ireland before the session of 1719 hoping to obtain a total repeal of the sacramental test, both Conolly and Midleton told him that this would be impossible. The viceroy accepted Conolly's advice that the government should leave it to parliament 'to frame such heads of a bill as they shall think reasonable for that purpose, for it is impossible to know how far gentlemen will go'.[61]

Communicating parliamentary opinion in this way could have its disadvantages. Midleton certainly believed that he derived no benefit from advising the earl of Sunderland that a repeal of the test would be impossible to achieve:

> I know that my Lord S[underland] thought I did not do all in my power about the sacramental test, for in effect he was of opinion I was cool in the matter when I gave him and the other ministers my advice that it would be an impracticable thing to aim at a total repeal of it ...[62]

The lord chancellor undoubtedly had been correct to offer such advice but Sunderland obviously suspected that he was simply being obstructive. Ministers sometimes forgot that undertakers had to deal not only with the government but also with their own followers in parliament. It seems that some ministers simply did not believe that members of parliament would refuse to follow the lead of undertakers. Sunderland clearly felt this way over the test and Walpole and Townshend were equally suspicious about Conolly's refusal to support Wood's patent. For historians also it is sometimes difficult to decide whether undertakers were genuinely communicating the mood of parliament or whether they were raising difficulties which did not in fact exist. Conolly's claim in 1727 that the House of Commons would be 'disobliged' if his candidate for the vacant archbishopric of Cashel was not successful does appear disingenuous.[63] However, regarding religious legislation and any 'patriot' issues the warnings of undertakers were probably more genuine. The advice of the undertakers in May 1716, for example, to stop the payment of certain pensions which had been objected to by the Commons and to delay placing some new pensions on the establishment was probably sensible. They also felt obliged to warn the government that they would be unable to prevent the passing of a motion calling for a reduction in the establishment 'because the opposing such a motion would destroy their credit with the country, and consequently their power of serving the King in another sessions'.[64]

The most difficult aspect of the viceroy-undertaker relationship about which to be precise is the question of who was ultimately in charge. Although the balance of power seems to have varied with changing circumstances, in general the viceroy appears to have been able to retain ultimate power. Carteret, for example, appears to have become the dominant factor in the coalition which directed the government of Ireland after 1727, taking a leading role in parliamentary management and the distribution of patronage.[65] However, the ultimate authority of the lord lieutenant can be seen in operation even during the viceroyalty of Grafton, perhaps the weakest and least able of the early Hanoverian lords lieutenant. In 1720, Conolly objected to Grafton's scheme to replace Midleton with Jeffrey Gilbert and to appoint Sir Richard Levinge as chief justice of the Common Pleas. Conolly argued that Gilbert's appointment would 'give universal dislike and dissatisfaction ... after what passed in the House of Lords here. As to Sir R. Levinge's being Lord Chief Justice of the Common Pleas, that will not be agreeable in this country.'[66] Conolly did not hesitate to raise the spectre of parliamentary opposition to these appointments, warning 'I dread the consequences of it to his Majesty's affairs and the ease of your Grace's administration'. To ensure that the viceroy understood the gravity of the situation, the speaker added 'it will not be in the power of your Grace's friends to answer your expectation'.[67] Conolly's stance was perfectly clear. If Grafton insisted upon these appointments there would be trouble in parliament which Conolly and his friends would not be able (nor perhaps willing) to prevent. Grafton, however, ignored Conolly's implicit threat to withdraw his support and went ahead with Levinge's appointment, although Gilbert himself turned down the lord chancellorship. When the letter arrived in Dublin appointing Levinge to his post, Conolly is reported to have said that 'he never signed anything with a worse will'.[68] Such an episode demonstrates the limited ability of even the most dominant of undertakers to influence a viceroy. The eventual fate of Midleton, moreover, indicates that, in the long run, even the most powerful of political magnates in Ireland were in no position to dictate terms to the government.

The relationship between the government and the undertakers was neither a stable nor a constant one. Each viceroy made his own arrangements with the individual parliamentary managers and operated in a different fashion. However, some consistent strategies are apparent. Although a lord lieutenant normally favoured a particular undertaker it was important, in public at least, to try to avoid giving offence to the others. This was particularly important when both Conolly and Midleton were members of the administration for the court needed the cooperation of both men to ensure a smooth-running session of parliament. Some viceroys were better at maintaining this appearance of impartiality than others but most tried to avoid alienating the leaders of parliamentary factions unnecessarily. After Grafton's return to Ireland in August 1723, Midleton informed his brother that 'We are at the Castle just as formerly, Mr. C[onolly] entirely confided in and caressed, not but that care is taken to appear upon every public occasion as civil as possible elsewhere; but it is all from the tooth outward.'[69] When the duke of Dorset first arrived in Ireland in 1731 it was noted that he 'appears very steady, and not near so loquacious as Lord Carteret nor so intriguing; but seems to leave people to themselves' and that he 'speaks very little to anybody, so that he doth not give offence by distinguishing persons'.[70] Dorset, obviously playing his cards close to his chest in 1731, faced a much more difficult and sensitive situation when he returned to Dublin in 1733 for, following the death of Sir Ralph Gore earlier in the year, the government had eventually decided to support Henry Boyle as his successor. At the same time, however, the viceroy tried not to alienate those who had followed Gore and Marmaduke Coghill until Boyle had time to consolidate himself in power. This was not an easy task for parliamentarians had a high opinion of themselves and were prone to take offence over what, on the surface, might appear to have been relatively minor issues. A good example of this can be seen from a misunderstanding which occurred prior to the opening of the session of 1733 and resulted in wounded pride and ill-feeling. On the eve of the opening of the parliamentary session, Dorset had gathered at the Castle the leading Irish parliamentarians to frame the customary parliamentary address to the king. The day before the viceroy had apparently indicated that Arthur Hill should move the address in the Commons and that this had been intimated to the latter. However, probably on the prompting of Henry Boyle, Dorset then changed his mind for at the meeting at the Castle it was decided that the member for Boyle, Richard Wingfield, should move the address. Marmaduke Coghill claimed that, although Hill did not resent this disappointment, 'he was desired to second Wingfield, which he very justly thought a great indignity, but this he could not refuse, got up and made a low bow, and the next day, said no more but that he seconded the motion'.[71] Clearly Hill felt that salt was being rubbed into a wound and that his honour was being slighted. Such apparently minor matters were obviously capable of causing great offence to men who took their public reputations extremely seriously.

Despite an official appearance of impartiality, it is clear that an hierarchy always existed among the government's advisers. An unofficial cabinet consisting of the speaker, lord chancellor, the three chief judges, the attorney and solicitor generals, the deputy vice-Treasurer, and chancellor of Exchequer was normally formed to assist the viceroy and chief secretary. However, a more exclusive inner circle of trusted advisers almost always existed to make the key policy decisions. Conolly was clearly excluded from the meetings where important decisions were made during Bolton's first session of parliament when the lord chancellor was the foremost adviser to the viceroy.[72] During Grafton's viceroyalty, on the other hand, the situation was reversed. Midleton alleged that prior to the session of 1723 he had dined with the duke of Grafton and Conolly, and that after he left the viceroy, the speaker and the chief secretary went into an upper room and 'were together for two hours and then settled the measures to be taken in the public affairs'.[73] A few months later the lord chancellor informed his brother that the 'cabinet' was meeting at Castletown. In addition to Conolly, this consisted of Grafton, chief secretary Hopkins, Lord Fitzwilliams, Bishop Hort, and the postmaster general, Isaac Manley.[74] During the first months of Carteret's viceroyalty, on the other hand, the lord lieutenant's 'cabinet' apparently consisted only of the government's legal officers, the only people whom he felt he could trust.[75]

The correspondence of successive chief secretaries makes clear the difficult job facing the Castle administration in managing parliament. Although like the viceroy an absentee, the chief secretary had a key role to play in the management of the session. Always sitting as an Irish MP, the viceroy's secretary was effectively the personal representative of the Castle administration in the House of Commons. A chief secretary, however, had to behave with considerable discretion in the house as MPs were always liable to object to any sign of undue pressure by the court over the proceedings of the lower house. Lord Brodrick repeatedly complained during the session of 1715-16 that the secretaries to the lords justices were exceeding their proper jurisdiction. Indeed St John Brodrick openly clashed with Martin Bladen in the Commons. Responding to an attack by Bladen the previous day, the lord chancellor's son suggested that it was inappropriate for a man who had no property in Ireland to be taking such a leading part in its affairs.[76] The behaviour of Walter Cary also seems to have been less than helpful on at least one occasion. Towards the end of a debate in the Commons over whether the details of payments on the military contingency fund (a favourite target of the 'patriots') should be laid before the house, Cary 'made a speech which was in a sort of bullying manner and accusing the house of disrespect to my Lord Lieutenant'. Marmaduke Coghill alleged that Cary's intervention 'exasperated to so great a degree' that the house, which before Cary's speech appeared to be prepared to let the matter drop, proceeded to vote that the details of this fund should be made available in future.[77]

Some indication of the relentless nature of the chief secretary's task can be gleaned from the respective comments of Charles Delafaye, Edward Webster and Walter Cary. In 1731, Delafaye was on the receiving end of Cary's complaints even before parliament had met:

> We are in this honeymoon of government (as you properly call it) so full of ceremony, noise and feasting, that I can scarce get a minute to myself. My back is almost broke with bowing, and my belly with eating, and what will become of my head, I can't tell. But what is most vexatious, amongst all this crowd, there are but few members of parliament come,

as yet, to Dublin, so that we can do, but little business in our cups.[78]

In 1719 Webster had complained to Delafaye that 'I don't find that the recess gives me any leisure but that my attendance on business is the same as at other times, it is very rare that I get to bed before two in the morning, nor do I see any likelihood of its being otherwise while I am here'.[79] If the prologue to the session and the recess were busy it was inevitable that the pressure of work should be even greater when parliament was in session. Delafaye himself had complained of the tribulations of the session when he acted as joint-chief secretary in 1715-16.

> Upon the whole we have made a good sessions of it but it was not with-
> out much application and industry, we were forced to meet every night
> with the chief of our friends to provide against the next day's battle, the
> rest of the day was spent either in the house or in running about to solicit
> the members and keep our forces together whom Brodrick with as much
> diligence endeavoured to debauch ...[80]

Viceroys, secretaries and undertakers, already facing an uphill task in piloting through the Irish parliament the government's money bills, could do without additional complications which made their task even more difficult. However, the job of these men was always likely to be made even more irksome by the regular appearance of apples of discord, normally of British origin.

Following the death of William Conolly at the beginning of the session of 1729, the court initially found it difficult to re-establish its authority in the Commons. Uncertainty caused by the speaker's death made it inevitable that the ensuing session would be a problematic one. Fortunately for the court the opposition appears to have been as confused as its own supporters and the government's business was eventually approved 'after a good deal of wrangling'.[81] However, the alteration of a money bill by the British privy council threatened to undo all of the painstaking work previously carried out by the Castle administration. Carteret explained to Townshend that the main alteration in the bill made in London had already been proposed and rejected in the Commons before its transmission to England. The viceroy claimed that he had personally spoken to 'near fifty of the principal members' to try to obtain their acquiescence to the alteration but without much success.[82] Although the altered money bill was eventually approved, Marmaduke Coghill claimed that it would undoubtedly have been rejected but for the fact that Carteret kept it from the Commons for several days in order to give the court and its supporters time to prepare a defence.[83] The frustration of the Dublin administration over the trouble which resulted from the alteration can be gauged from the chief secretary's forthright comments on the subject which are worth quoting at length:

The alterations in our Money Bill will give us a great deal of trouble here. It is a difficulty laid upon the King's servants, who I can assure you had enough before. I am persuaded they will exert themselves to the utmost to carry it through the House, but they seem uncertain what the success may be. Whatever his Majesty is pleased to do in Council is beyond dispute perfectly right; the ministers have their reasons for advising it; and it is our duty to support it here; nor can there be the least doubt but that the bill is much more accurately drawn than it was when it went from hence: but the bill as it went would have raised the money, for the subscription was full. I don't apprehend it will do more now. If some concessions have been made, which it were to be wished, could have been avoided, that must be attributed to the true cause, which is a want of power in the government and however well satisfied my Lord Lieutenant may be under that want those who expect to be obliged by him will not be so. I must tell you freely 'tis a very indifferent situation to serve under a government that has neither power nor party to support it, but is left at the mercy of a parliament.[84]

Clutterbuck's complaint about the weakness of the court and the unreliability of its parliamentary supporters is by no means unique. Three years later, at the end of his first (relatively unproblematic) session of parliament, the clearly disenchanted chief secretary to the duke of Dorset described the Castle's parliamentary forces as 'a divided, undisciplined militia, without leaders, and without pay'.[85] Although hard-pressed chief secretaries, weary from the seemingly endless task of courting members of parliament (often well into the early hours) may understandably have been liable to overstate the difficulties of supervising a session of parliament in Ireland, they were certainly more open and blunt about such matters than their masters in their correspondence with their counterparts in London. The underlying themes of such complaints, the lack of a court party in the Commons and the unreliability of those who were supposed to be the servants of the administration, are clear and consistent.

In addition to thoughtless, and perhaps needless, interventions by the British privy council, the management of the Irish parliament was regularly complicated by the introduction of divisive religious issues. This problem was normally of the government's own making, with successive Whig administrations in Britain making repeated attempts to pass legislation favourable to protestant dissenters in Ireland, in spite of repeated advice to the contrary. The introduction of religious issues not only had the effect of rallying the Tory party, it also divided the Irish Whigs, making it difficult for people who differed in their religious views to cooperate in other matters. The early Hanoverian period witnessed two major attempts to repeal the sacramental test, in 1719 and 1733. In spite of Midleton's advice to Sunderland and Bolton that such a project stood no chance of success, the latter arrived in Ireland in 1719 with instructions to try to achieve a repeal of the test. Bolton sensibly soon abandoned all thoughts of repeal and sought to obtain a toleration instead. However, even a toleration bill had the effect of disrupting the parliamentary session, as the lord lieutenant explained to James Craggs: 'It is not to be imagined what a confusion and heat people are in about the ease to be given to the dissenters. It has made great caballing with people that were of different sentiments before, but agree in this, in giving no ease to the dissenters but purely a toleration.'[86] A week previously, Bolton had explained that if the government was to attempt to achieve more than a bare toleration for the dissenters 'it would very probably produce such heats as would obstruct the more necessary business of the session, and unite such a number of Whigs with the Tories as to give great perplexity'.[87] The government resurrected the repeal issue again in 1733, this time with even less success. A repeal of the test had been considered during Dorset's first session of parliament in 1731-2 but the idea had been dropped at that time on the advice of Primate Boulter, Lord Chancellor Wyndham and the speaker of the Commons, Sir Ralph Gore, who were 'morally certain it could not succeed in the House of Commons'.[88] However, even rumours of an attempted repeal had encouraged more members to attend parliament than was usual after the recess which made necessary a 'strict attendance' on the part of the government's servants.[89] Knowing that the government would not introduce a bill to repeal the test before the money bills had been passed, members of parliament naturally suspected that an attempt would be made to rush such a bill through a thin house towards the end of the session. In 1719 similar suspicions had resulted in over 200 MPs attending the House of Commons after the recess.[90]

When Dorset returned to Dublin for the 1733 session he once more had instructions to attempt a repeal of the test. It is unlikely that either he or his secretary viewed this project with any enthusiasm. The session was already likely to be a difficult one since a new manager would have to direct the court's business due to the death of Sir Ralph Gore earlier in the year. Shortly after the beginning of the session, Cary confided to Delafaye that it was likely to be a troublesome one 'from a concurrence of many causes, some of which, and not the least, come from your side of the water'.[91] Marmaduke Coghill's account of a meeting with Dorset just before the start of the session suggests that the viceroy's commitment to the cause of the dissenters was lukewarm at best. Having spoken to Coghill 'very freely ... on that subject', Dorset apparently accepted without undue concern Coghill's admission that he could not support a repeal.[92]

Widespread rumours that a bill would be introduced to repeal the test made the early weeks of the session more problematic than it might otherwise have been. Cary told Delafaye that:

The apprehension of an attempt to repeal the test made our Committee of Accounts very dilatory, and uneasy, and keeps the House of Commons perpetually full, which, you know, is an ugly circumstance here. They endeavoured by all ways to delay the money bills, being well assured we should undertake nothing with regard to the dissenters till they were gone and passed.[93]

In order to prevent the introduction of a bill to repeal the test after the recess (and presumably to allow gentlemen to return to the country), the Commons voted that they would not accept any bill after 14 December which sought to amend any act to prevent the further growth of popery. On the morning of 13 December Boulter, Wyndham, Boyle, Archbishop Hoadly of Dublin, Lord Chief Justice Rogerson, General Wynne, Lords Allen and Duncannon, 'and about eight of the dissenters' met at the Castle. All of the government's advisers believed repeal to be impossible and Dorset flatly refused to contemplate the request of the dissenters to 'use his influence' with members of parliament.[94] The following day the lord lieutenant wrote to London explaining why he had dropped any thoughts of attempting to repeal the test. Dorset assured the duke of Newcastle that repeal of the test had been 'one of the great points in my view' and claimed that he had 'neglected no proper occasion, ever since my arrival here, to engage people of influence in both Houses in favour of that design'. In contrast to the account given by Coghill of the viceroy's meeting with the dissenters on 13 December, Dorset then explained that, although all of his advisers believed that repeal stood no chance, he had assured the dissenters that if they 'thought fit to persist, I would support them to the utmost of my power, both in my public and private capacity'.[95] It would appear that, while acting with considerable discretion in Ireland over the question of the test, Dorset was naturally keen to convince his masters in London that he had done all in his power on behalf of the dissenters.

As well as controversy over religious legislation, economic or 'patriotic' issues had the effect of disrupting stable parliamentary management. The raising of issues relating to the pensions and salaries of absentees, the national debt, British restrictions on Irish trade, or the rights of the Irish parliament relative to Westminster were always likely to weaken the Castle's strength in the Commons. Indeed, if the issue was sufficiently serious or 'popular' (Wood's halfpence, for example), the government's supporters in the Commons might have no choice but to 'swim with the tide' and join with the majority. To do otherwise would shatter their credibility and expose them as 'dupes' of the court.[96]

V

Essential to the effective management of parliament was an open and clear relationship between the Castle and its undertakers. MPs needed to know who was in the court's confidence and consequently whom they should follow in order to serve the government. One of the factors which made the session of 1725-26 so troublesome was the confusion caused due to uncertainty as to who was supposed to be directing government business. Carteret faced a similar situation in 1729 following the death of William Conolly at the start of the session. Although Conolly was succeeded as speaker by Sir Ralph Gore and as a revenue commissioner by Marmaduke Coghill it inevitably took time for members of parliament to get used to the new situation. As Carteret's chief secretary explained to Charles Delafaye, 'the people who had long served under him [Conolly], not caring immediately to list under a new leader'.[97] Gore and Coghill were to act as the main parliamentary managers until the former's death on 23 February 1733. Although Gore took over Conolly's roles as speaker of the Commons and lord justice and was, therefore, the senior partner, Coghill inherited the crucial post of revenue commissioner giving him a share in the vast patronage of the customs and excise. Together these men effectively performed the role which Conolly had undertaken alone. The session of parliament which followed Gore's death was also characterised by instability in that members of parliament were once again uncertain as to who was directing the court's business.

The nature of the negotiations which eventually led to Dublin Castle supporting Henry Boyle as successor to Gore are obscure, the best information on the developments between February and October 1733 coming from a single, generally hostile, source. However, within a fortnight of Gore's death, the primate and lord chancellor had written to Dorset recommending that Boyle be supported by the government as the new speaker. Informing Newcastle of their view, Boulter commented that:

> Mr. Henry Boyle (of a younger branch of the Burlington family) had before written to us to recommend him to my Lord Lieutenant for his favour; and has, we find by the letters come in by yesterday's post, begun to sollicit the interest of his friends for obtaining the chair. He has of himself a very good interest among the members; and we think, in our present circumstances, it will be most for His Majesty's service, and for the good of the common interest of England and Ireland, that he should be supported by the government in this affair.[98]

There is no hint here of why Boulter favoured Boyle over other possible candidates. The primate merely added that the government should take this opportunity to end the practice of routinely appointing the speaker of the Commons as a lord justice since there was a danger that this would soon assume the status of a precedent.

Boyle, however, was not the only candidate for the speaker's chair. The day before Gore's death Marmaduke Coghill ruled himself out as the speaker's successor believing that it was essential that there should be 'one of this country in the government in whom there may be a proper confidence placed by the country gentlemen'.[99] Coghill presumably felt that he was unable to fill such a role. Coghill named Thomas Carter (master of the rolls), Henry Singleton (prime serjeant), Henry Boyle, Eaton Stannard (member for Midleton and a noted 'patriot'), and Thomas Trotter (master in Chancery) as the most likely candidates to succeed to the chair. Two weeks later Coghill added Agmondisham Vesey to the list of candidates but believed that only Carter, Boyle and Singleton were serious contenders. He felt that should there be a competition for the chair it would be between Singleton and Boyle and that the government would have the power to decide the winner. Significantly, however, he added that, whereas Singleton would defer to the government's decision should Boyle receive official support, Boyle would probably oppose if the court backed the prime serjeant. Coghill's recommendation was that the government should back Singleton as speaker, that he himself should be given Gore's post as chancellor of the Exchequer, and that Boyle replace him as revenue commissioner.[100]

It soon became clear, however, that Singleton stood little chance of becoming speaker. On 5 April Coghill referred to objections being raised against Singleton in London:

> the objections made against Singleton I believe comes from hence, for I well know the primate and the archbishop of Cashel are as great enemies as Christianity will permit, and Singleton being a friend of Cashel's, having been contemporary with him in the college, it is presumed by the one great man, this may be an addition of power to the other.[101]

This connection with Theophilus Bolton would certainly explain why Boulter had been so keen to support Boyle's candidature. Bolton had been a thorn in Boulter's side ever since the latter's arrival in Ireland, having been a close associate of Archbishop King of Dublin, William Conolly and Lord Carteret. Boulter regarded Bolton as successor to William King as the leader of the 'Irish interest' in the House of Lords and Church of Ireland and would certainly have regarded the prospect of a friend of the archbishop of Cashel occupying the speaker's chair with horror.[102] Singleton was also vulnerable to attack on the grounds that he was a former Tory and this issue seems to have raised its head during the spring and summer of 1733. Despite Coghill's wish that 'these names were pretty well over, and forgotten amongst us' the raising of previous party affiliations cannot have helped Singleton's cause.[103] An association with Archbishop Bolton, Archbishop King and Carteret firmly identified the prime serjeant with a 'church' interest, particularly among members of the 'Munster squadron', long-standing opponents of the Tory and 'church' party. The final obstacle to Singleton's chances of succeeding Gore was the apparent perception that he was 'proud and haughty'.[104] The third serious challenger for the chair named by Coghill, Thomas Carter, appears to have accepted himself that he had little chance of success. Boulter had been an enemy of Carter's since 1725 and would, in all probability, have raised strong objections to his candidature. Just as important perhaps was Coghill's belief that, although Singleton would accept Boyle's succession to the chair, he would oppose any attempt by Carter to succeed Gore.[105] Under the circumstances, Carter seems to have settled for seeking to have Boyle elected in order to prevent Singleton's success.

Within a month of Gore's death, therefore, the situation as to who should be speaker seemed to have clarified itself to a considerable extent and to the advantage of Henry Boyle. Possessing the crucial recommendation of Boulter (who opposed his two main rivals) was a major advantage for Boyle. Carter, moreover, was actively campaigning on Boyle's behalf and the government had probably been informed that Singleton would accept Boyle's election as speaker, although no doubt with some reluctance. Under the circumstances, a decision by Dorset to support anyone but Boyle would have been difficult to comprehend.

What is more difficult to understand is Dorset's reluctance to finally declare for Boyle. What private negotiations were being carried out it is impossible to say. Rumours that Carter, Cary, Boulter, and Luke Gardiner were directing affairs may have contained more than an element of truth but in public there was a long period of silence from London on the question of Gore's successor.[106] Boyle's response to the prevarication of the court was to arrive in Dublin in April 1733 and openly declare that he would stand for the chair with or without the government's support. Coghill speculated that Boyle had either 'made his interest pretty certain, or hopes to make the Government think so'.[107] Boyle may have been already confident of the government's support or he may have been trying to force the issue. What is clear is that the court's failure to openly declare for any candidate gave Boyle the opportunity to secure the votes of many men who would normally follow the direction of the court. Moreover, once such promises of support were given, they would not be lightly withdrawn, this being a matter of 'honour'. By 19 April Coghill believed that the situation had developed so far in Boyle's favour that the government would have great difficulty in opposing him if they now chose to do so. On 21 June Coghill wrote that he believed Carter had persuaded Dorset that Boyle's 'interest is so great that it can't be withstood' and to support the latter's election as speaker.[108] The tone of Coghill's letters after this point indicates his growing

estrangement from the government and suggests that a decision to back Boyle
had been all but made by June 1733. Perceiving the direction in which the wind
was now about to blow, Coghill's main concern thereafter was to obtain the
post of chancellor of Exchequer in exchange for his post as commissioner of
the revenue.

Throughout the summer the perception that the court would support Boyle
seems to have become more widespread and as a consequence the latter's position was further strengthened.[109] However, even after his arrival in Ireland Dorset
continued to delay naming Boyle as the court's candidate for the chair. Eventually the viceroy summoned Singleton to the Castle (probably on 20 September)
to inform him that Boyle would receive the court's backing. Singleton accepted
Dorset's decision but could not help remarking that he believed that he himself
could have been elected as speaker given the support of the government 'though
His Grace was made to believe otherwise by those who favoured Mr. Boyle'.[110]
Dorset had to be careful at this point not to alienate seriously the former confidants of the court so close to the opening of parliament. Having informed
Marmaduke Coghill that Boyle would be the court's candidate for speaker,
Dorset went on to discuss the forthcoming session. When Coghill indicated his
desire to be appointed as chancellor of the Exchequer, Dorset responded that:

> the place I had was better, and I had a power, that Mr Conolly had, of
> obliging several persons, by which I might have an influence that might
> be serviceable to the government. I told him I was growing old and in-
> firm, and an employment of ease, though of less profit and power, would
> be more agreeable, and the person he put in my place might do what he
> thought I might in that station, upon which he said nothing would soon
> be done in that affair, and he would consider of it, and this coldly enough,
> so that I judge that place is determined for Mr Boyle.[111]

This was clearly an awkward meeting for both men. One of the government's
longest serving and most loyal of supporters realised that a new set of men
were about to take charge of the management of the court's business. Dorset
seems to have felt aggrieved that Coghill was seeking to take a back seat in
public affairs and may have had doubts about his loyalty to the court in the
coming session. By delaying a decision over the chancellorship of the exchequer, the viceroy probably hoped to ensure Coghill's good behaviour in
parliament, although the latter seems to have drawn the (correct) conclusion
that the post was promised to Boyle.

Boyle's election as speaker may not have clarified the parliamentary situation entirely for uncertainty seems to have remained as to the nature of the
relationship between the court and the new speaker. Writing on 20 October
Coghill claimed that:

> I can't find whether the government and he are upon any certain foot of confidence, nor do I really know where they have communicated their intentions, if any they have more than are in the speech, nor can I find to whom they have committed the conduct of the session, as has been usual in other governments. People generally imagine the Master of the Rolls is the chief advisor, whether he is or no I can't form any certain judgement.[112]

Significantly, Coghill added that 'I think all my Lord Carteret's and Mr Conolly's friends are treated with great coldness and indifference'.[113] The following month Coghill claimed that the court's affairs in parliament were faring badly, that people still did not know who was in the viceroy's confidence, and that 'the servants of the crown make but a sorry figure in all the divisions for they are almost left to stand by themselves'.[114] Coghill's version of events cannot be taken entirely at face value but it does appear that Boyle's relationship with the court took some time to settle down.[115] Coghill related an extraordinary incident, which probably took place at the house of Theophilus Clements, that indicates just how fragile was the relationship between Dublin Castle and Boyle at the end of 1733.

> After the company had drank very hard, Mr Cary reproached Mr Boyle that he had not kept his Munster Squadron in better order and more attached to the interest of the court. The speaker told him his friends were men of honour, and would support him on all occasions, he had no obligations to the court for he set up on the foot of the country party, and the court when they found they could not hinder him, they concurred to make him speaker, but whatever the court suffered was by their own mismanagement, having no confidence or intimacy with anybody, and by throwing amongst us a bone of contention about the test, which had raised animosities and divisions not easily to be quieted.[116]

It is impossible to imagine William Conolly uttering such words. Boyle was describing a relationship between the court and his followers which was very different to those which had existed since 1714. The new speaker was emphasising the independence of his followers and the conditional nature of his relationship with the government. He clearly felt under no particular obligation to the court for his election as speaker. According to Boyle, the government had had no alternative but to accept his candidature having delayed naming a candidate of their own until Boyle was too powerful to oppose. If Boyle seriously meant what he said (we should bear in mind, after all, that the company seems to have indulged fairly heavily in drink) then the basis of his relationship with the court was very different from that which had existed between the gov-

ernment and either Conolly, or Gore and Coghill. Boyle was explicitly portray-
ing himself as leader of the 'country party', something which previous
undertakers (with the possible exception of Midleton) would never have done.
The implication of Boyle's stance was that his position depended upon his
personal following among the 'Munster squadron' and the country gentlemen
rather than upon his relationship with the government. The implications of
Boyle's conditional relationship with the court were to become only too obvious in the 1750s.[117]

VI

The relationship between viceroy and undertaker was one of mutual dependence. Neither could prosper without the aid of the other. However, the lord
lieutenant always remained the more powerful partner in this coalition. While
there was only one viceroy, there were always at least two potential undertakers. On the other hand, without the support of an undertaker with enough interest
to manage parliament a viceroy could not hope to govern effectively. The relationship between viceroy and undertakers was, therefore, a coalition between
men whose interests were fundamentally the same. The viceroy wanted a quiet
session and enough additional revenues to meet the costs of the civil and military establishments. The undertakers for their part were prepared to frame and
pilot through the Commons the administration's money bills and keep in check
any 'patriot' opposition. In return, they demanded office for themselves and
their colleagues and asked that attention should be paid to their views in the
disposal of Irish patronage. In addition, they hoped that the government would
take their advice in avoiding steps such as increasing the establishment, making unpopular appointments, and sponsoring contentious legislation which would
only succeed in making their job more difficult. In theory, this was a mutually
beneficial arrangement which should have worked well. However, an examination of the parliamentary history of the early Hanoverian period shows only too
clearly the fragility of the government-undertaker relationship. Even when a
viceroy and his parliamentary managers understood each other and worked
well together, the relationship was always likely to come under strain from
interference by Westminster. The appointment of John Evans to the bishopric
of Meath; the attempts to repeal the sacramental test in 1719 and 1733; the
passage of the Declaratory Act of 1720; the granting of seven large pensions to
absentees in 1722-23; the alteration of a money bill by the British privy council
in 1729; and, most famously, the granting of a patent to William Wood to coin
halfpence, all of these 'external' factors had a significant impact upon the management of the Irish parliament. Although a viceroy and an undertaker could
come to a mutually beneficial arrangement based on the distribution of patron-

age in return for parliamentary support, such an agreement was constantly threatened by events beyond the control of both parties. There was no shortage of parliamentary factions in Ireland ready and willing to disrupt the business of the session. More importantly, insensitive behaviour on the part of the British crown, ministry, and parliament repeatedly undermined the efforts of English viceroys and Irish undertakers to establish stable government in Ireland in the early Hanoverian period.

7

The Irish and English Interests

George I's accession to the throne in 1714 had, as has been seen, important consequences for the functioning of Irish parliamentary politics. The most significant of these was the relegation of the Irish Tory party to a relatively weak and ineffectual force and the establishment in Ireland of a 'Whig ascendancy'. The subsequent split which occurred within the Irish Whig party after 1714 has previously been examined. Whereas the schism within the Whig party in the House of Commons resulted in the formation of two rival factions struggling for influence within the government, a different situation soon prevailed in the House of Lords. In the upper house, Whig bishops and lay peers also quickly discovered grounds for conflict, but here the division took a different form. Throughout the reign of George I and for several years afterwards, the politics of the House of Lords was dominated by an increasingly bitter rivalry between what quickly became known as the Irish and English 'interests'. As this terminology suggests, the division was based primarily on national identity. However, other considerations also came into play. For instance, some of the issues which had been to the fore during the Whig-Tory conflict under Queen Anne continued to occupy the minds of members of the upper house. Therefore, the Irish-English dichotomy was often complicated by the Whig-Tory divide. In an assembly in which, relatively speaking, Tories had greater influence than in the Commons, most Tory bishops and peers (Irish and English) who continued to attend after 1715 normally chose to side with the Irish interest against an English interest which was strongly identified with successive Whig administrations at Westminster.[1]

I

A striking feature of the national politics of Ireland in the first half of the eighteenth century was the leading role played by the episcopate of the Church of Ireland. One need think only of figures such as William King, Jonathan Swift, William Nicolson, Hugh Boulter, Edward Synge, and Andrew Stone to realise the importance of the clergy in the politics of the post-revolutionary period. A number of factors explains the prominence of the Anglican episcopate in national politics and particularly in the activity of the House of Lords. In addition to the moral authority enjoyed by bishops in their role as religious leaders of the dominant community and the local influence which their wealth gave them, Anglican bishops also had very considerable formal political powers. The most obvious source of the political power of the episcopate was in the role of the eighteen bishops and four archbishops as life members of the House of Lords. In the early Georgian period, moreover, the bishops were among the most assiduous attenders of the Lords in contrast to the infrequent attendance of most lay peers. Indeed, the 'unimpressive' nature of the resident Irish aristocracy is perhaps the most important reason for the prominence of the episcopate.[2] In an upper house which was sparsely-attended and where men of intelligence, authority, and charisma were thin on the ground, well-educated, experienced and articulate bishops were likely to stand out.

The relative influence of the bishops within the House of Lords varied with each session of parliament. For example, during the 1715-16 session the bishops were outnumbered by lay peers on sixty-three days out of seventy; in the 1717 session they were outnumbered on only thirty-three days out of fifty-four; in the 1719 session the bishops never outnumbered the lay peers; but during the 1725-6 session the bishops were outnumbered less than half of the time.[3] Although the relative power of the episcopal bench varied from session to session it is nevertheless true that the bishops were disproportionately influential in the upper house, simply because at least half of them usually turned up to attend parliamentary sessions whilst the great majority of lay peers for one reason or another stayed away. In May 1730, for example, John Percival claimed that towards the end of that parliamentary session the House of Lords 'were almost all bishops'.[4] This relatively assiduous attendance of the bishops meant that if the episcopal bench was united on any issue it was extremely difficult to defeat. Charles Delafaye commented during the parliamentary session in 1716 that 'the Rt. Rev. Bench when all of a side is too strong for any one side of the temporal Lords'.[5] The fact that after 1714 the episcopal bench was very rarely united on any single issue does not detract from the relatively powerful position held by the bishops within the House of Lords.

As well as their membership of the Lords, some of the more senior figures among the Irish bishops sat on the Irish privy council. The primate, the archbishops of Dublin and of Tuam, and the bishop of Meath were normally members of the council along with several other influential bishops.[6] In addition to its judicial and administrative functions, the Irish privy council had extremely important legislative powers. On this body too, therefore, the bishops could bring their weight to bear, especially if legislation affecting the religious establishment was under discussion. The Church of Ireland was also normally represented within the commission of lords justices which acted as the Irish executive in the absence of the lord lieutenant. Normally the primate of all-Ireland, the archbishop of Armagh, would be appointed as a lord justice along with one or two leading politicians or a general. Between September 1714 and the appointment of Hugh Boulter as primate in November 1724, however, the archbishop of Dublin took the primate's place as the church's representative on the commission. Thomas Lindsay, the primate between 1714 and 1724, had been an active supporter of the Tory governments in Ireland during Queen Anne's reign and had been a lord justice when she died. Due to widespread suspicions about Lindsay's commitment to the Hanoverian succession, the primate was snubbed by successive Whig administrations after 1714. With Boulter's appointment, however, the primate was restored to his customary position as a lord justice.

The bishops also formed the upper house of the convocation of the Church of Ireland which had met regularly during the reign of Queen Anne. After the queen's death, however, convocation was never recalled. It had been mainly used by the Tory lower clergy to attack their bishops and to carry on the party political battle. There were suggestions that it should be recalled in 1715 but Archbishop King refused to 'undertake' for its good behaviour and the government dropped the idea.[7] Primate Lindsay unsuccessfully sought its recall in 1717. When the question of a convocation was once more raised in 1728, both the ministry and Boulter opposed the idea, the latter explaining that he would be in favour of its meeting only if 'they had some useful business to do, and I was thoroughly certain they would confine themselves to that'.[8] The political influence of the Irish bishops was not confined to the House of Lords, privy council, commission of lords justices, and, under Queen Anne, convocation. Some bishops directly or indirectly controlled the return of members to the Irish House of Commons. Four bishops (the archbishop of Armagh and the bishops of Ferns, Ossory and Clogher) had permanent control of parliamentary boroughs in their dioceses. Other bishops, such as Archbishop King at Swords and Trinity College and Archbishop Vesey at Tuam, built up personal electoral interests in particular boroughs. In addition, bishops who came from Irish gentry families may have had some influence in the disposal of their family's electoral influence.[9] It is clear then that the bishops of the Church of Ireland exercised considerable political influence at all levels and that at the national level they were well-represented within the executive and the legislature. Given the actual and potential political power of the bishops, combined with the fact that once they had been appointed they could not be removed, it is understandable that any government would only appoint to the episcopal bench men whom they considered to be politically reliable. In this sense all bishops were political appointees and they were expected to behave as such.

It might appear from the above discussion that the episcopate of the Church of Ireland was in an extremely powerful position from which to influence Irish politics in this period. It is indeed true that bishops could be very powerful and influential men but their political influence should not be exaggerated. Although virtually all of the members of the Irish parliament, Irish executive, and the

British government were members of the established church this did not mean that the bishops could get their own way all of the time, even on religious issues. Indeed in the early Hanoverian era there was a strong distrust of the church leadership among many members of the Irish House of Commons. Moreover the British government rarely saw eye to eye with the church leadership over the sensitive question of relief for protestant dissenters. Finally, the bishops in Ireland very rarely agreed among themselves on any single issue.[10] All of these factors combined to prevent the Irish episcopate as a body from becoming a dominant force in Irish politics, however influential individual prelates might become.[11]

II

The Hanoverian Accession was to have long-lasting and important implications for the political role of the Church of Ireland. The Anglican clergy had been prominent in their support of the Tories during the party conflict of the reign of Queen Anne. On the latter's death, furthermore, the majority of Irish bishops were Tories. The archbishop of Dublin was in no doubt about the political allegiance of most of the Irish bishops, telling secretary of state, James Stanhope, in November 1715 that 'most of the bishops of this kingdom were very zealous for the late ministry'.[12] King feared that the Whig gentry, 'much irritated and soured' by the behaviour of the clergy, would take revenge on the church for ecclesiastical interference in the political arena. As he himself admitted, 'most of the clergy under the late management set themselves against the gentlemen, traversed them in their elections, endeavoured to turn them out of their boroughs, and in their convocation opposed the votes of the House of Commons by contrary votes'.[13] The Irish gentry had particularly resented the way in which the clergy had interfered in parliamentary elections. Although the clergy normally intervened in support of the Tories, the resentment against this interference in 'civil' matters was not confined to the Whigs. The Tory earl of Abercorn, for example, commented in 1713 that:

> I should be very sorry to see a Parliament altogether chosen, by dint of implicit faith, in our spiritual guides; for I fancy that we who profess bending our thoughts about temporal affairs, might be allowed to understand as much thereof, as those who ought to employ a great part of their time, in directing us of the laity right, beyond the verge of this world [14]

After 1714 the Whig gentry of Ireland who now dominated the House of Commons were repeatedly to demonstrate their unwillingness to forget the strong support given by the Anglican clergy to their political enemies. The bishops certainly found it very difficult to have legislation passed by the Commons which would have benefited the church. Bills to enable the purchase of glebes to encourage clergy to reside in their cures, for example, were consistently blocked by the Commons out of fear that the clergy's electoral influence would thereby increase. Henry Downes, bishop of Elphin, reporting that a bill to encourage residence had been 'hastily thrown out' by the Commons, explained 'I doubt anything in favour of the clergy will not easily pass there, [a] great part of the gentry being pretty much prejudiced against them on the account of the behaviour of too many of them in the late reign, and the cry that they had too much land already, and that more might enable them to multiply votes at elections'.[15] The bill's promoter explained its failure in a similar way commenting 'many, even churchmen, are of opinion that the clergy have too much already'.[16] The bishop of Kilmore concluded in 1721 that 'the House of Commons will not suffer any church bill to pass that may do us good'. This resentment of clerical power on the part of the laity did not quickly pass. After the lower house had rejected several church bills in 1732, the bishop of Elphin commented that 'the Commons have plainly discovered that they think the bishops have power enough'.[17] This legacy of distrust from the 'rage of party' may well be one explanation for the lack of enthusiasm shown by the Anglican laity for schemes to convert Catholics to Protestantism. Some may have felt that a significant increase in the number of Anglican communicants would only serve to increase the political influence of the clergy.

An obvious priority of the new government after August 1714 was to weaken the Tory majority on the Irish episcopal bench. The bishops, of course, could not be removed from their posts but, fortunately for the new administration, no less than three Irish sees lay vacant on the queen's death. All three bishoprics (Raphoe, Killaloe, and Kilmore) were quickly filled with men who were generally regarded as reliable Whigs. Two of these vacancies were filled by Irishmen and one by an Englishman who had been chaplain to the late lord lieutenant, the duke of Shrewsbury.[18] In filling these posts the ministry had accepted the recommendations of the archbishop of Dublin. This meant that the appointments were received favourably in Ireland but it may also have raised the expectation (not least in the mind of William King himself) that the archbishop of Dublin's views would be given equal weight on future occasions. When this expectation was dashed following the filling of the next vacancy on the Irish episcopal bench trouble quickly ensued. The circumstances surrounding this appointment engendered bitterness and rancour within the church and between the Irish clergy and the government. This controversy established the pattern which was to characterise almost every episcopal appointment in Ireland for the next twelve years and beyond.

In November 1715 the lucrative and politically important bishopric of Meath fell vacant following the death of William Moreton. The recently arrived lords justices, Lords Grafton and Galway, recommended for the post Edward Synge (appointed bishop of Raphoe in 1714); that Bishop Forster of Killaloe should succeed Synge; and that Dr Henry Leslie ('who is strongly recommended by the Archbishop of Dublin') be translated to Killaloe. Unfortunately for the lords justices the king had already promised the see of Meath to John Evans, the bishop of Bangor, and felt unable to go back on his word.[19] This misunderstanding demonstrates clearly the careless, indeed cavalier, attitude of many influential figures at court and in the ministry to the practicalities of the government of Ireland. The lords justices, unaware of the king's promise to Evans, had sought the recommendation of their advisers in Ireland regarding the filling of this see. Only after having received and forwarded this advice were they informed that the post had been promised to another. As a result, Grafton and Galway were made to look foolish shortly after having arrived in Ireland. Desperately trying to regain their authority with their Irish advisers, the lords justices wrote to Stanhope explaining why Evans should be persuaded to await a future vacancy:

> ... this being the first vacancy of any importance that has happened in this country since our arrival here, and we being ignorant of his Majesty's intentions, having already so far engaged in this matter as to recommend another person at the earnest request of several of his Majesty's best friends, we submit it to the King's consideration, whether our credit, and consequently his service may not be a good deal concerned in this matter, and whether his Majesty's affairs here may not suffer if it should be thought there has not been a consideration had to the persons recommended by us upon this first instance.[20]

Evidently the king was more concerned about the preservation of his own authority than that of his representatives in Dublin for, unmoved by their arguments, he confirmed Evans' appointment.[21] The duke of Grafton wrote to a correspondent in Britain stressing the possible consequences of this action:

> We last post received a letter from Mr. Secretary Stanhope in which we find the bishopric of Meath is disposed of, I wish it had not been just at this time of the Parliament where we have people even in the King's service ready to catch at any opportunity to do disagreeable things, and if our friends find we have not interest to get some of the preferments for them, how is it possible to think they will have that regard to us which is necessary for his Majesty's affairs[?][22]

Charles Delafaye, joint-chief secretary to the lords justices, expressed the an-

ger of the Castle administration in even more forthright terms. Delafaye claimed
that the opposition in Ireland were making the most of the Dublin administration's apparent lack of interest at court:

> If the Lords Justices had recommended any favourites of their own it
> might have been borne better; but God knows their recommendation
> was merely calculated to please the nation and particularly those in the
> House of Commons (and Lords too) who have exerted themselves and
> are best affected to the King's service: and whenever you send anyone to
> govern a nation you cannot make them too great nor too considerable;
> they must appear powerful enough to reward as well as punish.[23]

Clearly Evans' appointment had caused the Irish administration considerable
embarrassment. On the first occasion when a major post fell vacant following
their arrival in Ireland, the recommendation of the lords justices had been over-
ruled from London. The prestige of the lords justices was already a problematic
issue since they had been appointed to deputise for a lord lieutenant who refused to travel to Ireland. It was all the more important to them, therefore, to
have their authority and status confirmed by strong and public support from
London. Such a loss of face was even more difficult to accept whilst parliament
was sitting, for members of the Irish gentry who were disappointed by the
decision had an immediate opportunity to vent their frustrations in a very public way. That the decision had an impact on Irish MPs can be seen from the
comments of the member for Donegal borough who wrote to Stanhope after
the decision became known in Ireland. Henry Maxwell complained that 'I could
have wished that at a time when we are doing the utmost in our power to show
our zeal to serve the King it had been thought to have given us a bishop of our
own nation.' Maxwell objected to the government's decision because it blocked
a series of promotions within the Irish church from which he hoped his cousin
would have benefited.[24]

In an attempt to atone for what can only be described as a public humiliation, George I promised the lords justices the nomination of the next vacant
Irish bishopric and when the archbishopric of Tuam fell vacant in April 1716
Grafton and Galway were indeed allowed to appoint Bishop Synge (their candidate for Meath) to the post. Nicholas Forster succeeded Synge and was in
turn succeeded by the chaplain to the House of Commons, Dr Charles Carr.[25]
Despite this promotion of three Irish clergymen only a few months later, the
resentment aroused by the appointment of Evans seems to have run very deep,
possibly because the new bishop of Meath came to Ireland with a poor reputation.[26] Archbishop King in particular seems to have been deeply offended that
his views over the disposal of Meath had been disregarded. A letter to the secretary to the Prince of Wales, Samuel Molyneux, in May 1716 discussing the

possible removes following the death of Archbishop Vesey of Tuam makes this clear. Having said that it was likely that Synge would go to Tuam and be succeeded by Forster, he speculated about who might succeed the latter:

> Some say we are to have one from your side of the water, pray give me leave to deal freely with you on this subject. Four bishoprics have been filled since his Majesty's happy accession to the throne; that is, Kilmore, Raphoe, Killaloe, and Meath. Two of these, that is Meath and Kilmore, have been filled from England which are near double in value to the other two. If then another be sent on this occasion, consider with yourself what a discouragement that will be to the university and clergy here ...[27]

These comments by Dr King demonstrate the very difficult task facing the government of Ireland in maintaining an harmonious relationship with (and within) the Anglican episcopate in Ireland. The analysis offered by William King of senior church appointments which had taken place since the accession of George I was, it has to be said, a rather subjective one. It is understandable, of course, when lobbying for particular appointments to be made that the archbishop would put a gloss on the situation which would tend to support his recommendations. Since 1714, it is true, two bishoprics had been filled from England, but two had been filled from Ireland and three further sees were filled by Irishmen as a result of the death of Archbishop Vesey. A ratio of five to two does not indicate a policy of systematic discrimination against the Irish clergy. Such conflicting perceptions helps to explain the depth of the schism which soon affected the Irish episcopal bench and the government's difficulty in applying an appointments policy which would be regarded by both factions as 'even-handed'.

It was when he informed the archbishop of Canterbury in January 1716 of Dr King's resentment over Evans' appointment, that the English-born bishop of Kilmore, Timothy Godwin, employed the terminology which was to characterise the division within the Anglican episcopate for the following fifteen years. Godwin claimed that Archbishop King 'is wholly in the Irish interest as distinct from the English, and thinks all Church preferments do of right belong to the natives'.[28] As early as January 1716, therefore, identifiable Irish and English interests were beginning to form within the episcopate due to disputes over episcopal appointments. The impression that the appointment of Evans had made a significant contribution to the emergence of this 'national' conflict is strengthened by Lord Chancellor Midleton's view, expressed in 1720, that the origins of the Irish-English rivalry, then at its height, could be traced back to the personal antipathy which grew up between William King and John Evans.[29] Like the archbishop of Dublin, Evans had a reputation for being a rather indiscreet and combative figure, an impression which is certainly confirmed by the tone and content of Evans' letters to the archbishop of Canterbury. In October 1716, even Timothy Godwin confided to Archbishop Wake that 'The Bishop of Meath has not that guard upon him I could wish and speaks too openly his opinion of the English Natives here. I have told him of it but he can't hold his tongue.'[30]

After Evans' appointment every vacancy on the ecclesiastical bench became a trial of strength between what quickly became known as the Irish and English interests. These rivalries over the disposal of ecclesiastical patronage were certainly not new but the Whig-Tory party conflict of Queen Anne's reign had prevented the resentment of the Irish clergy from assuming an overt political manifestation. In the context of a 'Whig ascendancy', however, there was nothing to prevent these grievances coming to the fore. That the appointment of Evans was the catalyst for the outbreak of this conflict can be seen from the dramatic change in the attitude of the bishop of Kilmore. In December 1715, Godwin had expressed regret to the archbishop of Canterbury that Synge had been denied the post at Meath, maintaining that the provision of a post for Evans in England would have been preferable. Only seven weeks later, however, Godwin was emphasising to Wake the necessity of appointing Englishmen to Irish sees 'for the advantage of the English interest in this Kingdom'. As attitudes on both sides hardened throughout 1716, Godwin was consistently to repeat this exhortation.[31]

At this stage the rivalry between the Irish and English interests appears to have been primarily over patronage combined, perhaps, with clashes of personality. However, other factors soon drove the two groups further apart. In March 1716, for example, an unknown correspondent wrote to Robert Molesworth claiming that he could no longer recommend Irish clergymen for bishoprics although he had 'once thought it my duty and interest' to do so. He claimed that 'there is not one of them that can be justly called a Whig, no not even among them that were made since the King's happy accession to the throne'.[32] This resentment over the perceived 'Toryism' of the Irish bishops – which was undoubtedly exaggerated – was probably due to the controversy over the attempts by the government at that time to grant protestant dissenters a degree of relief from the restrictions imposed by the sacramental test. The differing stances adopted by the Irish and English Whig bishops over the question of relief for protestant dissenters was a recurring feature of the national conflict within the episcopate in the years to come.[33] In the early years of George I's reign, however, it was a more overtly 'national' issue which turned simmering resentments over the disposal of church patronage into outright political conflict.

III

The constitutional implications of the Sherlock–Annesley case were to sour relations between the Irish and English bishops for nearly four years.[34] For the first time the resentments within the episcopate over patronage could take on a political manifestation. In the parliamentary sessions of 1717 and 1719 the Irish and English interests in the House of Lords openly clashed over the question of the judicial rights of the Irish upper house. Most bishops, both Irish and English, supported what they regarded as the right of the Irish House of Lords to be the final court of appeal in Irish legal cases. However, those English bishops who had been sent to Ireland since the accession of George I, loyally supported the British government in arguing that the British Lords was the superior court. As far as the Irish bishops were concerned, this was unforgivable. A schism within the episcopal bench quickly appeared at the beginning of the dispute. A letter from Archbishop Synge to Archbishop Wake in September 1717 reflects the way in which the resentment of Irish clerics over the distribution of ecclesiastical patronage had become entangled with the judicature controversy:

> His Majesty no doubt may from time to time supply the vacancies of the bishops' bench with persons from England. But if such persons (as they one by one come in) shall be found to oppose what both Lords and Commons are (I think I may say) universally persuaded to be the right of the Kingdom, they will have but an uneasy time of it.[35]

The following month, the bishop of Kilmore confirmed that the Sherlock–Annesley dispute had created a divide among the Irish bishops based upon nationality. His recommendations demonstrate how the distribution of ecclesiastical patronage was now inseparable from the political conflict: 'In our house the great affair has been to assert our jurisdiction ... Now the Tories are brought low I find the distinction between the English and Irish grows more wide. Some care must be taken to preserve the English interest by sending us as vacancies happen more English bishops and judges.'[36] The experience of William Nicolson following his appointment as bishop of Derry in 1718 demonstrates the extent to which the conflict over the judicial rights of the Irish House of Lords had deeply divided the Irish and English bishops in Ireland. Archbishop King was furious over Nicolson's appointment to the see which the former described as 'my first love'.[37] Having discovered that, ignoring the recommendation of the Irish lords justices (one of whom, of course, was the archbishop of Dublin himself), Archbishop Wake had recommended Nicolson for Derry, King wrote to Wake vividly expressing his anger. Characteristically eschewing understatement, King complained:

... since the person nominated for the bishopric of Derry is so very useful to your Grace, I have been thinking of a way, by which your Grace may have the benefit of his assistance, without hurting his wife and family. I do consider that a man may govern a country diocese in Ireland as well if he live in London as in Dublin; that he may live as cheap there as here, and houses are cheaper; that he will have so many and strong precedents to justify him on the practice, that he need not bear any condemnation from the world for his absence, most of his bretheren being examples to justify him in it. If an act of parliament be cheaper than a journey into Ireland, he may, I doubt not, procure one for taking the oaths there, as well as so many civil officers; and so without any trouble, or giving himself the pain of visiting a miserable country, he may get above two thousand pounds per annum instead of eight or nine hundred. This will, in my opinion, be a precedent of very commendable frugality, and very grateful to his family, as well as to your Grace who will thereby have the benefit of his advice and assistance. As for the diocese of Derry, I see no reason why it may not do as well without a resident bishop for 15 years to come, as it did for the 15 years last past.[38]

Archbishop Synge wrote to Wake apologising for King's 'unwary expressions', attempting to excuse them by claiming that he was 'much fatigued' by work. At the same time, Synge felt obliged to convey the frustration of Irish clergymen who felt, with some justice, that the best posts in the church were being reserved for Englishmen:

... I have always thought it my duty, without any murmuring or resentment, to allow His Majesty the free exercise of his prerogative in the disposing of the great preferments in this church; nor have I ever thought it unreasonable that a good part of them should be bestowed upon men of worth from England: At the same time I hope His Majesty and the ministry will not forget, that there are some here amongst us, who deserve very well, and therefore ought not to be wholly overlooked.[39]

Conveying his delight to Wake upon Nicolson's appointment, John Evans added that Archbishop King 'is horn-mad that his scheme did not take place'.[40] Bishop Godwin told Wake that King was 'downright angry' about Nicolson's appointment, but admitted that he was pleased to have another English bishop 'for I find no friendships equal to those of my own countrymen'.[41]

Considering the anger of Archbishop King and others about Nicolson's appointment it is hardly surprising that the latter received a less than warm welcome in Ireland. King insisted that Nicolson, despite his many years as a bishop in England, should occupy a junior position on the bishops' bench in the House of

Lords. When Nicolson made the (in the circumstances) rather insensitive suggestion that the Irish Lords' journal should be drawn up according to the practice in England, he found himself 'being grinned at (in a libellous pamphlet) as one of the foreign prelates, sent hither to instruct and civilise my betters'.[42]

The 1719-20 parliamentary session saw the Sherlock–Annesley dispute reach its dramatic climax when the Irish Lords ordered that the Irish barons of the exchequer be taken into custody for following the orders of the British, rather than the Irish, House of Lords. Four Englishmen appointed to Irish bishoprics since George I's accession were joined by the Tory, but English-born, bishop of Kildare and only three more peers in registering their protest at the arrest of the barons.[43] By the time the British parliament had decided to pass the Declaratory Act which confirmed the supremacy of the Westminster parliament over that in Dublin, the situation in Ireland had become extremely tense. William Nicolson wrote in February 1720 that he and most other 'English foreigners', as he put it, were regarded as 'enemies to the public interests of this kingdom'. Nicolson was in no doubt about the leading role played by the Irish bishops in the judicial dispute alleging 'all the present ferment that we are in, has been raised by men of our order; ... Two or three lords spiritual managed the whole procedure against the barons. They drew up the report; and they framed the representation'.[44] Nicolson singled out Archbishop King, supported by Jonathan Swift, as the leader of what he called the 'new sect of state-independents':

> The whole fit of madness is owing to the resentments of a single ecclesiastical grandee; who feeling himself to sink in the esteem of his late associates in power, resolved to make himself considerable by an aftergame with the mob; whose darling he now is, as amply as he was (a few months ago) their aversion. The Angel of St Patrick's is now the Guardian of the Kingdom.[45]

In the midst of the constitutional dispute, the Irish and English bishops also found themselves on opposite sides of an argument over proposed religious legislation. Both on a bill to grant a measure of relief to the protestant dissenters in Ireland and on a 'popery bill', all five English bishops who had been appointed since 1714 once more found themselves in opposition to the rest of their brethren on the episcopal bench.[46] There does seem to have been a genuine difference of opinion between the Irish and English bishops regarding the status of Catholics and protestant dissenters. The Irish and Tory bishops appear to have regarded the dissenters as presenting the greater threat to the established church. They, after all, supported by the Scottish Kirk, were building new churches and winning converts from Anglicanism, especially in Ulster. The Catholics on the other hand were seen to be much less of a threat to the established church and could either be left alone or attempts could be made to convert them. In political terms these attitudes of the Irish bishops manifested themselves in opposition to any measure of relief to the dissenters and reluctance to extend the penal legislation against Catholics.[47]

Many English bishops found these attitudes difficult to comprehend. After 1714, all English bishops appointed to Irish sees were Whigs and, coming from an overwhelmingly Protestant country, it is understandable that they found it difficult to adjust to being surrounded, in most areas, by a large Catholic majority. They had been brought up to believe that all Catholics were potential traitors and enemies of the state. It seemed only reasonable to these men from England that all of the protestants in Ireland should unite to oppose this common enemy. The English bishops, therefore, were prepared, perhaps reluctantly, to grant some measure of toleration to the dissenters (although never a complete repeal of the test) and they consistently urged the necessity of further penal legislation against the Catholics.[48] The English bishops simply could not understand the opposition of many Irish bishops to further anti-Catholic legislation. Commenting upon the defeat of a popery bill in the Irish privy council in 1723, William Nicolson remarked that 'Many of us seem to be exceedingly afraid of provoking our Roman neighbours'.[49] John Evans reacted to rumours of an impending insurrection by the Catholics in 1719 with something approaching hysteria. Displaying a paranoia which was admittedly exceptional, Evans had visions of 'those Blood Thirsty Villains' carrying out a massacre like that of 1641 and blamed 'perjuring Tories' for giving encouragement to the Catholics.[50]

The Irish bishops took a very different view of the potential threat from the Catholics. They appear to have been satisfied that the political and military potential of the Catholics had been crushed. Archbishop King was dismissive of the Catholic threat in 1715, taking a mischievous delight in assuring his friends in England that the Protestants of Ireland were safer from the Jacobites than were their counterparts in Britain.[51] King took a pragmatic view of the Catholic question. In February 1715 he wrote to the lord lieutenant pointing out the weakness in the policy of trying to eliminate Catholicism through legislation, arguing that 'As to the Roman Catholics ... our laws are already too severe against them, but meet with no execution'.[52] Archbishop Synge of Tuam took a similar view about the Catholic question. Justifying to Archbishop Wake his opposition to a popery bill in 1719, he wrote:

> It is a melancholy reflection that the true Christian way of reducing Popery is not much regarded: nor can I but fear that there are too many amongst us, who had rather keep the Papists as they are, in an almost slavish subjection, than have them made Protestants, and thereby entitled to the same liberties and privileges with the rest of their fellow subjects.[53]

This relatively 'soft' line towards the Catholics was not, it must be emphasized, widespread among the Protestant community in Ireland. At the level of national politics it was confined almost entirely to the Irish-born and Tory bishops and a few lay peers (often recent converts) in the House of Lords.[54] The House of Commons was generally just as keen as were the English bishops to pass anti-Catholic legislation, although they were extremely reluctant to grant relief to the dissenters, a repeal of the sacramental test being completely out of the question.

When a bill for relieving protestant dissenters came before the House of Lords in 1719, the English bishops appointed since 1714 once more found themselves isolated from their bretheren. The votes of these 'five (Presbyterian) prelates' enabled the bill to progress. In retaliation, the Irish and Tory bishops united with certain lay lords to throw out a popery bill which was supported by 'four English schismatics'.[55] It is difficult to avoid the impression that the bitterness engendered by the Sherlock–Annesley dispute was partially responsible for these conflicting stances on the legislation affecting protestant dissenters and Catholics. The lord lieutenant, for example, could not understand why the popery bill 'should be opposed after its return from Great Britain (without any other alteration than a mitigation of the punishments) by some of those very lords whom had before thought most favourably of it in council. I doubt these proceedings will appear not enough consistent'.[56] There is some evidence to suggest that some of those bishops and peers who originally supported the popery bill, but later voted against it, had opposed it all along and had hoped that it would be dropped by the British privy council.[57] However, it may also be the case that the conflict between the Irish and English interests over the Sherlock–Annesley case and the bill to relieve dissenters encouraged some Irish peers and bishops to oppose a piece of legislation largely on the grounds that it had the support of the English bishops.

The parliamentary session of 1719 was of fundamental importance in establishing the national division among the Anglican bishops. It is not surprising that issues such as the judicial rights of the Irish House of Lords and attempts to alter the religious establishment should have engendered controversy and ill-feeling on both sides. What is noticeable, however, is that this national conflict did not diminish when these issues were resolved or given a lower profile. The original cause of the conflict, after all, had been disagreements over the disposal of ecclesiastical patronage and this rivalry was certain to continue.

IV

Disputes over the nature of Ireland's constitutional relationship with Britain or the status of Catholics and protestant dissenters exacerbated a schism within the episcopate the fundamental cause of which was rivalry over patronage. Clergymen born and educated in Ireland clearly felt that they were being unfairly treated by the government in the early Hanoverian period. The Irish clergy objected to the practice of granting bishoprics to perceived 'foreigners', not simply because it deprived an Irishman of that particular see but also because of the knock-on effect. If a bishopric was given to an Irishman it might allow a whole series of translations to take place whereby many clergymen could be promoted. By giving a bishopric to an outsider, all of these Irish clergymen were deprived of promotion. As Archbishop King argued following Evans' appointment to Meath:

> the more his Majesty obliges, the more he enlarges his interest. Now I will put the case, that instead of sending us a bishop of Meath from England, they had preferred a bishop of Ireland and a clergyman to fill his place, and then another into his etc., here a great many had by this tasted of his Majesty's bounty. In the scheme I proposed ten clergymen would have been advanced and obliged, whereas by sending us a bishop out of England all these were stopped and a damp put on the whole clergy ... [58]

Another objection of the Irish clergy was that English bishops often gave the best benefices in their dioceses to their friends and family from England, so that these posts were denied to Irish clergymen as well.[59] Finally, there were allegations that those Englishmen appointed to Irish sees did not take their duties seriously enough. As Dr King put it:

> I am sure it doth not serve the church to have men put into the principal posts, that are entirely strangers to the business, persons and concerns of the dioceses where they are to govern, the truth is, the common way practised by them hitherto is to take a house in Dublin spend their time there or in England and let their dioceses shift for themselves. Thus the diocese of Derry has been served by my two successors, thus the diocese of Meath, Kilmore and several others have been used, in all which there have not only been great neglects but destructions and delapidations.[60]

King became so convinced that the best posts in the Irish church were being reserved for English clergymen that he advocated that Irish bishops should deliberately keep down the value of their sees in order to make them less attractive to outsiders. Arguing that he could have made the see of Derry worth an extra £1,000 per annum when he was bishop there, King claimed that he had chosen not to do so because he thought that 'none of Irish education was then like to get it'.[61] Writing from London to the archbishop of Tuam in 1717, King argued that:

> it is our interest that some of our bishoprics should be very poor, for the value of them has such a reputation here, that we are extremely envied, and our bishoprics greedily coveted by the hungry clergy who withall are so proud and selfish, that they think no body deserveth anything but themselves and grudge every preferment that is disposed of to any in Ireland.[62]

The archbishop claimed in 1726 to have played up the disadvantages of the bishopric of Cloyne in order to discourage applications from England. He also advocated the separation of the dioceses of Kilmore and Ardagh to form two sees worth around £1,000 per annum each. No doubt his reasoning was that an Englishman would have been much less likely to want either of these dioceses than he would a combined see with an annual income of about £2,000. By 1727 King had concluded that the most lucrative Irish bishoprics would inevitably go to Englishmen. As he put it, 'We must not expect anything from the government that any of their friends will accept'.[63]

King does seem to have been correct in complaining that English-born candidates, in general, fared better than Irish clergymen in getting the best posts in the Irish church. On the other hand, his complaint to the lord lieutenant in 1720 'that a resolution is taken that none educated in this kingdom shall be made a bishop or a judge' overstated the problem.[64] In 1714 there were thirteen Irish-born bishops on the ecclesiastical bench to nine who were English-born. By 1727 there were eleven of each and the proportion was the same in 1760. This represents a transfer of two sees from Irishmen to Englishmen which, in itself, is not perhaps a significant difference. However, the English bishops do seem to have fared better in terms of promotions. Of a total of thirty-four episcopal appointments made between 1714 and 1727, twenty-one (61.7 per cent) went to Englishmen and thirteen to Irishmen. Promotion, therefore, came more easily to the English-born clergy than to the Irish. Englishmen also seem to have been given the better posts. Of the four archbishoprics, two each were held by Irishmen and Englishmen in 1714 and the proportion was the same in 1727. After the death of Archbishop King in 1729, for the remainder of the eighteenth century, the archbishoprics of Armagh and Dublin (that is, the more senior and wealthy archbishoprics) tended to have English occupants while Cashel and Tuam were reserved for the Irish. On two occasions, however, three of the archbishoprics were held by English occupants – briefly in 1729 and from 1742 to 1752 when Josiah Hort was archbishop of Tuam. English clergymen also tended to be given the most lucrative bishoprics. Apart from the four archbishoprics, the sees of Derry, Raphoe, Kildare, and Meath were probably those most sought after. In the period from 1690 to 1752, 67.5 per cent of appointments to these sees went to Englishmen.[65]

Although the patronage of the Church of Ireland was controlled by a variety of people, the single patron with the most ecclesiastical patronage at his disposal was the lord lieutenant. With the exception of the bishoprics, he controlled all ecclesiastical patronage in the crown's gift and those best placed to obtain lucrative benefices were the lord lieutenant's chaplains. Each viceroy, when he came to Ireland for the parliamentary session, brought a number of chaplains with him. One of these men was usually given precedence as his official chaplain and this man was almost certain to obtain one of the first bishoprics or wealthy deaneries which became vacant. The viceroy's other chaplains were also virtually guaranteed a bishopric or deanery. In recommending that his chaplain be appointed to the bishopric of Killala in 1720, the duke of Bolton remarked that 'the Lord Lieutenant's chaplain has always an expectation of supplying the first vacant bishopric'.[66] In December 1716 the earl of Sunderland's chaplain, Henry Downes, was still expected to be appointed to the first vacant bishopric even though Sunderland himself had resigned the viceroyalty over a year previously. Similarly Timothy Godwin, the duke of Shrewsbury's chaplain, was appointed to the bishopric of Kilmore after Shrewsbury had been removed from office. By 1725 Archbishop King thought that it had become accepted in England that every chaplain of a lord lieutenant must have either a bishopric or a benefice worth at least £400 per annum.[67]

To be appointed as a chaplain to the lord lieutenant was by far the quickest route to promotion in the Irish church. In June 1725 Carteret appointed William Cotterel to the deanery of Raphoe which was worth around £1,000 per annum. The bishop of Kilmore informed Archbishop Wake that this appointment had made the archbishop of Dublin 'cry out loudly' because Cotterel was a very young man who had been ordained only the year before at Carteret's request.[68] Archbishop King, however, was unlikely to have been surprised that such preferential treatment was given to the viceroy's chaplain. In November 1724 upon finding out that Carteret had brought three chaplains to Ireland he was resigned to the fact that they would have to be provided for before anyone else could hope to gain preferment.[69] The privileged position of the viceroy's chaplains quite naturally led to resentment among the Irish clergy. It must have been galling for men who had served for many years in the church to see many of the best posts in the Irish church given to outsiders who often had little or no experience. In December 1714, Archbishop King wrote to the bishop of Norwich about this grievance: 'Our chief governors are changed commonly once in three years, and they commonly bring chaplains with them, who succeed to bishoprics, if they fall, or to the best preferments, these being generally in the crown: and hence your Lordship may guess, what encouragement there is for the clergy educated here.'[70]

It should not be assumed, however, that the lord lieutenant's control of ecclesiastical patronage always worked in the interests of English clergymen.
The duke of Grafton certainly angered some of the English bishops by his
appointment of a number of Irishmen to posts in the church. Timothy Godwin
repeatedly alleged that the lord lieutenant was neglecting the English interest
in Ireland, complaining that Grafton had treated the English bishops 'with much
more reserve than when he was over here before'.[71] Claiming that his brother-
in-law had failed to obtain the post of counsellor to the revenue commissioners
because he was English, Godwin declared that Grafton had ignored 'us English' because he knew that he could rely on their support in parliament. According
to Godwin, the English bishops had hoped that Grafton's attitude would alter
when the session of parliament ended and the need to curry favour with the
Irish would be of less import. Such expectations, however, were quickly dashed
and the resentment of the English bishops towards Grafton increased over the
next two years.[72] Godwin was certainly not the only English bishop to grumble
about alleged ill-treatment by Grafton. Bishop Nicolson of Derry, for example,
complained that Grafton refused to tell him who he was going to appoint to the
deanery of Derry.[73] Bishops Evans and Godwin claimed, furthermore, that
Grafton's policy of granting favours to the Irish had been counterproductive.
Evans alleged that 'these people have had their wills in all they desired, and
were denied nothing, they almost (now) think themselves independent again'.[74]
After the controversy over Wood's halfpence had threatened to disrupt the parliamentary session of 1723-4, Godwin laid the blame squarely at Grafton's
door, remarking that 'tis certain our Lord Lieutenant's conduct has not succeeded well. He has courted these people till they have despised him.'[75]

During Grafton's viceroyalty the men who had been the staunchest supporters of the English interest in the past felt that their political support was now
being taken for granted. Men who had remained loyal to the government during the very difficult parliamentary sessions of 1717 and 1719-20, when loyalty
to the government could have unpleasant consequences, quite understandably
felt aggrieved when Grafton appeared to be adopting a distant or cool stance
towards them. It appeared that the Irish, on the other hand, who had proved
only too willing to cause trouble for the government, were being bought off
with posts in the church and elsewhere. Archbishop King, who had openly led
the 'Irish party' in the Lords during the Sherlock–Annesley dispute, was courted
by Grafton in 1722 to persuade him to accept a position in the commission of
lords justices. The English bishops were incredulous at Grafton's actions and
felt betrayed by the ministry in London. Bishop Downes, writing to Nicolson
in February 1722, expressed the dismay which was felt, no doubt, by all of
English Whig bishops:

What you told me is (beyond my expectation) come to pass. The Archbishop of Dublin, after mature deliberation, has accepted of the
Government, as Mr Fairfax did of the Deanery of Down. But my opinion is, that they who long hesitate about preferment should go without
it: especially such who think their acceptance a matter of obligation, and
consequently not worth thanks. Whether our friends on the other side
wanted power, or wanted courage, I cannot tell; I may say that they
wanted regard to us foreigners, who are put entirely into the hands of the
natives.[76]

It would seem that Grafton's dependence upon William Conolly to manage the
House of Commons on his behalf was particularly resented. Godwin alleged
that 'His Grace is governed by one on this side of the water with whom it is no
merit to be born in England or to own the dependence of this kingdom on it'.[77]
That it was resentment over Conolly's influence over the disposal of patronage
which was at the root of Godwin's complaints is made clear by his thoughts on
the prospect of the appointment of a new viceroy in January 1723:

We expect a new chief governor. We shall soon know what his conduct
will be by the persons he makes choice of here to confide in. If the great
commoner among us be Prime Minister it will be all alike to us, who
comes over. He gives us, English-born, good words, and no more is to
be expected from him.[78]

The extent of Conolly's influence with Grafton was demonstrated when, at the
height of the Wood's halfpence dispute, the lord lieutenant recommended
Conolly's candidate (Arthur Price) for the bishopric of Clonfert and this was
approved by the ministry. Bishop Evans was understandably aggrieved that, in
spite of the turbulent session of 1723, Grafton was still, in his words, 'Irishly
governed'.[79] However, perhaps the best evidence to support the complaints of
English clergymen that Irishmen were being given more favourable treatment
than had hitherto been the case, comes in a characteristically grudging remark
of William King. Even the foremost advocate of the Irish interest had to admit
that Grafton 'was something more indulgent to the [Irish] clergy' than had
been his predecessors.[80]

On the other hand, it was during Grafton's viceroyalty that Josiah Hort was
appointed to the bishopric of Ferns and Leighlin, a preferment which created
perhaps more resentment among the Irish clergy than any other in this period.
The viceroy's chaplains had been competing with each other for this bishopric
but Nicolson thought that the chaplain to the House of Commons, Dr William
Gore, would get it as he had the 'powerful interest' of Speaker Conolly. In the
end, however, Hort did get the post becoming with Charles Cobbe (bishop of

Killala, 1720-27) one of only two bishops of the Church of Ireland during the reign of George I not to have a doctorate.[81] Indeed Archbishop King claimed that Hort had never taken any degree at all and, furthermore, that he had never been episcopally ordained.[82] It does seem that Hort had made a poor impression in Dublin since arriving as chaplain to the earl of Wharton (a not uncontroversial figure himself) in 1709 and his non-conformist background would not have endeared him to Irish churchmen. Dr King claimed that Hort's behaviour had 'not been very clerical' and believed that 'hardly a more ungrateful person to all sorts of people could have been pitched on for a promotion'.[83] King, in fact, refused to consecrate Hort and a commission comprising bishops Evans of Meath, Godwin of Kilmore, and Lambert of Dromore had to carry out this task.[84] The English bishops, on the other hand, were delighted at Hort's preferment, although the bishop of Derry had to admit that the Irish deeply resented his appointment and that they 'represented him as one of the most ignorant and wicked wretches that ever yet officiated at God's altar'.[85] Of a total of six episcopal appointments made during the viceroyalty of Grafton, three went to Irish clergymen and three to Englishmen. It would appear, therefore, that Grafton was doing his best to keep both camps relatively content. The deep resentment which such an apparently even-handed policy aroused on both sides is indicative of the polarisation which had occurred within the episcopate by the early 1720s.

The resentment of the English bishops at the perceived neglect of the English interest by Grafton was to continue under his successor, Lord Carteret, and clashes between the English bishops and the lord lieutenant became a constant feature in the government of Ireland in the 1720s. The viceroy's prime objective was to keep the House of Commons relatively content in order to have the government's money bills passed. In order to keep the leaders of the Irish gentry in good humour he would often accept their recommendations for the disposal of vacant posts, including, of course, ecclesiastical benefices. The appointment of an Irish clergyman to a vacant bishopric or deanery was, therefore, an important opportunity for a lord lieutenant to win much-needed support in the House of Commons. Naturally, the English bishops who were responsible for opposing the Irish interest in the House of Lords viewed the matter rather differently. This tension between the English bishops and the Castle administration suggests that there was no clear uniformity of objectives between those who have been traditionally regarded as the representatives of the English interest in Ireland. The viceroyalties of Grafton and Carteret clearly demonstrated that there was often serious conflict between the ecclesiastical and lay wings of the English interest.

V

One figure has come to be regarded as the personification of the English interest in Ireland at this time – Hugh Boulter, archbishop of Armagh, 1724-42.
Boulter's correspondence shows that virtually from the day of his arrival in
Dublin he viewed the Irish political situation in terms of an Irish-English conflict.[86] Throughout the remainder of his primacy, Boulter vigorously argued in
favour of a systematic policy of strengthening the English interest by the appointment of English bishops, judges, and privy councillors. In the past,
historians argued that the period 1724-5 witnessed a deliberate change in government policy regarding the government of Ireland. The ministry's anger over
the unreliability of its Irish servants during the Wood's halfpence dispute, it
was said, led it to strengthen the English presence in the Dublin administration
by the appointment of Boulter and the replacement of Lord Chancellor Midleton
with Richard West. Simultaneously, management of the House of Commons
was handed over to William Conolly, the first 'undertaker'.[87] As has been pointed
out, however, undertakers were in existence long before 1724. It is evident that,
with the exception of the parliamentary session of 1717, William Conolly had
acted as the government's chief undertaker since 1715. Overall, it is difficult to
find firm evidence of a decision in Westminster to strengthen systematically
the English interest in Ireland as a result of the Wood's halfpence dispute.[88]
    Even if, contrary to the traditional view, Boulter's appointment did not sig-
nal a radical or systematic change in government policy, his arrival in Ireland
can be regarded as an important turning point in the history of the Irish-English
conflict within the Anglican episcopate. It has been seen how, as early as 1716,
English-born bishops in Ireland had been consistently urging the necessity of
strengthening the English interest so Boulter's support for such a policy was
certainly nothing new. However, Boulter's appointment did make a difference
for the leadership of the Church of Ireland was transferred from Archbishop
King, leader of the Irish interest, to Boulter, the leader of the English. More
importantly, Boulter's influence over the disposal of the ecclesiastical patronage in the gift of the crown thereafter enabled him to consolidate the English
interest within the Irish church. As has been pointed out, however, the extent to
which the English presence on the episcopal bench was increased should not
be exaggerated, there being eleven Irish and eleven English bishops in 1727.
What was different after 1724 was that the head of the Church of Ireland was
committed to the strengthening of the English interest in the House of Lords
and in the privy council through the appointment of reliable English candidates
to Irish sees and that Boulter could normally depend upon the wholehearted
support of the ministry in London.
    The aim which Boulter had set himself upon his appointment was to break
up the 'Dublin faction' on the Irish episcopal bench, that is the one led by

Archbishop King.[89] In the end it was only with King's death in 1729 and the Irish interest was deprived of its most charismatic leader that this aim was achieved. Even before King's death, however, Boulter had asserted his authority both within the church and in the House of Lords. His chief strength was the strong backing which he normally received from the ministry at Westminster. This enabled him, not only to weaken the Irish interest within the church, but also on occasion to confront and frustrate the lord lieutenant. Carteret, like Grafton before him, had other priorities besides strengthening the English interest within the Church of Ireland – namely, ensuring the passage of money bills through the Irish House of Commons. Boulter was fortunate in that he was on much better terms with the ministry than was Carteret. The latter indeed was regarded by Walpole as his most dangerous political adversary. With Boulter at its head, the English interest within the episcopate was in a much stronger position to overrule the wishes of the lord lieutenant regarding ecclesiastical appointments than it had been during the viceroyalty of Grafton who received full support from the ministry.

Due to the tension which existed between the ministry and Carteret, the split between the clergy and laity within the English interest became even more serious during the latter's viceroyalty. Carteret, for example, appears to have made a point of consulting Archbishop Wake about the disposal of Irish ecclesiastical posts.[90] Wake had long since fallen out with Walpole and had been replaced as the British government's ecclesiastical adviser by the bishop of London, Edmund Gibson. Carteret's decision to involve Wake in the affairs of the Church of Ireland can only be seen as a deliberate snub to Walpole, the duke of Newcastle, and their representative in Ireland, Hugh Boulter. More importantly, however, was the lord lieutenant's consistent recommendation of Irish candidates for posts in the church, judiciary, and privy council. Such recommendations repeatedly brought Carteret into conflict with Boulter.[91] The most serious of these conflicts between Carteret and Boulter occurred in 1727 following the death of the archbishop of Cashel. Carteret recommended for this see the Irish-born bishop of Elphin, Theophilus Bolton, the candidate of William Conolly and a protégé of Archbishop King. Carteret determinedly stuck to this recommendation despite the vigorous opposition of Boulter who described Bolton as 'as dangerous an Irishman as any on the bench' who 'would set himself, if he had that station, at the head of the Irish interest here'.[92] Boulter was incensed when he heard of a rumour that Conolly had written to England to say 'that the House of Commons will be very much disobliged' if Bolton was not appointed to Cashel. Claiming that 'the giving the archbishopric to Bishop Bolton will be a very great blow to the English interest in this kingdom', Boulter told the bishop of London that he would write to the duke of Newcastle asking 'the ministry to consider who is the proper person to recommend to bishopricks here, an Irish Speaker, or an English Primate'.[93]

On this occasion Boulter was successful in preventing Bolton's appointment, an impressive demonstration of the extent of his influence (and Carteret's lack of interest) with the ministry at that time. However, when the see of Cashel again became vacant in December 1729 Boulter had to agree to Carteret's recommendation that Bolton be appointed. Dublin Castle's control of the House of Commons had been seriously weakened by the death of Conolly in October of that year and Carteret was determined to use the vacancy at Cashel to try to win parliamentary support, especially as he found himself with the delicate and difficult task of piloting through the Commons a money bill which had been altered in London. Under the circumstances, the appointment of an Englishman to another Irish archbishopric was the last thing that Carteret needed, especially if it was at the expense of such a dangerous politician as Theophilus Bolton. After a meeting with Carteret on 14 December, Boulter reluctantly agreed to recommend Bolton for Cashel, explaining to the bishop of London that this was necessary in order 'to keep things quiet in this country'.[94] Writing to Gibson two weeks later Boulter admitted that he would have preferred to have had the bishop of St David's for Cashel if 'we had not been in a very uneasy situation in the House of Commons'.[95] It is clear that, faced with the possibility of losing a money bill in the House of Commons, the policy of strengthening the English interest was temporarily abandoned, even by Boulter, its foremost advocate.

VI

From a very early stage in the reign of George I the English-born bishops in Ireland consciously began to regard themselves as the representatives of an English interest in Ireland. As time passed this emphasis upon the importance of nationality came to predominate over all other political considerations as far as the recently-appointed English bishops were concerned. As early as 1718, one English-born bishop wrote to the archbishop of Canterbury expressing the hope that the arch-Tory, probably Jacobite, but English-born, Primate Thomas Lindsay might be persuaded to 'soften' his stance a little so 'that we English might join together'.[96] With the passage of time, even Tory bishops could expect preferment so long as they identified themselves with the English interest. Even Bishop Evans sought a better post for an elderly dean who, although 'a Stiff Tory', was at least an Englishman.[97] Bishop Ellis of Kildare, a Tory bishop from the reign of Queen Anne, eventually regained political respectability through support of the English interest in the House of Lords. During the 1719 session of parliament Ellis was described by Bishop Godwin as 'the Honest Bishop of Kildare', a significant adjective to apply to a former Tory.[98] However, at this stage Ellis' loyalties were still ambiguous. Whilst siding with the Tories and the Irish interest in opposing the toleration bill for protestant dissenters, he joined with the English interest in supporting the actions of the barons of the Exchequer over the Sherlock–Annesley case. However, his actions were clearly winning him over to the English Whig bishops. Noting that 'the Bishop of Kildare joined with us in everything', Bishop Godwin remarked that 'only my Lord Primate voted as a thorough Irishman'.[99] Ellis' rehabilitation was not, however, achieved quickly. When in 1727 he sought the archbishopric of Cashel on the grounds that, with the exception of Archbishop King, he was the most senior bishop on the bench, Primate Boulter admitted that, although 'a hearty Englishman' and an enemy to the Pretender, Ellis was 'rather counted a Tory here'. On the other hand, Boulter did not object to Ellis' appointment on these grounds.[100] Although Ellis failed to obtain this post he was eventually rewarded for his loyalty with an appointment in 1732 to the important and sought-after bishopric of Meath, a post which brought with it an automatic seat on the Irish privy council. Recommending Ellis for Meath, the duke of Dorset praised him as being, 'as zealous for the interest of England, as any person in the House of Lords'.[101]

It has been shown that the Irish clergy quickly began to resent the appointment of Englishmen to some of the best posts in the Irish church. However, there is little evidence of a conscious sense of national identity on the part of the Irish clergy. References to the 'Irish interest' are normally found only in the letters of English politicians and bishops who also referred to the Irish-born Anglican clergy as 'the natives'. When Archbishop Synge did refer to 'The Irish Bishops' in 1724 he was careful to add in parenthesis 'as it seems we are distinguished' to indicate that he and his colleagues did not regard themselves in these terms.[102]

Although the conflict between the English interest and the Irish interest which was formed to oppose it was clearly a very serious one, it is important not to overstate its significance. It is easy to overestimate the importance of this Irish-English rivalry because of the prominence which it is given in the surviving correspondence of some of the leading personalities of this period. The correspondence of William King, Hugh Boulter, and William Wake all give the impression that Irish-English rivalry was the central feature of Irish politics in this period. However, it is no coincidence that all of these men were churchmen and when the letters of Conolly, Midleton and other Irish laymen are examined the rarity of references to any conflict based upon nationality is striking. Furthermore, some English bishops seem to have been on good terms with Irish laymen. William Nicolson, for example, on a number of occasions expressed his admiration for Speaker Conolly. The latter was apparently also on close terms with the much-maligned Josiah Hort. For his part, Conolly offered to recommend Timothy Godwin for the bishopric of Derry in opposition to an Irish candidate. The 'national' conflict was of limited importance to the Irish Protestant gentry simply because in the main theatre of their political activity, the House of Commons, there was effectively no English interest for them to oppose. Disputes between the Irish and English interests were confined almost wholly to the House of Lords with the numbers involved on both sides amounting to, perhaps, no more than two dozen.[103]

The Irish-English divide, furthermore, was never completely rigid. Although as keen as anyone to uphold the English interest in Ireland, Timothy Godwin stood out among the English-born Whig bishops as sharing with his Irish colleagues a more lenient attitude towards Catholics. Following the rejection of a popery bill in 1724, he admitted 'I am not a little pleased that the Popery Bill is dropped. It was a cruel one and I could never have come into it. I wish the priests were allowed to officiate on condition they took the oath of allegiance and were under some regulation of the government – which would be better for the state than a base connivance.'[104] Josiah Hort was another English bishop who, perhaps because of his non-conformist background, came to share the attitude of many of the Irish clergy regarding penal legislation. In 1731 Hort argued that 'coercive laws … can never convince nor convert anybody; they may bind men's hands and tongues, but can never reach their hearts'.[105] Godwin's tolerance of Catholicism was part of the more generally 'moderate' position adopted by him within the English interest. In 1717, for example, he complained that 'my bretheren of Meath and Kildare are as national almost as his Grace of Dublin, that is in my mind to some extreme'.[106] Even Archbishop King seems to have regarded Godwin in a different light to the other English bishops. Discussing Dr King's 'national' politics in 1716, Godwin remarked that 'I have had the best treatment from him of any English man I know'.[107] Claiming that after the Sherlock–Annesley dispute he 'never delighted in Dublin' and preferred to reside in his diocese, Godwin informed Archbishop Wake that 'Since my residing here I must own the Archbishop of Dublin has not only spoken very civilly to me but has taken many occasions to speak of me to my advantage as my friends have told me.'[108] Godwin's arrival in Ireland in 1713 at the height of the Whig-Tory conflict as the duke of Shrewsbury's chaplain probably explains King's more favourable opinion of the bishop of Kilmore. Those English bishops who arrived after 1714 were thrust into a very different political context.

Bearing the above qualifications in mind, it is clear that the period between 1716 and 1719 witnessed the emergence of clearly-defined Irish and English interests among the Anglican bishops in the House of Lords. The root cause of the rivalry between the Irish and English bishops in Ireland was undoubtedly resentment on the part of the Irish clergy over the disposal of ecclesiastical patronage to perceived 'foreigners'. The religious disputes which had played a leading role in the Whig-Tory party conflict of the previous reign also caused tension between newly appointed Whig bishops from England and the Irish clergy who tended to support 'Tory' stances over religious questions. From the appointment of Boulter to the primacy in 1724, the conflict between the Irish and English interests was gradually transformed from being primarily a conflict within the Irish episcopate carried on in the House of Lords, to a struggle within the Irish executive between an Irish speaker of the Commons and the English primate and lord chancellor, with the lord lieutenant attempting to walk a fine line somewhere in-between.

The deaths of John Evans (1724), William Nicolson (1727), Timothy Godwin (1729), and, most importantly, William King (1729) acted to remove most of the leading actors who had dominated the Irish-English conflict until 1724 and facilitated the transformation of the Irish English conflict as noted above. This change in the nature of the Irish-English conflict was one part of the more general transformation which affected Irish politics between 1727 and 1730 largely due to the deaths of most of the leading political figures. The consequences of this redefinition of the Irish-English conflict can be witnessed from Boulter's joining with the viceroy, lord chancellor and archbishop of Dublin in recommending two Irish-born bishops for promotion in 1734. Both men were described by Boulter as being 'in the English interest'.[109] Clearly, the politics of the Anglican episcopate had undergone something of a sea change in the previous five years.

8

Patriotism

Chapter five analysed the role played by patronage in early eighteenth-century Irish parliamentary politics. The pursuit of patronage was a (arguably the) major factor which determined the political behaviour of Irish politicians in the early Hanoverian period. The link between patronage and political behaviour, normally implicit, was at times blatant. However, it has also been seen that patronage was a crude tool of parliamentary management, of only limited utility. The distribution of patronage was a problematic process in that it could lose as well as win the government support in parliament. Politicians, furthermore, were motivated by considerations in addition to the pursuit of patronage. Sean Connolly has rightly pointed out that considerations of honour, personal connection, 'a sense of the public interest ('patriotism') and the power of parliamentary oratory could all influence voting behaviour in parliament.[1] A determination to preserve the Anglican religious establishment from the perceived threat of Catholicism and, more realistically, protestant dissent could also be added to the list of additional factors which motivated the political behaviour of early Hanoverian Irish politicians. Members of both houses of the Irish parliament consistently proved themselves resistant to government influence over questions of religion. Successive undertakers had to explain to the government that a repeal of the sacramental test, for example, was out of the question. There is no doubt, however, that the single most important factor, after the pursuit of patronage, which influenced political behaviour at this time was a sense of 'patriotism'.

What was the nature of 'Protestant patriotism' in eighteenth-century Ireland? This is an immensely difficult question to answer. The evidence is often contradictory and historians have been unable to agree on how the terminology should be employed. A major difficulty is that the word 'patriotism' meant different things in different contexts. Specifically, the patriotism of a parliamentary opposition should be treated separately from the wider phenomenon of Protestant patriotism which represented a more general consensus among the Anglican community. The former was clearly closely related to the latter but, as shall be seen, parliamentary patriotism was not simply motivated by a selfless desire to defend the rights of one's country. Before analysing the motivation behind the patriotism of the parliamentary opposition an examination of the nature of Protestant patriotism in general is necessary.

I

The nature of Protestant patriotism in eighteenth-century Ireland remains a subject of controversy and debate among historians. A recent illuminating analysis of this complicated, contradictory, and often confusing phenomenon has consciously attempted to locate 'Anglo-Irish patriotism' in the context of similar phenomena elsewhere in eighteenth-century Europe.[2] The similarities between Irish patriotism and the related philosophy of patriotism in Britain in the early Hanoverian era should immediately be apparent. In its widest sense, a 'true' or 'worthy' patriot was a person who acted in the best interests of his entire community, for the 'common weal'. Patriotism, therefore, did not necessarily have 'constitutional' or even 'political' connotations. The promotion of agricultural improvement, for example, was widely considered to be a patriotic activity. Figures such as Robert, Viscount Molesworth or Arthur Dobbs clearly fall into this category of patriots who attempted to further the economic well-being of Ireland. This variety of patriotism received institutional recognition in the early eighteenth century with the foundation of the Linen Board (1711) and the Dublin Society (1731). Patriotic deeds, moreover, could be carried out by men to whom the mantle of patriotism was not normally conceded, even arch-enemies of the 'Irish interest'. In the wake of harvest failure in Ulster in the late 1720s Primate Boulter and his fellow lords justices organised the buying of food in Munster for transportation to the north in an attempt to stave off famine, a patriotic act in perhaps its most genuine sense.[3]

Although it is important to acknowledge the existence of this very broad concept of patriotism which can be completely separated from the political arena, it is necessary when examining the political culture of early Hanoverian Ireland not to employ a definition of patriotism so broad as to render it practically meaningless. If all politicians can legitimately be regarded as patriots all of the time, the word loses the political significance which it undoubtedly had for contemporaries. Protestant patriotism, therefore, should be regarded as having been a multi-layered phenomenon. The first layer represented the broad and non-political definition which referred to the desire to improve the state of the country, economically in particular. The second, although still representing a broad definition of patriotism, was more political in nature in that it reflected a consensus among the Protestant community on issues such as Ireland's relationship with Britain, the nature of the religious establishment, and the rights of the Irish parliament. The final layer represented the patriotism of the parliamentary opposition and related to the specific motivation of individual or groups of politicians in opposing an administration. The motivation (as opposed to the rhetoric) behind this activity might have little or no connection with the philosophy of patriotism in general.

Although it is the case that many similarities can be discerned between Irish patriotism and the related phenomenon in Britain, the former did have a quite distinctive and problematic additional feature. Whereas patriotism in Britain was motivated by an anti-court philosophy, Irish patriotism was not simply anti-court, it was also anti-English. 'Patriotism had a specifically Irish meaning, as the defence of local or national interests against English interference.'[4] Such a development was inescapable for Irish patriots, for the 'court' they were opposing was an English court, appointed by and taking its orders from the ministry in London. The disputed Treaty of Limerick; the attempts to resume the forfeited estates; the Woollen Act; the controversy over the judicial rights of the Irish House of Lords culminating in the Declaratory Act; Wood's patent; the repeated vetoing of Irish bills to encourage tillage; absentee landlords, office-holders and pensioners – all of these 'patriotic' issues had overtly anti-English aspects. Even the apparently politically 'neutral' desire to encourage economic improvement in Ireland very quickly encountered the restrictions placed upon Irish economic activity by the Westminster parliament. Because of this anti-English characteristic, some historians have argued that Irish Protestant patriotism developed into a form of 'colonial nationalism' akin to that of the North American colonists in the second half of the eighteenth century. Few would today subscribe to the 'colonial nationalism' thesis. Historians such as George Boyce, David Hayton, Joep Leerssen, Thomas Bartlett and Sean Connolly have each in their own ways rejected the validity of the colonial label. The fact that all of the most important historians working on eighteenth-century Ireland in recent years accept that Irish Protestants explicitly rejected the 'colonial' appellation should finally bury the 'colonial nationalism' label once and for all.

The validity of the other half of the term, 'nationalism', is much more difficult to assess and opinion is very much divided on the 'nationalist' credentials of Protestant patriotism. J.G. Simms clearly regarded Protestant patriotism as akin to the 'colonial nationalism' which allegedly developed in the former British colonies in North America. George Boyce also confers 'Anglo-Irish patriotism' with nationalistic credentials but rejects the 'colonial' label out of hand. Arguing that 'What is commonly called "colonial nationalism" is really an important strand in the complicated skein of Irish nationalism', Boyce says that 'Protestant nationalism' was one of place, Ireland, and of faith, Anglicanism.[5] Thomas Bartlett takes a similar view, arguing that 'if the use of the adjective "colonial" is problematic, the reality of the nationalism is beyond question'.[6] Bartlett has claimed that 'Protestant nationalism' in the eighteenth century consisted 'in roughly equal measure' of confidence that the Catholic threat had been crushed once and for all and resentment over discriminatory treatment at the hands of, and interference in Irish affairs by, Great Britain. Bartlett emphasises that 'Freedom from fear was essential to the development of the Protestant nationalism of the eighteenth century', that is, freedom from the 'Catholic, Stuart, and Presbyterian threats'.[7] This sense of confidence (engendered by the absence of fear) combined with resentment of English interference in Irish affairs to produce the distinctive 'nationalism' of the Protestant Irish. Therefore, whereas Simms appeared to regard Protestant patriotism as part of a wider colonial movement and Boyce places it firmly in the context of the long term development of Irish nationalism in general, Bartlett regards it as having arisen in circumstances peculiar to Ireland between 1690 and the early 1790s.

Another complicating factor has been added to the debate by David Hayton, who has argued that a distinction should be made between Protestant self-perception in the early eighteenth century and later. Hayton posits the view that, whereas in the 1690s Irish Protestants regarded themselves as the 'English in Ireland', by the middle of the eighteenth century they had come to consider themselves as 'Irish'.[8] Hayton's contribution to the debate is important because he correctly highlights the very real confusion which existed in the minds of Irish Protestants as to national identity in the early eighteenth century. Such confusion in the minds of contemporaries goes a long way towards explaining the disagreement among historians about the nature of Protestant patriotism or nationalism for it is a relatively simple matter to produce evidence to support whichever case one wishes to uphold. J.G. McCoy has responded to the contradictory evidence of the sources by concluding that 'The Ascendancy mind was capable of considering itself Irish, English and/or British at both different and simultaneous times.'[9] The confusion in the minds of contemporaries and historians alike is merely re-emphasised.

One historian, Joep Leerssen, has sought to resolve the confusion surrounding this subject by rejecting out of hand any 'nationalistic' credentials of 'Anglo-Irish Patriotism'. Arguing that Protestant patriotism 'must be liberated from the straightjacket of an Irish-English national manicheism and, terminologically, from the national connotations with which the word has anachronistically been burdened', Leerssen maintains that Protestant patriotism should be regarded, *pace* Boyce, not as a forerunner of nineteenth- and twentieth-century Irish nationalism, but of a liberalism which, in the Irish context, was still-born.[10] Whether such an interpretation, which strips the patriotism of the Anglican élite of all nationalist credentials, will achieve general acceptance is as yet unclear, although Sean Connolly, for one, has endorsed at least part of Leerssen's thesis.[11] An insistence on a precise use of language on the part of historians in this context is, however, surely justified. To describe eighteenth-century patriotism as a form of nationalism (colonial or otherwise) is, as Leerssen says, anachronistic. A convincing case can be made for the view that what would generally be regarded as nationalism in the nineteenth and twentieth centuries simply did not exist in the eighteenth. What is absolutely certain is that the form of romantic nationalism which emerged in Europe in the first half of the nineteenth century did not exist among the Anglican gentry of early eighteenth-century Ireland. A romantic view of Ireland's past (particularly the Gaelic past) was a fundamental component of Irish nationalism from the time of the Young Ireland movement. Moreover, modern nationalism normally defines nationality in terms of place of birth. Religion, class, or ethnic origin (although very often complicating factors) are not usually obstacles to membership of the nation, officially at least. Such a concept of the nation is clearly inappropriate to eighteenth-century Ireland where religious affiliation and wealth were its defining characteristics. More fundamentally, modern nationalists can justify their claim for political independence on the simple grounds that they consider themselves to be a separate people. Early eighteenth-century Irish Protestants quite obviously did not consider themselves to be a people separate from their brethren in England. Modern nationalists can also resort to historical or legal-constitutional arguments such as those employed by Molyneux and Swift,[12] but in the end they are not the underlying justification for national independence. In short, patriotism, anti-English resentments and an ambiguous sense of 'Irishness' did exist among the Anglican élite but nationalism did not. The use of the latter term has only served to confuse and it is best avoided.

Most historians, including Leerssen, do accept that some kind of Irish national identity began to emerge among at least some Irish Protestants by the middle of the eighteenth century. This was in part due to a growing feeling of 'belonging' in Ireland among some of the Anglican gentry and in part due to an increased awareness of Irish history. There seems little doubt, however, that the prime factor leading to the development of a sense of Irish identity among Irish Protestants was the recognition among many of them that they were perceived as 'Irish' by the English.[13] Just as the Anglican élite reacted to the rejection of their request for a parliamentary union in the reign of Queen Anne by loudly proclaiming the rights of their own parliament, they dealt with the fact that they were perceived in England as Irish by gradually reconciling themselves to the idea and making the best of it by giving Irishness positive connotations. They also altered the meaning of the term. Whereas it was sufficient at the start of the century to describe Catholics as 'the Irish', by mid-century adjectives such as 'native', 'original', 'natural' or 'mere' had to be added to the noun to maintain the division between Catholic and Protestant.[14] Noting the emergence of this 'new, shared sense of identity, based on a feeling of distinction' from the English, Joseph McMinn has accurately described it as 'an almost joyless discovery'.[15] It is evident, therefore, that Irish Protestants did not assume an Irish identity whole-heartedly, indeed that it was to a large extent forced upon them, and that much ambiguity about how they perceived themselves remained. What is unambiguous is that a sense of national identity which was inclusive of the Catholic and protestant dissenting communities (that is, around ninety per cent of the people of Ireland) played little or no part in the patriotism of the

Irish Anglican élite throughout the eighteenth century.[16]

In the context of the early Hanoverian era, it is important to emphasise that the widespread acceptance of an Irish identity among the Protestant community had not yet emerged. It is clear that at this stage Irish Protestants still preferred to be regarded as 'the English in Ireland'. A classic exposition of Protestant patriotism, Jonathan Swift's *Letter to the Whole People of Ireland* (1724), shows just how gradual was the alleged transformation in thinking among Irish Protestants over the question of national identity.[17] Although addressed to 'the whole people of Ireland' (not, it should be noted, to 'the Irish people'), Swift reserves the label 'Irish' for the Catholics. William Molyneux, for example, is described by Swift as 'an English gentleman born here', an antilogy to the modern mind. More tellingly, in response to Wood's complaint that 'the Irish' refused his coinage, Swift argues that 'he is mistaken, for it is the true English people of Ireland who refuse it'. On this occasion, as on many others, Swift based his claim for equality of rights for Irish Protestants on the grounds that they were 'the English in Ireland': 'by the laws of GOD, of NATURE, of NATIONS, and of your own Country, you ARE and OUGHT to be as FREE a people as your brethren in England'. Only once does Swift employ the label 'Irish' to describe Irish-born Protestants and it is surely significant that he uses it in the context of the conflict between the Irish and English interests within the Church of Ireland when, as we have seen, English bishops employed the label 'Irish' to identify their Irish-born opponents.[18] There is little ambiguity here and certainly no sign of proto-nationalistic sentiments. A man who complains about the 'misfortune' of being born in Ireland cannot be regarded as a nationalist in any meaningful sense.[19]

If Protestant patriotism was not based upon an unambiguous sense of Irish (as opposed to English/British) national identity, what then distinguished it from, for example, the provincial pride of the people of Yorkshire, Cornwall or Herefordshire? As Hayton has pointed out, the words 'country' and 'county' were often employed interchangeably in eighteenth-century Britain and Ireland.[20] Two factors differentiated Protestant patriotism from a merely provincial identity. Firstly, the patriotism of Irish Protestants was not only one of place, it was also one of faith – Anglicanism.[21] Moreover, Ireland was not simply a province or county, it was a kingdom with national, not provincial, institutions. It was the most important of these national institutions, the Irish parliament, which provided the focus for and rationale behind eighteenth-century Protestant patriotism.

J.G. McCoy has argued that an over-emphasis on the work of Jonathan Swift has led to the emergence of a false impression of the patriotism of the Anglican community in Ireland. His description of Irish patriotism in the eighteenth century differs from most standard accounts in that he argues that, although the Irish 'élite was happy enough to describe itself as Irish', Irish Protestants 'developed a brand of Patriotism which did not seek to assert Ireland's constitutional equality with Great Britain'.[22] Protestant patriotism, according to this account, was based on the emergence of an Irish national identity (although not exclusively Irish) among an Anglican élite who, particularly after the Declaratory Act, reconciled themselves to constitutional subjection to Great Britain. Such an interpretation is obviously in direct contradiction to the sentiments expressed by people such as Swift and William King both of whom, even after the passage of the Declaratory Act, continued to argue for the equality of the Irish parliament with that of Westminster. Swift was unambiguous on this point rejecting out of hand the theory of the subordination of the Irish parliament to that at Westminster:

> A "depending kingdom" is a *modern term of art*, unknown, as I have heard, to all ancient *civilians* and *writers upon government;* ... I have looked over all the English and Irish statutes without finding any law that makes Ireland *depend* upon England, any more than England does upon Ireland. We have indeed obliged ourselves to have the *same king with them*, and consequently they are obliged to have the *same king with us.* [23]

Swift, as usual, allowed himself to be carried away by his own rhetoric but his point was well made. Ireland was annexed to the English crown, not to the English parliament. The 'Representation' to the king drawn up by the Irish House of Lords in defence of its judicial rights in 1719 is unambiguous in asserting that only the crown in consultation with the Irish parliament had the right to pass laws binding Ireland:

> though the Imperial Crown of this Realm, was formerly inseparably annexed to the Imperial Crown of *England*, and is now to that of *Great Britain*, yet this Kingdom, being of itself a distinct Dominion, and no Part of the Kingdom of *England*, none can determine concerning the Affairs thereof, unless authorised thereto by the known Laws and Customs of this Kingdom, or by the express Consent of the King.[24]

It is certainly the case that Irish Protestants were prepared to accept a degree of dependence upon Britain, but they were emphatic that such dependence was upon the British crown, not upon the British parliament. John Toland made precisely this point in a pamphlet written in opposition to the Declaratory Act – 'there is a vast difference between *Ireland*'s being annext to the Crown of *Great-Britain*, and being subject to the Lords of *Great-Britain*'.[25] There was undoubtedly a gulf of understanding between the political élites of Britain and Ireland on this crucial constitutional point, in the case of the former perhaps a

wilful misunderstanding. Irish Protestants never questioned Ireland's dependence upon the English crown. However, when they commonly objected to any
form of subjection to the Westminster parliament this was perceived in England as a bid for 'independency'. Such muddled thinking on the part of British
parliamentarians is best exemplified by the text of the Declaratory Act itself:

> ... for the better securing of the dependency of *Ireland* upon the crown
> of *Great Britain*, ... be it declared ..., That the said kingdom of *Ireland*
> hath been, is, and of right ought to be subordinate unto and dependent
> upon the imperial crown of *Great Britain*, as being inseparably united
> and annexed thereunto; and that the King's majesty, by and with the
> advice and consent of the lords spiritual and temporal, and commons of
> *Great Britain* in parliament assembled, had, hath, and of right ought to
> have full power and authority to make laws and statutes of sufficient
> force and validity, to bind the kingdom and people of *Ireland*.[26]

Whereas no one in Ireland disputed the veracity of the first part of this declaration, they vehemently rejected the notion that the second (that Westminster had
the right to legislate for Ireland) followed logically from it. The establishment
of rival parliaments in London and Dublin after 1688, combined with the shift
in power from the monarchy to parliament in Britain in the succeeding decades, meant that a constitutional relationship which had been more or less
appropriate to a situation in which the monarch was the most powerful factor
rapidly became anachronistic. The realities of the power relationship between
Britain and Ireland meant that if a conflict arose between the Irish and British
political establishments, the latter would emerge victorious, as indeed occurred
during the Sherlock–Annesley dispute. Irish Protestants were clearly aware of
this basic fact of life. However, such a recognition of political reality on the
part of men such as Viscount Midleton who warned of the consequences of
opposing the British House of Lords over the Sherlock–Annesley case should
not be taken to imply that they were completely happy with this interpretation
of the Anglo-Irish constitutional relationship.[27] As the judicature dispute began
to gather momentum in 1717, Charles Dering admitted to Lord Percival that 'I
think as you do that this dispute may very probably be of ill consequence',
however he added defiantly 'but the not asserting their own jurisdiction must
necessarily be so, and if privileges are to be taken away from a body of men, a
decent resistance is what is very commendable'.[28]

It may still be objected that men such as Swift, King, Percival and Dering
cannot be regarded as being representative of the Irish Protestant community
as a whole. It is probably true that historians have tended to over-estimate the
extent to which the writings of Jonathan Swift and William King are representative of the wider Anglican community. It is certainly the case that the

leaders of the Irish-born clergy, resentful at the disposal of the patronage of the Church of Ireland to 'foreign' Englishmen, played a leading role in the Sherlock–Annesley dispute. The centrality of Archbishop King's role in the affair is beyond dispute. Those who loudly proclaimed the equality of the Irish parliament were in all probability a vociferous minority and it is likely that most of the Protestant élite took a more pragmatic view of their country's relationship with Britain than that expressed by the leading patriots in parliament. On the other hand, because some men advocated that Irish Protestants should accept a degree of dependency upon Britain and operate within the parameters set out by the British government, it does not follow that they were necessarily content with that situation. In other words, that some (or even most) members of the Anglican community were prepared to recognise the realities of the power relationship between Britain and Ireland did not mean that they abandoned the view that the Irish parliament should be regarded as the equal of that at Westminster. Although most members of the Anglican community were prepared to accept that Ireland was to a certain extent a 'dependent kingdom', all were determined to stress that it was a kingdom nonetheless and that such dependency had its limitations.

Few in Ireland, furthermore, appeared to disagree, publicly at least, with the version of the constitutional relationship outlined by the House of Lords in 1719. When the Lords approved their 'Representation' outlining the rationale behind their defence of their judicial powers only eight peers dissented: the lord chancellor; the brother of one of the barons of the Exchequer who had been taken into custody on the orders of the Irish lords; Lord Shelburne; and, most significantly, five English bishops, four of whom had been appointed to their Irish sees since the accession of George I. The barons of the Exchequer and the English-born bishops, moreover, clearly felt under enormous social pressure during the Sherlock–Annesley dispute, suggesting that a considerable degree of consensus existed among the Anglican community on this overtly constitutional issue.[29] Just before the passage of the Declaratory Act, Bishop Nicolson informed Archbishop Wake that 'Whatever the fate of your Bill relating to this Kingdom, the progress already made in that matter has created [for] me (and I believe most other English foreigners) a good deal of disquiet. We are all treated by friends and foes, Whigs and Tories, as enemies to the public interests of this Kingdom'. Nicolson added that 'the general cry for Independency ... universally prevails'.[30] It would seem that the situation was even worse after the Act was finally passed. Nicolson wrote that the 'rage' of 'our gentlemen ... is not to be described. "Here's an end", says one of the wisest of them in my hearing, "of all the liberties and properties of Ireland. The house of lords is already demolished, and we are all slaves &c." This sort of seditious talk is so general, that conversation is become extremely hazardous.' Interestingly, however, Nicolson believed that 'within a few weeks this heat will abate', a judgement which was probably correct.[31] Not surprisingly, the barons of the Exchequer seemed to bear the brunt of the Anglican community's resentment. Whilst on his circuit at Longford, Chief Baron Gilbert had to endure the indignity of lodging in the local army barracks as 'no house would receive him' and Baron St Leger's reception at Phillipstown was described as 'but very indifferent'.[32] In the absence of alternative evidence, it seems reasonable to assume that more Irish Protestants agreed with the actions of the House of Lords than disagreed.

The Lords' Representation, however, which on the face of it asserts the rights of the Irish parliament in confident and combative terms, also contains evidence that even the most vociferous Irish patriots were prepared to recognise that the alterations in the operation of the constitution since 1688 required some modification to their case for the full equality of their parliament with that at Westminster. Despite the ambiguities of the 'revolution settlement', the ultimate supremacy of the Westminster parliament (over the monarchy, never mind the Irish parliament) was scarcely in doubt after the Williamite revolution. Irish Protestants reacted to the vast increase in the power of the Westminster legislature by accepting its supremacy in imperial matters (diplomacy, war and trade) but by continuing to reject its right to interfere in internal 'Irish' matters. The Lords' Representation emphasised on no less than four separate occasions that what they were seeking to defend was their jurisdiction over 'all Matters that wholly relate to this Realm'.[33] Two years previously, Archbishop Synge had argued just this case:

It must indeed be allowed that England is the Principal Kingdom, and Ireland an accessory to it; but still they are both Kingdoms: and although it may not seem reasonable that the accessory Kingdom should finally determine any matter where the principal may be affected by such a determination; yet where a matter lies wholly within ourselves, and England is not at all concerned in it, what reason can be given why it should not be finally determined by our own Parliament[?][34]

By the reign of George I, therefore, Irish Protestants were apparently prepared to accept that the Westminster parliament should have the final say in imperial matters, but that the internal affairs of Ireland should be regulated by their own legislature. In this respect, it is correct to say that the patriotism of the Anglican élite recognised the superiority of the Westminster legislature. This did not amount, however, to an acceptance of the premise of the Declaratory Act that the British parliament had the right to interfere in wholly internal Irish affairs. Even Archbishop Boulter was prepared to defend the right of the Protestants of Ireland to regulate their own affairs without unwarranted interference from England. In 1735 Boulter asked the duke of Newcastle to oppose a bill introduced in the Westminster parliament 'for securing the title of Protestants'. The primate argued that 'it must be dangerous to give way to passing bills originally in England wholly relating to affairs in Ireland and especially to our private property here, without the least pretence that his Majesty's service or the interest of England are anyways concerned in the affair'.[35] William King could not have put it (much) better.

This version of the Anglo-Irish constitutional relationship (which effectively recognised Irish autonomy within the broader imperial framework) rapidly gained acceptance on both sides of the Irish Sea, not because Irish Protestants reconciled themselves to the Declaratory Act but, because the British parliament did not attempt to use the powers theoretically available to it after 1720. Certainly some commentators realised the potential impact of the Act, they were outlined with admirable clarity by Lord Percival to Archbishop King:

> my Lord, I plainly perceive by that clause in the Bill (so foreign to the dispute of Judicature) namely that Great Britain has power to make laws for Ireland, that for the future, when ever our Parliaments refuse to give the sums required by the Crown, we shall be threatened with dissolutions and a taxing law from hence. This cloud will always hang over our heads, and we shall be awed into compliances not only in money matters but even the taking off the Test or any other thing that a future corrupt Ministry shall propose.[36]

None of these dangers was ever to materialise. One gains the strong impression that, having made their point and established their superiority, British parliamentarians quickly lost interest in Ireland. Many in both Britain and Ireland, no doubt, had regarded the dispute as being primarily between the respective upper houses. So long as legislation passed at Westminster affecting Ireland related to imperial affairs, it met with little opposition in Ireland. Restrictions on Irish trade with the rest of the empire continued to rankle in Ireland, of course, but they did not produce a constitutional crisis.[37] So long as the Anglican élite was permitted to govern Ireland largely as it saw fit, a relatively amicable relationship was preserved. The significance of the Declaratory Act, therefore, should not be overstated. In fact, the government of Ireland continued after 1720 exactly as it had done before. The undoubted absence of widespread protest in Ireland following the passage of the Declaratory Act was not due to an acceptance of its claim that the British parliament had the right to legislate for Ireland, but because the Act made no difference to the operation of practical politics. The 'Sixth of George I' did not lead to greater British interference in Irish affairs, nor did it lead to the creation of the undertaker system, and it did not change Anglican patriot thinking in any significant way.[38] The decision in the late 1760s of Lord Lieutenant Townshend to reside permanently in Dublin had a far greater impact on the government of Ireland and the Anglo-Irish constitutional relationship than did the Declaratory Act.[39]

II

The acceptance of a subordinate status for their parliament on the part of the Anglican élite, therefore, should not lead to the conclusion that the question of the rights and status of their parliament was a minor aspect of the philosophy of Protestant patriotism. Irish peers and MPs consistently displayed extreme sensitivity about the rights of the Irish parliament in relation to the British privy council and the Westminster parliament. Advising against 'tacking' a clause to repeal the sacramental test to a popery bill, Primate Boulter warned that 'most that set up for patriots will on that very account reject it'.[40] The vigorous assertion of the status and rights of the Irish parliament was probably the single most important and consistent ingredient of eighteenth-century Protestant patriotism. The functions and status of the Dublin parliament were central to Anglican self-perception and it is difficult to overestimate the significance of the Irish parliament in the evolution of Protestant patriotism. Without the emergence of the Irish parliament as a permanent and influential institution in the aftermath of the Williamite revolution, Protestant patriotism could not have developed in the form in which it did.

The central dilemma which faced Irish Protestants throughout the eighteenth century was a result of their desire for greater autonomy (although never independence, of course) from Britain while simultaneously continuing to deny political and economic rights and privileges to the majority of the Irish people. Given the relative numerical weakness of their position in Ireland, Protestants had to choose carefully the grounds upon which they demanded constitutional equality with Britain. Isolde Victory has claimed that one of the consequences of the Declaratory Act was that Irish Protestants were forced to base their claims for political rights on the grounds of 'Lockean Natural Right'.

> Until 1720, the Anglo-Irish had rooted their political legitimacy in being the inheritors of common law rights. Historical, judicial and legislative precedents were the bulwarks of their constitutional construct. The Declaratory Act undermined the foundations of these beliefs by providing an overriding precedent against all such claims.[41]

This interpretation raises two difficulties. In the first place, there is little evidence to support the view that Irish Protestants accepted the premise of the Declaratory Act that the Westminster parliament had the right to legislate for Ireland. The fact that this theoretical power was not used by the British establishment after 1720 is clear evidence that it would have aroused strong opposition in Ireland. If Irish Protestants did reconcile themselves to the Declaratory Act, why then did they seek to have it repealed in 1782? More importantly perhaps, is the fact that if Irish Protestants had abandoned the constitutional basis of their arguments for equality in favour of those arising out of 'natural right', this would have had serious potential implications for the status of Irish Catholics. Were only Protestants entitled to 'natural rights'?[42]

The greatest advantage of basing patriotic arguments for constitutional equality on the historic rights of the Dublin parliament was that it allowed Irish Protestants to assert autonomy from Britain without raising the thorny question of the political rights of Irish Catholics. For Protestant patriots did not assert the rights of 'the people', but (at first) the rights of 'free born Englishmen'. When it became clear that they were increasingly coming to be regarded in England as 'Irish', they concentrated on a defence of the rights of parliament, an institution safely under the control of the Anglican squirearchy. Whereas it was safe to defend the rights of their parliament from attempted encroachment by Westminster, arguments which stressed the natural rights of 'the people' raised questions which could have unforeseen and unfortunate consequences, particularly as it became increasingly obvious as the eighteenth century progressed that it was not at all clear in the eyes of the British establishment who exactly were 'the people of Ireland'. The Irish parliamentary reformers of the early 1780s were to face precisely this dilemma as soon as they moved beyond the limits which had defined Protestant patriotism since the 1690s. Whereas the Protestant élite was prepared to support Grattan's claim for the 'independence' of parliament (as soon as the British government made it clear that it would accede to such a demand), more power for 'the people' (even if confined to the Protestant community) was quite another matter. As Grattan famously put it, 'having given a parliament to the people, the Volunteers will, I doubt not, leave the people to Parliament'.[43] As soon as the question of extending political power beyond the Anglican élite was raised, the patriotic united front was destroyed. Irish Protestants in the eighteenth century, like European liberals in the nineteenth, were only too aware that the theory of parliamentary sovereignty allowed those who dominated parliamentary institutions to demand greater rights for themselves while continuing to deny those rights to the rest of the population. Leerssen's proposition that 'Anglo-Irish Patriotism' should be regarded as a proto-liberal rather than a proto-nationalist phenomenon may well have real merit.

The theory of the independence of the Irish parliament based on its historic rights allowed Irish Protestants to argue for autonomy from Britain whilst maintaining the continued connection with the British crown. Ideally, British military protection could coexist with the freedom to govern Ireland more or less as they pleased. Ironically, an institution which had served the purposes of the

Anglican élite extremely well began to lose some of its attractiveness soon after the achievement of legislative independence in 1782. When in the 1790s it became increasingly obvious that the closely related questions of political rights for Catholics and parliamentary reform could not be postponed indefinitely, the Dublin parliament became more of a threat than an asset. An institution which had been used to protect the political and economic privileges of the Anglican élite for a hundred years could no longer serve this purpose due to an increasingly 'direct' form of government by London which became evident after the Regency crisis and, especially, the outbreak of war in Europe. The manner in which the British government bullied this 'independent' legislature into repealing virtually all anti-Catholic legislation in 1793 graphically demonstrated the extent to which parliament was no longer a bulwark of the Anglican virtual monopoly of political power and economic privilege. As is well known, the Dublin parliament had rejected similar proposals out of hand a year previously accompanied by a stream of anti-papist abuse. At the start of 1793, however, Henry Dundas had bluntly outlined the British government's attitude to Lord Lieutenant Westmoreland: 'If it is a mere question of whether one description of Irishmen or another are to enjoy a monopoly of preeminence, I am afraid that is not a question which they would feel either their passions or their interests so materially concerned in as to justify any application of the reserves of Great Britain in the decision of it'.[44] This bombshell undermined the entire rationale behind Protestant patriotism which had rested upon the assumption that the Westminster government would defend the right of the Anglican élite to be considered the 'people of Ireland'. Now it seemed, as far as the government was concerned, Irish Protestants were merely 'one description of Irishmen'. It was at this point that those Irish Protestants who, in earlier and quieter decades could afford 'to play with the idea of themselves as Irishmen',[45] were finally compelled to face the reality of their relationship with Britain and with the non-Anglican communities in Ireland. The Irish parliament and the patriotism which depended upon its continued existence could not long survive in this new harsher climate.

Noting the transformation which occurred in Irish Protestant thinking in the 1790s as a result of the revival of the Catholic threat, Thomas Bartlett has commented that 'By 1793, if not before, Protestant nationalism had yielded to Protestant Ascendancy.'[46] This comment illustrates the problematic nature of employing the terminology of nationalism in an eighteenth-century context. For Irish Protestants in the 1790s did not abandon a nationalist philosophy in favour of a unionist one. Rather many Protestant patriots lost confidence in the institution which hitherto had served their purposes so well. Protestant parliamentary patriotism and 'Protestant Ascendancy' were fundamentally one and the same thing. It is indicative of the importance of the Dublin parliament to Anglican self-perception and self-esteem that so many Irish Protestants fought so hard to preserve it even in the harrowing context of the late 1790s.

III

The above analysis of Protestant patriotism has highlighted the confusion, in the minds of both contemporaries and historians alike, as to its true nature. In terms of parliamentary politics, however, patriotism had a much more specific meaning and it is this political or parliamentary patriotism which will now be examined. In the parliamentary context, a patriot was a man who was committed to no party or faction and certainly not to the government. His role was to prevent the political system from being abused, particularly by the government. Court corruption, excessive or unfair taxation, absentee landlords and office-holders, infringements of the liberties of the subject, the waging of unnecessary wars and so on were issues of particular concern to patriots. Clearly such a patriotic agenda had much in common with a country platform and the concerns of the Commonwealthmen of the seventeenth and early eighteenth centuries.[47] From the 1690s, furthermore, the Tory party in Britain became increasingly identified with such issues. The overlap between Commonwealth, Old Whig, country, Tory, and patriot philosophies makes it difficult to differentiate them clearly and it is probably futile to attempt to do so, the terminology often being interchangeable. In 1710, for example, some at least of the Tory opponents of the Whig administration of the earl of Wharton adopted the label of the 'country party'.[48] Likewise the Whig opponents of Shrewsbury's administration in 1713-14 referred to themselves as the 'country party' although they were described sardonically as 'great Patriots' by a government supporter.[49] After 1715, the opposition in the Irish House of Commons (a combination of Tories, discontented Whigs led by the Brodricks, and patriotic 'country gentlemen') was also sometimes disparagingly called the 'patriots'. In the 1725-6 parliamentary session those opposition MPs who disputed the veracity of the government's accounts apparently called themselves the 'Country party'. In 1732, Marmaduke Coghill warned that any attempt to repeal the sacramental test would 'increase the country party'.[50] In truth, the terminology employed is less important than the motivation behind such opposition to the court. It is perhaps significant, however, that the only party label employed by politicians adopting a patriotic stance in parliament was that of the 'country party'.

Like Protestant patriotism in general, the nature of parliamentary patriotism in eighteenth-century Ireland (and Britain) remains an area of debate among historians. One reason for the continued disagreement over the motivation behind parliamentary patriotism is the respective preconceptions of individual historians. Whilst one person might regard patriotism as the selfless pursuit of the common good, another will view it as a cloak of legitimacy cynically employed by self-seeking politicians intent on creating mischief for those in power. This dichotomy will never be resolved. Contemporaries, as well as historians, displayed a similar uncertainty as to the motivation of patriots.[51] Not surprisingly, those in power were universally hostile to and deeply suspicious of the motivation behind parliamentary patriotism. In government correspondence the word 'patriot' was always employed in a pejorative sense, often heavily laced with sarcasm. Chief baron of the Exchequer, Bernard Hale, called those who were organising opposition to Wood's patent in 1724 as 'our great patriots'.[52] In 1731 chief secretary Cary complained that because the government's money bills were being delayed at Holyhead, the administration was 'being kept in continual alarm with the daily motions of Patriots'.[53] When the opposition in the Commons questioned aspects of the government's accounts in 1733-4, baron of the Exchequer, John Wainwright, commented that 'This they did as Patriots'.[54] Possibly the best summary of the official view of parliamentary patriotism in this period is that which was offered by the chief secretary in 1723. Drawing parallels with the situation at Westminster, Edward Hopkins commented:

> Patriots in this country, as well as in another we are acquainted with, arise out of disappointments, and country gentlemen are caught by popular points by those for whom they have personally no esteem. The increase of pensions and the coinage of copper half-pence have been artfully improved and worked up into grievances ...[55]

There is no doubt that 'artful' politicians regularly used patriot or country issues to rally the country gentlemen in opposition to the court. The administration's plan in 1719 to seek a bill offering protestant dissenters a limited toleration, provided the opposition with an ideal issue with which to muster support. After Sir Ralph Gore agreed to head a committee to draw up such a bill, 'the Br[odric]ks met the Country party and many of those whom they had formerly ill used assuring them no old sores should be ripped or railings for past things but that they should unanimously join in this matter'.[56] The opposition was successful in defeating Gore's bill and having their own measure passed instead. Although no doubt genuinely opposed to concessions to protestant dissenters, the Brodricks certainly exploited the issue as an opportunity to attack an administration which had recently dismissed Midleton as its chief undertaker in favour of William Conolly. In the Commons indeed, St John Brodrick accused Conolly of undertaking for the dissenters' bill, a charge vehemently denied by the latter.[57]

In the aftermath of the Wood's halfpence dispute, an opposition of Tories and discontented Whigs led by the Brodricks (calling themselves the 'Country Party')[58] were able to exploit the confused state of the government's accounts due to the arrest of the deputy vice-Treasurer and win the country gentlemen to their side. Marmaduke Coghill claimed that although everything done by the court had been 'fair and honest', it had been impossible to calm the fears of the country gentlemen who 'by insinuation of crafty men do really believe they are to be cheated'.[59] Coghill was not alone in his cynicism towards the motivation of such patriots. Informing his father of the success of the parliamentary opposition, Philip Percival commented that 'this majority may rather be called the Anti Courtiers than the Country party, for I believe their zeal and vehemence proceeded more out of pique to the former than affection to the latter, though the pretence was as usual the good of the Nation but I believe as usual it will be left in the lurch at last'.[60]

The exploitation of fears of new taxes or alterations to the religious establishment were the most common means by which patriots stirred up parliamentary opposition. When the government presented a money bill to open the first session of George II's parliament, Agmondisham Vesey moved that the house should not receive a money bill until the committee of accounts had reported, the implication being that additional taxation might not be necessary. Government supporters cleverly responded by similarly playing upon the country gentlemen's fears of new taxation. Arguing that any delay in passing the money bill would mean that the civil and military establishments could not be supported, they warned that 'this must inevitably bring a land tax upon us'. Marmaduke Coghill, a government supporter, commented that the opposition's 'motion was made with an intention to try if a party could be framed upon some topic of patriotism, which you know has often deceived young members, (of which I have been one) which in the end have always proved mischievous to the country, and a success only to help designing men to what they aim at'.[61] Five years later, following the election of Henry Boyle as speaker of the Commons, Coghill described the collapse of the patriot opposition. Claiming that Arthur Dawson and Mr Malone were the only surviving patriots, Coghill commented ironically that 'Mr Stannard appears hitherto quiet, and Vesey's heart has not bled this session, nor does he appear to be much troubled as formerly, for the distress of his country'.[62] The previous year, Vesey had promised to end his opposition to the court in return for the appointment of his son-in-law as dean of Ardfert. It is not surprising that official sources portrayed patriots in a less than complimentary light. From the government point of view, such men were no more than self-seeking, cynical troublemakers who would exploit any opportunity to create mischief for the court.

Those in opposition to (or merely outside of) the government could afford to adopt a more objective or even generous stance. In this context, the noun 'patriot' was preceded by adjectives such as 'good', 'noble' or 'worthy', but in order to convey praise and appreciation rather than sarcasm or irony. It has to be said, however, that praise of 'noble patriots' normally arose in the context of patron-dependant relationships. It is, therefore, difficult to estimate the genuineness or otherwise of such panegyrics.[63]

IV

Protestant patriotism, as we have seen, emerged in the immediate aftermath of the Williamite war. The decade of the 1690s provided a number of high-profile issues which facilitated the emergence of an explicit patriotic philosophy. The controversy surrounding the claim of the Irish House of Commons to have the 'sole right' to initiate financial legislation in 1692; the long-running disagreement between the Irish parliament and the government over the final form of the Treaty of Limerick; the tangled mess over the confiscated estates; the dispute between the bishop of Derry and the London Society over the right to final appeal in Irish legal cases; and, most famously, the Woollen Act of 1699. The latter controversy resulted, of course, in the publication of what was to become the 'bible' of Protestant patriotism, William Molyneux's *The Case of Ireland's being bound by Acts of Parliament in England Stated*. By the time of Queen Anne's accession, therefore, the main themes of the patriotic disputes which were to dominate Anglo-Irish relations for the remainder of the century had emerged – rejection of the assumed right of the Westminster parliament to legislate for Ireland; resentment over the control of the Irish economy by England; and exception to what was perceived as unwarranted interference by the English government and parliament in internal 'Irish' affairs, especially regarding the status of non-Anglicans. A strong degree of consensus could normally be found among Irish Protestants on these issues. Indeed it was this general consensus which made patriotism such a powerful weapon in the hands of government opponents and, consequently, so difficult an attack for those Irishmen in office to withstand.

The emergence of a full-blown and explicit party conflict in the latter half of Queen Anne's reign seriously complicated the politics of patriotism. Politicians in opposition could still, as before, adopt a 'patriotic' or 'country' platform in order to attack the administration but as the Whig-Tory dichotomy intensified such a stance became increasingly difficult to defend. Each change in the party composition of the administration (as occurred in 1703, 1707-8, 1710 and 1714) saw the increasingly distasteful spectacle of former government servants employing patriotic terminology in order to attack their party opponents who were now in office. When Ormonde was replaced as lord lieutenant by Pembroke in 1707 and Alan Brodrick was returned to office, one observer wrote contemptuously of his abandonment of opposition to the government: 'The speaker having been made attorney general fell in now with the demands of the court, though he was too great a patriot to do it in the duke of Ormonde's government for which he is heartily dispised by many of his quondam friends'.[64] The parliamentary session of 1707, indeed, witnessed perhaps the most blatant example of such *volte-faces* on the part of Irish politicians. Those Whigs who had opposed the request of the late Tory government for a two year money bill in the previous session of parliament now had to attempt to achieve just such a measure for their own Whig administration. The device eventually employed to overcome this difficulty was the rather crude one of a money bill which would last for twenty-one months. Thus the Whigs were enabled, superficially at least, to save face.[65] Such blatant attempts by so-called patriots to abandon the principles which they had apparently so sincerely professed shortly before must have led to a widespread distrust of and cynicism towards the motivation of those who employed patriotic terminology to attack political opponents.

The establishment of a Whig ascendancy after 1714 brought stability to the Irish political system but it also transformed the tactics of the parliamentary opposition. During the party conflict members of parliament had generally served under party banners and ambitions for office and patronage were pursued through the party system. The Whig schism and expulsion of Tories from government and office complicated the picture. Men who found themselves out of favour with the dominant faction no longer had the option of joining an organised parliamentary opposition with a realistic prospect of gaining power. The Brodrick-Conolly conflict, of course, gave men the option of joining one of these factions but this dichotomy was a very different one from the Whig-Tory dispute and neither faction had the coherence of the old Whig party. Conolly, moreover, was usually in the ascendant. More importantly, until 1725 both men were members of the government and could not openly place themselves at the head of a country or patriot opposition. The only option open to ambitious politicians under these circumstances was to cut a figure in parliament by employing patriotic rhetoric in order to bring themselves to the attention of those in power. The intention was to persuade the court that it was better to have such men in office than in opposition. Men such as Henry Singleton, Thomas Carter, Theophilus Bolton and, of course, Henry Boyle used such tactics with considerable success. However, not all of those who took up the banner of patriotism did so in order to achieve personal advancement. It is clear that some men who had long since given up hopes of preferment simply hoped to wound a government which, for whatever reason, they particularly disliked. Others, taking pride in their independence, opposed particular measures rather than the government as such. These 'country gentlemen' provided the main reservoir of support for the more able and motivated patriot leaders. Unless the country gentlemen could be persuaded to lend their support to a particular patriot campaign it was doomed to failure. The support of such 'independent' members, moreover, was notoriously unstable often disappearing as quickly as it had arrived.

The tactics of the patriot opposition were fairly straightforward. The proposal of motions relating to the state of the nation were the most common means by which patriots raised the issues which concerned them. Such motions might be presented as addresses to the king, ostensibly designed to bring to his attention the concerns of his Irish subjects. The main topics for complaint were the size of the national debt, the level of taxation, restrictions on Irish trade, and the state of the economy in general. The granting of pensions to individuals considered 'unworthy' in some way might also be the subject of a motion. The focus of the patriotic attack normally came at the beginning of the session when the question of additional taxation was discussed in the committee of accounts and by the whole House of Commons. Patriots would often argue that no additional taxation was needed or would not be necessary if the court managed its finances properly. This attack was often accompanied by complaints about the state of the Irish economy. During the proceedings over the supply in 1729, for example, Robin Allen moved that the Commons resolve that 'this country was in a miserable condition' and Thomas Carter proposed that the importation of lace, wines and other luxuries 'tended to the immediate ruin of this Kingdom'.[66] Motions were regularly proposed to cut government expenditure (usually by removing pensions) or to tax the salaries and pensions of absentees, a tax of 4 shillings in the pound on such incomes being routinely passed after 1715.

Clearly economic issues were at the forefront of patriotic opposition and it is certainly the case that such issues were most likely to attract support from the country gentlemen. However, other issues were also employed to attack the court. Attempts to pass legislation favourable to the protestant dissenters was a favourite object of opposition. The great advantage of this issue was that it could be used by discontented Whigs to attract the support of both Tories and country gentlemen. Although the avoidance of controversial party political issues was essential for the success of the patriotic opposition, Irish patriots were fortunate in that Whigs in Ireland had rarely shown much sympathy for protestant dissenters. The most serious episodes of this kind were those of 1719 and 1733 when opposition to government-sponsored attempts to repeal the sacramental test seriously threatened to disrupt the parliamentary session. During the former session the duke of Bolton claimed that 'really this matter of the Dissenters made them shy of trusting one another and has made them cabal and be together with people of different opinions that it is not easy for them to come together again'.[67] In 1733 the chief secretary observed that the committee of accounts delayed the money bills 'being well assured, we should undertake nothing with regard to the Dissenters, till they were gone, and passed'.[68] Suspecting that the government intended to introduce a bill to repeal the test late in the session after most members had gone home, the opposition finally passed a resolution declaring that the Commons would not receive such a bill after a certain date.

Other non-economic issues which were employed by patriots to attack the court related to the way in which the country was governed. Resentment at the domination of the government by English-born officials after 1726 had implications for the smooth-running of the parliamentary session. The dominance of Primate Boulter and Lord Chancellor Wyndham was, it seems, particularly objected to and this resentment occasionally manifested itself in opposition to measures sponsored by them. Following the rejection of a riot bill in 1730, for example, Marmaduke Coghill commented that many had opposed it because it was framed by the primate and lord chancellor. Although there were some genuine objections to the bill, Coghill believed that Boulter's and Wyndham's 'warmth about it was one great means of rejecting it, for some people have a mind to show them, that they shall govern but by the people of Ireland, with whom at present they have little correspondence or confidence, nor endeavour to have any, and yet seem desirous to carry everything as they have a mind'.[69] Boulter also complained that those who opposed his scheme to reform the Irish currency in 1729 represented it as 'an *English* project, formed in *England*, and carried on by my Lord Chancellor, myself, and other *English* here, with a design to drain this Kingdom of their gold, as they are already drained of their silver'.[70]

A dominant theme of patriot rhetoric was assertion of the rights and status of parliament. When in 1730 the House of Commons sought the removal of the prohibition on the export of corn (imposed the year before due to the threat of famine in Ulster), Carteret not unreasonably sought the advice of the revenue officials. A noted patriot, Caesar Colclough chose to interpret this, however, as an affront to the Commons complaining that the lord lieutenant 'had taken no notice of the address of the house desiring the prohibition against exportation of corn might be taken off, but as he heard had so little regard for the opinion of the Commons, that he waited to have the opinion of little collectors and custom house officers, and that he stood up in behalf of a distressed nation and an injured House of Commons'.[71] In itself, such posturing had little impact. Only when a combination of circumstances occurred to make already disaffected country gentlemen particularly receptive to such rhetoric did such patriotic opposition seriously threaten government business. On the occasion referred to above, for example, Colclough's proposed motion attacking Carteret received little or no support.

The employment of patriotic rhetoric to complain of alterations to the religious establishment, to allege court corruption, to bemoan English interference in Irish affairs, to object to the appointment of English officials to senior positions in church and state, to question whether additional taxation was really necessary, to lament the drain upon the Irish economy of absenteeism, and to cry out about alleged slights to the dignity of parliament were part and parcel of the parliamentary culture of early Hanoverian Ireland. Such beating of breasts and gnashing of teeth could at times be extremely effective in winning the sympathy of parliamentarians. However, patriotism, always a nuisance to the court, only became a serious menace when a concomitant 'real' issue was of sufficient import to rally the country gentlemen and the Tories to the banner of the small number of committed patriots. Even then, because such an opposition tended to coalesce around a single issue, the coalition of forces eventually broke up once that particular cause had been addressed. In the long run clashes of personality and ideological differences inevitably resulted in the collapse of powerful opposition forces. Under normal circumstances, patriotic rhetoric was liable to be seen by most parliamentarians and members of the politically educated public for what it usually was – the attempts of young, ambitious or embittered individuals to cause trouble for the court or simply draw attention to themselves by enacting the by now ritualised patriotic performance. The pertinence of Samuel Johnson's later ironic description of a patriot as 'a factious disturber of government' would have been immediately recognised by many Irish parliamentarians in the early Hanoverian era.[72] A few, especially if in office, would perhaps even have been persuaded to admit the propriety of the noun 'scoundrel'.

9

Conclusion

The four decades which followed the Williamite victory in 1691 witnessed major changes in Irish politics and society. The immediate consequence of William III's triumph was the establishment of Protestant dominance in Ireland, the Catholic challenge having been well and truly crushed. The decade of the 1690s also witnessed the key steps towards the establishment of permanent parliamentary government in Ireland. The Irish House of Commons established its predominant role in drawing up financial legislation; the Irish parliament regained the legislative initiative by systematically undermining Poynings' Law through the practice of introducing 'heads of bills'; leading Irish parliamentarians were brought into the Castle administration and given an influence over government policy and a say in the distribution of patronage. The establishment of a 12,000 standing army in Ireland after 1697 virtually guaranteed the existence of the Dublin parliament as an permanent institution. The reign of Queen Anne saw parliament become accepted as a permanent feature of the political landscape but also retarded, perhaps, the development of stable government because of the strain and disruption imposed by the Whig-Tory party conflict. The two decades following the accession of George I, on the other hand, established the manner in which Ireland would be governed for fifty years at least. The elimination of disruptive party politics allowed the dominance of the undertakers to take hold.

Three main themes were to dominate the parliamentary politics of the early Hanoverian period. In ascending order of importance, they were religion, a sense of 'patriotism', and the pursuit of patronage. Debate over the status of Catholics had played a leading role in the parliamentary politics of the 1690s and differing stances regarding religion were central to the Whig-Tory party conflict of the reign of Queen Anne. With the benefit of hindsight it is possible to see that the Catholic threat had effectively been eliminated, at least in the short term, by military defeat and penal legislation. Contemporaries, of course, did not possess the advantage of hindsight and Irish Protestants in the five decades after the Battle of the Boyne remained very much on the alert for any signs of a possible Catholic resurgence. Anti-Catholic legislation continued to be introduced into the Irish parliament (and enacted) long after any serious threat from the Catholics had receded. The continued preoccupation of the Protestant ruling élite with the 'Catholic question' makes it clear that, to some extent at least, their concerns and objectives went beyond merely containing a physical threat. The continued existence of an overwhelmingly Catholic population was obviously unsettling even if that population was effectively powerless. Many Anglicans, on the other hand, quite obviously saw the threat from protestant dissent as being at least as great as that from the Catholics. Although it would appear that the initiative for the imposition of the sacramental test in 1704 had not come from within Ireland, Irish Protestants proved themselves only too keen to retain it over the next three decades. The attempts by successive Whig administrations to revoke the test foundered on the determination of the Anglican community to continue to exclude protestant dissenters from the full benefits of citizenship, confident in the knowledge that the latter could always be relied upon to join their fellow protestants in the unlikely event of a Catholic military threat. The willingness of Ulster Presbyterians to enlist (illegally) in the militia during the Jacobite scare of 1715-16 seemed to justify Anglican self-assurance in this regard.

As in so many other periods, the attitude of the British government towards Ireland in the two decades following the accession of George I was predominantly characterised by neglect. Except for the several attempts to pass legislation favourable to protestant dissenters (which in all likelihood were only undertaken with the aim of setting a precedent for Britain), the ministry showed very little interest in Irish affairs. This was not, however, an unreasonable stance to take. Ireland did not present a major security threat at this time. The country seemed relatively quiet and peaceful for once, certainly in contrast to Scotland and even parts of England itself. Bearing in mind the continued existence of the Jacobite threat, serious factional rivalry within the British Whig party, the conflict within the royal family, the economic crisis following the collapse of the South Sea Company, not to mention Britain's relations with the European powers, it is not surprising that Ireland and Irish affairs were very low on the government's list of priorities. Given these circumstances, it would be unreasonable for historians to expect to find a clearly defined 'Irish policy' emanating from Westminster.

On the other hand, the British government was forced on occasion to pay attention to Irish affairs whether it wanted to or not. After all, Anglo-Irish relations in this period cannot be described as having been cordial. It is significant, however, that serious conflict between the Irish and British political establishments almost always came about as a result of the actions of the latter. The role of the Anglican political élite in such conflicts was normally a reactive one. The two great crises in Anglo-Irish relations during the early Hanoverian period, the Sherlock–Annesley case and the Wood's halfpence dispute, initially arose from the actions of, respectively, the British House of Lords and the British government. Similarly, the government's attempts to interfere in the relationship between the rival religious communities in Ireland can only have been regarded by the Anglican community as an unwarranted interference in internal Irish affairs.

The disposal of patronage could also, it is clear, sometimes strain the relationship between the British ministry and the Irish political establishment. The granting of pensions by the government was often regarded as excessive and insensitive by Irish Protestants and this resentment could have serious consequences for the Irish administration's relations with the House of Commons. Even more damaging to Anglo-Irish relations was the opposition aroused by the ministry's appointments to Irish ecclesiastical posts. The Irish bishops were extremely influential members of the House of Lords and privy council. To give offence to people such as William King, Edward Synge and Theophilus Bolton was simply inviting trouble in parliament.

The virtual removal of the Catholic threat to the position of the Anglican community by the defeat of James II, meant that the Protestant community in Ireland could feel more secure than had ever before been possible. Under these circumstances, Irish Protestants could afford the luxury of questioning some aspects of the constitutional relationship between Ireland and Britain. Initially, their main concern was their lack of a formal means to influence the decisions of the executive power. This problem could be resolved in two ways – by abolishing Poynings' Law and making the Castle administration directly responsible to the Irish parliament; or by an act of union, giving Ireland representation at Westminster. It seems clear that in the early years of the eighteenth century Irish Protestants favoured the latter solution. The attempts of the Irish parliament to obtain an act of union in 1703 are well known. Even leading Irish 'patriots' such as William Molyneux, William King and Jonathan Swift thought a union the best solution to the Anglo-Irish constitutional muddle.[1] When it became clear that the English government had no intention of agreeing to such a measure, Irish Protestants had little option but to strengthen the position of the Dublin parliament in order to obtain as much control over their own affairs as possible. The determination of Irish Protestants to defend what they regarded as the historic rights of their parliament, therefore, had a very practical rationale and was not done for its own sake. Similarly, the anti-English feeling of the Anglican community was a response to specific grievances – economic rivalry, patronage disputes, and the interference of the Westminster parliament in internal Irish affairs.

A conscious division does appear to have existed in Ireland at this time between Protestants who had been born and educated in Ireland and English-born Protestants. This schism was certainly exacerbated following the accession of George I and the rapid decline in party conflict. Whether this division was regarded in 'national' terms is more debatable. The practical grievances underlying this distinction were made clear by Viscount Midleton who claimed that the distinction was between the 'old and new English, that is between those who have estates here and those who have not but came over very hungry and think themselves entitled to everything till they are filled'.[2] It is interesting that Midleton (a man with property and political interests on both sides of the Irish Sea) believed that this was 'a very ill distinction' and that whoever introduced it should have been 'hanged'.[3] However, the longevity of even this distinction is called into question by Bishop Nicolson's comment about the English-born bishops in Ireland: 'After our quarantine is over, we are all clean, and our posterity (of the very next generation) will be as true-born Irishmen as if they had been brought out of Egypt in Scota's lap.'[4] In the long run, English-born residents in Ireland and their offspring, like converts from Catholicism, appear to have had relatively little difficulty in being assimilated into the Irish Protestant community .

The anti-English resentment which was common among certain sections of the Anglican community at this time, therefore, cannot be described as 'colonial nationalism' in the modern sense of that term. The contemporary term 'patriotism' is a far more accurate way in which to describe this phenomenon. The anti-English feeling of many Irish Protestants was based on specific and practical issues, with economic grievances often to the fore. The size of the national debt, government demands for additional taxes, restrictions on Irish trade, the size of the Irish establishment, the appointment of Englishmen to 'Irish' jobs, and a determination to uphold the status and dignity of the Dublin parliament – these were the issues which led to the emergence of a patriot opposition in parliament. Many of these same issues, of course, also motivated patriots at Westminster. A sense of separate national identity, based on religion, culture, language, race, or historical experience (fundamental to nineteenth- and twentieth-century notions of nationalism) played little part in the patriotism of the Anglican community in early Hanoverian Ireland.

A number of historians have noted the ostentatious nature of Protestant patriotism in the eighteenth century. The best example of such ostentation was, of course, the building of a new parliament house, consciously intended to rival that at Westminster. The Irish-born bishop of Elphin, Robert Howard, wrote to his brother in England soon after the new building was completed. Having complained about the extremely depressed state of the Irish economy at that time, he added 'Notwithstanding all this, we have got a most magnificent parliament house, with as few faults as could well be in so large a building, it is indeed too fine for us, but it hath chiefly employed our own hands.'[5] In a few words Howard encapsulated some of the fundamental tenets of Protestant patriotism. Pride in the institution of parliament, a recognition that such ostentation was perhaps excessive, but above all a real concern for the well-being of the Irish economy.

A conclusion that the pursuit of patronage played a central role in the politics of early Hanoverian Ireland is neither original nor surprising. Patronage, after all, plays a central role in the operation of any political system and historians have traditionally highlighted the political importance of patronage in eighteenth-century Britain and Ireland. The overwhelming importance of the pursuit of patronage to the management of the British parliament in the early Hanoverian period was perhaps put most forcefully in the introduction to the relevant volume of that great 'Namierite' enterprise, the *History of Parliament*: 'Not that there are no honest men but one will seldom be wrong in attributing the conduct of an individual to reasons of interest and nearly always wrong in supposing that there are any others.'[6] Implicit in this comment is the interesting view that men who act because of 'reasons of interest' are necessarily dishonest. It is such comments which Sean Connolly has rightly criticised on the grounds that they apply anachronistic standards of public morality to an eighteenth-century political culture. Such a comment is also simplistic in that it effectively dismisses factors other than patronage in affecting political behaviour at this time.

It has been seen that the employment of patronage to manage the Irish parliament was no straightforward matter. Patronage was not the all-powerful weapon in the hands of British ministers which enabled them to 'bribe' the Irish parliament into agreeing to anything with which it was presented by the government. The British ministry did not control the disposal of all state patronage. The granting of patronage did not necessarily bind the future actions of its recipients. The disposal of patronage could alienate more people than it gained to the government side. Most importantly, on some political issues, specifically those relating to religion and the economic well-being of the country, the promise of patronage was unable to influence political behaviour. On the other hand, it is abundantly clear that without the ability to appoint people to office the government could not have managed the Irish parliament. Leading Irish politicians simply would not have cooperated with the Castle administration if they had not been offered posts in the government. Such able and ambitious politicians (like their counterparts in all eras) were motivated primarily by the desire for office and the power and patronage which accompanied it. This lesson had been learnt in the 1690s when Lord Deputy Capel brought Alan Brodrick and Robert Rochfort into the government. In 1714 the new Whig administration had no choice but to appoint the leading Irish Whigs to office. To have excluded men such as Alan Brodrick, William Conolly, William Whitshed, and John Forster from the new administration would have rendered parliament unmanageable. It was, of course, in the government's interest to appoint such men to positions of responsibility. They had the ability to perform their official duties with competence and to serve the government in parliament. They also, of course, had the ability to cause trouble in parliament if they were so inclined. The ability to 'buy off' or win the goodwill and cooperation of the leading Irish parliamentarians was the first and most important use to which government patronage was put.

The purge of the Castle administration, the privy council, the judiciary, the army, and the revenue service after 1714 had made it clear that the holding of public office was dependent upon loyalty to the current régime. With the exception of Midleton (who resigned), however, there are no further examples of Irish office-holders being dismissed or forced from office in the following two decades for opposing the court in parliament. It is possible to draw from this two very different conclusions. It could be argued that the government did not have to dismiss people because they were loyal supporters of Dublin Castle in parliament. The fear of dismissal, in other words, was a sufficient incentive for office-holders to toe the line. On the other hand, it may have been the case that the lack of dismissals indicates the inability of the government to discipline office-holders who went into opposition. To dismiss government servants who occasionally departed from the Castle's line in parliament might have caused more trouble than it was worth. A dismissed office-holder might well be able to persuade his friends, relations and dependants in parliament to join him in permanent opposition. On the other hand, by refraining from disciplining disloyal government employees the government might simply encourage more behaviour of this kind, a point made by a number of government servants. In general, however, government employees were usually loyal to the Castle. Such loyalty was relatively easy to maintain because the government made remarkably few demands on its followers and those which it did make were not excessive. All that the Castle usually required of its 'friends' was that they attend the session, support the government's money bills and refrain from open opposition. Under normal circumstances this was relatively easy to do for the court rarely tried to pass contentious legislation which might arouse opposition in parliament.

The great test of the government's control over its servants came, of course, during the Wood's halfpence dispute. More than any other, this controversy graphically demonstrated the limitations of the ministry's ability to employ patronage to obtain parliamentary support. All of the government's servants in Ireland, except for the judges, abandoned the court on this occasion and the ministry discovered that under these circumstances it was, to all intents and purposes, powerless. At the peak of the crisis Robert Walpole outlined the ministry's inability to influence events in Ireland:

> The popular frenzy and aversion to the taking this money, I am afraid, is now carried to such a degree that it will scarce be prudent to attempt the forcing their inclinations, especially when they are supported and countenanced in their obstinacy by their governors and those that are in authority under his Majesty ... This makes it impracticable to hope to change the mind of the people and to repeat the orders of the King to the Lords Justices, when they have already told you in effect that they will not obey them, is but a second time to expose the King's honour without

any hopes of success. At the same time I cannot but be of opinion to
suffer the Lords Justices to continue in authority under such a behaviour
is at once to give up all the power and authority of the Crown of England
over Ireland from this time forever ... To remove them avowedly and
expressly for this behaviour would possibly make them so popular all
over the kingdom that with the interest and influence they have already
they might be able to render the King's government absolutely impracticable. I think therefore the only expedient is to send over immediately
the lord lieutenant ... as 'tis plain no Irishman will venture to stem this
torrent ...[7]

In fact the situation was even more desperate than Walpole realised for the
arrival of an English viceroy did little to solve the problem. The real difficulty
lay not in the attitude of the lords justices but in that of parliament. The ministry could replace Irish lords justices with an English lord lieutenant but it could
do nothing in the face of the determined opposition of the Dublin parliament.
No promises of patronage or threats of dismissal were able to influence the
behaviour of Irish politicians during this dispute and the government had no
choice but to retreat. It is significant that none of those Irish office-holders
who, with all respect, had opposed the government over Wood's halfpence were
dismissed from their posts. In fact, throughout the Wood's halfpence affair there
appears to have been a strong sense of safety in numbers among the government's advisers in Ireland. It was even rumoured that Conolly and Midleton
'have both agreed to forget all former disputes and differences and have sworn
friendship to each other and to stand by one another in this affair'.[8] Given the
intense rivalry between these men, the existence of such an agreement seems
highly improbable but the very fact that a rumour to this effect was circulating
in London demonstrates the extent to which the situation had deteriorated as
far as the government was concerned.[9] The lesson of the dispute over Wood's
patent appeared to be that if the crown's Irish servants united in opposing the
ministry they were effectively immune from the wrath of English ministers.
After all, the government could not dismiss the entire Irish administration for
no one would remain to govern the country. To dismiss only selected officers
for their disloyalty would have been equally unwise.

Under normal circumstances, however, it was the government's ability to
employ state patronage which enabled it to have its legislation passed by the
Irish parliament. In the House of Lords this was done directly. In an assembly
with an average attendance of around thirty people it was possible to build up a
relatively loyal following of dependent peers and bishops. A high proportion of
the regular attenders of the House of Lords were pensioners or government
office-holders. In addition, the government had direct control over the membership of the upper house. The government appointed the bishops and could,

in extremis, resort to the creation of sufficient peers to give it a majority. Given these circumstances, the difficulty which the government faced in controlling the Irish upper house is all the more surprising. Irish bishops and peers showed themselves only too willing to oppose the court on a number of occasions in the early Hanoverian period. Special circumstances were at work, however. The Tory presence in the upper house was still troublesome until 1727 at least; the Sherlock–Annesley dispute was bound to bring the Irish Lords into conflict with the government; the strength of Tory attitudes towards religion among Irish peers and bishops was also certain to lead to conflict with a Whig ministry with a favourable attitude toward protestant dissent; and issues such as the attempt to found a national bank and Wood's patent encouraged normally supportive members of the upper house to go into opposition. What all of these episodes demonstrated was that, in spite of the government's ability to employ patronage to obtain support in the upper house, the support of bishops and peers could not be taken for granted. The trouble caused to the British ministry, particularly from 1715 to 1725, by an Irish House of Lords which in theory should have been 'subservient' is an important indication of the limitations of patronage.

The government's use of patronage in regard to the House of Commons was more indirect. Some government employees did sit in the Commons – officials at Dublin Castle, revenue officers, legal officers, and army officers. These office-holders did not, however, form a sufficiently large party to enable the government to directly control the lower house. Furthermore, the government had very little control over the return of MPs so the Commons was potentially a much more 'independent' institution than the Lords. Unable to return its own nominees and with insufficient patronage to employ directly sufficient MPs to give it a majority, the Castle administration had to employ local politicians to manage the lower house on its behalf. The patronage of the Castle administration, revenue service, army, church, and judiciary was employed in order to reward these undertakers and their followers.

When examining the nature of the relationship between government and undertakers, the Irish parliament must also be taken into account. The job of the undertaker was first and foremost to pilot through the House of Commons the government's money bills. Viscount Midleton gives a rare insight into how the negotiations between government, undertakers and their followers over the supply may have operated. Midleton claimed that before the 1715 session he told his 'friends' from the House of Commons 'that if they would come roundly into two years additional duties and not publicly find fault with the establishment, I should not press them to more' and that this was agreed to by the lords justices.[10] Midleton alleged that Conolly and the secretaries later tried to obtain more money than had been agreed and that he refused to support such a demand.[11] As well as persuading parliament to approve the government's money bills, the undertakers also warned the government of possible causes of conflict, normally relating to religious legislation or the size of the establishment. In order to keep parliament relatively content the government also had to support favourite legislation (anti-popery bills, for example) and also distribute government patronage to members of parliament and their dependants. In the distribution of this patronage, the undertakers acted as mediators, primarily by receiving requests and recommendations and forwarding them to the government. It was in this role as mediators between the ultimate dispensors of and the recipients of patronage that the undertakers were able to exert considerable influence in the disposal of government patronage. However, it must be stressed that they did not control the disposal of this patronage. They could only advise the government as to its disposal and regarding the more important offices in church and state the government had a tendency regularly to override the undertakers' wishes. Despite their undoubted power and influence the undertakers of the early Hanoverian period were not in a position of dominance over the viceroy.

Religious controversy, resentment over perceived English interference in Irish affairs and competition for state patronage regularly caused conflict in the early Hanoverian period. In addition to these sensitive issues, certain structural flaws in the constitutional relationship between Britain and Ireland and in the mechanisms of the Irish government made regular conflict virtually inevitable. As has been seen, the emergence of the Westminster parliament after 1689 as the dominant factor in the government of Britain and the empire quickly highlighted the problematic nature of the constitutional relationship between the kingdoms of Britain and Ireland. The existence of two parliaments under one crown was bound to lead to conflict, particularly when one legislature regarded itself as superior to the other and possessed the power ultimately to enforce such a superiority. In addition, the practice of lords lieutenant residing in Ireland only during the parliamentary session made the government in London dangerously reliant upon the cooperation of its resident officials in Ireland. The need to appoint lords justices to officiate in the absence of the viceroy brought further problems. The decision as to whom should officiate was fraught with difficulties for someone who had been left out was likely to be extremely unhelpful in the future. In 1721, for example, when Archbishop King suggested to Midleton that parliament should vote a supply for only one year, the lord chancellor believed that this suggestion was a result of the archbishop's exclusion from the commission of lords justices.[12] Another problem was that acceptable candidates for this vital post were few and far between. Between 1714 and 1724, for example, two of the leading candidates to serve in the commission were Archbishop King and Midleton, men who in their own ways had often been the government's most troublesome parliamentary opponents. King was excluded from the commission of lords justices on several occasions only to be reinstated at a later date because there was no one else suitable to serve. Appointments to the commission of lords justices also became another aspect of the factional rivalry between Conolly and Midleton as each sought to have the other excluded. Obviously, the resentments and conflicts surrounding the appointment of lords justices could have been avoided if the lord lieutenant had stayed in Ireland.

The most important structural weakness in the Irish political system was the lack of formal links between the executive and the legislature. Not only was the executive not responsible to parliament but the government had very little direct presence within parliament. The judges and certain bishops and lay peers formed something akin to a 'Castle party' in the House of Lords but the government had virtually no interest in the House of Commons. Only the viceroy's chief secretary and under-secretary could be regarded as direct representatives of the Castle administration. Other office-holders, of course, would normally act as the representatives of the Castle but they cannot be regarded as having been the mouthpieces of the court. The main cause of the absence of a solid 'Castle party' in the lower house was the government's lack of a significant electoral interest. With the exception of eight members returned for boroughs under the control of four bishops, the government did not control the return of any MPs.[13] Furthermore, the government seems to have made few if any efforts to influence the election of MPs. Virtually the only evidence of attempts by viceroys to return members of parliament relates to the arrangements for the election of the chief secretaries of incoming lords lieutenant.[14]

Constitutional muddle, a non-resident viceroy, the absence of a strong 'Castle party' in the Commons, the lack of party discipline after 1714, the government's dependence upon the goodwill of the Anglican élite, and the unsettling effect of religious and 'national' disputes, made the government of Ireland no easy task in the early Hanoverian period. It is not surprising to discover, therefore, that in 1720 the ministry seriously considered the option of governing without parliament again. By this time, however, there was no ready alternative. Parliamentary government had now become firmly established in the political and social culture of the Irish Anglican élite. The regular sessions of the Dublin parliament had given the Protestant community something which they had signally lacked prior to 1692, that is, an opportunity every other year to discuss their country's affairs and to pass appropriate legislation. More importantly, the government's need to obtain additional taxation every two years to support its standing army in Ireland meant that never again could a British government disregard the views of the Irish Protestant community over issues which they felt were of fundamental importance. The plan to dispense with the 'necessity of calling a parliament' in Ireland quickly foundered when the ministry calculated that the price to be paid for such a luxury, among other things, was a cut of 2,000 men in the military establishment.[15] The financial and military needs of the expanding British state required that Ireland make a major contribution to British and imperial defence. In return for such a contribution, the government had to allow the Dublin parliament to meet on a regular basis and to pay attention to the views of the Irish Protestant community. The only alternative was a union of the two kingdoms. When the parliamentary system of government in Ireland began to break down under a combination of pressures at the end of the century, the government indeed resorted to precisely this alternative. By that time, of course, for other reasons, union was a much more problematic proposition than it would have been in the early decades of the Hanoverian régime.

Notes

INTRODUCTION

1   W.E.H. Lecky, *A history of Ireland in the eighteenth century* (5 vols, London, 1892), i, 458.
2   James Anthony Froude, *The English in Ireland in the eighteenth century* (3 vols, London, 1872-4), i, 657 – quoted by F.G. James, *Ireland in the Empire, 1688-1770* (Cambridge, Mass., 1973), p 182.
3   J.L. McCracken, 'The undertakers in Ireland and their relations with the lord lieutenant, 1724-1771' (unpublished MA thesis, QUB, 1941); idem, 'Central and local administration in Ireland under George II' (unpublished PhD thesis, QUB, 1948); idem, 'Irish parliamentary elections, 1727-68', *IHS*, 5, 19 (Mar. 1947), 209-30; idem, *The Irish parliament in the eighteenth century* (Dundalk, 1971); idem, in *New History of Ireland*, iv, 31-122.
4   J.G. Simms, *Jacobite Ireland* (London, 1969); idem, *The Williamite Confiscation in Ireland, 1690-1703* (London, 1956); idem, *Colonial Nationalism 1698-1776: Molyneux's* 'Case of Ireland ... Stated' (Cork, 1976); idem, in *New History of Ireland*, iii, 420-53; 478-508; 634-95; ibid., iv, 1-30; 629-56. The most important of Simms' published articles have been collected and published in David Hayton and Gerard O'Brien (eds.), *War and Politics in Ireland, 1649-1733* (London, 1986).
5   J.I. McGuire, 'Politics, opinion, and the Irish constitution, 1688-1707' (unpublished MA thesis, UCD, 1968); idem, 'The Irish parliament of 1692', in Thomas Bartlett and David Hayton (eds.), *Penal Era and Golden Age: essays in Irish history, 1690-1800* (Belfast, 1979), pp 1-31; David Hayton, 'Ireland and the English Ministers, 1707-1716' (unpublished DPhil thesis, Oxford, 1975); idem, 'The crisis in Ireland and the disintegration of Queen Anne's last ministry', *IHS*, 22, 87 (Mar. 1981), 193-215; idem, 'Walpole and Ireland', in Jeremy Black (ed.), *Britain in the Age of Walpole* (London, 1984), pp 95-119; idem, 'The beginnings of the "Undertaker System"', in Bartlett and Hayton, *Penal Era and Golden Age*, pp 32-54.
6   David Dickson, *New Foundations. Ireland 1660-1800* (Dublin, 1987).
7   Patrick McNally, 'Patronage and Politics in Ireland, 1714 to 1727' (unpublished PhD thesis, QUB, 1993).

EARLY EIGHTEENTH-CENTURY IRISH SOCIETY

1   See Sean Connolly, 'Eighteenth-Century Ireland: Colony or *ancien régime*?' in D. George Boyce and Alan O'Day (eds.), *The Making of Modern Irish History. Revisionism and the Revisionist Controversy* (London, 1996), pp 15-33.
2   E.P. Thompson, *Customs in Common* (London, 1993), p 42.
3   Ibid., p 33.
4   Ibid., p 37, p 39.
5   *Whalley's Newsletter*, 5 Aug. 1721.
6   Louis Cullen, 'Catholics under the Penal Laws', *Eighteenth-Century Ireland*, 1 (1986), 23-36.

7   Nicolson to Wake, 7 May 1723 (BL Add MS 6116, fos 131-2).
8   Maule to Wake, 22 Aug. 1724 (Christ Church, Oxford, Wake MSS, 14, fol 213).
9   Percival to Taylor, [   ] Aug. 1715 (BL Add MS 46966, fol 96).
10 Lord Castledurrow to Sir John St Leger, 15 July 1738 (NLI MS 11478/11).
11 Owen Gallagher to Oliver St George, 19 Feb. 1730 (PRO C 110/46/719-20); Same to Same, 6 Aug. 1730 (ibid., 769).
12 Cary to Delafaye, 10 Dec. 1731 (PRO SP 63/394/141-2).
13 Boulter to Bp of London, 9 Sept. 1734 (*Boulter Letters*, ii, 97-8).
14 Evans to Wake, 11 Dec. 1718 (Christ Church, Oxford, Wake MSS, 13, fol 31).
15 For a discussion of some of the problems which can arise from the attempts of historians to periodise eighteenth-century Ireland see Thomas Bartlett, 'A New History of Ireland', *Past and Present*, 116 (Aug. 1987), 206-19; 209-11.
16 For the significance of the annual commemoration of the 1641 uprising see Toby Barnard, 'The uses of 23 October 1641 and Irish Protestant celebrations', *English Historical Review*, 106, 421 (Oct. 1991), 889-920, and Bartlett, 'New History of Ireland', 213-16.
17 Evans to Wake, 11 Apr. 1719 (Christ Church, Oxford, Wake MSS, 13, fol 50).
18 Nicholas Rogers, *Whigs and Cities. Popular politics in the age of Walpole and Pitt* (Oxford, 1989), p 355.
19 *The Dublin Post-Man*, 27 Aug. 1725; Nicolson to Wake, 3 May 1720 (BL Add MS 6116, fos 98-9); Same to Same, 9 June 1720 (ibid., fos 99-100); Owen Gallagher to Oliver St George, 31 Aug. 1725 (PRO C 110/46/388-9).
20 Rogers, *Whigs and Cities*, p 358.
21 Ibid., pp 351-2; Linda Colley, *Britons. Forging the nation 1707-1837* (New Haven and London, 1992), pp 18-30.
22 Barnard, '1641', 914.
23 Celebrated by shoemakers in both Britain and Ireland.
24 *Weekly Miscellany*, 26 Oct. 1734.
25 For the celebration of St Patrick's Day in the early eighteenth century see Jacqueline Hill, 'National festivals, the state and "protestant ascendancy" in Ireland, 1790-1829', *IHS*, 24, 93 (May 1984), 30-51; 31.
26 Philip Percival to Lord Percival, 18 June 1717 (BL Add MS 47028, fol 193).
27 Barnard, '1641', 914.
28 Boulter to Newcastle, 11 June 1726 (*Boulter Letters*, i, 65-6). See Patrick Fagan, 'The Dublin Catholic mob (1700-1750)', *Eighteenth-Century Ireland*, 4 (1989), 133-42.
29 Bartlett, 'New History of Ireland', 214-17.
30 Cullen, 'Catholics under the Penal Laws', 24.
31 Connolly, *Religion, Law, and Power*, p 312.
32 Sean Connolly, 'Religion and History', *Irish Economic and Social History*, 10 (1983), 66-80; 75.
33 Connolly, *Religion, Law and Power*, p 263.
34 J.G. Simms, 'The making of a Penal Law (2 Anne, c. 6), 1703-4', *IHS*, 12, 46 (Oct. 1960), 105-18; Connolly, *Religion, Law and Power*, p 263.
35 King to Bp of Lincoln, 19 July 1715 (TCD MS 2533/23-5).
36 A similar argument has been put forward by Jim Smyth, 'The making and undoing of a confessional state: Ireland, 1660-1829', *Journal of Ecclesiastical History*, 44, 3 (July 1993), 506-13.
37 James Joll, '1914: the unspoken assumptions', in H.W. Koch (ed.), *The origins of the First World War: great power rivalry and German war aims* (London, 1972), pp 307-28.
38 See the review of Connolly's *Religion, Law and Power* by Tommy Graham in *History Ireland*, 1, 1 (Spring 1993), 58.

39 Percival to King, 10 Mar. 1720 (BL Add MS 47029, fol 26).

40 Delafaye to Manley, 14 Apr. 1720 (PRO SP 35/21/16).

41 R. Dudley Edwards and T.W. Moody, 'The History of Poynings' Law: Part 1, 1494-1615', *IHS*, 2, 8 (Sept. 1941), 415-24; Aidan Clarke, 'The History of Poynings' Law, 1615-41', *IHS*, 18, 70 (Sept. 1972), 207-22.

42 J.P. Greene, *Peripheries and Center: constitutional development in the extended polities of the British Empire and the United States, 1607-1788* (Athens, Ga., 1986), p 14.

43 R.F. Foster, *Modern Ireland 1600-1972* (London, 1989), p 170.

THE GLORIOUS REVOLUTION AND IRELAND

1 For the debate surrounding the origins of this term see Jacqueline Hill, 'The meaning and significance of "Protestant Ascendancy" 1787-1840', in *Ireland after the Union: Proceedings of the second joint meeting of the Royal Irish Academy and the British Academy* (London, 1989), pp 1-22; W.J. McCormack, 'Vision and revision in the study of eighteenth-century Irish parliamentary rhetoric', *Eighteenth-Century Ireland,* 2 (1987), 7-36; idem, 'Eighteenth-Century Ascendancy: Yeats and the historians', *Eighteenth-Century Ireland,* 4 (1989), 150-81; James Kelly, 'The genesis of "Protestant Ascendancy": the Rightboy disturbances of the 1780s and their impact upon Protestant opinion', in Gerard O'Brien (ed.), *Parliament, Politics and People: essays in eighteenth-century Irish history* (Dublin, 1989), pp 93-127; idem, 'Eighteenth-Century Ascendancy: a commentary', *Eighteenth-Century Ireland,* 5 (1990), 173-87.

2 J.G. Simms, *The Williamite Confiscation in Ireland 1690-1703* (London, 1956), p 195; Connolly, *Religion, Law and Power*, pp 311-2.

3 James McGuire, 'Richard Talbot, earl of Tyrconnell (1603-91)', in Ciaran Brady (ed.), *Worsted in the Game. Losers in Irish history* (Dublin, 1989), pp 73-84.

4 The seven were Bishop Compton, the Earl of Danby, Lord Lumley, Edward Russell, Henry Sidney, the Earl of Devonshire and the Earl of Shrewsbury.

5 John Miller, 'The earl of Tyrconnell and James II's Irish policy, 1685-1688', *Historical Journal*, 20, 4 (1977), 803-24; 807-8.

6 For a detailed account of the Williamite war see J.G. Simms, *Jacobite Ireland, 1685-91* (London, 1969).

7 See Raymond Gillespie, 'The Irish Protestants and James II, 1688-90', *IHS*, 28, 110 (Nov. 1992), 124-33 for an analysis of Protestant attitudes towards James.

8 Dickson, *New Foundations*, p 40.

9 Simms, *Williamite Confiscation*, p 195.

10 Ibid., pp 17-20.

11 It has recently been suggested that the land of Catholic converts to Anglicanism should be included in any calculation of the amount of land owned by Catholics, the assumption being that such converts continued to act in a broader 'Catholic interest'. At present this remains an assumption rather than a demonstrable phenomenon. See Cullen, 'Catholics under the penal laws', 27-8, and Kevin Whelan, 'An underground gentry? Catholic middlemen in eighteenth-century Ireland', in *The Tree of Liberty. Radicalism, Catholicism and the construction of Irish identity 1760-1830* (Cork, 1986), pp 5-7.

12 W. A. Speck, *Reluctant Revolutionaries. Englishmen and the Revolution of 1688* (Oxford, 1988), p 246.

13 The Scottish parliament also increased in power and influence as a result of the revolution of 1688. See Rosalind Mithchison, *A History of Scotland* (2nd ed., London, 1982), pp 273-90, and Keith M. Brown, *Kingdom or Province? Scotland and the regal union, 1603-1715* (London, 1992), pp 107-92.

14	Dickson, *New Foundations*, pp 9-15.
15	Only six Protestants sat in the House of Commons; five Protestant peers and four Anglican bishops sat in the Lords. J.G. Simms, *The Jacobite Parliament of 1689* (Dundalk, 1966) remains the most authoritative and useful account.
16	This discussion of the 1692 Parliament and its aftermath relies heavily upon J.I. McGuire, 'The Irish Parliament of 1692', in Bartlett and Hayton, *Penal Era and Golden Age*, pp 1-31.
17	*Journals of the House of Commons of the Kingdom of Ireland* (2nd ed., 23 vols, Dublin, 1763-86), ii, 35-36, quoted by McGuire, 'Irish Parliament of 1692', p 21.
18	J.G. Simms, *The Treaty of Limerick* (Dundalk, 1961). McGuire, 'Irish Parliament of 1692', pp 15-6; Dickson, *New Foundations*, pp 40-2.
19	E.A. Reitan, 'From revenue to civil list, 1689-1702: the revolution settlement and the "mixed and balanced" constitution', *Historical Journal*, 13 (1970), 571-88; Clayton Roberts, 'The constitutional significance of the financial settlement of 1690', *Historical Journal*, 20, 1 (1977), 59-76.
20	McGuire, 'Irish Parliament of 1692', p 28.
21	Ibid., pp 28-31.
22	In 1707 and 1713.
23	Parliament did not meet between 1699 and 1703.
24	Dudley Edwards and Moody, 'Poynings Law, 1494-1615'; Clarke, 'Poynings Law, 1615-41'.
25	Coghill to Southwell, 4 Dec. 1732 (BL Add MS 21123, fos 11-14); Cary to Delafaye, 10 Jan. 1734 (PRO SP 63/397/17-8).
26	David Hayton has calculated that 88.8 per cent of public bills passed by the Irish parliament between 1707 and 1716 started as heads of a bill – Hayton, 'Ireland and the English ministers', p 97. According to Joseph Griffin, 94.8 per cent of Irish legislation during the 1715-27 Parliament was initiated as heads of a bill – Joseph Griffin, 'Parliamentary politics in Ireland during the reign of George I' (unpublished MA thesis, UCD, 1977), Appendix A. After the granting of legislative independence to the Irish parliament in 1782 either house of parliament could draw up bills proper.
27	Hayton, 'Beginnings of the Undertaker System', p 44; Connolly, *Religion, Law, and Power*, pp 74-8; Dickson, *New Foundations*, pp 40-44.
28	Hayton, 'Ireland and the English ministers', pp 121-2
29	McGuire, 'Irish Parliament of 1692', pp 1-31; Hayton, 'Beginnings of the Undertaker System', 43-4; Connolly, *Religion Law and Power*, pp 74-8.
30	James Kelly, 'The origins of the Act of Union: an examination of unionist opinion in Britain and Ireland, 1650-1800', *IHS*, 25, 99 (May 1987), 236-63; David Hayton, 'Anglo-Irish attitudes: changing perceptions of national identity among the Protestant Ascendancy in Ireland, ca. 1690-1750', *Studies in Eighteenth-Century Culture*, 17 (1987), 145-57; Jim Smyth, '"Like amphibious animals": Irish Protestants, Ancient Britons, 1691-1707', *Historical Journal*, 36, 4 (1993), 785-97; [Henry Maxwell], *An essay towards an union of Ireland with England, most humbly offer'd to the consideration of the Queen's most excellent Majesty and both houses of parliament* (London, 1703).
31	Percival to Dering, 5 Mar. 1720 (BL Add MS 47029, fos 22-5).
32	Jonathan Swift, *A Letter to the Whole People of Ireland*, in H. Davis (ed.), *The Drapier's Letters* (Oxford, 1941), p 62.
33	But see Hayton, 'Walpole and Ireland' in Black (ed.), *Britain in the age of Walpole*, p 97.
34	King to Lord King, [ ] June 1726 (TCD MS 750/8/101-02).
35	Forth to Hopkins, 19 Nov. 1722 (NLI MS 16007/110-11); Lowndes to the Irish revenue commissioners, 22 Jan. 1715 (PRO T 14/9/607).

36 Webster to Delafaye, 15 Aug. 1719 (PRO SP 63/377/15-16).
37 For the legal disabilities against Catholics and protestant dissenters see Maureen Wall, *The Penal Laws, 1691-1760* (Dundalk, 1976); *New History of Ireland,* iv, 16-25.
38 J.G. Simms, 'Irish Catholics and the parliamentary franchise, 1692-1728', *IHS,* 12, 66 (Mar. 1960), 28-37.
39 The earl of Rochester and Lord Carteret were exceptions. Rochester resided in Ireland as lord lieutenant from 1700 to 1702. Carteret was sent to Ireland at the height of the Wood's halfpence crisis in October 1724 although parliament did not meet until the following September.
40 The two other leading British politicians who were appointed to the Irish viceroyalty in this period, Charles, 3rd earl of Sunderland, and Charles, 2nd Viscount Townshend, never set foot in Ireland.
41 BL Add MS 23636, fos 70-2; King to Hopkins, 8 Jan. 1723 (TCD MS 750/7/269-72).
42 The disposal of the following civil and military posts was reserved to the Crown: the lord chancellor; lord treasurer; vice-treasurer; all judges of the courts of Exchequer, Kings Bench and Common Pleas; master of the rolls; attorney general; solicitor general; master of the ordnance; and muster master general – (PRO SP 63/371/74-80).
43 Conolly, Medlicott, and Southwell to Sunderland, 18 Jan. 1715 (NLI MS 16007/6-9); Forth to Thompson, 19 Jan. 1730 (ibid., 210-11).
44 '16 July 1719, Names of the people whom my Lord Lieutenant summoned the night before the Parliament was to open to sound their sense how far they would go in favour of the Dissenters.' (PRO SP 63/377/175-6); Bolton to Craggs, 30 July 1719 (PRO SP 63/377/103-4).
45 Midleton to Thomas Brodrick, 1 Nov. 1723 (SRO, Midleton MSS, v, fos 325-8).
46 Warrant for Irish lords justices pay, 14 Sept. 1714 (PRO SO 1/16/36).
47 King to Bp of Dromore, 6 Oct. 1715 (TCD MS 2533/97-9).
48 Bladen to Delafaye, 9 Feb. 1717 (PRO SP 63/375/13-4).
49 King to Synge, 2 Mar. 1717 (TCD MS 2534/97-8).
50 Memorandum, 15 Feb. 1722 (SRO, Midleton MSS, v, fos 186-7).
51 King to Molyneux, 29 Sept. 1722 (TCD MS 750/7/217-8).
52 Downes to Nicolson, 1 Mar. 1721, in John Nichols (ed.), *Letters on various subjects, literary, political, and ecclesiastical, to and from William Nicolson, D.D., successively Bishop of Carlisle, and of Derry; and Archbishop of Cashell;...* (2 vols, London, 1809); ii, 535-7 – (hereafter cited as *Nicolson Correspondence*).
53 King to Gourney, 2 July 1723 (TCD MS 750/7/359).
54 Conolly to Delafaye, 18 Oct. 1717 (PRO SP 63/375/212-3).
55 Downes to Nicolson, 24 Nov. 1719 (*Nicolson Correspondence,* ii, 496-9).
56 Conolly to Delafaye, 14 Jan. 1718 (PRO SP 63/376/1).
57 Addison to Godolphin, 30 Aug. 1709, in Walter Graham (ed.), *The Letters of Joseph Addison* (Oxford, 1941), p 184.
58 King to Whitshed, 6 Jan. 1718 (TCD MS 2535/55-7).
59 King to Bp of Carlisle, 8 Mar. 1718 (TCD MS 2535/105-8).
60 King to Story, 18 Sept. 1714 (TCD MS 750/13/70-71); King to Foster, 28 Sept. 1714 (ibid., 79-80).
61 Coghill to Southwell, 31 Mar. 1733 (BL Add MS 21123, fos 30-1)
62 Newcastle to Boulter, 19 Feb. 1732 (PRO SP 63/395/62).
63 Carteret to Townshend, 9 Jan. 1725 (PRO SP 63/385/9-12); Newcastle to Carteret, 13 Mar. 1725 (ibid., 64-5).
64 Brodrick to Addison, 14 Apr. 1715 (BL Add MS 61636, fol 171).

65   Cox to Southwell, 10 July 1707 (BL Add MS 38155, fos 75-6).

66   Boulter to Newcastle, 19 Mar. 1730 (*Boulter Letters,* i, 287-8).

67   Coghill to Southwell, 18 Apr. 1730 (BL Add MS 21123, fos 1-5).

68   Same to Same, 22 Jan. 1730 (BL Add MS 21122, fos 107-10).

69   Boulter to Newcastle, 16 Dec. 1729 (*Boulter Letters,* i, 272-3); Grafton to Carteret, 12 Feb. 1724 (PRO SP 63/383/63-7); Irish lords justices to James Stanhope, 24 Feb. 1716 (PRO SP 63/374/105-7).

70   King to Wake, 24 Mar. 1716 (TCD MS 2533/160-71); Same to Same, 1 Aug. 1719 (BL Add MS 6117, fos 60-61).

71   Nicolson to Wake, 13 Jan. 1722 (BL Add MS 6116, fos 104-5).

72   Midleton to Thomas Brodrick, 10 Jan. 1722 (SRO, Midleton MSS, v, fos 170-72).

73   West to Newcastle, 27 Jan. 1726 (PRO SP 63/387/13-4); Boulter to Newcastle, 22 Mar. 1726 (*Boulter Letters,* i, 54-6).

74   Dickson, *New Foundations,* p 80. For a more detailed discussion of Boulter's policy after 1724 see chapter seven below.

75   Carteret to Newcastle, [_] May 1726 (PRO SP 63/387/184-5); Boulter to Newcastle, 19 May 1726 (*Boulter Letters,* i, 59); Newcastle to Boulter, 21 June 1726 (PRO SP 63/387/212-3).

76   Boulter to Newcastle, 10 Mar. 1730 (*Boulter Letters,* i, 285-6).

77   The number of people eligible to sit in the Irish House of Lords in the early eighteenth century was around 120 – James, *Ireland in the Empire,* p 45.

78   Edward Southwell to Sir Charles Hedges, 1 Mar. 1705 (PRO SP 63/365/101); quoted in Hayton, 'Beginnings of the Undertaker System', p 34.

79   Webster to [Delafaye?], 29 July 1719 (PRO SP 63/377/107).

80   See list of bills taking their rise in House of Lords, 1731-2 – Dorset to Newcastle, 2 Jan. 1732 (PRO SP 63/395/9).

81   See chapter seven below and Patrick McNally, '"Irish and English interests": national conflict within the Church of Ireland episcopate in the reign of George I', *IHS,* 29, 115 (May 1995), 295-314.

82   Hayton, 'Ireland and the English ministers', pp 39-40.

83   J.L. McCracken, 'Central and local administration in Ireland under George II' (unpublished PhD thesis, QUB, 1948), pp 110-12.

84   Romney Sedgwick (ed.), *The History of Parliament: the House of Commons 1715-54* (2 vols, London, 1970), i, 489-90.

85   Lena Boylan, 'The Conollys of Castletown', *Quarterly Bulletin of the Irish Georgian Society,* 11, 4 (Oct.-Dec. 1968), 4.

86   Accurate statistics regarding the size of the Irish population and its denominational make-up are unavailable for this period.

87   J.L. McCracken, *The Irish Parliament in the Eighteenth Century* (Dundalk, 1971), pp 7-9. Between 1714 and the passage of the Octennial Act in 1768 general elections in Ireland occurred only on the death of the monarch, that is, in 1727 and 1760.

88   However, Louis Cullen has suggested that converts from Catholicism comprised a 'third force' or even part of a wider 'Catholic interest' in Irish electoral politics – Cullen, 'Catholics under the Penal Laws', 29-35.

89   Figures compiled from L.J. Hughes, *Patentee officers in Ireland, 1173-1826* (Dublin, 1960).

90   Figures compiled from Charles Dalton, *George the First's Army, 1714-27* (2 vols, London, 1910-12). Hayton has estimated that there were at least thirty-five army officers or half-pay officers in the House of Commons in 1713 – Hayton, 'Ireland and the English ministers', p 89.

91 Charles Stewart who was also a Westminster MP – Sedgwick, *History of Parliament,* ii, 447-8.
92 Rowley Lascelles (ed.), *Liber Munerum Publicorum Hiberniae...; or the Establishments of Ireland...* (2 vols, London, 1824-30), i, Part 2, 1-90 – (hereafter cited as *Liber Munerum*).
93 'A list of the commissioners and officers appointed for management of His Majestys Revenue in Ireland with their respective salaries. 1720.' (Bod Lib, MS Rawl. B.511) The nine were William Conolly, Thomas Medlicott, James Forth, James Topham, Henry Sandford, George Macartney, William Maynard, Theophilus Clements, and Edward May. This list does not include those who held patentee revenue posts.
94 Martin Bladen and Charles Delafaye, joint chief secretaries to the lords justices; Eustace Budgell, under-secretary at Dublin Castle; William Conolly, speaker of the House of Commons; George Gore, attorney general; Isaac Manley, post-master general; Benjamin Parry, register of memorials of deeds; Matthew Pennefather, muster master general; John Pratt, deputy vice-treasurer; John Rogerson, solicitor general; and Michael Tisdall, advocate general. Parry and Pratt were, in addition, both in receipt of pensions on the Irish civil establishment – (*Commons Journals,* iii, Appendix, xxi-xxii).
95 PRONI T 2825/A/8a.
96 According to the government, the Irish national debt increased from £23,000 in 1715 to £130,000 in 1727 - Griffin, 'Parliamentary politics in Ireland', Appendix B, pp 188-9.
97 Eveline Cruickshanks, 'The political management of Sir Robert Walpole', in Black (ed.), *Britain in the age of Walpole*, pp 23-44; 35.

THE HANOVERIAN ACCESSION

1   Philip Percival to Lord Percival, 30 Jan. 1724 (BL Add MS 47030, fos 57-8)
2   For the party conflict of Anne's reign see Hayton, 'Ireland and the English Ministers', chapters 4 and 5; idem, 'Crisis in Ireland'; idem, 'Beginnings of the Undertaker System', pp 41-6; James, *Ireland in the Empire*, 51-83; and Connolly, *Religion, Law, and Power*, pp 77-84.
3   King to Bp of Lincoln, [_] Aug. 1715 (TCD MS 2533/42-3).
4   The Jacobite MP was Robert Saunderson, member for Co Cavan (1713-14) - Hayton 'Ireland and the English ministers', p 136; Cox to Southwell, 15 July 1707 (BL Add MS 38157, fol 29); Cox to Southwell, 14 Aug. 1714 (ibid., fol 108).
5   J.H. Plumb, *Sir Robert Walpole* (2 vols, London, 1956-60), i, 377.
6   Lord Brodrick to Thomas Brodrick, 20 Mar. 1716 (SRO, Midleton MSS, iii, fos 322-4).
7   William Percival to Sir John Percival, 19 Aug. 1710 (BL Add MS 47026, fos 25-6).
8   Hayton, 'Crisis in Ireland', 203; J.G. Simms gives a figure of nine in 'The Irish Parliament of 1713', *War and Politics in Ireland*, p 84.
9   Percival to Berkeley, 10 Sept. 1713 (BL Add MS 47027, fos 47-9).
10 Hayton, 'Ireland and the English ministers', pp 120-41; Simms, 'Irish Catholics and the parliamentary franchise, 28-37; F.G. James, 'The Church of Ireland in the early eighteenth century', *Historical Magazine of the Protestant Episcopal Church,* 48, 4 (1979), 442-51.
11 Connolly, *Religion, Law, and Power*, p 80.
12 Abercorn to Southwell, 3 Nov. 1713 (PRONI D 623/A/3/2).
13 Daniel Dering to Percival, [undated – between 4 and 11 May 1714] (BL Add MS 47027, fos 107-9).

14   Lord Brodrick to Thomas Brodrick, 10 June 1716 (SRO, Midleton MSS, iii, fos 386-7).
15   Hayton, 'Ireland and the English ministers', pp 118-19, 141-3.
16   Jonathan Swift, *A Short Character of His Excellency, Thomas Earl of Wharton, Lord Lieutenent of Ireland* (1710).
17   Hayton, 'Ireland and the English ministers', pp 182-5.
18   Dralle, Louis A. 'Kingdom in reversion: the Irish viceroyalty of the Earl of Wharton, 1708-1710', *Huntington Library Quarterly*, 15 (1951-2), 393-431; 398-407.
19   Hayton, 'Crisis in Ireland', 195-98.
20   Cox to Southwell, 1 Dec. 1713 (BL Add MS 38157, fol 29).
21   Hayton, 'Beginnings of the Undertaker System', pp 39-40; Simms, 'The Irish Parliament of 1713'.
22   Abercorn to Southwell, 5 Jan 1714 (PRONI, Abercorn Papers, D 623/A/3/12).
23   Lindsay to Charlett, 8 July 1714 (Bod Lib, Oxford, MS Ballard 8, fol 109).
24   Dering to Percival, 24 June 1714 (BL Add MS 47027, fos 132-3) The 'Pretender men' were men who had been sentenced to death for enlisting men for the service of James III.
25   Dering to Percival, 7 Aug. 1714 (ibid., fos 151-3).
26   William, 1st earl Cowper, 'An account of political parties at the accession of George I, 1714', in D.B. Horn and Mary Ransome (eds.), *English Historical Documents, 1714-1783*, vol 10 (London, 1957), 194-7.
27   W.A. Speck, 'The General Election of 1715', *English Historical Review*, 90, 356 (July 1975), 507-22; 510, 518.
28   King to Molyneux, 5 Oct. 1715 (TCD MS 2533/95-6).
29   Hayton, 'Ireland and the English ministers', pp 182-6.
30   Molesworth to King, 28 Sept. 1714, in C.S. King, *A Great Archbishop of Dublin, William King 1650-1729: his autobiography, family, and a selection from his correspondence* (London, 1906), pp 168-9.
31   King to Bp of Dromore, 26 Aug. 1714 (TCD MS 750/13/39-40).
32   Cox to Southwell, 31 Aug. 1714 (BL Add MS 38157, fol 112).
33   King to Lord Merion, 24 Nov. 1714 (TCD MS 750/13/120-21); revenue commissioners to Lords of the Treasury, 19 Oct. 1717 (NLI MS 16007/28); King to Sunderland, 29 Oct. 1714 (TCD MS 750/4/10-11); Same to Same, 9 Nov. 1714 (ibid., 12).
34   King to Bp of Clogher, 24 Nov. 1714 (TCD MS 750/13/123-4); King to Bp of Cloyne, 20 Nov. 1714 (ibid., 114-15).
35   William Berry to Sunderland, 29 Feb. 1715 (BL Add MS 61639, fos 118-19); King to Jemmett, 7 Dec. 1714 (TCD MS 750/13/138-9).
36   Sunderland to Conolly, 13 Jan. 1715 (BL Add MS 61652, fos 247-9).
37   Whitshed to Sunderland, 17 Nov. 1714 (BL Add MS 61639, fos 62-3).
38   Addison to King, 12 Apr. 1715 (*Addison Letters*, p 316).
39   Earl of Kildare to Sunderland, 16 Nov. 1714 (BL Add MS 61635, fol 205); Sunderland to Conolly, 28 July 1715 (BL Add MS 61652, fos 311-12); revenue commissioners to Sunderland, 9 Aug. 1715 (NLI MS 16007/11-13).
40   Memorial of William Maynard, 7 Aug. 1717 (ibid., 24); Charles Stanhope to revenue commissioners, 9 Aug. 1717 (PRO T 14/9/95); revenue commissioners to Lords of the Treasury, 16 Sept. 1717 (NLI MS 16007/26-7); Same to Same, 19 Oct. 1717 (ibid., 28); William Berry to Sunderland, 29 Feb. 1715 (BL Add MS 61639, fos 118-19).
41   Revenue commissioners to Lords of the Treasury, 19 Oct. 1717 (NLI MS 16007/28-30); Lords of the Treasury to revenue commissioners, 13 Nov. 1717 (ibid., 32).
42   King to Sunderland, 27 Nov. 1714 (TCD MS 750/4/16); Same to Same, 31 Dec. 1714 (ibid., 26-7); King to Sir Richard Levinge, 15 Mar. 1715 (TCD MS 750/13/211); Lord

Chief Justice Parker to Sunderland, 10 May 1715 (BL Add MS 61639, fos 151-2); Sunderland to King, 18 Dec. 1714 (BL Add MS 61652, fos 230-31); Sunderland to Alan Brodrick, 18 Dec. 1714 (ibid., fos 231-2); Sunderland to Lord Cowper, 14 May 1715 (ibid., fos 281-3); Alan Brodrick to Addison, 16 Nov. 1714 (BL Add MS 61636, fos 119-20); Lord Brodrick to Thomas Brodrick, 12 Apr. 1715 (SRO, Midleton MSS, iii, fos 230-31); Alan Brodrick to Sunderland, 26 Oct. 1714 (BL Add MS 61636, fos 115-16).

43   Hayton, 'Ireland and the English ministers', p 304.

44   King to Bp of Killala, 20 Nov. 1714 (TCD MS 750/13/116-18).

45   Irish lords justices to Bolingbroke, 14 Aug. 1714 (PRO SP 63/371/85-6).

46   Molesworth to King, 2 Sept. 1714 (King, *A Great Archbishop of Dublin,* pp 163-4); King to Molyneux, 16 Sept. 1714 (TCD MS 750/13/60-63).

47   Cox to Southwell, 23 Sept. 1714 (BL Add MS 38157, fos 126-7); Same to Same, 9 Oct. 1714 (ibid., fol 133); Irish lords justices to James Stanhope, 12 Oct. 1714 (PRO SP 63/371/99-100); James Stanhope to Irish lords justices, 30 Sept. 1714 (PRO SP 67/6/1-2); Same to Same, 5 Oct. 1714 (ibid., 6).

48   Cox to Southwell, 16 Oct. 1714 (BL Add MS 38157, fol 136).

49   King to Purcell, 6 Nov. 1714 (TCD MS 750/13/107-8); Alan Brodrick to Addison, 12 Jan. 1715 (BL Add MS 61636, fos 129-30).

50   For a list of deputies of government officials see Nat. Arch. M 2537/196-7.

51   *Liber Munerum*, ii, 1-194.

52   King to Mountjoy, 2 Nov. 1714 (TCD MS 750/13/105-6).

53   King to Shrewsbury, 20 Nov. 1714 (ibid., 118-19); King to Bp of Killala, 20 Nov. 1714 (ibid., 116-18); King to Merion, 24 Nov. 1714 (ibid., 120-21); *Liber Munerum*, i, Part 2, 100-27.

54   King to Merion, 24 Nov. 1714 (TCD MS 750/13/120-21); Abercorn to Southwell, 3 Dec. 1713 (PRONI D 623/A/3/3).

55   F.E. Ball, *The Judges in Ireland, 1221-1921* (2 vols, London, 1926), ii, 75-85.

56   Alan Brodrick to Thomas Brodrick, 4 Nov. 1714 (SRO, Midleton MSS, iii, fos 199-201).

57   Ibid.

58   Molesworth to King, 28 Sept. 1714 (King, *A Great Archbishop of Dublin,* pp 168-9).

59   Irish lords justices to James Stanhope, 11 Apr. 1716 (PRO SP 63/374/195-6).

60   Alan Brodrick to Thomas Brodrick, 4 Nov. 1714 (SRO, Midleton MSS, iii, fos 199-201); Alan Brodrick to Addison, 16 Nov. 1714 (BL Add MS 61636, fos 119-20).

61   *Liber Munerum*, i, Part 2, 133-5.

62   Sedgwick, *History of Parliament, i,* 506-7; ibid., ii, 250-51; King to Bp of Carlisle, 13 May 1715 (TCD MS 750/13/276-7); Irish lords justices to James Stanhope, 10 May 1715 (PRO SP 63/372/41-2); Delafaye to Pringle, 4 June 1715 (ibid., 58-9); Alan Brodrick to Sunderland, 26 Oct. 1714 (BL Add MS 61636, fos 115-16).

63   British lords justices to revenue commissioners, 24 Dec. 1714 (NLI MS 16007/1); Lords of the Treasury to revenue commissioners, 8 Jan. 1715 (ibid., 2); Same to Same, 2 Dec. 1714 (ibid., 4); revenue commissioners to Sunderland, 18 Jan. 1715 (ibid., 6-9); Same to Same, 9 Aug. 1715 (ibid., 11-13).

64   King to Annesley, 24 May 1715 (TCD MS 750/13/294-6); BL Add MS 47087, fol 99 (quoted in Hayton, 'Ireland and the English ministers', p 270); King to Molyneux, 3 Nov. 1715 (TCD MS 750/4/115-17).

65   King to Addison, 25 Jan. 1715 (TCD MS 750/4/28-9).

66   Revenue commissioners to Sunderland, 18 Jan. 1715 (NLI MS 16007/6-9).

67   Sunderland to Conolly, 28 July 1715 (BL Add MS 61652, fos 311-12).

68 Ibid.
69 Dalton, *George 1's Army*, i, 325-66; *Liber Munerum*, i, Part 2, 100-3; Thomas Collins to Stanhope, 6 Aug. 1715 (PRO SP 63/373/74-5); *Commons Journals*, iii, Appendix, xii.
70 Dalton, *George 1's Army*, ii, 129-46.
71 Alan Brodrick to Thomas Brodrick, 16 Oct. 1714 (SRO, Midleton MSS, iii, fos 193-4); King to Sunderland, 29 Oct. 1714 (TCD MS 750/4/10-11); Whitshed to Sunderland, 17 Nov. 1714 (BL Add MS 61639, fos 62-3); 'Petition of Brinsley Butler', [undated] (BL Add MS 61635, fol 79); '29 June 1719: Warrant granting Col. Brinsley Butler a pension of 10 shillings a day' (PRO T 14/10/261). See also Addison to Delafaye, 4 June 1715 (*Addison Letters*, p 330) referring to a Major Champaigne who was recommended to be removed because he had 'as bad a character as can be given him'.
72 Collins to Stanhope, 6 Aug. 1715 (PRO SP 63/373/74-5).
73 Philip Percival to Lord Percival, 12 Oct. 1725 (BL Add MS 47031, fos 17-18).
74 Hayton has estimated that twelve of the Irish bishops in August 1714 were Tories – Hayton, 'Ireland and the English ministers', p 304.
75 See chapter seven below.
76 Molesworth to King, 28 Sept. 1714 (King, *A Great Archbishop of Dublin*, p 168-9).
77 Whitshed to Sunderland, 17 Nov. 1714 (BL Add MS 61639, fos 62-3); Same to Same, 25 Jan. 1715 (ibid., fos 104-5).
78 Lord Tullamore to Addison, 7 Aug. 1717 (PRO SP 63/375/171-2).
79 King to Gustavus Hamilton, 2 Sept. 1715 (TCD MS 2533/74); Sunderland to King, 20 Aug. 1715 (BL Add MS 61652, fos 313-14); Alan Brodrick to Thomas Brodrick, 30 Oct. 1714 (SRO, Midleton MSS, iii, fos 195-6).
80 Figures from attendance lists in *Lords Journals*, ii, 451-544.
81 Alan Brodrick to Thomas Brodrick, 20 Jan. 1716 (SRO, Midleton MSS, iii, fos 300-1).
82 Same to Same, 4 Nov. 1714 (ibid., fos 199-201).
83 Alan Brodrick to Sunderland, 25 Jan. 1715 (BL Add MS 61636, fos 131-2); Sunderland to Conolly, Feb. 1715 (BL Add MS 61652, fos 260-62).
84 Whitshed to Sunderland, 15 Mar. 1715 (BL Add MS 61639, fos 124-6); Addison to King, 2 July 1715 (King, *A Great Archbishop of Dublin*, pp 183-4); BL Add MS 61637C, fos 2-10; *Commons Journals,* iii, Appendix, xxi-xxii.
85 BL Add MS 61637C, fos 2-10.
86 Ibid., fos 3-5 [Original in French, author's translation].
87 King to Sunderland, 19 Apr. 1716 (TCD MS 2533/210-11); King to Addison, 2 June 1716 (ibid., 245-6).
88 Same to Same, 4 Mar. 1717 (TCD MS 2534/110).
89 *DNB*, iii, 224-5; Alan Brodrick to Thomas Brodrick, 4 Nov. 1714 (SRO, Midleton MSS, iii, fos 199-201).
90 BL Add MS 61637C, fos 4-7.
91 Cox to Southwell, 23 Dec. 1714 (BL Add MS 38157, fol 145).
92 Lindsay to Charlett, 23 Oct. 1714 (Bod Lib, Oxford, MS Ballard 8, fol 110).
93 King to Mountjoy, 24 Nov. 1714 (TCD MS 750/13/121-3); King to Merion, 24 Nov. 1714 (ibid., 120-21).
94 Delafaye to _____, 3 Nov. 1715 (PRO SP 63/373/207); King to Molyneux, 3 Nov. 1715 (TCD MS 2533/115-17).
95 King to James Stanhope, 1 Nov. 1715 (PRO SP 63/373/203-4).
96 The party affiliation of those MPs elected in 1715 is based on a series of parliamentary lists from the reign of Queen Anne, a summary of which is given in Hayton, 'Ireland and the English ministers', pp 105-8 and Appendix (BL Add MS 9715, fos 150-53, 34; BL Add

MS 34777, fol 67, 68v, 70, 71, 72-3, 46-7, 90-91.)
97 4 George I c. 15; 4 George I c. 16.
98 Hayton, 'Ireland and the English Minsters', pp 305-6; Ball, *Judges in Ireland*, ii, 85-8.
99 Dering to Percival, 14 Jan. 1716 (BL Add MS 47028, fos 119-21); Lord Tullamore to Percival, 21 Jan. 1716 (ibid., fos 121-2); Dering to Percival, 12 June 1716 (ibid., fol 156).
100 King to Mountjoy, 2 Nov. 1714 (TCD MS 750/13/105-6).
101 Lord Brodrick to Thomas Brodrick, 20 Jan. 1716 (SRO, Midleton MSS, iii, fos 300-1); Delafaye to _____, 19 Apr. 1716 (PRO SP 63/374/215-16).
102 Bolton to [Carteret], 16 July 1728 (PRONI D 562/92/167-70).
103 Delafaye to _____, 30 Jan. 1716 (PRO SP 63/374/59-60).
104 Delafaye to _____, 31 May 1716 (ibid., 246-7).
105 Plumb, *Walpole*, i, 244-85; Clyve Jones, 'Whigs, Jacobites and Charles Spencer, Third Earl of Sunderland', *English Historical Review*, 109, 430 (Feb. 1994), 52-73; 54.
106 Delafaye to _____, 30 Jan. 1716 (PRO SP 63/374/59-60).
107 Godwin to Wake, 24 Jan. 1724 (Christ Church, Oxford, Wake MSS, 14, fol 152); Hort to [Delafaye?], 3 Jan. 1724 (PRO SP 63/383/6-8).
108 Coghill to Southwell, 30 Oct. 1725 (BL Add MS 21122, fos 24-6).
109 Bolton to [Carteret], 16 July 1728 (PRONI D 562/92/167-70).
110 Godwin to Wake, 12 Apr. 1719 (Christ Church, Oxford, Wake MSS, 12, fos 252-3).
111 Same to Same, 30 July 1719 (Christ Church, Oxford, Wake MSS, 13, fol 95).
112 Same to Same, 14 Apr. 1722 (Christ Church, Oxford, Wake MSS, 14, fol 4).
113 Same to Same, 5 Oct. 1723 (ibid., fol 103).
114 Irish lords justices to Stanhope, 23 Nov. 1715 (PRO SP 63/373/256-8); Midleton to [Walpole?], 21 Sept. 1723 (PRO SP 63/381/135-6); Conolly to Delafaye, 25 Feb. 1726 (PRO SP 63/387/77-8).
115 *Liber Munerum*, i, Part 2, 38, 71, 76.
116 William Percival to Lord Percival, 31 Oct. 1724 (BL Add MS 47030, fos 107-8).
117 Coghill to Southwell, 5 Apr. 1733 (BL Add MS 21123, fos 32-4).
118 David Hayton, 'The "Country" interest and the party system, 1689-c.1720', in Clyve Jones (ed.), *Party and management in Parliament, 1660-1784* (Leicester, 1984), p 38. See also Sedgwick, *History of Parliament*, i, 62-78; Eveline Cruickshanks, *Political Untouchables. The Tories and the 45* (London, 1979); Linda Colley, *In Defiance of Oligarchy* (Cambridge, 1982); John Cannon (ed.), *The Whig Ascendancy* (London, 1981); J.C.D. Clark, 'A general theory of party, opposition and government 1688-1832', *Historical Journal*, 23, 2 (1980), 295-325; idem, 'The politics of the excluded: Tories, Jacobites and Whig Patriots', *Parliamentary History*, 2 (1983), 209-22.
119 Clark, 'Politics of the Excluded', 218.
120 Cruickshanks, *Political Untouchables*, pp 3-6; Bruce Lenman, *The Jacobite Risings in Britain 1689-1746* (London, 1980), p 287.
121 Cruickshanks, 'The political management of Sir Robert Walpole'; Hayton, 'The "Country" interest and the party system'; W.A. Speck, '"Whigs and Tories dim their glories": English political parties under the first two Georges', in Cannon (ed.), *The Whig Ascendancy*, pp 51-76.
122 Hayton, 'The "Country" interest and the party system', p 65.
123 Cruickshanks, 'The political management of Sir Robert Walpole', p 32.
124 Delafaye to _____, 30 Jan. 1716 (PRO SP 63/374/59-60).
125 _____ to Coningsby, 30 July 1719 (PRONI D 638/83).
126 King to Bp of Dromore, 26 Aug. 1714 (TCD MS 750/13/39-40); Alan Brodrick to Thomas Brodrick, 4 Nov. 1714 (SRO, Midleton MSS, iii, fos 199-201).

127 Irish lords justices to James Stanhope, 23 Nov. 1715 (PRO SP 63/373/256-8); Same to Same, 29 Nov. 1715 (ibid., 252-3); Lord Brodrick to Thomas Brodrick, 27 Dec. 1714 (SRO, Midleton MSS, iii, fos 289-90).
128 Delafaye to _____, 19 Apr. 1716 (PRO SP 63/374/215-16).
129 Delafaye to _____, 31 May 1716 (ibid., 246-7).
130 Midleton's brother, Thomas Brodrick, was MP for Stockbridge, 1713-22 and Guildford, 1722-27; his son, St John Brodrick, sat for Bere Alston 1721-27 (Sedgwick, *History of Parliament*, i, 489-92).

PATRONAGE AND POLITICS

1 Lecky, *Ireland in the Eighteenth Century*, i, 197.
2 E.M. Johnston, *Ireland in the Eighteenth Century* (Dublin, 1974), pp 59-60.
3 Beckett, *Modern Ireland*, p 162.
4 Hayton, 'Beginnings of the "Undertaker System"', p 36.
5 Dickson, *New Foundations*, p 63.
6 Connolly, *Religion, Law, and Power*, p 74.
7 Ibid., pp 88-9.
8 Ibid., pp 91-4.
9 Dalton, *George I's Army*, i, 325-71; ibid., ii, 152-3.
10 King to Grafton, 18 Dec. 1722 (TCD MS 750/7/258-9).
11 *Liber Munerum*, i, Part 2, 133-64; 'Offices in Lord Lieutenant's Gift', [undated, c. Dec. 1714] (PRO SP 63/371/75-80).
12 'A list of the commissioners and officers appointed for management of His Majesty's Revenue in Ireland with their respective salaries. 1720.' (Bod Lib, Oxford, MS Rawl. B. 511); 'Offices in Lord Lieutenant's Gift', [undated, c. Dec. 1714] (PRO SP 63/371/75-80).
13 'A list of the commissioners and officers appointed for management of His Majesty's Revenue in Ireland with their respective salaries. 1720.' (Bod Lib, Oxford, MS Rawl. B. 511).
14 King to Bp of Norwich, 11 Dec. 1714, in Richard Mant, *History of the Church of Ireland from the reformation to the union of the churches of England and Ireland, Jan. 1, 1801* (2 vols, London, 1840), ii, 289.
15 *New History of Ireland*, iv, 66-70.
16 *Liber Munerum*, i, Part 2, 20-77.
17 *Commons' Journals*, iii, Appendix, clxvii-clxviii, ccxlv, cccv, cccxxxvii.
18 Ibid., iii, Appendix, xxi-xxii, cccxxxvii.
19 In addition, two new Irish titles were conferred upon George I's German mistresses – Baroness Schulenburg was created Duchess of Munster in 1716 and the Countess of Platen was created Countess of Leinster in 1721.
20 *Liber Munerum*, i, Part 1, 1-51.
21 Boulter to Newcastle, 22 Mar. 1725 (*Boulter Letters*, i, 55)
22 King to Tollet, 14 Jan. 1715 (TCD MS 750/13/173-4).
23 Delafaye to _____, 4 May 1716 (PRO SP 63/374/219-20); Grafton and Galway to [Stanhope?], 17 May 1716 (ibid., 225-7); Grafton and Galway to [Stanhope?], 17 May 1716 (ibid., 225-7). On the other hand, an unprecedented twenty-seven new pensions were awarded between 1725 and 1727 – McNally, 'Patronage and Politics', p 185.
24 PRO CUST 1/15/83 (24 Mar. 1721); Conolly to Clutterbuck, 18 July 1726 (NLI MS 16007/167).

25 McNally, 'Patronage and Politics', p 86.
26 Bladen to Delafaye, 6 Apr. 1717 (PRO SP 63/375/76); Dalton *George i's Army*, ii, 181.
27 J.W. Hayes, 'The social and profesional background of the officers of the British army, 1714-63' (unpublished MA thesis, University of London, 1956), p 116.
28 Henry St John to Lord Orrery, 12 June 1711, in Gilbert Parke (ed.), *Letters and Correspondence of Henry St John, Lord Viscount Bolingbroke* (London, 1798), i, 245-6.
29 Coghill to Southwell, 5 Apr. 1733 (BL Add MS 21123, fos 32-4).
30 Godwin to Wake, 28 Mar. 1716 (Christ Church, Oxford, Wake MSS, 12, fol 28).
31 Dorset to Newcastle, 27 Oct. 1731 (PRO SP 63/394/101-2).
32 Same to Same, 29 Sept. 1731 (ibid., 75-6).
33 Boulter to Carteret, 26 Aug. 1727 (*Boulter Letters*, i, 156-7).
34 Boulter to Sir Robert Walpole, 14 June 1729 (ibid., i, 253-4); Boulter to Newcastle, 3 Jan. 1730 (ibid., i, 276-7). See also Same to Same, 10 June 1729 (ibid., i, 250-51); Same to Same, 23 Oct. 1729 (ibid., i, 262-5).
35 Berkeley to Lord Percival, 9 Jan. 1722 (BL Add MS 47029, fol 95).
36 Robert Wilson to Oliver St George, 27 Aug. 1724 (PRO C 110/46/338-9); Owen Gallagher to Oliver St George, 22 Sept. 1724 (ibid., 340-1).
37 Lord Brodrick to Thomas Brodrick, 1 Mar. 1717 (SRO, Midleton MSS, iii, fol 406).
38 A distinction has been made between the composition of those groups coming under the general headings 'the Irish' and 'the Irish interest'. The term 'Irish interest' refers to those Irish-born Anglican bishops who opposed the English interest in the House of Lords. For a detailed discussion of the composition of the Irish and English interests and the causes of conflict between these groups, see chapter seven below.
39 Godwin to Wake, 11 Apr. 1722 (Christ Church, Oxford, Wake MSS, 14, fol 6-7).
40 Boulter to Wake, 23 May 1727 (*Boulter Letters*, i, 133-4); Boulter to Gibson, 21 Feb. 1727 (ibid., i, 114-6); Same to Same, 25 Apr. 1727 (ibid., i, 126-7); Same to Same, 14 Dec. 1729 (ibid., i, 271-2).
41 Godwin to Wake, 18 Dec. 1723 (Christ Church, Oxford, Wake MSS, 14, fol 135).
42 Whitshed to Sunderland, 15 Mar. 1715 (BL Add MS 61639, fos 124-6).
43 Coghill to Southwell, 20 Oct. 1733 (BL Add MS 21123, fos 62-4).
44 King to Sir George St George, 18 Dec. 1714 (TCD MS 750/13/154); Daniel Dering to Lord Percival, 6 Aug. 1715 (BL Add MS 47028, fos 51-3).
45 Figures from attendance lists in *Lords' Journals*, ii, 451-544.
46 Ibid., iii, Appendix, xv, cxxii, clxvi, ccxiii, ccxlvi, cccv, cccxxxvi.
47 King to Sunderland, 19 Apr. 1716 (TCD MS 2533/210-11); King to Addison, 2 June 1716 (ibid., 245-6).
48 BL Add MS 61637C, fos 4-7.
49 Bolton to Lords of the Treasury, 6 May 1719 (*Calendar of Treasury Papers*, 1714-19, vol ccxi, 450-1); Same to Same, 31 May 1720 (ibid., 1720-28, vol ccxxviii, 12).
50 *Commons' Journals*, iii, Appendix, cccxli.
51 The five Tories were the earls of Charlemont and of Bellamont, Viscount Strabane, and Lords Altham and Kerry. The ten peers in employment were Lord Brodrick (lord chancellor); earl of Cavan (half-pay officer and civil pensioner); earl of Mount-Alexander (military pensioner); Viscount Strangford (civil pensioner); Lord Blayney (military pensioner); Lord Ferrard (governor of Drogheda); Lord Ranelagh (civil pensioner); Lord Santry (governor of Charlemont Fort); Lord Stackallen (military pensioner); and Lord Tyrawley (commander-in-chief of the army in Ireland). *Commons' Journals*, iii, Appendix, xxi-xxii, cxvii-cxviii,cxxi; Dalton, *George i's Army*, ii, 151-3.

52   Note of voting by Charles Delafaye, 14 Feb 1716 (PRO SP 63/374/94-6); *Lords' Journals*, ii, 626-8 (29 July 1719).
53   Note of voting by Charles Delafaye, 14 Feb 1716 (PRO SP 63/374/94-6).
54   McNally, 'Patronage and Politics', p 204.
55   Charles Irvine to King, 8 Feb. 1715 (King, *A Great Archbishop of Dublin*, pp 177-8).
56   Irish lords justices to Stanhope, 23 Nov. 1715 (PRO SP 63/373/256-8).
57   Same to Same, 28 May 1716 (PRO SP 63/374/244-5).
58   Stanhope to Irish lords justices, 25 Feb. 1716 (PRO SP 67/7/150).
59   Bolton to Craggs, 18 July 1719 (PRO SP 63/377/131-2).
60   Lord Tyrawley to Sunderland, 1 Jan. 1715 (BL Add MS 61636, fol 7); King to Flower, 6 Aug. 1715 (TCD MS 2533/44).
61   Irish lords justices to Stanhope, 6 Feb. 1716 (PRO SP 63/374/84-5); Delafaye to [Pringle?], 6 Feb. 1716 (ibid., 90-91).
62   Irish lords justices to Stanhope, 8 Mar. 1716 (ibid., 131-2); 'Persons recommended that were not upon the Half-pay list in Ireland.' [undated, with papers of July 1716, but probably enclosed with letter of 8 March 1716] (ibid., 306-7).
63   Stanhope to Irish lords justices, 27 Mar. 1716 (PRO SP 67/6/135-6).
64   Galway to Methuen, 10 Nov. 1716 (PRO SP 63/374/274-5).
65   Dalton, *George 1's Army*, ii, 129-46.
66   King to earl of Pembroke, 30 June 1722 (TCD MS 750/7/146).
67   King to S. Molyneux, 15 Feb. 1715 (ibid., 186).
68   'Reasons for building a barracks at Cloghnakilty, Co. Cork.', c. Mar. 1715 (BL Add MS 61639, fol 137).
69   Sunderland to Conolly, 25 Jan. 1715 (BL Add MS 61652, fol 254); *Commons' Journals*, iii, Appendix, cxxxiii. Ten barracks were built in the end.
70   *Liber Munerum*, i, Part 2, 100-27; Dalton, *George 1's Army*, ii, 152-5; ibid., ii, 153-5; *Commons' Journals*, iii, Appendix, cxxi.
71   Midleton to Thomas Brodrick, 9 July 1727 (SRO, Midleton MSS, vii, fos 77-8).
72   Coghill to Southwell, 20 Nov. 1733 (BL Add MS 21123, fos 64-8).
73   See Thomas Bartlett, 'The Townshend Viceroyalty', in *Penal Era and Golden Age*, pp 88-112; and 'Viscount Townshend and the Irish Revenue Board', in *Proceedings of the Royal Irish Academy*, 79, sect. C (1979), 153-75.
74   Swift, *Journal to Stella*, 28 Sept. 1710 – quoted in Lena Boylan 'The Conollys of Castletown – a family history', in *Quarterly Bulletin of the Irish Georgian Society*, 40, 4 (Oct.-Dec. 1968), 6; Alan Brodrick to Sunderland, 19 Oct. 1714 (BL Add MS 61636, fos 113-4).
75   Katherine Conolly to Delafaye, 17 June 1729 (PRO SP 63/391/71).
76   Coghill to Southwell, 14 Jan. 1735 (BL Add MS 21123, fos 84-6).
77   Sunderland to Conolly, 4 Jan. 1715 (BL Add MS 61652, fos 241-2); John Forster to Sunderland, 13 Nov. 1714 (BL Add MS 61639, fos 57-8); Oliver St George to Sunderland, 25 Mar. 1715 (ibid., fos 130-31).
78   Midleton to Thomas Brodrick, 14 June 1717 (SRO, Midleton MSS, iv, fos 35-6).
79   Conolly to [Delafaye], 14 July 1724 (PRO SP 63/384/9-10); Downes to Nicolson, 16 July 1724 (*Nicolson Correspondence*, ii, 579-81).
80   Midleton to Thomas Brodrick, 22 Jan. 1720 (SRO, Midleton MSS, iv, fos 200-01); Same to Same, 21 Feb. 1720 (ibid., iv, fol. 228).
81   Downes to Nicolson, 24 Mar. 1724 (*Nicolson Correspondence*, ii, 565-7); Townshend to Grafton, 17 Mar. 1724 (PRO SP 63/384/103-4).
82   Midleton to Thomas Brodrick, 22 May 1720 (SRO, Midleton MSS, iv, fos 265-6).
83   Connolly, *Religion, Law, and Power*, p 94.

84   Cox to Southwell, 22 Apr. 1707 (BL Add MS 38155, fol 21).

85   Boulter to Newcastle, 16 Nov. 1725 (*Boulter Letters*, i, 43-5).

86   Coghill to Southwell, 5 April 1733 (BL Add MS 21123, fos 32-4).

87   Same to Same, 21 June 1733 (ibid., fos 41-2).

88   Same to Same, 5 Apr. 1733 (ibid., fos 32-4).

89   Bp of Killaloe to Midleton, 22 Apr. 1728 (SRO, Midleton MSS, vii, fos 63-4).

90   Boulter to Townshend, 9 May 1728 (*Boulter Letters*, i, 192-3); see also Boulter to Newcastle, 30 April 1728 (ibid., i, 190-91).

91   Coghill to Southwell, 5 April 1733 (BL Add MS 21123, fos 32-4).

92   Boulter to Dorset, 13 Mar. 1735 (*Boulter Letters*, ii, 107-8); Same to Same, 3 Aug. 1736 (ibid., ii, 134-5); Same to Same, 17 Mar. 1737 (ibid., ii, 161).

93   Coghill to Southwell, 20 Sept. 1733 (BL Add MS 21123, fos 51-2). Purdon was MP for Castlemartyr, 1715-37.

94   Anon. to Wake, 17 April 1716 (Christ Church, Oxford, Wake MSS, 12, fol 37).

95   Revenue commissioners to Sunderland, 18 Jan. 1715 (NLI MS 16007/6-9).

96   PRO CUST 1/15/27 (5 Oct. 1720); ibid., 35 (29 Oct. 1720); ibid., 34 (24 Oct. 1720); Conolly to [Delafaye], 3 Dec. 1720 (PRO SP 63/379/85).

97   Boulter to Dorset, 11 May 1732 (*Boulter Letters*, ii, 60-1).

98   Ibid.

99   King to S. Molyneux, 12 July 1715 (TCD MS 2533/11).

100 Midleton to Thomas Brodrick, 21 Oct. 1723 (SRO, Midleton MSS, v, fos 323-4).

101 Grafton to Stanhope, 22 May 1716 (PRO SP 63/374/240-41).

102 West to Newcastle, 27 Jan. 1726 (ibid., 13-4).

103 Bolton to Craggs, 18 July 1719 (PRO SP 63/377/131-2).

104 'A list of the commissioners and officers appointed for management of His Majesty's Revenue in Ireland with their respective salaries. 1720.' (Bod Lib, Oxford, MS Rawl. B. 511); Midleton to Thomas Brodrick, 17 Dec. 1721 (SRO, Midleton MSS, v, fos 122-3); Same to Same, 21 Oct. 1723 (ibid., fos 323-4).

105 Same to Same, 3 June 1718 (SRO, Midleton MSS, iv, fol 118).

106 Boulter to Newcastle, 16 Nov. 1725 (*Boulter Letters*, i, 44-5).

107 Same to Same, 22 Mar. 1726 (ibid., i, 54-5).

108 Same to Same, 22 Mar. 1726 (ibid., i, 56).

109 Walpole to Newcastle, 1 Sept. 1724 (PRO SP 63/384/54-5).

110 Coghill to Southwell, 13 Dec. 1733 (BL Add MS 21123, fos 76-7).

111 Same to Same, 18 Oct. 1733 (ibid., fos 58-61).

112 Philip Percival to Lord Percival, 24 Apr. 1724 (BL Add MS 47030, fol 64).

VICEROYS, UNDERTAKERS AND PARLIAMENTARY MANAGEMENT

1   Charles Delafaye to _____, 19 Apr. 1716 (PRO SP 63/374/215-6).

2   McGuire, 'Irish Parliament of 1692'; Hayton, 'Beginnings of the "Undertaker System"'.

3   McNally, 'Patronage and Politics', pp 213-4.

4   Lord Brodrick to Thomas Brodrick, 14 Apr. 1715 (SRO, Midleton MSS, iii, fos 232-3).

5   Same to Same, 18 Dec. 1715 (ibid., fos 280-85).

6   Ibid.

7   Delafaye to _____, 17 Dec. 1715 (PRO SP 63/373/336-7).

8   Abercorn to Southwell, 5 Jan. 1714 (PRONI D 623/A/3/12). See also Hayton, 'Beginnings

of the "Undertaker System"', pp 37-8.
9   Brodrick to Sunderland, 25 Jan. 1715 (BL Add MS 61636, fos 131-2).
10 Alan Brodrick to Thomas Brodrick, 14 Dec. 1714 (SRO, Midleton MSS, iii, fos 205-7).
11 Same to Same, 6 Aug. 1725 (SRO, Midleton MSS, vi, fos 277-80); Same to Same, 17 Nov. 1725 (ibid., fos 336-41).
12 Same to Same, 30 Dec. 1715 (SRO, Midleton MSS, iii, fos 291-4); Same to Same, 16 Aug. 1719 (SRO, Midleton MSS, iv, fos 156-9).
13 [_____] to Wake, 16 July 1719 (Christ Church, Oxford, Wake MSS, 13, fol 90).
14 Ibid.
15 Midleton to Thomas Brodrick, 1 Nov. 1723 (SRO, Midleton MSS, v, fos 325-8).
16 Same to Same, 27 Aug. 1725 (SRO, Midleton MSS, vi, fos 289-91).
17 Conolly to Delafaye, 2 Sept. 1725 (PRO SP 63/386/52).
18 Charles Dering to Lord Percival, 6 Aug. 1717 (BL Add MS 47028, fol 196).
19 Connolly, *Religion, Law and Power*, pp 91-7; James Kelly, *'That damn'd thing called honour'. Duelling in Ireland, 1570-1860* (Cork, 1995), pp 48-66.
20 Midleton to Thomas Brodrick, 21 Oct. 1723 (SRO, Midleton MSS, v, fos 323-4).
21 Same to Same, 28 Dec. 1723 (ibid., fos 344-5).
22 Same to Same, 7 Dec. 1719 (SRO, Midleton MSS, iv, fol 180).
23 Cox to Southwell, 21 Sept. 1714 (BL Add MS 38157, fol 124).
24 Midleton to Thomas Brodrick, 22 Jan. 1720 (SRO, Midleton MSS, iv, fos 200-01).
25 Same to Same, 22 Mar. 1725 (SRO, Midleton MSS, vi, fos 179-81).
26 Same to Same, 11 Nov. 1717 (SRO, Midleton MSS, iv, fos 92-4).
27 Conolly to Delafaye, 9 Oct. 1717 (PRO SP 63/375/208-9).
28 Addison to Bolton, 5 Nov. 1717 (PRO SP 67/7/23-4).
29 Conolly to Grafton [draft], 18 Oct. 1720 (PRONI, T 2825/A/15).
30 Midleton to Thomas Brodrick, 5 June 1721 (SRO, Midleton MSS, v, fos 37-9).
31 Same to Same, 6 June 1721 (ibid., fos 43-6).
32 Ibid.
33 Thomas Brodrick to Midleton, 17 June 1721 (SRO, Midleton MSS, v, fos 49-50); Midleton to Thomas Brodrick, 13 July 1721 (ibid., fol 59).
34 For accounts of the Wood's halfpence dispute see Albert Goodwin, 'Wood's Halfpence', *English Historical Review*, 51, 204 (Oct. 1936), 647–74; David Hayton, 'Walpole and Ireland', in Black (ed.), *Britain in the age of Walpole*, pp 95-120; Burns, *Parliamentary politics in Ireland*, i, 134-216. A detailed analysis of the dispute's implications for the relationship between viceroys and undertakers can be found in McNally, 'Wood's halfpence, Carteret and the government of Ireland, 1723-26', *IHS*, forthcoming.
35 King to Grafton, 10 July 1722 (TCD MS 750/7/159 a,b,c); revenue commissioners to Hopkins, 7 Aug. 1922 (PRO SP 63/380/110).
36 Grafton to Walpole, 22 Aug. 1723 (PRO SP 63/381/3-5).
37 Townshend to Grafton, 17 Mar. 1724 (PRO SP 63/384/103-4).
38 Walpole to Townshend, 6 Nov. 1723 (Coxe, *Walpole*, ii, 285-6).
39 Conolly to Delafaye, 15 Aug. 1724 (PRO SP 63/384/40).
40 Carteret to Newcastle, 28 Oct. 1724 (ibid., 139-56); Boulter to Newcastle, 19 Jan. 1725 (*Boulter Letters*, i, 9-10).
41 Thomas Brodrick to Midleton, 4 Apr. 1724 (SRO, Midleton MSS, vi, fos 1-3).
42 Owen Gallagher to Oliver St George, 22 Dec. 1724 (PRO C 110/46/352-3); Same to Same, 22 May 1725 (ibid., 366-7). The change in the relationship between Carteret and Conolly was demonstrated when the viceroy spent Christmas 1727 at Castletown – Coghill to Southwell, 30 Dec. 1727 (BL Add MS 21122, fos 37-8).

43 Gallagher to St George, 9 Jan. 1725 (PRO C 110/46/313-4).
44 For indications of Carteret's policy and contemporary reaction to it see Carteret to New-
    castle, 14 Nov. 1724 (PRO SP 63/384/182-8); Same to Same, 24 Nov. 1724 (ibid., 196-
    200); Midleton to Thomas Brodrick, 12 Dec. 1724 (SRO, Midleton MSS, vi, fos 106-7);
    Carteret to Newcastle, 16 Dec. 1724 (PRO SP 63/384/226-8); Nicolson to Wake, 1 Jan.
    1725 (BL Add MS 6116, fos 137-8); King to Annesley, 28 Jan. 1725 (TCD MS 2537/208-
    9); Carteret to Newcastle, 31 Jan. 1725 (PRO SP 63/385/25-34); Same to Same, 27 Mar.
    1725 (ibid., 72-5); King to Southwell, 15 May 1725 (TCD MS 2537/339-41); Godwin to
    Wake, 18 May 1725 (Christ Church, Oxford, Wake MSS, 14, fol 263); Carteret to Newcas-
    tle, 8 June 1725 (PRO SP 63/385/137-8); Same to Same, 6 July 1725 (ibid., 263-5); Godwin
    to Wake, 14 July 1725 (Christ Church, Oxford, Wake MSS, 14, fol 276); Lord Perceval to
    Philip Perceval, 30 July 1725 (BL Add MS 47030, fol 147); King to Molyneux, 3 Oct.
    1725 (TCD MS 750/8/31-2); Manley to [Delafaye?], 28 Jan. 1726 (PRO SP 67/387/25-6).
45 Carteret to Newcastle, 6 Aug. 1725 (PRO SP 63/386/5-8); West to Newcastle, 6 Aug. 1725
    (ibid., 9-10).
46 Boulter to Newcastle, 21 Sept. 1725 (*Boulter Letters*, i, 34-5); Boulter to Wake, 24 Sept.
    1725 (ibid., i, 36-8); Midleton to Thomas Brodrick, 24 Sept. 1724 (SRO, Midleton MSS,
    vi, fos 314-9).
47 Coghill to Southwell, 30 Oct. 1725 (BL Add MS 21122, fos 24-6).
48 The relationship between the two men cannot have been helped when Carteret's chief but-
    ler accidentally fell to his death at Castletown in August: Gallagher to St George, 21 Aug.
    1725 (PRO C 110/46/386-7). I am indebted to David Hayton for this reference.
49 Townshend to Carteret, 29 Dec. 1724 (PRO SP 63/384/231-5); Carteret to Townshend, 23
    Sept. 1725 (PRO SP 63/386/84-99); Newcastle to Townshend, 1 Oct. 1725 (ibid., 171-3).
50 West to Newcastle, 26 Oct. 1725 (ibid., 214-16); Coghill to Southwell, 30 Oct. 1725 (BL
    Add MS 21122, fos 24-6); Carteret to Newcastle, 16 Nov. 1725 (PRO SP 63/386/292-4);
    West to Newcastle, 16 Nov. 1725 (ibid., 308-9); Boulter to Newcastle, 16 Nov. 1725 (*Boulter
    Letters*, i, 43-5).
51 Coghill to Southwell, 23 Dec. 1725 (BL Add MS 21122, fos 27-8).
52 Philip Percival to Lord Percival, 1 Feb. 1726 (BL Add MS 47031, fos 92-4).
53 Coghill to Southwell, 23 Dec. 1725 (BL Add MS 21122, fos 27-8); Newcastle to Townshend,
    5 Nov. 1725 (BL Add MS 32687, fol 178); Southwell to Lord Percival, 31 Dec. 1725 (BL
    Add MS 47031, fos 67-9).
54 Coghill to Southwell, 23 Dec. 1725 (BL Add MS 21122, fos 27-8).
55 Boulter to Newcastle, 28 Oct. 1725 (*Boulter Letters*, i, 40-1).
56 Southwell to Lord Percival, 31 Dec. 1725 (BL Add MS 47031, fos 67-9).
57 Midleton to Thomas Brodrick, 15 Oct. 1725 (SRO, Midleton MSS, vi, fos 330-31).
58 Boulter to Newcastle, 12 Oct. 1725 (*Boulter Letters*, i, 39-40).
59 Boulter to Delafaye, 22 Feb. 1726 (PRO SP 63/387/50-1); West to Newcastle, 27 Jan. 1726
    (ibid., 13-4); Carteret to Newcastle, 28 Jan. 1726 (ibid., 17-9); Manley to [Delafaye?], 28
    Jan. 1726 (ibid., 25-6).
60 Lord Brodrick to Thomas Brodrick, 26 Apr. 1717 (SRO, Midleton MSS, iv, fos 13-4).
61 Bolton to Craggs, 27 June 1719 (PRO SP 63/377/234-5).
62 Midleton to Thomas Brodrick, 4 Dec. 1720 (SRO, Midleton MSS, iv, fos 367-9).
63 Boulter to Gibson, 25 Apr. 1727 (*Boulter Letters*, i, 126-7).
64 Grafton and Galway to [Stanhope?], 17 May 1716 (PRO SP 63/374/225-7).
65 Carteret to Townshend, 14 Dec. 1729 (PRO SP 63/391/254); Forth to Thompson, 19 Jan.
    1730 (NLI MS 16007/210-11).
66 Conolly to Grafton [draft], 18 Oct. 1720 (PRONI T 2825/A/15).

67   Ibid.
68   Midleton to Thomas Brodrick, 4 Dec. 1720 (SRO, Midleton MSS, iv, fos 367-9).
69   Same to Same, 24 Aug. 1723 (SRO, Midleton MSS, v, fos 296-7).
70   Robert Howard to Hugh Howard, 12 Oct. 1731 (NLI, Wicklow Papers, PC 227, unfoliated).
71   Coghill to Southwell, 18 Oct. 1733 (BL Add MS 21123, fos 58-61).
72   Conolly to Delafaye, 3 Nov. 1717 (PRO SP 63/375/214).
73   Midleton to Thomas Brodrick, 1 Nov. 1723 (SRO, Midleton MSS, v, fos 325-8).
74   Same to Same, 9 Mar. 1724 (ibid., fos 384-5).
75   Carteret to Newcastle, 28 Oct. 1724 (PRO SP 63/384/139-56).
76   Lord Brodrick to Thomas Brodrick, 30 Dec. 1715 (SRO, Midleton MSS, iii, fos 291-4);
     Same to Same, 12 Apr. 1716 (ibid., fos 360-62); Dering to Lord Percival, 10 Dec. 1715 (BL
     Add MS 47028, fos 109-11).
77   Coghill to Southwell, 20 Nov. 1733 (BL Add MS 21123, fos 64-8).
78   Cary to Delafaye, 26 Sept. 1731 (PRO SP 63/394/73-4).
79   Webster to Delafaye, 1 Sept. 1719 (PRO SP 63/378/35-6).
80   Delafaye to _____, 17 Dec. 1715 (PRO SP 63/373/336-7).
81   Clutterbuck to Delafaye, 20 Nov. 1729 (PRO SP 63/391/236-7).
82   Carteret to Townsend, 14 Dec. 1729 (PRO SP 63/391/263-5).
83   Coghill to Southwell, 3 Jan. 1730 (BL Add MS 21122, fos 103-6).
84   Clutterbuck to Delafaye, 14 Dec. 1729 (PRO SP 63/391/260-2).
85   Cary to Delafaye, 11 Mar. 1732 (PRO SP 63/395/98-9).
86   Bolton to Craggs, 8 July 1719 (PRO SP 63/377/167-8).
87   Webster to Craggs, 2 July 1719 (ibid., 226-7).
88   Boulter to Newcastle, 18 Jan. 1732 (PRO SP 63/395/5-6).
89   Cary to Delafaye, 22 Feb. 1732 (ibid., 64-5).
90   Bolton to Craggs, 15 Oct. 1719 (PRO SP 63/378/83-4).
91   Cary to Delafaye, 30 Oct. 1733 (PRO SP 63/396/91-2).
92   Coghill to Southwell, 18 Oct. 1733 (Add MS 21123, fos 58-61).
93   Cary to Delafaye, 20 Nov. 1733 (PRO SP 63/396/99-101).
94   Coghill to Southwell, 13 Dec. 1733 (BL Add MS 21123, fos 76-7).
95   Dorset to Newcastle, 14 Dec. 1733 (PRO SP 63/396/121-4).
96   See Swift's attack on those peers who changed their votes under pressure from Carteret in
     1725, 'On Wisdom's Defeat in a Learned Debate', in Harold Williams (ed.), *The Poems of
     Jonathan Swift* (2nd ed., 3 vols, Oxford, 1958), iii, 1117-8.
97   Clutterbuck to Delafaye, 20 Nov. 1729 (PRO SP 63/391/241-3).
98   Boulter to Newcastle, 6 Mar. 1733 (PRO SP 63/396/15)
99   Coghill to Southwell, 22 Feb. 1733 (BL Add MS 21123, fos 20-21).
100 Same to Same, 8 March 1733 (ibid., fos 24-5).
101 Same to Same, 5 Apr. 1733 (ibid., fos 32-4).
102 Boulter to Bp of London, 11 [*recte* 21] Feb. 1727 (*Boulter Letters*, i, 114-6).
103 Coghill to Southwell, 5 Apr. 1733 (BL Add MS 21123, fos 32-4).
104 Same to Same, 15 Mar. 1733 (ibid., fos 26-7).
105 Boulter to Newcastle, 22 Mar. 1726 (*Boulter Letters*, i, 56); Coghill to Southwell, 5 April
     1733 (BL Add MS 21123, fos 32-4).
106 Ibid.
107 Same to Same, 19 Apr. 1733 (BL Add MS 21123, fos 36-7).
108 Same to Same, 21 June 1733 (ibid., fos 41-2).
109 Same to Same, 27 July 1733 (ibid., fol 47).
110 Same to Same, 20 Sept. 1733 (ibid., fos 51-2); Same to Same, 18 Oct. 1733 (ibid., fos 58-
     61).

111   Same to Same, 18 Oct. 1733 (ibid., fos 58-61).
112   Same to Same, 20 Oct. 1733 (ibid., fos 62-4).
113   Ibid.
114   Same to Same, 20 Nov. 1733 (BL Add MS 21123, fos 64-8).
115   James, *Ireland in the Empire*, pp 167-8.
116   Coghill to Southwell, 4 Dec. 1732 [*recte* 1733] (BL Add MS 21123, fos 64-8).
117   Declan O'Donovan, 'The Money Bill dispute of 1753', in Bartlett and Hayton, *Penal Era and Golden Age*, pp 55-87.

THE IRISH AND ENGLISH INTERESTS

1   Welbore Ellis, a Tory bishop who identified strongly with the English interest, is an exception in this respect.
2   See Hayton, 'Ireland and the English minsters', pp 7-12.
3   These calculations are based on the attendance records as recorded in the *Lords' Journals*. These figures do not take into account the attendance of the Irish judges which is not recorded in the journals.
4   John Percival to Lord Percival, 3 May 1730 (BL Add MS 47032, fos 175-6).
5   Delafaye to [Pringle?], 6 Feb. 1716 (PRO SP 63/374/90-1).
6   'A list of the privy councillors of Ireland with the dates of their being sworn, from the 3rd of July 1711.' (PRONI T 1019).
7   King to Stanhope, 5 Nov. 1715 (PRO SP 63/373/209-11). For more on the activities of convocation under Queen Anne see Sean Connolly, 'Reformers and highflyers: the post-revolution church', in A. Ford, J. McGuire, and K. Milne (eds.), *As by Law Established. The Church of Ireland since the Reformation* (Dublin, 1995), pp 152-65.
8   Addison to Bolton, 3 Aug. 1717 (*Addison Letters*, p 369); Boulter to Wake, 13 Jan. 1728 (*Boulter Letters*, i, 166-7).
9   Hayton, 'Ireland and the English minsters', pp 109-13; J.L. McCracken, *The Irish Parliament in the eighteenth century* (Dundalk, 1971), p 13; Conolly to Grafton [draft], 24 Sept. 1720 (PRONI, T 2825/A/14); King to Molesworth, 14 Dec. 1714 (TCD MS 750/13/144-7).
10   Refusal to contemplate a total repeal of the sacramental test was a notable exception.
11   Mant, *Church of Ireland*, ii, 293; King to Francis Annesley, 1 Nov. 1723 (TCD MS 2537/19-21); King to Howard, 10 Apr. 1716 (TCD MS 2533/187-8).
12   King to J. Stanhope, 5 Nov. 1715 (PRO SP 63/373/209-11).
13   King to Charlett, 20 Apr. 1715 (King, *A Great Archbishop of Dublin*, pp 179-80).
14   Abercorn to Southwell, 3 Nov. 1713 (PRONI D 623/A/3/2).
15   Downes to Wake, 15 Oct. 1720 (Christ Church, Oxford, Wake MSS, 13, fol 200).
16   Synge to Wake, 15 Aug. 1720 (BL Add MS 6117, fos 155-7).
17   Godwin to Wake, 23 Dec. 1721 (Christ Church, Oxford, Wake MSS, 13, fos 213-4); Bp of Elphin to H. Howard, 22 Apr. 1732 (NLI, Wicklow MSS, PC 227, [unfoliated]).
18   Mant, *Church of Ireland*, ii, 286-8.
19   Irish Lords Justices to J. Stanhope, 23 Nov. 1715 (PRO SP 63/373/256-8); J. Stanhope to Irish Lords Justices, 10 Dec. 1715 (PRO SP 67/6/115).
20   Irish Lords Justices to J. Stanhope, 17 Dec. 1715 (PRO SP 63/373/308-9).
21   J. Stanhope to Irish Lords Justices, 27 Dec. 1715 (PRO SP 67/6/117).
22   Grafton to _____, 6 Jan. 1716 (PRO SP 63/374/12-3).

23 Delafaye to _____, 8 Jan. 1716 (ibid., 18-9).
24 Maxwell to [J. Stanhope], 24 Nov. 1715 (PRO SP 63/373/254); Same to Same, 13 Dec. 1715 (ibid., 302).
25 J. Stanhope to Irish Lords Justices, 27 Dec. 1715 (PRO SP 67/6/117); Same to Same, 14 Jan. 1716 (ibid., 118-20); Same to Same, 1 May 1716 (ibid., 142-3).
26 *DNB*, vi, 928.
27 King to S. Molyneux, 2 May 1716 (TCD MS 2533/221-4).
28 Godwin to Wake, 24 Jan. 1716 (Christ Church, Oxford, Wake MSS, 12, fos 318-9).
29 Midleton to Mrs Ally Brodrick, 30 Dec. 1720 (SRO, Midleton MSS, iv, fol 385).
30 Godwin to Wake, 31 Oct. 1716 (Christ Church, Oxford, Wake MSS, 12, fos 90-1).
31 Same to Same, 20 Dec. 1715 (ibid., fos 11-12); Same to Same, 11 Feb. 1716 (ibid., fos 16-7); Same to Same, 3 May 1716 (ibid., fos 45-6); Same to Same, 31 Oct. 1716 (ibid., fos 90-1); Mant, *Church of Ireland*, ii, 288-90; King to S. Molyneux, 2 May 1716 (TCD MS 2533/221-4).
32 _____ to Robert Molesworth, 27 Mar. 1716 (PRO SP 63/374/185-6).
33 James, 'The Church of Ireland in the early eighteenth century', 442-51.
34 See Isolde Victory, 'The making of the Declaratory Act of 1720', in O' Brien (ed.), *Parliament, Politics and People*, pp 9-29.
35 Synge to Wake, 30 Sept. 1717 (BL Add MS 6117, fos 126-9).
36 Godwin to _____, 9 Oct. 1717 (PRO SP 63/375/208-9).
37 King to Wake, 10 May 1718 (TCD MS 2535/166-71).
38 Same to Same, 25 Mar. 1718 (ibid., 125-6).
39 Synge to Wake, 29 Apr. 1718 (BL Add MS 6117, fol 137).
40 Evans to Wake, 25 Mar. 1718 (Christ Church, Oxford, Wake MSS, 12, fol 246).
41 Godwin to Wake, 12 Apr. 1719 (ibid., fos 252-3). See Norman Sykes, *William Wake, Archbishop of Canterbury, 1657-1737* (2 vols, Cambridge, 1957), ii, 222-34.
42 Nicolson to Wake, 17 Jan. 1720 (BL Add MS 6116, fos 94-5).
43 The three others were Viscount Midleton (lord chancellor), Viscount Doneraile (brother of Sir John St. Leger, one of the barons), and earl Fitzwilliam, a strong supporter of the government – (*Lords' Journals, Ireland*, ii, 626-8).
44 Nicolson to Wake, 30 Nov. 1719 (BL Add MS 6116, fos 92-3).
45 Same to Same, 31 Oct. 1719 (ibid., fos 91-2).
46 Same to Same, 17 Oct. 1719 (ibid., fos 90-1); Same to Same, 30 Nov. 1719 (ibid., fos 92-3).
47 Connolly, *Religion, Law, and Power*, pp 280-94.
48 See below p 172 for some exceptions to this general attitude.
49 Nicolson to Wake, 14 Dec. 1723 (BL Add MS 6116, fol 127).
50 Evans to Wake, 11 Apr. 1719 (Christ Church, Oxford, Wake MSS, 13, fol 50).
51 King to S. Molyneux, 30 July 1715 (TCD MS 2533/37-8); King to Nicolson, 30 July 1715 (ibid., 40-2); Same to Same, 16 Sept. 1715 (ibid., 86-7).
52 King to Sunderland, 8 Feb. 1715 (TCD MS 750/4/29).
53 Synge to Wake, 19 Nov. 1719 (BL Add MS 6117, fos 142-3); see also King to Bp of Lincoln, 19 July 1715 (TCD MS 2533/23-5); Synge to Wake, 29 June 1722 (BL Add MS 6117, fos 163-4).
54 F.G. James, 'The active Irish peers in the early eighteenth century', *Journal of British Studies*, 18, 2 (1979), 52-69, esp 67-9; Toby Barnard, 'Protestants and the Irish language, c.1675-1725', *Journal of Ecclesiastical History*, 44, 2 (Apr. 1993), 243-72.
55 Nicolson to Wake, 17 Oct. 1719 (BL Add MS 6116, fos 90-1); Same to Same, 30 Nov. 1719 (ibid., fos 92-3).

56   Bolton to Craggs, 3 Nov. 1719 (PRO SP 63/378/133-4).

57   Pocklington to Wake, 3 Nov. 1719 (Christ Church, Oxford, Wake MSS, 13, fol 122). For a more thorough analysis of the circumstances surrounding the rejection of this bill (including a discussion of the notorious 'castration clause') see Connolly, *Religion, Law, and Power*, pp 281-2.

58   King to S. Molyneux, 2 May 1716 (TCD MS 2533/221-4).

59   Same to Same, 24 Nov. 1724 (TCD MS 2537/187-90); Same to Same, 2 May 1716 (TCD MS 2533/221-4).

60   Ibid.

61   King to Trench, 12 Feb. 1717 (TCD MS 2534/87-8).

62   King to Synge, 21 Mar. 1717 (ibid., 129-30).

63   King to Bp of Cloyne, 24 Dec. 1726 (TCD MS 750/8/170-72); King to Carteret, 6 June 1727 (ibid., 204); Boulter to Newcastle, 1 Jan. 1727 (*Boulter Letters*, i, 94); King to Bp of Cloyne, 6 June 1727 (TCD MS 750/8/205).

64   King to Grafton, 20 Dec. 1720 (TCD MS 8191/169).

65   Figures from Mant, *Church of Ireland*, ii, 781-92.

66   Bolton to Wake, 19 Apr. 1720 (Christ Church, Oxford, Wake MSS, 13, fol 168).

67   King to Coghill, 22 Dec. 1716 (TCD MS 2534/36-7); King to Rev John Blair, 18 May 1725 (TCD MS 2537/245).

68   Carteret to Wake, 17 Apr. 1724 (Christ Church, Oxford, Wake MSS, 14, fol 192); Godwin to Wake, 14 July 1725 (ibid., fol 276). Cotterel was appointed as bishop of Ferns and Leighlin in 1743.

69   King to S. Molyneux, 24 Nov. 1724 (TCD MS 2537/187-90).

70   King to Bp of Norwich, 11 Dec. 1714 (Mant, *Church of Ireland*, ii, 289).

71   Godwin to Wake, 3 Mar. 1722 (Christ Church, Oxford, Wake MSS, 13, fos 323-4).

72   Godwin to Wake, 11 Apr. 1722 (Christ Church, Oxford, Wake MSS, 14, fos 6-7). The appointment to this post would have been, officially at least, decided by the Treasury. The viceroy had no official influence in the filling of revenue posts.

73   Nicolson to Wake, 29 Feb. 1724 (BL Add MS 6116, fos 130-1).

74   Evans to Wake, 15 Mar. 1723 (Christ Church, Oxford, Wake MSS, 14, fol 60).

75   Godwin to Wake, 24 Jan. 1724 (ibid., fol 152).

76   Downes to Nicolson, 17 Feb. 1722 (*Nicolson Correspondence*, ii, 549-50).

77   Godwin to Wake, 2 June 1722 (Christ Church, Oxford, Wake MSS, 14, fos 22-3).

78   Same to Same, 16 Jan. 1723 (ibid., fol 48).

79   Evans to Wake, 29 Jan. 1724 (ibid., fol 155).

80   King to Francis Annesley, 26 Nov. 1725 (TCD MS 750/8/53-5). The context of King's letter makes it clear that he is referring to the Irish clergy.

81   Nicolson to Wake, 6 Jan. 1722 (BL Add MS 6116, fos 103-4); Same to Same, 20 Jan. 1722 (ibid., fol 105).

82   King to Grafton, 16 Feb. 1722 (King, *A Great Archbishop of Dublin*, pp 231-2).

83   King to Wake, 3 Feb. 1722 (BL Add MS 6117, fos 71-2).

84   None of these bishops were Irish-born and all had been appointed since the accession of George I – W.A. Phillips (ed.), *History of the Church of Ireland from the earliest times to the present day* (3 vols, London, 1933), iii, 198.

85   Nicolson to Wake, 4 Mar. 1722 (BL Add MS 6116, fos 120-21); Synge to Wake, 26 Mar. 1722 (BL Add MS 6117, fos 162-3).

86   Boulter to Newcastle, 4 Mar. 1725 (*Boulter Letters*, i, 12-13).

87   McCracken, 'The undertakers in Ireland'. A similar interpretation has more recently been placed on the events of 1724-5 in Burns, *Irish Parliamentary Politics*, i, 167.

88   Hayton, 'Beginnings of the "Undertaker System"', 32-3; Dickson, *New Foundations*, pp 66-79.
89   Boulter to Newcastle, 4 Mar. 1725 (*Boulter Letters*, i, 12).
90   Henry Maule to Wake, 9 June 1724 (Christ Church, Oxford, Wake MSS, 14, fol 202).
91   Boulter to Townshend, 29 Apr. 1725 (*Boulter Letters*, i, 17-8); Boulter to Newcastle, 12 Oct. 1725 (ibid., i, 39-40); Carteret to Delafaye, 28 Oct. 1725 (PRO SP 63/386/222); Boulter to Newcastle, 19 May 1726 (*Boulter Letters*, i, 58-60); Boulter to Carteret, 7 Mar. 1727 (ibid., i, 116-8).
92   Boulter to Wake, 23 May 1727 (ibid., i, 133-4); Boulter to Gibson, 21 Feb. 1727 (ibid., i, 114-6).
93   Boulter to Gibson, 25 Apr. 1727 (ibid., i, 126-7).
94   Same to Same, 14 Dec. 1729 (ibid., i, 271-2).
95   Same to Same, 2 Jan. 1730 (ibid., i, 275-6).
96   Godwin to Wake, 2 Aug. 1718 (Christ Church, Oxford, Wake MSS, 12, fos 298-9).
97   Evans to Wake, 14 Mar. 1718 (ibid., fol 245).
98   Godwin to Wake, 2 July 1719 (Christ Church, Oxford, Wake MSS, 13, fol 76).
99   Evans to Wake, 23 Oct. 1719 (ibid., fol 118); Pocklington to Wake, 30 July 1719 (ibid., fol 94); Godwin to Wake, 30 July 1719 (ibid., fol 95).
100 Boulter to Carteret, 18 Feb. 1727 (*Boulter Letters*, i, 112-5); Boulter to Bp of London, 21 Feb. 1727 (ibid., i, 114-6).
101 Dorset to Newcastle, 9 Feb. 1732 (PRO SP 63/395/48-50).
102 Godwin to Wake, 24 Jan. 1716 (Christ Church, Oxford, Wake MSS, 12, fos 318-9); Synge to Wake, 3 Jan. 1724 (BL Add MS 6117, fos 175-7).
103 Nicolson to Wake, 21 Oct. 1720 (BL Add MS 6116, fos 113-4); Nicolson to Wake, 28 Oct. 1721 (ibid., fos 115-6); Godwin to Wake, 7 Feb. 1717 (Christ Church, Oxford, Wake MSS, 12, fos 126-7).
104 Godwin to Wake, 24 Jan. 1724 (Christ Church, Oxford, Wake MSS, 14, fol 152).
105 Quoted in Phillips, *Church of Ireland*, iii, 209.
106 Godwin to Wake, 31 Jan. 1717 (Christ Church, Oxford, Wake MSS, 12, fol 119).
107 Same to Same, 24 Nov. 1716 (ibid., fos 94-5); see also Same to Same, 24 Jan. 1716 (ibid., fos 318-9).
108 Same to Same, 1 Sept. 1722 (Christ Church, Oxford, Wake MSS, 14, fol 36).
109 Boulter to Newcastle, 6 Jan. 1734 (*Boulter Letters*, ii, 80)

PATRIOTISM

1   Connolly, *Religion, Law, and Power*, pp 87-97.
2   Joep Leerssen, 'Anglo-Irish Patriotism and its European context: notes towards a reassessment', *Eighteenth-Century Ireland*, 4 (1989), 7-24.
3   Boulter to Newcastle, 13 Mar. 1729 (*Boulter Letters*, i, 229-31).
4   Connolly, *Religion, Law and Power*, p 92.
5   D. George Boyce, *Nationalism in Ireland* (2nd ed., London, 1991), pp 105-7.
6   Bartlett, 'New History of Ireland', 212.
7   Thomas Bartlett, '"A people made rather for copies than originals": the Anglo-Irish, 1760-1800', *The International History Review*, 12, 1 (Feb. 1990), 11-25; 16-18.
8   Hayton, 'Anglo-Irish attitudes', 145-57.

9   J.G. McCoy, 'Local political culture in the Hanoverian empire: the case of Ireland, 1714-1760' (unpublished DPhil thesis, Oxford, 1994), p 269.

10   Leerssen, 'Anglo-Irish Patriotism', 8, 15.

11   Connolly, *Religion, Law, and Power*, p 123.

12   For example, the argument on the part of some members of the Scottish National Party that the Union of 1707 was illegal.

13   David Hayton, 'From Barbarian to Burlesque: English images of the Irish, c. 1660-1750', *Irish Economic and Social History*, 15 (1988), 5-31.

14   Hayton, 'Anglo-Irish Attitudes', 23, 29-31; Connolly, *Religion, Law, and Power*, pp 117-20.

15   Joseph McMinn, 'A weary patriot: Swift and the formation of an Anglo-Irish identity', *Eighteenth-Century Ireland*, 2 (1987), 103-13; 112.

16   But see Bartlett, '"A people made rather for copies than originals"', 17-18.

17   Jonathan Swift, *A Letter to the Whole People of Ireland* (1724), in Herbert Davis (ed.) *The Drapier's Letters* (Oxford, 1941), pp 53-68.

18   Ibid., p 62, 67, 63, 61.

19   Ibid., p 61. I am using 'nationalist' here in the sense in which it has commonly come to be understood since the middle of the nineteenth century. See also Swift's 'Holyhead Verses', in Harold Williams (ed.), *The Poems of Jonathan Swift* (2nd ed., 3 vols, Oxford, 1958), ii, 420-1.

20   Hayton, 'Anglo-Irish Attitudes', 152-3. This question of a provincial identity is clearly relevant to Steven Ellis' argument that Ireland in the sixteenth century is best treated as a region of the British Isles. Ellis' views, of course, have not gone unchallenged.

21   Boyce, *Nationalism in Ireland*, p 106.

22   McCoy, 'Local political culture', p 278, p 286.

23   Swift, *Letter to whole people of Ireland*, p 62. For King's unwillingness to accept the Declaratory Act see Nicolson to Wake, 24 Jan. 1721 (BL Add MS 6116, fos 105-6) and Patrick Kelly, 'William Molyneux and the spirit of liberty in eighteenth-century Ireland, *Eighteenth-Century Ireland*, 4 (1989), 133-48; 140-1, fn 31.

24   *Lords Journals*, ii, 655.

25   John Toland *Reasons Most Humbly Offer'd to the Honble House of Commons, Why the Bill Sent Down to Them from the Most Honble House of Lords; Entitul'd, An Act for the Better Securing the Dependency of the Kingdom of Ireland upon the Crown of Great Britain, Shou'd not Pass into a Law* (London, 1720) – cited by McCoy, 'Local political culture', p 56.

26   6 George I, c. 5.

27   Midleton to Thomas Brodrick, 26 June 1720, in William Coxe (ed.), *Memoirs of the Life and Administration of Sir Robert Walpole, Earl of Orford* (3 vols., London, 1798), ii, 176-7.

28   Dering to Percival, 27 Sept. 1717 (BL Add MS 47028, fol 203).

29   Pocklington to Wake, 7 Apr. 1720 (Christ Church, Oxford, Wake MSS, 13, fol 160); Nicolson to Wake, 23 Feb. 1720 (BL Add MS 6116, fos 95-6); Same to Same, 3 Apr. 1720 (ibid., fos 97-8); Same to Same, 9 Aug. 1720 (ibid., 100-01).

30   Nicolson to Wake, 23 Feb. 1720 (BL Add MS 6116, fos 95-6).

31   Same to Same, 3 Apr. 1720 (ibid., fos 97-8).

32   Pocklington to Wake, 7 Apr. 1720 (Christ Church, Oxford, Wake MSS, 13, fol 160).

33   *Lords Journals*, ii, 655-60.

34   Synge to Wake, 30 Sept. 1717 (BL Add MS 6117, fos 123-4).

35   Boulter to Newcastle, 18 Apr. 1735 (PRO SP 63/398/9-10).

36 Percival to King, 10 Mar. 1720 (BL Add MS 47029, fol 26).
37 Although the campaign for 'Free Trade' in the late 1770s eventually provoked the constitutional crisis which culminated in the granting of legislative independence.
38 For an alternative interpretation see Victory, 'The making of the Declaratory Act', p 28.
39 Thomas Bartlett, 'The Townshend Viceroyalty, 1767-72', in Bartlett and Hayton, *Penal Era and Golden Age*, pp 88-112.
40 Boulter to Newcastle, 15 Jan. 1732 (PRO SP 63/395/3-4).
41 Victory, 'The making of the Declaratory Act', p 28.
42 Patrick Kelly has previously noted that, despite 'the logical implications of the Declaratory Act', the rights of the Irish parliament (until the 1760s at least) continued to be defended in terms of history and precedent and not with arguments of 'natural right' – Kelly, 'Molyneux and the spirit of liberty', 140-1, 148.
43 M.R. O'Connell, *Irish politics and social conflict in the age of the American Revolution* (Philadelphia, 1965), p 328.
44 Dundas to Westmoreland, 7 Jan. 1793 (PRO HO 100/43/128-43) cited by Thomas Bartlett, 'The origins and progress of the Catholic question in Ireland, 1690-1800', in Power and Whelan (eds.), *Endurance and Emergence. Catholics in Ireland in the eighteenth century* (Blackrock, 1990), p 15.
45 The phrase is Sean Connolly's, *Religion, Law and Power*, p 124.
46 Bartlett, '"A people made rather for copies than originals"', 22.
47 Caroline Robbins, *The Eighteenth-Century Commonwealthman. Studies in the transmission, development and circumstance of English political thought from the restoration of Charles II until the war with the Thirteen Colonies* (New York, 1968).
48 William Percival to Sir John Percival, 29 Aug. 1710 (BL Add MS 47026, fos 25-6).
49 Southwell to Percival, 21 Jan. 1714 (BL Add MS 47027, fol 68); Hayton, 'Crisis in Ireland', 204-5.
50 Coghill to Southwell, 4 Dec. 1732 (BL Add MS 21123, fos 11-14).
51 For an excellent discussion of the motivations of those professing 'country' or 'patriot' principles in the Westminster parliament see Hayton, 'The Country interest and the party system, 1690-c.1720', pp 48-51.
52 Bernard Hale to Devonshire, 10 Sept. 1724 (PRONI T 3158/8).
53 Cary to Delafaye, 8 Dec. 1731 (PRO SP 63/394/135-6).
54 John Wainwright to Newcastle, 16 Jan. 1734 (PRO SP 63/397/19-200).
55 Edward Hopkins to Temple Stanyan, 22 Oct. 1723 (PRO SP 63/381/13-14).
56 [_____] to Wake, 16 July 1719 (Christ Church, Oxford, Wake MSS, 13, fol 90).
57 Ibid.
58 West to [Newcastle?], 16 Nov. 1725 (PRO SP 63/386/308-9).
59 Coghill to Southwell, 30 Oct. 1725 (BL Add MS 21122, fos 24-6).
60 Philip Percival to Lord Percival, 1 Feb. 1726 (BL Add MS 47031, fos 92-4).
61 Coghill to Southwell, 8 Dec. 1727 (BL Add MS 21122, fos 35-6).
62 Same to Same, 20 Oct. 1733 (BL Add MS 21123, fos 62-3).
63 See, for example, the dedication to Midleton in the preface to David Bindon *Some Reasons Shewing the Necessity the People of Ireland Are Under, for Continuing to Refuse Mr. Wood's Coinage* (Dublin, 1724), p 2 – cited in McCoy, 'Local political culture', p 131; also Connolly, *Religion, Law and Power*, p 92.
64 William Percival to John Percival, 7 Nov. 1707 (BL Add MS 47025, fol 80).
65 Hayton, 'Beginnings of the "undertaker system"', pp 38-9.
66 Coghill to Southwell, 8 Nov. 1729 (BL Add MS 21122, fos 64-8).
67 Bolton to Craggs, 18 July 1719 (PRO SP 63/377/131-2).

68 Cary to Delafaye, 20 Nov. 1733 (PRO SP 63/396/99-101).
69 Coghill to Southwell, 18 Apr. 1730 (BL Add MS 21123, fos 1-5).
70 Boulter to Carteret, 13 May 1729 (*Boulter Letters*, i, 243-6).
71 Coghill to Southwell, 18 Apr. 1730 (BL Add MS 21123, fos 1-5).
72 Hugh Cunningham, 'The language of patriotism, 1750-1914', *History Workshop Journal*, 12 (1981), 8-33. See Christine Gerrard, *The Patriot Opposition to Walpole. Politics, poetry, and national myth, 1725-1742* (Oxford, 1994), pp 10-11 for additional discussion of this definition.

CONCLUSION

1   *New History of Ireland*, iv, 7.
2   Midleton to Mrs Ally Brodrick, 30 Dec. 1720, (SRO, Midleton MSS, iv, fol 385).
3   Ibid.
4   Nicolson to Wake, 19 Mar. 1721 (BL Add MS 6116, fos 106-7).
5   Robert Howard, Bp of Elphin to Hugh Howard, 2 Nov. 1731 (NLI, Wicklow Papers, PC 227, unfoliated)
6   Sedgwick, *History of Parliament*, i, 23.
7   Walpole to Newcastle, 1 Sept. 1724 (PRO SP 63/384/54-5).
8   Newcastle to Walpole, 29 Aug. 1724 (ibid., 44-51).
9   For an indication of the rivalry between Conolly and Midleton see Philip Percival to Lord Percival, 30 Jan. 1724 (BL Add MS 47030, fos 57-8).
10 Lord Brodrick to Thomas Brodrick, 16 Apr. 1716 (SRO, Midleton MSS, iii, fos 364-5).
11 Ibid.
12 Midleton to Thomas Brodrick, 15 July 1721 (SRO, Midleton MSS, v, fos 61-2).
13 However, even in these cases the government could not automatically rely upon the bishops to return members supportive of the Castle administration.
14 Conolly to Grafton, 24 Sept. 1720 [draft] (PRONI T 2825/A/14); Lord Brodrick to Thomas Brodrick, 31 Mar. 1717 (SRO, Midleton MSS, iv, fos 1-4).
15 Series of documents relating to a plan to 'not be under a necessity of calling a Parliament there every two years' (PRO SP 63/379/61-71).

Bibliography

MANUSCRIPT SOURCES

BRITISH LIBRARY

Add MS 61,635-6; 61639: Letters to earl of Sunderland as lord lieutenant, 1714-15.

Add MS 61,637C: Pensions on the civil list with notes on the circumstances and political affiliations of the pensioners.

Add MS 61,652: Earl of Sunderland's letters to Abp.King, Alan Brodrick, William Conolly, and others, 1715.

Add MS 32,686-7: Letters to and from duke of Newcastle, 1723-25.

Add MS 38,157: Letters from Sir Richard Cox to Edward Southwell, 1713-26.

Add MS 34,778: Letters from Thomas Medlicott to Edward Southwell, 1703-27.

Add MS 21,122-3: Letters from Marmaduke Coghill to Edward Southwell, 1722-35.

Add MS 38,016: Letters from Lord Carteret to Edward Southwell, 1725-30.

Add MS 38,712: Papers 1705-27, mostly relating to military affairs.

Add MS 6,116-7: Letters to Archbishop Wake from William King, Edward Synge, and William Nicolson.

Add MS 47026-47032: Letters to John Percival, 1st earl of Egmont.

Add MS 34358: Letters about Wood's Patent.

Add MS 23636: Tyrawley Papers.

Egerton MS 1971: Papers relating to Irish affairs, 1715.

PUBLIC RECORD OFFICE, LONDON

SP 63/371-395: State Papers, Ireland

SP 67/6-9: Secretary's Letter Books

SP 35/21/16: State Papers, Domestic

CUST 1/13-22: Minute Books of Irish revenue commisioners

T 14: Treasury Papers: Out Letters, Ireland.

SO 1/16-17: Signet Office Records

C 110/46: Chancery Masters Exhibits (St George Correspondence)

Calendar of Treasury Papers, vol ccxi (1714-19); vol ccxxviii (1720-28)

CHRIST CHURCH, OXFORD

Wake Manuscripts, vols 12-14: Letters to William Wake, archbishop of
Canterbury, on Irish affairs

BODLEIAN LIBRARY, OXFORD

MS Rawl. B.511: 'A list of the commissioners and officers appointed for
management of His Majesty's Revenue in Ireland with their respective
salaries. 1720.'
MS Ballard 8: Letters from Irish prelates to Rev Dr Arthur Charlett
MS Carte 227 (10672): Letters mainly to Thomas Carte, 1732-3

CAMBRIDGE UNIVERSITY LIBRARY

Cholmondeley (Houghton) Manuscripts.

PUBLIC RECORD OFFICE, NORTHERN IRELAND

MIC 310/2: 'A list of the nobility and gentry who are generally esteemed to
have one hundred pounds a year and upwards in the Province of Ulster, as
divided into Churchmen, Dissenters and Papists' (1731)
D 623/A/3: Abercorn Papers
T 2825: Castletown (Conolly) Papers
T 3158: Chatsworth Papers [originals in possession of duke of Devonshire]
D 638: De Ros Papers
D 207; D 562: Foster-Massereene Papers
MIC 260: Grafton Papers: [Originals in Ipswich and E. Suffolk Record Office]
T 1075: Leslie Manuscripts
T 1019: List of Irish Privy Councillors, 1711-1905
MIC 308: Midleton Manuscripts [Originals in Surrey Record Office, MS 1248,
vols 3-7]
MIC 240: Nicolson-Wake Letters
D 2707/A/2-3: Shannon Papers
T 2827/1-5: Southwell Papers [xerox copies]
T 2774: Tickell Manuscripts
T 3071/3: Townshend (Sydney) Papers
T 448, T 519, T 546, T 580, T 610, T 659, T 693, T 722: Transcripts of State
Papers, Ireland
MIC 364: Upton Papers
D 429: Wynne Papers

TRINITY COLLEGE, DUBLIN

MSS 750/4-13, MSS 2533-2537: Letterbooks of Archbishop William King
MS 8191: xerox copy of MS 750/6
MSS 1995-2008: Lyons (King) Collection
MS 590 (E.3.27): Irish civil and military establishments, 1719

NATIONAL LIBRARY OF IRELAND

MIC p 1946: Account of secret service money, 1723

MS 12813: Calendar of Lismore Papers

MS 10756: F.S. Bourke Collection

MS 18993: Letter from Thomas Dawson to Henry Boyle

MS 16007: Letterbook of James Forth, secretary to the Irish revenue commissioners

MS 11481: Letters to William Flower

MIC p 3753: Molesworth Papers

MS 13296: Shannon Papers

MS 10171: Ussher Papers

PC 225 (5), 226, 227: Wicklow Papers

MIC p 1615: Castleward Papers [originals in possession of earl of Bangor]

NATIONAL ARCHIVES OF IRELAND

M 2537: list of officers on civil or military establishments and list of pensions, 1688-1729

M 2446-7: two volumes of copy correspondence from viceroys, chief secretaries and lords justices to British government, 1697-1798

M 2480: list of salaries and pensions payable as on 26 Oct. 1729

D 9353: agreement by Rt Hon Edward Southwell for the sale of various offices to Thomas Carter and Thomas Carter, junior, 14 Nov. 1717

NEWSPAPERS

The Dublin Daily Advertiser
The Dublin Post-Man
The Flying Post; or, The Post Master
The Post Boy
Reilly's Weekly Oracle
St James' Evening Post
Watson's Gentleman's and Citizen's Almanack
The Weekly Miscellany
Whalley's Newsletter

PRINTED SOURCES

A collection of the protests of the Lords of Ireland, from 1634 to 1770 (London, 1771)

Ainsworth, John (ed.), *The Inchiquin Manuscripts* (Dublin, 1961)

Cartwright, J.J. (ed.), *The Wentworth Papers, 1705-39* (London, 1883)

Coxe, William (ed.), *Memoirs of the Life and Administration of Sir Robert Walpole, Earl of Orford* (3 vols, London, 1798)

Dalton, Charles, *George the First's army 1714-27* (2 vols, London, 1910-12)

Fenning, Hugh (ed.), *The Fottrell Papers, 1721-39: an edition of the papers found on the person of Fr. John Fottrell, provincial of the Dominicans in Ireland, at his arrest in 1739* (Belfast, 1980)

Graham, Walter (ed.), *The Letters of Joseph Addison* (Oxford, 1941)

Grosart, A.B. (ed.), *The Lismore Papers* (5 vols, London, 1886-8)

Horn, D.B. and Ransome, Mary (eds.), *English Historical Documents*, vol x, 1714-83 (London, 1957)

Hughes, L.J., *Patentee officers in Ireland, 1173-1826* (Dublin, 1960)

Journals of the House of Commons of the Kingdom of Ireland (3rd ed., 23 vols, Dublin, 1796-1800)

Journals of the House of Lords [Ireland] (8 vols, Dublin, 1779-1800)

King, C.S. (ed.), *A great archbishop of Dublin, William King, 1650-1729: his autobiography, family and a selection from his correspondence* (London, 1906)

Lascelles, Rowley (ed.), *Liber Munerum Publicorum Hiberniae, or the Establishments of Ireland* (2 vols, London, 1824-30)

Letters written by His Excellency, Hugh Boulter, D.D., lord primate of all Ireland..., (2 vols, Dublin, 1770),

Levinge, Sir Richard G.A., *Jottings of the Levinge Family* (Dublin, 1877)

Lucas, Charles, *The Political Constitutions of Great-Britain and Ireland, Asserted and vindicated;* ... (2 vols, London, 1751)

Newman, A.N., *The parliamentary diary of Sir Edward Knatchbull 1722-1730* (Royal Historical Society, Camden Third Series, vol 94, London, 1963)

Nichols, John (ed.), *Letters on various subjects, literary, political, and ecclesiastical, to and from William Nicolson, D.D., successively Bishop of Carlisle, and of Derry; and Archbishop of Cashell;...* (2 vols, London, 1809)

Parke, Gilbert, *Letters and Correspondence of Henry St John, Lord Viscount Bolingbroke* (2 vols, London, 1798)

Reports of the Royal Commission on Historical Manuscripts:

Buccleuch, vol i

Egmont, vols i, ii

Ormonde, vol viii

Portland, vol v

Stopford-Sackville, vol i

Various Collections, vol viii

Ross, Angus and Wooley, David (eds.), *The Oxford Authors. Jonathan Swift* (Oxford, 1984)

Swift, Jonathan, *Gulliver's Travels* (Reprint, Harmondsworth, 1985)

Toland, John, *Reasons Most humbly offer'd to the Honble. House of Commons, Why the Bill sent down to them From the Most Honble. House of Lords, Entitul'd, An Act for the better securing the Dependency of the Kingdom of Ireland upon the Crown of Great-Britain, Shou'd not Pass into a Law* (London, 1720)

Williams, Harold (ed.), *The correspondence of Jonathan Swift* (5 vols, Oxford, 1963-5)

Williams, Harold (ed.), *The Poems of Jonathan Swift* (3 vols, 2nd ed., Oxford, 1958)

UNPUBLISHED THESES

Ferguson, K.P., 'The army in Ireland from the Restoration to the Act of Union' (PhD, University of Dublin, 1981)

Griffin, Joseph, 'Parliamentary politics in Ireland in the reign of George i' (MA, University College, Dublin, 1977)

Hayes, J.W., 'The social and professional background of the officers of the British army, 1714-1763' (MA, University of London, 1956).

Hayton, David, 'Ireland and the English Ministers, 1707-1716' (DPhil, Oxford, 1975)

Magennis, Eoin, 'Politics and administration of Ireland during the Seven Years' War, 1750-63' (PhD, Queen's University, Belfast, 1996)

McCoy, J.G., 'Local political culture in the Hanoverian empire: the case of Ireland, 1714-1760' (DPhil, Oxford, 1994)

McCracken, J.L., 'Central and local administration in Ireland under George ii' (PhD, Queen's University, Belfast, 1948)

McCracken, J.L., 'The undertakers in Ireland and their relations with the lord lieutenant, 1724-1771' (MA, Queen's University, Belfast, 1941)

McGuire, J.I., 'Politics, opinion, and the Irish constitution, 1688-1707' (MA, University College, Dublin, 1968)

McNally, Patrick, 'Patronage and Politics in Ireland, 1714 to 1727' (PhD, Queen's University, Belfast, 1993)

Victory, Isolde, 'Colonial Nationalism in Ireland, 1692-1725: from Common Law to Natural Right' (PhD, Trinity College, Dublin, 1985)

BOOKS AND JOURNAL ARTICLES

Akenson, D.H., *The Church of Ireland: ecclesiastical reform and revolution, 1800-1855* (London, 1971)

Ball, F.E., *The Judges in Ireland, 1221-1921* (2 vols, London, 1926)

Barnard, Toby, 'Lawyers and the law in later seventeenth-century Ireland', *Irish Historical Studies*, 28, 111 (May 1993), 256-82

Barnard, Toby, 'Protestants and the Irish language, c. 1675-1725', *Journal of Ecclesiastical History*, 44, 2 (Apr. 1993), 243-72

Barnard, Toby, 'Reforming Irish manners: the religious societies in Dublin during the 1690s', *Historical Journal*, 35, 4 (1992), 805-38

Barnard, Toby, 'The uses of 23 October 1641 and Irish Protestant celebrations', *English Historical Review*, 106, 421 (Oct. 1991), 889-920

Barnard, Toby, 'Crises of identity among Irish Protestants, 1641-1685', *Past and Present*, 127 (May 1990), 39-83

Barnard, Toby, 'Farewell to Old Ireland', *Historical Journal*, 36, 4 (1993), 909-28

Barnard, Toby, 'Improving clergymen, 1660-1760', in Ford *et al.*, *As by Law Established*, pp 136-51

Bartlett, Thomas, *The Fall and Rise of the Irish Nation. The Catholic question 1690-1830* (Dublin, 1992)

Bartlett, Thomas and Hayton, David (eds.), *Penal Era and Golden Age: essays in Irish history 1690-1800* (Belfast, 1979)

Bartlett, Thomas, '"A people made rather for copies than originals": the Anglo-Irish, 1760-1800', *The International History Review*, 12, 1 (Feb. 1990), 11-25

Bartlett, Thomas, 'A New History of Ireland', *Past and Present*, 116 (Aug. 1987), 206-19

Bartlett, Thomas, 'An end to moral economy: the Irish militia disturbances of 1793', *Past and Present*, 99 (May 1983), 41-64

Bartlett, Thomas, 'The Townshend Viceroyalty', in Bartlett and Hayton, *Penal Era and Golden Age*, pp 88-112

Bartlett, Thomas, 'Viscount Townshend and the Irish Revenue Board', in *Proceedings of the Royal Irish Academy*, 79, sect. C (1979), pp 153-75

Baxter, S., *William III* (Harlow, 1966)

Beckett, J.C., *The Making of Modern Ireland, 1603-1923* (2nd ed., London, 1981)

Beckett, J.C., *Protestant Dissent in Ireland* (London, 1948)

Beckett, J.C., *The Anglo-Irish Tradition* (London, 1976)

Beckett, J.C., 'The government of the Church of Ireland under William III and Anne', *Irish Historical Studies*, 2, 7 (Mar. 1941), 280-302

Beckett, J.C., 'The Irish parliament in the eighteenth century', *Belfast Natural History Society Proceedings*, 4 (1950-55), 17-28

Beckett. J.C., 'William King's administration of the diocese of Derry, 1691-1703', *Irish Historical Studies*, 4, 14 (Sept. 1944), 164-80

Beckett, J.V., *The Aristocracy in England 1660-1914* (Oxford, 1986)

Beddard, Robert (ed.), *The Revolutions of 1688* (Oxford, 1991)

Bennett, G.V., *The Tory Crisis in Church and State, 1688-1730* (Oxford, 1975)

Berlatsky, Joel, 'Roots of conflict in Ireland: colonial attitudes in the age of the penal laws', *Éire-Ireland*, 18 (1983), 40-56

Biddle, Sheila, *Bolingbroke and Harley* (London, 1975)

Black, Jeremy (ed.), *Britain in the age of Walpole* (London, 1984)

Black, Jeremy, *Robert Walpole and the nature of politics in early eighteenth-century England* (London, 1990)

Black, Jeremy and Cruickshanks, Evelyn (eds.), *The Jacobite challenge* (Edinburgh, 1988)

Bolton, G.C., 'The Anglo-Irish and the historians, 1830-1980', in McDonagh, Mandle and Travers, *Irish Culture and Nationalism*, pp 239-57

Boyce, D.G., *Nationalism in Ireland* (2nd ed., London, 1991)

Boyce, D.G. and O'Day, Alan (eds.), *The Making of Modern Irish History. Revisionism and the revisionist controversy* (London, 1996)

Boyce, D.G., Eccleshall, Robert and Geoghegan, Vincent (eds.), *Political thought in Ireland since the seventeenth century* (London, 1993)

Boylan, Lena, 'The Conollys of Castletown', *Quarterly Bulletin of the Irish Georgian Society*, 11, 4 (Oct.-Dec. 1968), 1-46

Bradshaw, Brendan, 'Nationalism and historical scholarship in Ireland, *Irish Historical Studies*, 26, 104 (Nov. 1989), 329-51

Bradshaw, Brendan and Morrill, John (eds.), *The British Problem, c.1534-1707. State formation in the Atlantic archipelago* (London, 1996)

Brady, Ciaran (ed.), *Worsted in the Game. Losers in Irish history* (Dublin, 1989)

Brady, Ciaran (ed.), *Interpreting Irish history. The debate on historical revisionism* (Blackrock, 1994)

Brady, John, 'Remedies proposed for the Church of Ireland (1697)', *Archivium Hibernicum*, 22 (1959), 163-73

Brewer, John, *The Sinews of Power. War, money and the English state, 1688-1783* (London, 1989)

Brooks, Colin, 'Public finance and political stability: the administration of the Land Tax, 1688-1720', *Historical Journal*, 17, 2 (1974), 281-300

Brown, Keith, *Kingdom or Province? Scotland and the regal union, 1603-1715* (London, 1992)

Burns, R.E., *Irish Parliamentary Politics in the Eighteenth Century* (2 vols, Washington, DC, 1989)

Burns, R.E., 'The Irish Penal Code and some of its historians', *Review of Politics*, 21 (1959), 276-99

Burns, R.E., 'The Irish Popery Laws: a study of eighteenth-century legislation and behaviour', *Review of Politics*, 24 (1962), 485-508

Burton, I.F., and Newman, A.N., 'Sir John Cope: promotion in the eighteenth-century army', *English Historical Review*, 78, 309 (Oct. 1963), 655-68

Cain, P.J. and Hopkins, A.G., *British Imperialism: innovation and expansion 1688-1914* (Harlow, 1993)

Cannon, John (ed.), *The Whig Ascendancy* (London, 1981)

Cannon, John, *Aristocratic Century. The peerage of eighteenth-century England* (Cambridge, 1984)

Canny, Nicholas, *Kingdom and Colony: Ireland in the Atlantic world 1560-1800* (London, 1988)

Childs, John, *The British army of William III, 1689-1702* (Manchester, 1987)

Clark, J.C.D., *English Society, 1688-1832: ideology, social structure and political practice during the* ancien régime (Cambridge, 1985)

Clark, J.C.D., *Revolution and Rebellion: state and society in England in the seventeenth and eighteenth centuries* (Cambridge, 1986)

Clark, J.C.D., 'A general theory of party, opposition and government 1688-1832', *Historical Journal*, 23, 2 (1980), 295-325

Clark, J.C.D., 'The decline of party, 1740-60', *English Historical Review*, 93, 368 (July 1978), 499-527

Clark, J.C.D., 'The politics of the excluded: Tories, Jacobites and Whig Patriots', *Parliamentary History*, 2 (1983), 209-22

Clark, J.C.D., 'Whig tactics and parliamentary precedent: the English management of Irish politics, 1754-56', *Historical Journal*, 21, 2 (1978), 275-301

Clark, Samuel and Donnelly, J.S. (eds.), *Irish Peasants. Violence and political unrest, 1780-1914* (Wisconsin, 1983)

Clarke, Aidan, 'The History of Poynings' Law, 1615-41', *Irish Historical Studies*, 18, 70 (Sept. 1972), 207-22

Clarkson, L.A. and Crawford, E.M., *Ways to Wealth. The Cust family of eighteenth-century Armagh* (Belfast, 1985)

Clarkson, L.A., 'The writing of Irish economic and social history since 1968', *The Economic History Review*, 33, 1 (Feb. 1980), 100-11

Colley, Linda, *Britons. Forging the nation 1707-1837* (New Haven and London, 1992)

Colley, Linda, *In Defiance of Oligarchy. The Tory party, 1714-60* (Cambridge, 1982)

Connolly, Sean, *Religion, Law, and Power. The making of Protestant Ireland 1660-1760* (Oxford, 1992)

Connolly, Sean, 'Reformers and highflyers: the post-revolution church', in Ford *et al., As by Law Established*, pp 152-65

Connolly, Sean, 'Religion and History', *Irish Economic and Social History*, 10 (1983), 66-80

Connolly, Sean, 'Eighteenth-century Ireland: colony or *ancien régime?*', in Boyce and O'Day, *The Making of Modern Irish History*, pp 15-33

Corish, P.J., *The Catholic Community in the Seventeenth and Eighteenth Centuries* (Dublin, 1981)

Corkery, Daniel, *The Hidden Ireland* (Cork, 1925)

Coward, Barry, *The Stuart Age: a history of England, 1603-1744* (Harlow, 1980)

Craig, Maurice, *Dublin 1660-1860* (Dublin, 1952)

Cruickshanks, Eveline, *Political Untouchables. The Tories and the '45* (London, 1979)

Cruickshanks, Eveline, 'The political management of Sir Robert Walpole', in Black, *Britain in the age of Walpole,* pp 23-44

Cruickshanks, Eveline (ed.), *By Force or Default? The revolution of 1688-9* (Edinburgh, 1989)

Cullen, L.M., *An Economic History of Ireland Since 1660* (London, 1972)

Cullen, L.M., *The Emergence of Modern Ireland, 1600-1900* (New York, 1981)

Cullen, L.M. (ed.), *Radicals, Rebels and Establishments* (Belfast, 1985)

Cullen, L.M., 'Catholics under the Penal Laws', *Eighteenth-Century Ireland*, 1 (1986), 23-36

Cullen, L.M. (ed.), *The Formation of the Irish Economy* (Cork, 1969)

Cullen, L.M. and Bergeron, Louis (eds.), *Culture et Pratiques Politiques en France et en Irelande xvie-xviiie Siècle* (Paris, 1988)

Cunningham, Hugh, 'The language of Patriotism, 1750-1914', *History Workshop Journal*, 12 (1981), 8-33

Dalton, Charles, *George the First's Army, 1714-27* (2 vols, London, 1910-12)

Davis, Herbert (ed.), *The Drapier's Letters* (Oxford, 1941)

Dickinson, H.T., 'The poor Palatines and the parties', *English Historical Review,* 82, 314 (July 1967), 464-85

Dickinson, H.T., 'The eighteenth-century debate on the "Glorious Revolution"', *History*, 61, 201 (Feb. 1976), 28-45

Dickinson, H.T., *Bolingbroke* (London, 1970)

Dickinson, H.T., *Walpole and the Whig Supremacy* (London, 1973)

Dickson, David, *New Foundations. Ireland 1660-1800* (Dublin, 1987)

Dickson, P.G.M., *The financial revolution.*(London, 1967)

Dralle, Louis A., 'Kingdom in reversion: the Irish viceroyalty of the Earl of Wharton, 1708-1710', *Huntington Library Quarterly*, 15 (1951-2), 393-431

Dudley Edwards, R. and Moody, T.W., 'The History of Poynings' Law: Part 1, 1494-1615', *Irish Historical Studies,* 2, 8 (Sept. 1941), 415-24

Eccleshall, Robert, 'Anglican political thought in the century after the Revolution of 1688', in Boyce *et al., Political thought in Ireland*, pp 36-72

Fagan, Patrick, 'The Dublin Catholic mob (1700-1750)', *Eighteenth-Century Ireland*, 4 (1989), 133-42

Flaherty, M.S., 'The Empire strikes back: *Annesley v. Sherlock* and the triumph of imperial parliamentary supremacy', *Columbia Law Review*, 87, 3 (Apr. 1987), 593-622

Flaningam, John, 'The Occasional Conformity controversy: ideology and party politics, 1697-1711', *Journal of British Studies*, 17, 1 (Fall, 1977), 38-62

Ford, Alan, McGuire, James and Milne, Kenneth (eds.), *As by Law Established. The Church of Ireland since the Reformation* (Dublin, 1995)

Foster, R.F., *Modern Ireland* (London, 1988)

Frankle, R.J., 'The formulation of the Declaration of Rights', *Historical Journal*, 17, 2 (1974), 265-80

Froude, James Anthony, *The English in Ireland in the Eighteenth Century* (3 vols, London, 1872-4)

Gillespie, Raymond, 'The Irish Protestants and James II, 1688-90', *Irish Historical Studies*, 28, 110 (Nov. 1992), 124-33

Goodwin, Albert , 'Wood's Halfpence', *English Historical Review*, 51, 204 (Oct. 1936), 647-74

Greene, J.P., *Peripheries and Center: constitutional development in the extended polities of the British Empire and the United States, 1607-1788* (Athens, Ga., 1986)

Gregg, Edward and Jones, Clyve, 'Hanover, Pensions and the "Poor Lords", 1712-13', *Parliamentary History*, 1 (1982), 173-80

Guy, A.J., *Oeconomy and Discipline. Officership and administration in the British army 1714-63* (Manchester, 1985)

Harris, Tim, *Politics under the Later Stuarts: party conflict in a divided society 1660-1715* (Harlow, 1993)

Hatton, Ragnhild, *George I. Elector and King* (London, 1978)

Hayton, David, 'A debate in the Irish House of Commons in 1703: a whiff of Tory grapeshot', *Parliamentary History*, 10, 2 (1991), 151-63

Hayton, David, 'Anglo-Irish attitudes: changing perceptions of national identity among the Protestant Ascendancy in Ireland, ca. 1690-1750', *Studies in Eighteenth-Century Culture*, 17 (1987), 145-57

Hayton, David, 'Divisions in the Whig Junto in 1709: some Irish evidence', *Bulletin of the Institute of Historical Research*, 55, 132 (Nov. 1982), 206-14

Hayton, David, 'From Barbarian to Burlesque: English images of the Irish, c. 1660-1750', *Irish Economic and Social History*, 15 (1988), 5-31

Hayton, David, 'The "Country" interest and the party system, 1689-c.1720', in Jones, *Party and Management in Parliament*, pp 37-86

Hayton, David, 'The beginnings of the "Undertaker System"', in Bartlett and Hayton, *Penal Era and Golden Age*, pp 32-54

Hayton, David, 'The crisis in Ireland and the disintegration of Queen Anne's last ministry', *Irish Historical Studies*, 22, 87 (Mar. 1981), 193-215

Hayton, David, 'Walpole and Ireland', in Black, *Britain in the Age of Walpole*, pp 95-119

Hayton, David and O'Brien, Gerard (eds.), *War and Politics in Ireland, 1649-1733* (London, 1986)

Hayton, David, 'Did Protestantism fail in early eighteenth-century Ireland? Charity schools and the enterprise of religious and social reformation, c.1690-1730', in Ford *et al., As by Law Established*, pp 166-86

Hayton, David, *Ireland after the Glorious Revolution* (Belfast, 1976)

Hayton, David, 'Moral reform and Country principles in the reign of William III', *Past and Present*, 128 (Aug. 1990), 48-91

Hayton, David, 'An Irish parliamentary diary from the reign of Queen Anne', *Analecta Hibernica*, 30 (1982), 97-149

Hayton, David, 'Two ballads on the County Westmeath by-election of 1723', *Eighteenth-Century Ireland*, 4 (1989), 7-30

Hill, B.W., *Robert Harley. Speaker, Secretary of State, and Premier Minister* (New Haven, 1988)

Hill, B.W., *Sir Robert Walpole: 'sole and prime minister'* (London, 1989)

Hill, B.W., *The Growth of Parliamentary Parties 1689-1742* (London, 1976)

Hill, Christopher, *Century of Revolution* (London, 1961)

Hill, Jacqueline, 'Popery and Protestantism, Civil and Religious Liberty: The disputed lessons of Irish history, 1690-1812', *Past and Present*, 118 (Feb. 1988), 96-129

Hill, Jacqueline, 'The meaning and significance of "Protestant Ascendancy" 1787-1840', in *Ireland after the Union: Proceedings of the second joint meeting of the Royal Irish Academy and the British Academy* (London, 1989), pp 1-22

Hill, Jacqueline, 'National festivals, the state and "protestant ascendancy" in Ireland, 1790-1829', *Irish Historical Studies*, 24, 93 (May 1984), 30-51

Holmes, Geoffrey (ed.), *Britain after the Glorious Revolution, 1689-1714* (London, 1969)

Holmes, Geoffrey, *Augustan England: professions, state, and society, 1680-1730* (London, 1982)

Holmes, Geoffrey, *British Politics in the Age of Anne* (revised ed., London, 1987)

Holmes, Geoffrey, *The Making of a Great Power. Late Stuart and early Georgian Britain, 1660-1722* (London, 1993)

Holmes, Geoffrey and Szechi, Daniel, *The Age of Oligarchy. Pre-industrial Britain, 1722-1783* (London, 1993)

Holmes, Geoffrey and Speck, W.A. (eds.), *The Divided Society: party and politics in England, 1694-1716* (London, 1967)

Houlding, J.A., *Fit for Service. The training of the British army, 1715-1795* (Oxford, 1981)

Hughes, L.J., *Patentee officers in Ireland, 1173-1826* (Dublin, 1960)

Innes, Joanna, 'Jonathan Clark, social history and England's *ancien régime*', *Past and Present*, 115 (May 1987), 165-200

James, F.G., *Ireland in the Empire, 1688-1770* (Cambridge, Mass., 1973)

James, F.G., *North Country Bishop: a biography of William Nicolson* (New Haven, 1956)

James, F.G., 'The active Irish peers in the early eighteenth century', *Journal of British Studies*, 18, 2 (1979), 52-69

James, F.G., 'Illustrious or Notorious? The historical reputation of Ireland's pre-Union parliament', *Parliamentary History*, 6 (1987), 312-25

James, F.G., 'Irish smuggling in the eighteenth century', *Irish Historical Studies,* 12, 48 (Sept. 1961), 299-317

James, F.G., 'The Church of Ireland in the early eighteenth century', *Historical Magazine of the Protestant Episcopal Church*, 48, 4 (1979), 433-51

James, F.G., 'The Irish lobby in the early eighteenth century', *English Historical Review,* 81, 320 (July 1966), 543-57

Johnson, E.M., *Great Britain and Ireland, 1760-1800. A study in political administration* (Edinburgh, 1963)

Johnston, E.M., *Ireland in the Eighteenth Century* (Dublin, 1974)

Johnston, Joseph, *Bishop Berkeley's* Querist *in historical perspective* (Dundalk, 1970)

Jones, Clyve, 'Whigs, Jacobites and Charles Spencer, Third Earl of Sunderland', *English Historical Review,* 109, 430 (Feb. 1994), 52-73

Jones, Clyve (ed.), *Party and Management in Parliament, 1660-1784* (Leicester, 1984)

Jones, J.R., *Court and Country. England 1658-1714* (London, 1978)

Kearney, H.F., 'The political background to English mercantilism, 1695-1700', *Economic History Review,* new series, 11 (1959), 484-96

Kee, Robert, *The Green Flag. A history of Irish nationalism* (London, 1972)

Kelch, R.A., *Newcastle – A duke without money: Thomas Pelham-Holles, 1693-1768* (London, 1974)

Kelly, James, *'That Damn'd Thing Called Honour'. Duelling in Ireland, 1570-1860* (Cork, 1995)

Kelly, James, 'Eighteenth-century Ascendancy: a commentary', *Eighteenth-Century Ireland,* 5 (1990), 173-87

Kelly, James, 'The genesis of "Protestant Ascendancy": the Rightboy disturbances of the 1780s and their impact upon Protestant opinion', in O'Brien, *Parliament, Politics and People,* pp 93-127

Kelly, James, 'The origins of the Act of Union: an examination of unionist opinion in Britain and Ireland, 1650-1800', *Irish Historical Studies*, 25, 99 (May 1987), 236-63

Kelly, Patrick, '"A light to the blind": the voice of the dispossessed élite in the generation after the defeat at Limerick', *Irish Historical Studies*, 24, 96 (Nov. 1985), 431-62

Kelly, Patrick, 'William Molyneux and the spirit of liberty in eighteenth-century Ireland', *Eighteenth-Century Ireland*, 4 (1989), 133-48

Kenny, Colum, 'The exclusion of Catholics from the legal profession in Ireland, 1537-1829', *Irish Historical Studies*, 25, 100 (Nov. 1987), 337-57

Kenyon, J.P., *Revolution Principles: the politics of party, 1689-1720* (Cambridge, 1977)

Kidd, Colin, 'Gaelic antiquity and national identity in Enlightenment Ireland and Scotland', *English Historical Review*, 109, 434 (Nov. 1994), 1197-1214

Kiernan, T.J., *History of the Financial Administration in Ireland to 1817* (London, 1930)

King, C.S., *A Great Archbishop of Dublin, William King 1650-1729: his autobiography, family, and a selection from his correspondence* (London, 1906)

Lammey, David, 'The growth of the patriot opposition in Ireland during the 1770s', *Parliamentary History*, 7, 2 (1988), 257-81

Langford, Paul, *A Polite and Commercial People. England 1727-1783* (Oxford, 1989)

Lascelles, Rowley (ed.), *Liber Munerum Publicorum Hiberniae...; or the Establishments of Ireland* ... (2 vols, London, 1824-30)

Lecky, W.E.H., *A History of Ireland in the Eighteenth Century* (5 vols, London, 1892)

Leerssen, Joep Th., *Mere Irish and Fíor-Ghael: studies in the idea of Irish nationality, its development and literary expression prior to the nineteeenth century* (Amsterdam, 1986)

Leerssen, Joep Th., 'Anglo-Irish patriotism and its European context: notes towards a reassessment', *Eighteenth-Century Ireland*, 4 (1989), 7-24

Leighton, C.D.A., *Catholicism in a Protestant Kingdom. A study of the Irish ancien régime* (Dublin, 1994)

Lenman, Bruce, *The Jacobite Risings in Britain, 1689-1746* (London, 1980)

MacMillan, Gretchen M., *State, Society, and Authority in Ireland. The foundations of the modern Irish state* (Dublin, 1993)

Maguire, W.A., 'The estate of Cú Chonnacht Maguire of Tempo: a case history from the Williamite land settlement', *Irish Historical Studies*, 27, 106 (Nov. 1990), 130-44

Malcomson, A.P.W., *John Foster: the politics of the Anglo-Irish Ascendancy* (Oxford, 1978)

Malcomson, A.P.W., *The Penal Laws* (Belfast, 1975)

Mant, Richard, *History of the Church of Ireland from the Reformation to the Union of the Churches of England and Ireland, Jan. 1, 1801* (2 vols, London, 1840)

McBride, Ian, 'The school of virtue: Francis Hutcheson, Irish Presbyterians and the Scottish Enlightenment', in Boyce *et al., Political thought in Ireland,* pp 73-99

McCormack, W.J., 'Eighteenth-Century Ascendancy: Yeats and the historians', *Eighteenth-Century Ireland,* 4 (1989), 150-81

McCormack, W.J., 'Vision and revision in the study of eighteenth-century Irish parliamentary rhetoric', *Eighteenth-Century Ireland,* 2 (1987), 7-36

McCracken, J.L., 'Irish parliamentary elections, 1727-68', *Irish Historical Studies,* 5, 19 (Mar. 1947), 209-30

McCracken, J.L., 'The conflict between the Irish administration and parliament, 1753-56', *Irish Historical Studies,* 3, 10 (Sept. 1942), 159-79

McCracken, J.L., *The Irish Parliament in the Eighteenth Century* (Dundalk, 1971)

McDonagh, Oliver, Mandle, W.F. and Travers, Pauric (eds.), *Irish Culture and Nationalism, 1750-1950* (London, 1983)

McDowell, R.B., *Ireland in the Age of Imperialism and Revolution* (Oxford, 1979)

McGrath, C.I., 'Securing the Protestant interest: the origins and purpose of the penal laws of 1695', *Irish Historical Studies,* 30, 117 (May 1996), 25-46

McGuire, J.I., 'The Irish parliament of 1692', in Bartlett and Hayton, *Penal Era and Golden Age,* pp 1-31

McKendrick, Neil (ed.), *Historical Perspectives. Studies in English thought and society in honour of J.H. Plumb* (London, 1974)

McMinn, Joseph, 'A weary patriot: Swift and the formation of an Anglo-Irish identity', *Eighteenth-Century Ireland,* 2 (1987), 103-13

McNally, Patrick, '"Irish and English Interests". National conflict within the Church of Ireland episcopate in the reign of George I', *Irish Historical Studies,* 29, 115 (May 1995), 295-314

McNally, Patrick, 'The Hanoverian accession and the Tory party in Ireland', *Parliamentary History,* 14, 3 (1995), 263-83

McNally, Patrick, 'Wood's halfpence, Carteret and the government of Ireland, 1723-26', *Irish Historical Studies,* forthcoming

Miller, D.W., 'Presbyterianism and modernisation in Ulster', *Past and Present,* 80 (Aug. 1978), 66-90

Miller, D.W., 'The Armagh Troubles, 1784-95', in Clark and Donnelly, *Irish Peasants,* pp 155-91

Miller, John, 'The Earl of Tyrconnel and James II's Irish policy, 1685 to 1688', *Historical Journal,* 20, 4 (1977), 803-24

Miller, John, *James II: A study in kingship* (Hove, 1978)

Miller, John, 'The Glorious Revolution: "contract" and "abdication" reconsidered', *Historical Journal*, 25, 3 (1982), 541-55

Miller, John, *Restoration England. The reign of Charles II* (London, 1985)

Miller, John, *The Glorious Revolution* (London, 1983)

Mitchison, Rosalind (ed.), *Essays in eighteenth-century history* (London, 1966)

Mitchison, Rosalind, *A History of Scotland* (2nd ed., London, 1982)

Monod, Paul, *Jacobitism and the English people, 1688-1788* (Cambridge, 1989)

Monod, Paul, 'Jacobitism and Country principles in the reign of William III', *Historical Journal*, 30, 2 (1987), 289-310

Moody, T.W., Martin, F.X., Byrne, F.I., and Vaughan, W.E. (eds.), *A New History of Ireland* (9 vols, Oxford, 1976-)

Munter, Robert, *History of the Irish Newspaper, 1685-1760* (Cambridge, 1967)

Murphy, Sean, 'Charles Lucas and the Dublin election of 1748-1749', *Parliamentary History*, 2 (1983), 93-111

Murphy, Sean, 'Charles Lucas, Catholicism and nationalism', *Eighteenth-Century Ireland*, 8 (1993), 83-102

Namier, L.B., *The Structure of Politics at the Accession of George III* (2nd ed., London, 1957)

Naylor, J.F. (ed.), *The British Aristocracy and the Peerage Bill of 1719* (New York, 1968)

Nokes, David, *Jonathan Swift. A hypocrite reversed. A critical biography* (Oxford, 1985)

O'Brien, Gerard (ed.), *Catholic Ireland in the Eighteenth Century. The collected essays of Maureen Wall* (Dublin, 1989)

O'Brien, Gerard (ed.), *Parliament, Politics and People: essays in eighteenth-century Irish history* (Dublin, 1989)

O'Buachalla, Brendan, 'James our true king: the ideology of Irish royalism in the seventeenth century', in Boyce *et al.*, *Political thought in Ireland*, pp 7-35

O'Connell, Maurice, *Irish Politics and Social Conflict in the Age of the American Revolution* (Philadelphia, 1965)

O'Donovan, Declan, 'The Money Bill Dispute of 1753', in Bartlett and Hayton, *Penal Era and Golden Age*, pp 55-87

Petrie, Charles, *The Jacobite Movement* (London, 1932)

Phillips, W.A. (ed.), *History of the Church of Ireland from the Earliest Times to the Present Day* (3 vols, London, 1933)

Plumb, J.H., *England in the Eighteenth Century* (Harmondsworth, 1950)

Plumb, J.H., *Sir Robert Walpole* (2 vols, London, 1956-60)

Plumb, J.H., *The Growth of Political Stability in England, 1675-1725* (London, 1967)

Porter, Roy, *English Society in the Eighteenth Century* (Harmondsworth, 1982)

Power, T.P. and Whelan, Kevin (eds.), *Endurance and Emergence. Catholics in Ireland in the eighteenth century* (Blackrock, 1990)

Rafferty, Oliver P., *Catholicism in Ulster. An interpretative history* (London, 1994)

Reid, James Seaton, *History of the Presbyterian Church in Ireland* (3 vols, Belfast, 1867)

Reitan, E.A., 'From revenue to civil list, 1689-1702: the revolution settlement and the "mixed and balanced" constitution', *Historical Journal*, 13, 4 (1970), 571-88

Robbins, Caroline, *The Eighteenth-Century Commonwealthman. Studies in the transmission, development and circumstance of English liberal political thought from the restoration of Charles II until the war with the Thirteen Colonies* (New York, 1968)

Roberts, Clayton, *Schemes and Undertakings. A study of English politics in the seventeenth century* (Columbus, Ohio, 1985)

Roberts, Clayton, 'The constitutional significance of the financial settlement of 1690', *Historical Journal*, 20, 1 (1977), 59-76

Rogers, H.C.B., *The British Army in the eighteenth century* (London, 1977)

Rogers, Nicholas, *Whigs and Cities. Popular politics in the age of Walpole and Pitt* (Oxford, 1989)

Ryder, Michael, 'The bank of Ireland, 1721: land, credit, and dependency', *Historical Journal*, 25, 3 (1982), 557-82

Sedgwick, Romney (ed.), *The History of Parliament: the House of Commons 1715-54* (2 vols, London, 1970)

Simms, J.G., *The Williamite Confiscation in Ireland, 1690-1703* (London, 1956)

Simms, J.G., *Jacobite Ireland* (London, 1969)

Simms, J.G., *Colonial Nationalism 1698-1776: Molyneux's 'Case of Ireland ... Stated'* (Cork, 1976)

Simms, J,G., 'The Irish Parliament of 1713', in Hayes-McCoy, G.A. (ed.), *Historical Studies*, 4 (London, 1963), pp 82-92

Simms, J.G., 'Irish Catholics and the parliamentary franchise, 1692-1728', *Irish Historical Studies*, 12, 66 (Mar. 1960), 28-37

Simms, J.G., *The Jacobite Parliament of 1689* (Dundalk, 1966)

Simms, J.G., *The Treaty of Limerick* (Dundalk, 1961)

Simms, J.G., 'The Bishops Banishment Act of 1697 (9 Will. III, c.1)', *Irish Historical Studies*, 17, 66 (Sept. 1970), 185-99

Simms, J.G., 'The making of a penal law, (2 Anne, c.6) in 1703-04', *Irish Historical Studies*, 12, 46 (Oct. 1960), 105-18

Smyth, Jim, *The Men of No Property. Irish radicals and popular politics in the late eighteenth century* (Dublin, 1992)

Smyth, Jim, '"Like amphibious animals": Irish Protestants, ancient Britons, 1691-1707', *Historical Journal*, 36, 4 (1993), 785-97

Smyth, Jim, 'The making and undoing of a confessional state: Ireland, 1660-1829', *Journal of Ecclesiastical History*, 44, 3 (July 1993), 506-13

Smyth, Jim, 'Anglo-Irish unionist discourse, c.1656-1707: from Harrington to Fletcher', *Bullán*, 2, 1 (summer 95), 17-34

Speck, W.A., *Reluctant Revolutionaries. Englishmen and the revolution of 1688* (Oxford, 1988)

Speck, W.A., *Stability and Strife. England 1714-1760* (London, 1977)

Speck, W.A., '"Whigs and Tories dim their glories": English political parties under the first two Georges', in Cannon (ed.), *The Whig Ascendancy*, pp 51-75

Speck, W.A., 'The General Election of 1715', *English Historical Review*, 90, 356 (July 1975), 507-22

Stephen, Leslie and Lee, Sidney (eds.), *Dictionary of National Biography* (21 vols, Oxford, 1937-8)

Stone, Lawrence (ed.), *An Imperial State at War. Britain from 1689 to 1815* (London, 1994)

Sykes, Norman, *Church and State in England in the Eighteenth Century* (Cambridge, 1934)

Sykes, Norman, *William Wake, Archbishop of Canterbury, 1657-1737* (2 vols, Cambridge, 1957)

Szechi, Daniel, *Jacobitism and Tory politics, 1710-14* (Edinburgh, 1984)

Thompson, E.P., *The Making of the English Working Class* (London, 1968)

Thompson, E.P., *Whigs and Hunters* (London, 1975)

Thompson, E.P., *Customs in Common* (London, 1993)

Thomson, M.A., *The Secretaries of State, 1681-1782* (London, 1932)

Townend, G.M., 'Religious radicalism and conservatism in the Whig party under George I: the repeal of the Occasional Conformity and Schism Acts', *Parliamentary History*, 7, 1 (1988), 24-44

Victory, Isolde, 'The making of the Declaratory Act of 1720' in O' Brien, *Parliament, Politics and People*, pp 9-29

Walcott, Robert, *English politics in the early eighteenth century* (Oxford, 1956)

Wall, Maureen, *The Penal Laws, 1691-1760* (Dundalk, 1976)

Whelan, Kevin, *The Tree of Liberty. Radicalism, Catholicism and the construction of Irish identity 1760-1830* (Cork, 1996)

Williams, Basil, *Carteret and Newcastle: a contrast in contemporaries* (Cambridge, 1943)

Williams, Basil, *The Whig Supremacy* (2nd ed., Oxford, 1961)

Willman, Robert, 'The origins of "Whig" and "Tory" in English political language', *Historical Journal*, 17, 2 (1974), 247-64

Index